PASS ME THE RICE

PASS ME THE RICE

ROBERT G. KAY

AuthorHouse™
1663 Liberty Drive
Bloomington, IN 47403
www.authorhouse.com
Phone: 1-800-839-8640

First published by AuthorHouse 05/12/2011

ISBN: 978-1-4634-0153-5 (sc)
ISBN: 978-1-4634-0152-8 (dj)
ISBN: 978-1-4634-0151-1 (ebk)

Library of Congress Control Number: 2011906817

Printed in the United States of America

This book is printed on acid-free paper.

This book is dedicated to the memories of:

Senior Chief Gunners Mate
Earl A. Shipp
US Navy—Retired

Boatswains Mate First Class
Juan L. Montoya
US Navy—Retired

PROLOG

I wrote this book in response to the repeated urgings of my friends to whom over the years I had related many of the events that occurred during my tours in Vietnam. When the time finally came for me to sit down and recall all my stories, I decided that the book should not be a "War Story" per se, but rather, a glimpse into some of the events that befell me and my shipmates, some humorous and some not. There were many boring hours of patrol, both at sea and on the rivers that I felt did not belong in this book: But the occasions where something out of the ordinary had occurred, I included in the narrative in order to present a different picture of the war in Vietnam through the eyes of a Naval Advisor. Additionally, even if I were not fortunate enough to get the book published, there would be a written document as a legacy for my children that would answer the question, "What did you do during the war, Dad?"

It should be noted that I had volunteered for duty in Vietnam and because of that, I will appear somewhat biased. I thoroughly enjoyed my two years of active duty in-country and my ensuing six years as a civilian adviser to the Vietnamese Navy. It was the high point of my naval career. And lastly, many individual's names have been altered for obvious reasons, while others, for whom I hold the utmost respect, have remained unchanged.

PART ONE

NEWPORT NAVAL STATION, RHODE ISLAND

The sky was somber and completely blanketed by ugly dark gray-green clouds that were typical of a winter's day in Newport, Rhode Island. A damp, cold brisk wind was driving sleet in from Narragansett Bay and the two largest piers of the Naval Station were slowly being covered by a thin sheet of ice.

The USS Wilkinson (DL-5) was the only ship at Pier One and was moored on the port side, occupying a little over five hundred feet of pier space. She was a sleek haze gray warship designated by the Navy as a Destroyer Leader, which placed her size-wise somewhere between a standard destroyer and a light cruiser.

Wilkinson was one of two Test and Evaluation ships for the experimental AN-SQS-26X Sonar system and the last in a class of five ships. She was the test platform for the aluminum covered bow mounted sonar dome, while her sister ship, the USS Willis A. Lee (DL-4), had a rubber coated dome. Wilkinson had just returned to her homeport of Newport after three weeks of intensive refresher training in Guantanamo Bay, Cuba. The training at Gitmo was standard procedure for any ship returning to duty after a stint in a Naval Shipyard for major repairs in an Extended Overhaul. We had spent seventeen months in the Boston Naval Shipyard where new modifications had been retrofitted into our Sonar equipment and the yard workers started referring to us as "Building 5" since that was our hull number. On this particular morning, a steady stream of sailors in foul weather gear were lethargically carrying stores aboard from one of two big tractor trailers positioned side by side at the foot of the brow. Working parties such as this were common in the navy and were made up of personnel selected by the leading petty officers of each division assigned to the evolution. The number of people required was predetermined by the particular task at hand, and today's working party consisted of people from Engineering, Operations and the Weapons Departments. Since this one involved dry stores and provisions, the Supply Department only required one Storekeeper on the trailer to check off each item, one in the storeroom and one on the reefer deck to validate receipt of the foodstuff. These checks and balances were necessary because certain items had a way of mysteriously vanishing aboard ship somewhere between point A and point B.

Case in point aboard this ship happened last summer. Twenty watermelons were off-loaded from the truck but only nineteen made it to the reefer deck. When the final tally was made and the disappearance was noted, the Senior Chief Commissaryman went ballistic. He and his cooks proceeded to scour the entire ship for the wayward melon. After about an hour of intensive searching, the missing melon was discovered in the "B" Division's berthing compartment stuffed inside their dirty laundry bag.

Those of you familiar with navy ships know that "B" Division's living spaces are among the grungiest onboard compared to the other divisions. For some reason, Boilertenders seem to naturally prefer this grease and oil inundated lifestyle, much to the dismay of the Executive Officer whenever he conducted his periodic Zone Inspections. The liberated fruit was ultimately returned safely to the reefer and reunited with the other melons.

Performing this or any other type of manual, drone-like labor is not the high point of a sailor's idea of shipboard adventure. Considering the present inclement weather, this working party most definitely qualified as a genuine shit detail.

The current loading of stores was in preparation for the ship being scheduled to participate in a UNITAS cruise which would take them to the warm waters of South America. Navy ships from several South American countries join in annually for the multilateral naval and amphibious operations. These include at-sea exercises and inport activities among each other to increase operability and mutual understanding. Above all else however, most sailors looked forward to the various port visits in places where they up to now had only read about in books. With the exception of one person . . . . me!

I was a Lieutenant Junior Grade and one of four officers in the Weapons Department including, the Department Head. My official title was First Lieutenant and I was in charge of the 1st Division, which in reality made me the ship's Head Janitor.

My responsibilities included the physical maintenance and materiel upkeep of the main deck, the 0-1 level, which is the next deck above the main deck, all their bulkheads, the outer hull and both anchors and chains. When I initially reported aboard, I quickly observed that there was a lot to be desired with the outward appearance of the ship.

During the months in the Boston Naval Shipyard, a considerable amount of cosmetic work was performed by my people. As time went on, the crew began taking more pride and exerted a significant effort into getting the old girl into looking exceptionally good.

Just before we were to leave Boston, the Deck Force had managed to transform the Wilkinson into a genuine showboat. My sailors had slapped paint on every vertical and horizontal surface assigned to us, applied non-skid overlay to every deck area that required sure footing by the crew, stenciled white stars on every mooring bitt on deck and completely outfitted our three rows of lifelines with diamond-shaped black double braided hollow nylon polypropylene line. The acquisition of the latter was due solely to our highly resourceful Supply Officer who somehow found the way to fund its purchase for me. When we were finished, we looked so good that our Squadron Commander insisted on having his Change of Command ceremony on the fantail of our ship after we returned to our homeport of Newport.

In preparation for that occasion, we ran a long sound-powered phone line from the ship to the head of the pier where it was manned by one of my brighter First Division people. His job was to ask the driver of the incoming dignitary's car to identify his passenger and pass the word back to the Quarterdeck. As the distinguished person set foot upon the ship's brow, the Boatswain's Mate of the Watch rang the appropriate number of bells and announced over the ship's public address system the title of the individual, i.e. "COMSURFLANT, arriving." Once the visitor stepped aboard, the messenger of the watch would snap his picture with a Polaroid camera and note his title on the bottom. In this way, we were prepared to properly identify and "Bong off" each individual correctly upon their departure.

Under Navy protocol, Admirals rated 4 bells rang in a sequence of two, where Captains and below only rated two bells. A Captain of a ship would be announced with two bells and the name of his ship, i.e. "Bong-Bong, Wilkinson arriving."

With the ceremony well underway on the fantail, a late arrival pulled up to the brow. Since it had bypassed the phone talker at the head of the pier who had already secured, the Quarterdeck watch was taken by surprise. The startled Boatswain's Mate, upon seeing a Flag Officer approach the brow, quickly went to the PA system and announced tremulously, "Bong-Bong, Bong-Bong, another Admiral arriving," without actually ringing the bell. That's when time literally stood still aboard the ship. After a slight pause, smiles appeared on the faces of the guests at the procedural gaff, with exception of course of my Captain. His laser-like glare quickly found me standing just forward of the fantail and sent an unspoken message of "Give your soul to Jesus because your ass belongs to me!"

Fortunately, the breakdown in protocol was diminished because the tardy Admiral had later remarked to my Captain that it was the first time he was ever bonged vocally aboard a ship and thought it was hilarious. "Besides," he said, "I probably deserved it for being late."

The Captain, upon later hearing my explanation, simply stated that "Shit happens, but it had better not happen again."

Naturally, for some time to come I would be greeted with "Bong-Bong, Janitor arriving," whenever I entered the Ward Room.

Had it not been for the long and arduous hours of hard work that went into setting us apart from the rest of the ships in the Squadron, I'm sure the Captain would have insisted that I and my Division never set foot on dry land again. But being a highly professional officer, he praised us for our accomplishments despite the one goof-up during the ceremony.

ANCHOR'S AWAY

However, I was still not a contented individual. That's why on that cold blustery morning in November of 1966, I was huddled inside a wind and rain buffeted phone booth on the pier calling my Detailer in Washington. The Detailers in the Navy Bureau of Personnel are the men who make the duty assignments for officers by grade. Lieutenant Mike Kaleres was my detailer and would eventually rise to Flag Rank later in his career.

"Lieutenant's Detail Desk, Kaleres speaking," he said very businesslike.

"This is Robert Kay calling from the Wilkinson, DL-5 in Newport."

"What can I do for you Mr. Kay?"

"Being a fellow Greek, I thought you could help me volunteer for duty in Vietnam as an Advisor."

Without so much as a why would you want to do that, he replied, "Hang on a second while I look up your record." What seemed only a few moments later he announced, "OK, you've got it; I'll get the orders cut right away . . . and good luck, *Patrioti*."

From that short conversation, it was evident that the Navy must have been looking for Vietnam volunteers rather than having to arbitrarily assign some officer who had no such desires. That would explain the unbelievable ease with which my request was granted.

That afternoon just before lunch was served in the Ward Room, the officers stood at their respective places around the two tables awaiting the arrival of the Captain. A few of the younger officers, who for some reason always seemed to be hungry, were surreptitiously eating saltine crackers smeared with butter. The senior officers, on the other hand, showed maturity, patience and restraint lest the "old man" enters and catches them munching away like a bunch of food deprived squirrels.

The two tables were set up for the noon meal, with crisp white table linen, the ship's dinnerware and each officer's individual napkin ring holding equally white napkins flanking each place setting. The smaller of the two tables was for the Captain, the Executive Officer and the four Department Heads. The second and larger table was designated for the junior officers and had room to accommodate 18 people. Everyone took their seat once the Captain entered and assumed his place at the head of his table.

Once the meal was finished, dishes were cleared and coffee was served. The Captain looked over in my direction and said, "Bob, I want you to ensure that the paint locker has enough supplies aboard to last us through the cruise next month." Normally, he would have addressed this to my boss, the Weapons Department Head, but he was the Command Duty Officer today and was not present for lunch.

"I've already taken care of that sir, we're in good shape," I replied. "By the way Captain, I won't be making the cruise because I've just volunteered for duty in Vietnam. My orders should be on their way even as we speak."

A cold silence immediately fell over the wardroom and I got the distinct impression that everyone in the Mess must have considered me some kind of lunatic. After all, who would give up this choice sea-duty for a one year fun-filled tour in the rice paddies, jungles and polluted waters of Southeast Asia? Once again . . . me, that's who!

Pushing away from the table and slowly getting to his feet, the Captain said, "I'd like to see you in my cabin for a few minutes after we're through here Bob."

"Aye sir," I replied, thinking that he was going to give me hell for having blind-sided him in front of the other officers, especially since it was just before a major deployment. It definitely was not the right time or place to drop that bombshell on the CO because he didn't deserve that from me. I guess my elation of finally getting something I really wanted out of the Navy made me blurt it out for all to hear. Damn, what a stupid thing for me to do.

However, when I reported to his cabin, I found the XO and the CO sitting at the small round table in the corner of the room. I was surprised when the skipper calmly invited me to sit down and asked how I had come about my decision to go to Vietnam. It took me by surprise because I fully expected him to launch a tirade at me for my ill-timed proclamation. Make no mistake, once an officer attains command of his own ship or group, his ability to browbeat a junior officer verbally indicates that he had successfully completed the well-known Navy "ass-chewing" course. Fortunately for me, this did not turn out to be one of those times.

I explained that since I still had about another year to go before being rotated from the ship and because of my pending divorce, I found it difficult to remain focused on my job aboard ship. The fact that I was about seven years behind my age-grade because of the time it took me to complete college and attend Officer Candidate School, made it obvious that I had to do something to make up lost ground. I figured by getting my ticket punched for duty in a combat zone, it would definitely give me that opportunity. "Besides," I continued, "My ancestors came from Sparta, the home of Greece's fiercest warriors and felt that I was naturally driven in that direction."

The Captain nodded thoughtfully and said, "I would think it was more your domestic situation rather than laying it at the feet of your ancestors, but in either case, it's your decision. Best of luck," he said, dismissing me as the XO nodded in turn.

True to my Detailer's word, my orders arrived the next day. I was to be transferred to the Amphibious Base in Coronado, California for temporary duty at the Navy's Counter-Insurgency School. Thirty days leave was authorized for me to wrap up my personal affairs and it was to commence immediately.

It took me most of the morning to pack my gear and make the rounds of the ship, bidding enlisted men and brother officers alike, goodbye. Traditionally, I left seeing the CO and XO for last. Fortunately, the two men were together again in the Captain's cabin pouring over some navigational charts. The XO looked up and informed me that the Bureau had already assigned a relief for me and that he'd be aboard sometime next week. In addition he went on; there would be a "Hail and Farewell" party for you in the Officers Club on Saturday night at 1900 hours.

I shook hands with both men and said that it had been a distinct privilege to have served with them and hoped that our paths would again cross in the future.

With that out of the way, I went aft to my stateroom to get my bag and briefcase and was told that one of the Boatswain's Mates had already taken them up to the Quarterdeck for me. This was just another indication of the mutual respect the men in my division and I had for each other. Reaching the Quarterdeck, I found the seaman standing there still holding my bags.

"I'll give you a hand with these, Lieutenant," he said.

"I appreciate it Boats, thanks."

I turned and saluted Ensign Hanson, who was the Officer of the Deck and said, "Request permission to leave the ship."

"Permission granted," he replied returning my salute smartly.

I stepped onto the brow, turned and threw another salute towards the colors aft as the ship's bell "bonged me off." The words "Officer departing" echoed from the PA system and out over the snow covered pier.

HAIL AND FAREWELL

The party was typical of all the O-club's going away bashes. The married officers brought their wives; the bachelors brought dates or came solo hoping to cut a stray out of the herd. There was always the possibility that a lone female would be at the club, especially one whose spouse might be at sea or have the duty. But on that account, loners' chances increased exponentially if they were in the larger fleet ports such as San Diego, Norfolk or Charleston.

Prior to coming back into the Navy, I was married and had three young daughters who were the light of my life. But after seven years of marriage, we separated because my wife couldn't adapt to Navy life and the separations caused by sea duty. She had been extremely jealous of the Navy for taking up so much of my time and eventually found ways to occupy her lonely hours. In a Navy town, that wasn't too difficult.

My rationalization was that the children would benefit more if we divorced rather than to grow up in a home filled with suspicion and hostility. Although the divorce would cost me practically everything, including a brand new home in Rhode Island, I felt catharsis would eventually replace the pain and anger. Another reason for my getting away from her had to do with my Naval career. A little known fact is that as you attain higher rank in the service, more scrutiny is placed on you by the Bureau of Personnel. For example, if two officers are qualified in all respects for a highly visible billet or a promotion, the Bureau would then take a closer look at the spouses. The officer, whose wife kept a low profile, was a good hostess and mixed in well with the other wives, would always get selected over the one whose spouse had the reputation of being "the good time had by all." So in the end, it was a no-brainer.

From the day I moved out of the house, my work aboard ship became more endurable now that the nagging suspicions of where she was and what she was doing during my absences were no longer uppermost in my mind. So, that's why I came to the party as just "one me."

And so it was, the final breaking of ties with the ship and fellow officers punctuated with lots of drinking, toasting, and the ever-popular sea stories.

Taking his place at the microphone, the XO embarked on a long winded account of the first time that I was tested with a "Man Overboard" drill. It happened one quiet afternoon while we were steaming independently off the coast of Rhode Island. I was the Assistant Officer of the Deck at the time, when LT Anderson, the OOD, told me to take the Conn so he could make a head call. Since I didn't suspect anything unusual, I was taken by surprise a few minutes later when I heard, "This is a drill, this is a drill, Man Overboard, port side", announced over the ship's PA system.

I immediately ordered the helmsman to give me left full rudder and the annunciator man to put all engines ahead full. I went out to the port wing of the bridge and found the CO and XO leisurely watching my handling of the drill. As per procedure, I looked to the signal bridge where the duty signalman was supposed to be pointing his arm in the direction of "Oscar" the orange painted canvas dummy that was used for this drill. Surprisingly, there was no one there.

I frantically searched the sea with my binoculars but the two foot swells prevented me from locating "Oscar." The ship was just about completing its full circle when I finally spotted the orange life-jacketed dummy before it slipped into the trough of a wave. I made the mistake of ordering the port engine stopped which resulted in putting drag on the propeller and slowed the ship down considerably. A quick look at the Captain's frown told me that I was blowing it, big time. I finally managed to maneuver the ship so that we were able to snag Oscar with a boathook on the port side according to the manual. But, too much time had elapsed since the dummy had been over the side and if it were a live sailor in cold water, he'd already be dead from hypothermia. These drills are always conducted with the worst-case scenarios in mind.

LT Anderson had meanwhile returned to the bridge and reassumed the Conn once the drill was completed. I sheepishly had to endure the CO's critique of my performance on the bridge wing out of earshot of the watch standers. He pointed out my mistake of stopping the port engine which failed to result in making a much tighter, quicker turn. The fact that there was no signalman pointing towards the dummy was no excuse for panic. He had been ordered specifically beforehand not to be there as he would normally be in order to place more stress on me. I also failed to ask Combat Information Center for a location of the dummy's last known position when it went overboard. After that, I realized that I had more studying to do before I could become qualified as Officer of the Deck aboard this ship.

Continuing with his tale, the XO related that a few weeks after that ill-fated Man Overboard drill, another opportunity to test me presented itself. Luckily, this time I had been forewarned because one of the Stewards Mates overheard the Captain and the Exec talking about it alone after lunch in the Ward Room. A quick call to me on the bridge tipped me off about the plans to surprise me since I was once again the Assistant OOD. I quickly got word to my leading Boatswains Mate and told him what I wanted done.

Once again, LT Anderson turned over the Conn to me while he supposedly made another head call. No imagination there, I thought to myself. The XO nonchalantly appeared down below on the forward main deck, as expected, holding Oscar the dummy. He noticed several First Division seamen busily polishing brass fittings on the foc'sle lifelines and not suspecting anything out of the ordinary, proceeded to lift Oscar over the lifelines. At that precise moment, two of my seamen tackled the dummy and prevented it from going over the side while the XO was struggling and simultaneously yelling, "Man overboard!"

As I peered down from the bridge at the scene below, the XO finally realized that the sailors had been there by design. He glared up at me and yelled, "Play the game Kay, play the goddamned game." Then he angrily stomped away leaving Oscar safely in the grasp of the two seamen who were both grinning up at me from ear to ear.

He continued with his narration after the laughter died down and said, "I never did find out how you learned about the drill," raising his eyebrows in anticipation of a possible explanation.

"Trade secret XO, sorry I can't divulge my sources," I replied with conviction, not wanting to rat out the Stewards.

Finally, the CO took his turn at the microphone and with a deep sigh said, "That was not the end of the Kay method of handling a man overboard exercise. The XO and I, along with Bob's Department Head, Lieutenant Commander Adams, decided that we would run this drill again when the opportunity presented itself.

So the following week we assigned Bob as Officer of the Deck by himself while we were still steaming around independently. It was just before the noon meal and the non-watchstanding officers were gathered in the Wardroom awaiting my arrival. The XO and I were up on the signal bridge where Bob couldn't see us just as the cry of "Man Overboard, port side," was yelled out by the duty Signalman. For some reason, Bob immediately ordered left full rudder, all engines ahead flank instead of full.

Once the twin screws bit into the water, the ship lurched ahead and heeled over precariously as we sped into the turn. Everyone on the bridge grabbed for the nearest object or railing to keep from being knocked off their feet, that is, all except Bob who was calmly leaning against the splinter shield looking through his binoculars. He ordered the engines stopped at about five eighths of the way around the circle and then backed them one third. He ordered the helm to steady up as we smartly came alongside Oscar just under the port bow and stopped the engines.

The XO and I stomped down the ladder from the signal bridge and confronted Bob, who was standing there with a grin on his face. I asked him just what in the hell he thought he was doing and he calmly replied as he held up a stopwatch, that he had just saved a sailor from certain death in the frigid water by pulling him out one minute forty two seconds faster than the ship's previous record. Both XO and I stood there dumbfounded while the entire bridge watch stood around like smiling baboons. I finally regained my composure and announced that the effort was commendable, however in the future; flank speed was not to be used for this exercise.

When the XO and I entered the Wardroom, we found that all the crockery had been redistributed around the room and onto the deck. Fortunately, the food had not yet been served because of my absence, so it wasn't a total loss. Needless to say the physical conditions on the mess decks and the Chief's Mess resembled the scene from Pompei's destruction by Mount Vesuvius. I had no choice but to sign off on Bob's "Man Overboard" execution and vowed never to let him do that again on my ship."

Once the laughter died down, the Captain became serious and made a few complimentary remarks about me punctuated with such adjectives as resourceful, imaginative and self-determined. This was followed by his presenting me with the ship's plaque. In retrospect, I could hardly recognize the individual that the CO and XO had referred to in their speeches, but then again, these affairs were designed to end on an upbeat note for the honoree.

I had arrived alone at the party and left the same way after many hugs and kisses from the wives and the halfhearted promises to keep in touch. In seriousness, however, they all advised me to keep my head down in Vietnam.

Since the pending divorce, I no longer had a residence other than the ship, so I decided to stay overnight at the Bachelor Officers Quarters on the base. After all my consumption of rum and pineapple juice at the party, I thought it prudent to drive down to New Jersey the next morning after a good night's sleep. That way, I could visit friends and family fully refreshed. As I lay in bed that night, I thought back to the XO's last futile attempt at trying to finagle the source who warned me of the intended drill that lazy afternoon. I remained steadfast because my close affinity with the Stewards Mates, who up to that time were comprised of Negro and Filipino sailors, had actually begun while I was in the Reserves.

USS MIDWAY (CV-41), ALAMEDA, CA

In the winter of 1962, my Minneapolis Naval Air Station based Reserve Unit had orders to report for our annual two week ACDUTRA (Active Duty for Training) aboard the carrier USS Midway (CV-41). Seventy five members of my unit boarded a chartered Northwest Airlines flight to San Francisco and upon our arrival were loaded into two Navy busses and driven to Alameda Naval Air Station.

The old carrier was tied up to the pier and a wisp of economical light gray smoke was coming out of her stack. This showed that she had steam up in preparation for getting underway the next morning for two weeks of training at sea. Being a Quartermaster/Signalman First Class, I was assigned to a three section watch rotation on the bridge as QM of the Watch. The Officer of the Deck, with whom I was to share the watch, was the most senior Lieutenant on the ship. Lieutenant Muscato, a native of Uniontown, Pennsylvanian, was seven inches over five feet in height and as feisty as they came. He had close cropped curly dark black hair with hazel eyes that placed his ancestry somewhere in northern Italy near Trieste. It was evident that his short stature resulted in his having a severe

Napoleonic complex. He was constantly in an aggressive mode and went out of his way to intimidate those below him in rank and above him in height.

For some unexplained reason, he took me under his wing once he discovered that I was a Reserve Officer Candidate. During our watches together, he would explain in great detail all the varied functions of a Deck Officer's duties underway. On one particular mid-watch, he told me to go to the Ward Room pantry and ask the duty Steward to make him a sandwich. I hustled below and found a huge black Steward's Mate Third Class sitting in the pantry listening to music from a small 45 record player. His head was bobbing with the beat emanating from his earphones and his eyes were closed. A slight smile creased his otherwise smooth milk-chocolaty face that just barely revealed the whiteness of his teeth. The name "Davis" was embroidered in blue letters on the right breast of his white steward's jacket a few inches below the ship's emblem. He was in his early twenties and easily weighed two hundred and forty pounds, none of which I noticed, was fat. His eyes snapped open in surprise as I gingerly touched him on one of his massive arms and quickly informed him of the Officer of the Deck's request.

Removing the earphones and turning off the record player, he gave me a huge smile and said, "You must be one of those Reserves that came aboard in Alameda."

"That's right," I replied. "I spent a lot of sea time pumping fuel alongside the older carriers when I was stationed on fleet oilers, but never got to ride one until now."

"These babies ride like a city block, unless Mister Pacific decides to raise a fuss and then you'll learn to pray to the Lord without the help of a preacher. Who's the OOD wanting the sandwich?"

"Lieutenant Muscato," I replied

"That's the little Eye-talian," rumbled Davis from deep in his chest. "Now there's one gen-u-wine sumbitch and I've got just the sandwich for that man of misery," he said scowling maliciously. "Watch and learn shipmate."

Taking a roll of baloney from the refrigerator, he expertly lopped off two generous slices with a big kitchen knife. He then cut two slices of bread from a freshly baked loaf, coated each piece with mayonnaise and placed baloney on each slice. "Now, I want you to pay close attention to this next part," he said, lowering his voice conspiratorially.

He quickly unzipped his fly, pulled out one of the biggest penises that I had ever seen and proceeded to wipe it all over the baloney. I could hardly believe what I was witnessing as I stood there speechless. When he was satisfied that no part of the baloney had been missed, he wiped his crank on his apron, zipped up his fly, put the sandwich together, wrapped it up and said in his deep rumbling voice, "Take this up to the good Lieutenant and tell him with compliments from Junior Davis."

"Will do," I replied. As I turned to leave with the wax-paper wrapped sandwich in hand, he asked me if I wanted one too, seeing as he still had the fixin's on the counter. "No thanks," I answered a little too quickly, "I'll settle for watching him eat this one."

Davis chuckled as he shook his head and started clearing the counter. "You be sure and tell me how 'Massa' Muscato enjoys his sandwich, hear?"

I made my way back up to the darkened bridge and handed the sandwich to Lieutenant Muscato who was occupying the portside Captain's chair. I also passed on Davis' compliments, to which Muscato merely grunted. Leaning against the Quartermaster's table, I watched in awe as the Lieutenant began wolfing down the sandwich with obvious relish. The Boatswain's Mate of the Watch sidled over to me and whispered, "That 'Palomino Love-Stick' sandwich smells pretty good. How come you didn't get one for yourself?"

"Boats, most sailors always refer to a baloney sandwich as 'Horse Cock,'" I whispered, "And I just learned where that expression came from. I watched Davis wipe his dick all over that meat once he found out who it was for."

"No shit?" he asked incredulously, trying hard not to laugh out loud. "Wait till I tell the other guys."

"Be careful and make sure no one screws up and tips Muscato off," I cautioned; "otherwise it's Junior's ass."

"Roger that. Man, that's just fuckin' bee-u-ti-ful."

From that moment on, I made myself a solemn oath to never ever piss off a Steward's Mate for the rest of my naval career. So, when I first reported aboard the Wilkinson, I made it a point to befriend the Wardroom Stewards. On occasions when the food on the Wardroom menu didn't seem appetizing, I would wait until the meal was over and everyone had left. I would then slip into the pantry and share some "Gilly-Gilly" with the Stewards. It was a staple that one of the Filipinos concocted and consisted of seasoned rice, onion and garlic stir-fried with chicken, beef or pork. It turned out to be a beneficial relationship and I don't think anyone ever noticed that my dessert portions were slightly larger than everyone else's.

Then I recalled one of the most hilarious events of that trip that happened on our return flight after completing our two weeks aboard the Midway. We were several hours out of San Francisco with the crew quietly resting in their seats, when a voice piped up from the rear of the plane.

"Hey skipper, did you and XO get a chance to visit Pinocchio's before we left?" The gnarly voice belonged to the oldest member of our unit, "Popeye" Larson. He was a 52 year old Engineman First Class but looked 70. During his career, he took the Chief's exam every year since he became eligible, but for some reason, he failed to pass it. His diminutive size along with his wizened appearance naturally earned him the nickname "Popeye."

Everyone in the unit knew that Pinocchio's was a notorious establishment catering to homosexuals in San Francisco and realized that Popeye was affectionately trying to break the CO's stones.

"Sorry Popeye, I never had the chance to get there because XO kept dragging me up to see Carol Doda's renowned breasts at her club on Eddy Street." It was the CO's turn to break XO's stones, but it was all in fun because they were law partners in civilian life. "How about you, anything exciting happen?"

"Funny you should mention that boss. The last night of liberty downtown in a bar, I met a winsome lass that caught my fancy. No lie! After a few drinks, she asked me if I was in the mood to have some fun up at her place. Well, you know me; I had the check paid, hat on my head and a death grip on her arm as we beat feet out of there. To make a long story short, we wound up in her one bedroom walkup nearby and were on the bed naked as jaybirds. She wrestled me over and before I knew what was happening, she was down on me like a vacuum cleaner. After a few seconds she lifted her head and said, 'You know, this is the first time I've ever done this,' and I laughed right in her asshole."

With that, the entire crew cracked up laughing. The noise was so loud that the Captain came out of the cockpit to investigate the commotion. He looked inquiringly at the head flight attendant who was doubled over with laughter leaning against the galley counter and holding her stomach. When she regained her composure enough to speak, she wiped the tears from her eyes and related the entire conversation verbatim. The Captain chuckled as he returned to the cockpit shaking his head and closing the door behind him mumbling, "Sailors!"

Still lying there in the dark, recalling old Popeye's shenanigans, I started to think about food. My stomach was starting to growl since it had been several hours since I had eaten at the party. I tried to convince myself that I wasn't hungry and that I would soon be eating some good Greek cooking at home. Finally, I fell asleep.

The trip south to New Jersey was uneventful and I arrived at my mother's house just in time to be served a big bowl of my grandmother's Greek creamy egg and lemon soup brimming with rice. Boy, I had sure missed that. Both my mother and grandmother weren't too pleased when I told them that I had volunteered for Vietnam, but they respected my decision and thankfully kept their opinions to themselves.

After a few days of making the usual rounds, I found it extremely uncomfortable whenever the subject of my divorce came up in a conversation. At some point, thirty days leave seemed unbearably long and it became increasingly difficult for me to relax, especially when my grandmother would stay up and wait for me by the window until I came home at night. She had done the same thing with her three sons, so it wasn't out of character for her. However, it did become disconcerting after the first few nights.

With duty in a combat zone looming in my immediate future, I started dwelling on the thought that perhaps I might not get out of Vietnam unscathed. I also began to notice that I had less and less things in common to talk about with my closest friends and relatives as the days dragged by. In other words, I was getting bored and seemed to be in a complete social funk. It was then that I made my decision to cut short my time here at home and head out to the West Coast earlier than originally planned.

Once again, my mother and grandmother were not enthused when I told them of my plans to leave early. I think they sensed the uneasiness that I was experiencing and both managed to put up a brave front. With hugs and kisses, my grandmother made the sign of the cross over me for divine protection. I managed to leave the teary-eyed women in the doorway and left for the airport and boarded the crowded flight to San Diego.

PART TWO

THE JOURNEY BEGINS

I took a cab from the Charles Lindbergh Airport directly to Coronado because I wanted to settle in as soon as possible and I had no idea where it was. I was surprised when the cabdriver pulled aboard a ferry and turned around to tell me that it would only be a short trip. "They've been talking about building a bridge across the bay in the future so I guess that means the old ferries will have had it," he added.

The trip to the Amphibious Base took about ten minutes from the ferry slip and I was impressed with the neat, compact little town of Coronado. We passed a small marina housing all types of sailing craft with royal blue canvas on the left, while on the right, directly across the wide street, was the famous Del Coronado Hotel. It was huge, and from what I learned from the cabbie, was very luxurious. Well, that was probably one place that I wouldn't be able to afford on a Lieutenant's salary.

A little further down the road we arrived at the main gate of the Amphibious Base as the beautiful Pacific Ocean to our right cascaded its breakers along the beach known as the Silver Strand. I showed my ID and orders to the Marine sentry who after seeing them, saluted me smartly and waved us through. The BOQ was a three story squat brick building on the right and the cabdriver came to a stop in front of the main entrance. As I retrieved my gear from the trunk, the cabbie nodded to the building across the street and said, "That's the Officer's Club, in case you're interested."

"Many thanks and have a good one," I said as I handed him a hefty tip.

"Pardon my asking, but are you coming here to train for Vietnam?"

"As a matter of fact, I am,"

"Kinda thought so; if I was still in I'd be doing the same thing as you. I retired in '64 as a Senior Chief Torpedoman with twenty six years on tin cans and I still get homesick for the old days being around the Navy all the time. I push a hack because there's not much call for guys with my experience on the outside. Anyway, best of luck over there sir," he said quietly as he got into his cab and slowly drove away.

Now that was sad, I thought to myself as I watched him slowly disappear around the corner.

During the next eighteen weeks, we would be given instruction in the Vietnamese Culture, ideology, a brief overview of their history and Vietnamese language familiarization. We weren't expected to become proficient linguists in the short period that we had, but the course was designed to give us sufficient tools to allow us to better interact with our Vietnamese counterparts.

Strong emphasis would also be placed on the physical and mental conditioning of each officer. A strenuous week of SERE Training (Survival, Escape, Resistance and Evasion), was conducted at the Marine Base at Camp Pendleton and at an isolated area of northern San Diego County called Warner Springs. The training was intended to give us the knowledge and confidence necessary to survive in a hostile environment. The last phase was conducted in a POW setting complete with a fenced in compound. We were confined for long periods of time in boxes and crates, with malevolent guards who showered us with constant verbal and physical abuses. It was meant to teach us how to deal with fatigue, thirst, hunger, pain, extreme temperatures and boredom; but most of all, it provided an insight into one's self and the self-discipline required to complete the training.

Then finally one morning at the conclusion of the curriculum, my entire class was mustered in the parking lot after breakfast with all our gear. We were authorized to travel in wash khakis because of the long flight and when the busses pulled up, we quickly got aboard. At the airport in San Diego, we were split up into three groups of twenty.

My group departed first for San Francisco aboard a PSA DC-8 and I can verify that the female flight attendants were among the prettiest in the world. They seemed to possess the natural beauty and charm that can only be found on southern California beaches.

It was a short flight to San Francisco where we would be further transported by bus to Travis Air Force Base, the main point of departure for all Pacific destinations. The place was a beehive of activity and because our scheduled flight wasn't until 2 AM, it meant that we had twelve long hours to kill.

After baggage check-in, which by the way was thoroughly searched, we naturally gravitated to the Officer's Club. There's a belief in the military that the Air Force constructs their O-Clubs first and then builds the rest of the base around them. Travis was no exception. It was a first rate operation and due to the large volume of people traffic, the snack bars, lounges and large dining facilities remained open around the clock. Non-stop entertainment was offered in the lounge which helped pass the time for many of the transients.

One of the functions of the base administrative staff was the verification of each individual's orders and health records before anyone boarded an outbound flight. Those who were lacking the required immunizations for their particular destination were directed to a medical trailer set out in back of the O-Club where the required shots were quickly dispensed. Problems with personal records were addressed in an adjacent trailer.

Everywhere one looked, each chair, sofa and stairway, was occupied by military personnel in all manner of repose. The place was a veritable mass of humanity and we eagerly looked forward to strapping on our seatbelts and heading out as soon as possible.

After what seemed like an eternity, our flight was called away over the public address system and we were directed to board the busses at the foot of gate 5. We let out a collective sigh of relief knowing that we were finally on our way.

The busses drove onto the hardstand passing many commercial aircraft that were chartered by the Military Airlift Command and whose function was to ferry troops overseas. We pulled up along the left side of a Continental Air Lines Douglas DC-9 that had boarding ramps at its forward and after doors.

Once we were aboard and in our seats, the doors were closed. The plane was pulled back, turned around and then taxied along the hardstand until it reached the head of the active runway. We sat there for several minutes as the pilot revved up the engines and stood on the brakes in order to build up power. When final clearance from the tower was given, the brakes were released and the throttles pushed forward, propelling us rapidly down the runway. The blue side markers of the runway flashed by our windows faster and faster until enough speed was reached for the pilot to rotate the controls that would point us skyward.

A hush fell over the cabin as the plane's nose gently tilted skyward and the powerful thrust of the engines pushed the seats against our backs. As the plane's wheels lost contact with the ground, the rumbling from below faded away and was replaced by the whine of the landing gear assembly being retracted. Circling out over the rocky coastline below, the aircraft clawed at the dark sky reaching for more altitude. That's when we realized that we were leaving the continental United States behind us.

We were soon cruising at an altitude of 40,000 feet over the mighty Pacific Ocean, bound for Saigon in the Republic of South Vietnam. The passengers on this flight were made up of military personnel and civilians heading in-country for duty. There were approximately one hundred and fifty passengers aboard, of whom sixty of us were bound for Advisory billets, fifty-three assorted military and thirty seven civilians. Since it was now just half past three in the morning and nothing scheduled until breakfast, everyone gratefully crashed as the cabin lights were turned off.

As the hours passed and our plane soared effortlessly through the sky, we were all starting to get a little butt-sore and tired. Thankfully, the flight was interrupted by short interim fuel stops in Hawaii, Guam and Yokota Air Force Base in Japan. Total flying time was around twenty six hours of liquorless travel.

As you may or may not know, U. S. Government directives specifically prohibit MAC flights from carrying liquor onboard. This caused many of the passengers to try to correct this lapse in accommodation at each of the ensuing stops along the way.

YOKOTA AIR FORCE BASE, JAPAN

A most welcomed break occurred when we were forced to lay over at Yokota Air Force Base in Japan for a day due to a mechanical problem. We all disembarked and were assigned to various military billeting accommodations on the base while repairs were being made to the engine.

Luckily, this gave us the evening off and an opportunity to look around the town a bit. One of my traveling companions, who had been at the Counter-Insurgency School in Coronado with me, was LT John Rubeck. He had been a Chief Sonarman prior to being commissioned and fortunately for me, an old WestPac sailor who knew his way around this part of the world.

"Have you ever eaten Sushi?" he asked me as we walked through the main gate of the base and headed into town.

"Never have been exposed to it," I answered. "We never had much of a chance to eat real Japanese food in the Mediterranean."

"Well, this is your lucky day. Tell you what; I'll pay for all you can eat since this is your first trip to Japan."

Putting my trust in him completely, I followed him into a small, brightly lit establishment a short distance down the main street. The shop was long and narrow with a counter running its length down the right side similar to our diners in the States. Several customers were seated at the counter on round stools busily eating with chopsticks while simultaneously conversing with their companions. Boy was this going to be an experience, I thought to myself.

The counter was extremely clean and the tile back-splash was brilliantly white with spotless chrome trim. We found two vacant stools at the far end and sat down. An ice filled open shelf ran the length of the back of the counter where all sorts of fish delicacies were on display. I could see right away that the Japanese adhered to the esthetics of food preparation and presentation. A smiling young male behind the counter with an ultra white apron and a tall white chef's hat on his head, was displaying his prowess and speed with a very large, sharp knife. His hands were a blur as he chopped, sliced and deftly flicked pieces of fish onto a customer's plate. During all this, he kept up a steady stream of chatter that I naturally didn't understand.

"I'll order the white meat fish for you for starters," said John. "You can leave the red meat for later because it has a stronger taste and you might not take to it right away."

"You're the boss," I said, eagerly looking forward to my first taste of raw fish.

I was surprised when John ordered in fluent Japanese and more impressed that the Chef had understood without batting an eye.

"Where did you pick up the language?" I asked. "That was pretty neat."

"Three deployments to Westpac, two years shore duty in Yoko and my wife Fumiko is Japanese."

As I absorbed this bit of information, I was also thinking that so many young men in the States didn't know what they were missing by avoiding going into the service. Where else could they experience life in other parts of the world? But then again, everyone wasn't as Gung Ho as me when it came to visiting far off places with strange sounding names.

Our food had quickly been prepared and served with a flourish. I had three chunks of rice wrapped in seaweed with a piece of what looked like a caper and a sliver of roasted red pepper on top, two slices of white fish meat sprinkled with fresh dill and an orange curl of some kind of vegetable which turned out to be ginger. A small porcelain decanter containing hot Sake was set between us and John graciously filled both our little cups.

"Do you like your food hot, moderate or bland?" he asked.

"I like my food on the spicy side, but I'm not into suicide chilies."

"In that case go easy on the green sauce. That's Wasabi and a smidgen of that will be enough to have you running backwards tomorrow trying to keep your anus cool."

"Thanks for the heads-up. I'll have to try a little bit of it anyway just to satisfy my curiosity."

"Okay, but be real careful."

Well, the meal went off nicely and although the sauce was indeed hot, the Sake helped quench the fire somewhat. I really liked the sampling that I had and knew that I wouldn't hesitate to eat Sushi again, thanks to my benevolent shipmate.

"Now that the meal is over with, the next stop is a "Hotsy Bath"," he announced with a crooked smirk.

"What's a Hotsy Bath?" I asked feeling like a rube in the big city.

"You'll see when we get there and I promise you won't be disappointed."

As we left the Sushi Shack and headed back towards the base, we turned into a small side street. John pulled me gently by the arm through an open doorway that led to a long flight of very narrow stairs. At the top, we entered a large reception room with several couches facing a huge Panasonic television set that was showing Sumo wrestling. Other than the enormous man in a white tee shirt sitting behind the reception desk, we were the only other people in the room. When I say that the "receptionist" was big, I mean really big. There was no sideways to this guy. There must have been a large freight elevator somewhere in this place, because this giant would have trouble trying to negotiate the narrow stairway. Once again, John tossed out his Japanese and the bald-headed giant nodded his head several times showing three gold teeth and gently said "Hai."

"We're in luck," John said enthusiastically after a short dialogue with the keeper of the gate. He guided me back through some beaded curtains behind the Oriental Goliath while saying, "We're going to have our pick of the litter."

I followed him into another area that resembled a sitting room where there were six or seven young Japanese maidens sitting around in various poses of relaxation. They each wore a red silk robe, loosely tied and a white, two piece sharkskin bathing suit underneath. All eyes turned to us in quick appraisal as we entered the room.

"Pick one," said John as he pointed to one for himself.

I looked them over quickly and settled on a petite young lady with lustrous black hair cut in a page boy style. Her bangs just missed covering her almond shaped eyes and I put her age to be somewhere in her very early twenties. She immediately stood up and daintily came over, bowed demurely and took me by the hand as she led me towards another room. She helped me remove my shoes and placed them neatly in the hallway beside a door that opened into another small room. There were no windows and a standard size massage table occupied the center of the room. Here, she motioned for me to remove my clothes and hang them on the hooks that were provided on the wall.

I had no qualms about stripping down in the presence of a female; after all, I was a sailor. When I was totally naked, she again took me by the hand and led me through yet another door into a room that contained a sunken tub about 10 feet by 6 feet, three feet deep and filled with steaming hot water. She lithely slipped out of her robe and into the water whose surface was giving off tendrils of steam. Once again she motioned me to join her. Being the brave and courageous seafarer that I was, I threw caution to the wind and jumped in. Wow, was that a mistake. As the big toe of my right foot broke the surface; my nerve endings immediately screamed for me to stay the hell out of the water. But by that time gravity had kicked in and I discovered exactly how a live lobster feels when it's tossed into a pot of boiling water.

I think that I survived those first few seconds of immersion only because my inherent desire to salvage what little pride I had left in front of this sloe eyed smiling Oriental flower. Once the initial shock wore off, the water was extremely soothing. Little flower then began soaping my various body parts, rinsing and then repeating the process a second time. Man, was I relaxed. The bathing phase lasted about thirty minutes and then she deftly climbed out of the water and held up a fluffy white towel with which she helped me dry off. She then led me back to the other room and pointed to the massage table, nodding her head while her eyes were still laughing at me. I climbed aboard and lay on my stomach with the towel still wrapped around my waist. She shook her head and motioned for me to remove the towel, which I did. What followed next was the best body massage I had ever had. Her hands were small but surprisingly strong as she applied oil and kneaded my tired muscles. I was on the verge of falling asleep when she gently slapped me on the buttocks and indicated for me to turn over. Starting at my toes, she worked her way up both legs, bypassing my groin and concentrated on my chest, neck and head. When she had obviously finished the massage, her elbow softly nudged my penis as she sat lightly on the edge of the table. Up to now, my "peter" had been behaving itself. I said up to now, but when her elbow brushed against it, he immediately became rigid.

Noticing my erection, she turned and asked smilingly in broken English, "You wannee speshu, onry ten dollah Amelican?"

Unsure as to what a "special" was, I just knew that I wanted one. Nodding affirmatively, I pointed to my pants hanging against the wall and said, "The money is in my pocket."

She quickly retrieved my pants and let me take the money out myself. Tucking the bill into her waistband, she returned my pants to the hook just as she had found them. She then sat lightly on the edge of the massage table with her back to me as she undid her top and released her small, perky breasts out of confinement. I reached around her slowly, because I didn't want to give the impression that I was a horny round-eye and cupped each pear-shaped breast. As I gently rubbed her nipples with my thumbs and forefingers, I immediately felt them begin to harden. She delicately grasped my penis in her right hand and started a slow, rhythmic up and down motion, applying slight pressure on the down stroke. Her tempo increased as she started to feel the insistent throbbing of my penis and then suddenly, my stored up semen erupted over the end of the table onto the floor. She maintained the steady reciprocating motion until every last drop had been ejected.

Whooeee! I could have sworn that my sphincter was attached to the tail end of that monstrous ejaculation as I lay there totally exhausted, but extremely content. I could have lain there all night, but that's when she casually wiped her hand on a towel and slipped back into her top. I sat up slowly and accepted the warm moist towel she offered me to wipe off my well-spent member.

As I redressed myself, she retrieved my shoes and tied them for me once I had slipped them on. Without saying a word, she guided me back through another door that led to the reception room. John was already there carrying on a friendly conversation with King Kong and they both smiled knowingly when they caught sight of me. Guess who they had been discussing?

"Well, how was it?" asked John with eyebrows raised. "I assume you accepted the offer of a 'Special' too, you dirty old man."

"One more round like that and you would have to take me back to the base in a body bag," I replied.

John translated it for the amiable giant whose face split into the biggest grin accompanied by much animated head nodding.

"Think you can make it back to the Q?"

"Aside from the fact that my body feels as if it has been completely de-boned, it's affirmative on your last. Let's go before euphoria sets in and I miss the plane tomorrow. Man, I'm so relaxed, even my socks won't stand up."

The next morning, all the passengers surprisingly managed to show up at the departure terminal for the continuation of our flight to Vietnam. Once back aboard the aircraft, I settled back comfortably into my seat as I let my mind drift back over the preceding months that brought me to this point in my life.

"GOOD MORNING VIETNAM"

My reverie ended as our plane finally made landfall over the coast of South Vietnam. It was the first chance we had to get a glimpse of the country that would be our home for the next year providing we made it through in one piece. A chilling thought immediately crossed my mind that somewhere down below at this very moment, there were people who wanted to kill me. Where was that morbid thought when I called my Detailer in Washington and volunteered for duty in Vietnam? I had been safely tucked away aboard a ship in Newport RI, where life had started to become boring and repetitious, especially since our breakup. That precipitated my call to the Bureau of Personnel and it was a helluva of a thought to have just as I began a new tour of duty.

The sun reflected off a large river that meandered like an anodized silver ribbon through the shimmering water-filled rice paddies. The middle of May in 1967 found us at the start of the Southwest Monsoon season in South Vietnam and would last until September. This meant that we were just entering the wet season in this part of the world where we could expect rain almost every day. The Northeast monsoons, on the other hand, were basically dry and were prevalent from September through March. Beneath the wings of the airplane, a large city appeared spread out below in hues of brown dirty linen. The streets were crowded with people and the buildings possessed that shabby look of a tired, worn out taxi dancer.

As the plane banked to starboard, the pilot aligned the big bird with the long runway whose perimeters we noticed, were bordered by sand-bagged gun emplacements at evenly spaced intervals. The pilot made a better than average landing which made me think that he might have been an ex-Navy carrier pilot at one time. He taxied slowly on the hardstand, finally coming to rest in front of a squat, dirty looking building that served as the main terminal for Saigon's Tan Son Nhut International Airport. Here at last! My bottom was sore from being cooped up in the austere coach-like accommodations. After all, nothing was too good for our fighting men, right? Besides, that was the best that MAC flights had to offer since they usually selected the lowest bidder.

"WELCOME TO SAIGON, BUDDY"

We had landed in Saigon, a city that seemed to bulge at the seams trying to contain almost five million people. In the mid 19th century when the country was known as Cochin China, France with the aid of Spain invaded and began the colonization of French Indo-China until 1954. Following on the heels of their defeat by the Northern based Viet Minh and their leader Ho Chi Minh, all Catholics living in the north were permitted to emigrate to the south to avoid living under Communist rule. Then the struggle between north and south to unite the divided country began in earnest. The government in the south under President Diem requested help from the west and thus started the US involvement by providing military advisory assistance. Now here we were some twelve years later joining into the fray.

A blast of dry hot air hit us in the face as we disembarked down two antiquated, rusty mobile stairways onto a scorching hardstand. We were directed by flight attendants at the foot of each stairway towards a group of military personnel standing in the shade of an overhang just to the left of the terminal. This apparently was our welcoming committee. They were all dressed in neatly pressed greens with clipboards officially clutched under their arms and dark sun glasses. They were recognizable by their military insignia, so each of us gathered in small groups around our particular service representative. As each name was called, we were directed to the proper bus that would take us to our various destinations. Our Navy party was separated into two groups of officers and enlisted men, since the billets were located in different areas of the city. My group was assigned as Advisors to the Vietnamese Navy and consisted of nine Lieutenants and three Lieutenant Junior Grades. We were all in our 30s, and the majority of us were Mustangs; that is, officers who were originally enlisted men and had made the transition to the Commissioned Officer ranks through various routes. We were to find out later that the Navy had undertaken a new policy of sending older and hopefully a more mature group of replacements in-country because of casualties that had occurred to several of the younger officers who had preceded us.

Our bus was painted haze gray and the windows were covered with strong wire mesh. This reminded me of prison conveyance vehicles shown in the movies. The mesh was intended to deter any terrorist from lobbing a grenade or satchel charge into the bus. This later proved ineffectual as the Viet Cong counteracted that by coming alongside on their motor bikes and hanging a grenade with a hook onto the wire mesh. It would soon become apparent to me that this war was a constant battle of moves and countermoves.

As the bus left the fly-blown airport and made its way through the grime filled streets, I was amazed by the mass of humanity around us. Our ears were assaulted by the sounds coming from the ancient blue and yellow Renault taxies, 3-wheeled motorcycles that resembled front-end loaders, and all manner of motor bikes. The air was inundated with heavy gray smoke that was emitted from the exhausts from the many motors that propelled their passengers to their destinations.

After a short while, we pulled into a side street and stopped in front of another drab building whose second floor balcony was ringed with coils of barbed wire. There was a fifteen foot high wire enclosure in front of the building that was attached to the bottom of the second floor balcony. A small, wizened Oriental guard dressed in faded powder blue semi-military clothes, was casually sitting in a small guard booth at its entrance. He had a lit cigarette dangling from his lips as he gazed lethargically at the newcomers. A battered looking M-30 carbine lay casually across his lap and his sweat stained blue ball cap was pulled low over his heavy lidded eyes. These guards were comprised of old veterans from the French regime who were contracted by the U. S. Government to provide perimeter security for the various American installations. This one's quasi-alert demeanor didn't exactly convey a warm and fuzzy feeling to me.

Once inside, we were directed to large individual rooms on the first floor to the left of the entrance. In my particular room there were eight double bunks with mattresses folded over some sheets and pillow cases. The ceiling was about fifteen feet high and the inadequate lighting barely provided enough illumination to see our way around. We were told to make up our bunks, stow our gear in any available locker and prepare to eat lunch. The mess hall was in the rear of the building on the first floor.

Not knowing what to expect, we were surprised by the quality of food that was awaiting us cafeteria style. Three young Vietnamese girls with hair nets and white smocks stood behind the serving counter and upon seeing us, crowded together and giggled just like most other teenage girls in the world. The appraising looks we received were somewhat disconcerting and obvious, but this was probably not the time or place for fraternization.

After finishing our lunch, we were herded up to the second floor and shown into another dimly lit room by a bored American Petty Officer. The room contained fifteen battered and well worn desk-chairs where we were asked to have a seat.

Shortly, a ruddy faced Navy Lieutenant in work khakis entered the room and stood in front of our group. In a gruff voice that obviously belonged to an ex-Chief Boatswain's Mate, he said, "Welcome to Vietnam, people. My name is Lieutenant Pete Ross and I've been in this here land of enchantment for almost a year. In fact, I have twenty three days and a wakeup until I return to the land of the big PX. My job is to acquaint you with some of the various social pitfalls that you will no doubt encounter during your tour here in Viet Nam; specifically, the bars and the bar girls that inhabit them. There's no doubt in my mind that some of you will fall in love the minute you first set foot into one of these local establishments.

The first thing you'll notice is that the lighting is poor and it's designed this way purposely so you can't see the cockroaches that have free rein over the place. The beer is cold and the girls are warm and usually available. Believe me, it's a great temptation for any red blooded American. As you enter one of these places, you'll notice that every girl's head will immediately turn around to eyeball you. This is for two reasons: one, they're looking for their regular customers, and two, they're keeping an eye out for the 'White Mice' as the Vietnamese police are referred to because of their white uniforms. These police will harass a bar owner and his girls unmercifully unless some money changes hands on a frequent basis. It was a throwback to the Diem regime that previously ruled South Vietnam. The President had a sister known as Madame Nhu who was a strong moral force behind her brother. Under their leadership, bar girls had to sit behind the bar at all times and avoid any physical contact whatsoever with the male patrons. Young couples were not even allowed to hold hands in public and all signs of affection were strictly taboo. This all ended with the assassination of her brother causing the somewhat Puritanical morality to take a back seat throughout the country.

Getting back to the bars, the main item of the day is "Saigon Tea", which in reality is merely tepid iced tea sold as whiskey at inflated whiskey prices. The girls will caress, grope and put an occasional tongue in your ear in order to get you to spring for a 'Saigon Tea' . . . . or two or three. If in a very short time they don't succeed in getting into your wallet, they will move on to greener pastures. You can be certain of one thing in the event that you refuse to answer their plea for tea. You will be forever marked and shunned as a 'Cheap Charlie' in this or any other bar they happen to see you in. If on the other hand you weaken and buy the poor lass a drink, you will then belong to her exclusively and no girl will dare approach you as long as she's around the next time you come in. The Bamboo Grapevine is alive and functions extremely well in Vietnam.

'Pinch me, I think I've died and gone to heaven,' you will most likely say to yourself after one of these encounters. But shipmates let me assure you that the chances are pretty damned slim that you'll find any virgins in their line of work."

The rest of the classes were so mundane and dreary that I can't remember to this day what they were about, with the exception that they were mostly exact repetitions of the ones we had back at Coronado.

Two days later, having completed our short indoctrination, we were again herded into a military bus with all our gear. One of the more memorable pieces of information that we learned after leaving the Compound, was that directly across the street from our building, was a house of ill repute. Coincidentally, it was also called the "Compound", naturally taking its name from the building where we had been billeted. I filed that tidy bit of information away for future reference. Yeah, I know, once a sailor . . . blah, blah, blah.

RACH GIA, KIEN GIANG PROVINCE

We were again taken to Tan Son Nhut and further separated into groups heading north and south. There were six of us heading south and we were directed to board an old olive drab colored aircraft called a U-6A Beaver off to the left on the tarmac. Our destination was the town of Rach Gia, pronounced "Rock Jaw." This small city lay on the western side of Vietnam, close to the Cambodian border and was the capital of Kien Giang Province.

After a flight of about an hour and a half, we could see a beautiful city below us. A fifty foot wide canal led from the sea through the town. Rach Gia was the locale for a Vietnamese naval base that was home to three Junk Groups here in IV Corps. They were located in Kien An Province which was reputed to be inhabited by many Viet Cong and their sympathizers. The Junk Forces there were constantly having encounters with the enemy.

While we were still in Coronado, one of the instructors who had served his tour in this area, told us about PCF-4. The PCF, (or Swift Boat as it is known), was 50 feet long by 13.5 feet wide and fashioned after the World War II Nasty Boats. It had a crew of 6, consisting of 1 officer and 5 enlisted men. This particular boat was one of the original contingents of Swifts brought to beef up the coastal defense and interdiction effort.

PCF-4 was returning from a long and boring patrol on Valentine's Day, the 14th of February 1966, and the crew was tired and looking forward to a good night's sleep in-port. As she neared the shoreline in the Bay of Rach Gia, the crew spotted a small basket floating in the water. Sticking up from the basket was a long shaft of bamboo with a Viet Cong flag attached and fluttering in the breeze. The CO of the Swift, cognizant of the many types of booby traps employed by the enemy, was wary. He had his men throw a few grenades around the basket as they circled it several times, with no subsequent results. Finally, tossing caution to the wind, the CO ordered the Swift to be brought alongside thinking that the flag would make a good war souvenir to bring home to show the folks. Once the Swift was alongside, one of the crew grabbed the bamboo pole and proceeded to untie the flag. Simultaneously on the nearby shore hidden in amongst the mangrove trees, a Viet Cong touched a bare copper wire to a battery and exploded the mine that was tied beneath the basket. The ensuing explosion tore open the underbelly of the Swift Boat and sent a geyser of water some thirty feet into the air. The main deck buckled upward crushing the Cox'n against the overhead of the pilot house and killing him instantly. The gunner was blown out of his gun tub over the side and the Swift Boat quickly settled beneath the frothing dirty brown surface of the water.

One of the local Junk Force units happened to be in the area and heard the explosion. They quickly sent out a "Mayday" call reporting the mining of the Swift Boat and headed over to look for survivors. By the time PCF-3 responded, the Junk had already recovered two lone survivors, the CO and the radioman. Four other crewmen were fatalities and their bodies were later recovered during salvage operations. The remains of the Swift Boat was retrieved and sent back to the States for analysis where improvements to the hull were implemented in later boats of the class. Thus, PCF-4 was the first Swift Boat to be lost because of enemy action in Vietnam.

All this went through my mind as we passed over the bay and landed at the small local airport. After disembarking from the Beaver, we were met by two young Petty Officers with Jeeps, and driven to an ornate former Chinese funeral parlor where we would be temporarily billeted. The building was situated in a shady tree-lined street a few blocks from the waterfront. Inside, the large main room contained upwards of twenty cots complete with mosquito netting where we were assigned to empty ones and told to make ourselves at home. We were also informed that LTJG George Combs and I would be departing the next day for the base at An Thoi on the island of Phu Quoc.

The next morning after a quick breakfast of bacon and eggs in the small cafeteria, Combs and I were back in the Jeep and on our way to the airstrip. Our driver informed us that Phu Quoc was the largest island in Vietnam and was situated forty miles west of Rach Gia in the Gulf of Thailand. It was twenty two miles long by thirteen miles wide with the IV Coastal Zone Headquarters based at An Thoi on the southernmost part of the island. He also said that the Vietnamese maintained a huge Prisoner of War camp on the northern end which held some 35,000 prisoners. I sure hoped their security was good.

My travel companion, LTJG Combs was about five feet nine inches tall with a slight build. His black curly hair was cropped short with a cowlick on the top. He had large, washed out brown eyes that reminded me of a Lemur and it looked like he was trying real hard to grow a mustache. Although I never asked him where he was from, his slow drawl and twangy accent put him either from Texas or Oklahoma. He had orders to the Communication Center at An Thoi,(naturally with his accent), while I had been assigned as the Assistant Advisor to Junk Force Coastal Group 41, located on the small island of Poulo Obi.

The Vietnamese Navy Junk Force was comprised of 28 separate groups strategically located along the 1200 miles of South Vietnam's coastline. Each group consisted of 7 Junks and approximately 130 Vietnamese Naval personnel. There were usually 6 Yabuta Junks with a 371 Gray Marine Diesel 110 horsepower engine and 1 Command Junk, or *Chu Luk*, with a 671 Gray Marine with 348 horsepower. Weaponry aboard the Yabutas consisted of a .30 and .50 caliber machine gun and a .51mm mortar. The same armament was on the Command Junk, except that a heavier .81mm mortar replaced the smaller model.

These Junks were designed by a Japanese boat builder and were common in Southeast Asia. They were 10 meters long but considered a few meters too short for the bow to reach across the trough under normal conditions. Additionally, its 2 foot draft also made it notorious for pitching, pounding and porpoising while underway in a moderate sea.

Poulo Obi, I learned, was about eight miles south of the Camau Peninsula and was the southernmost part of Vietnam. It was approximately one hundred and fifty miles due south from An Thoi.

In February of 1965, a U. S. Army Huey helicopter pilot was flying a routine patrol over Vung Ro Bay near the city of Qui Nhon. He spotted what appeared to be a small island moving from one side of the bay to the other. As he flew lower he saw that it was a camouflaged motor vessel, obviously some VC trying to ferry in weapons. He immediately called in an air strike that resulted in the ship exploding like the Fourth of July. This awoke the brain trust in Saigon to the fact that a closer surveillance had to be maintained in order to interdict the enemy resupply routes along the 1200 miles of coastline from the South China Sea to the Gulf of Thailand.

By July of that year, Operation Market Time was implemented. It consisted of Navy DERs (Destroyer Escort-Radar), MSOs (Ocean Going Minesweepers), PCFs (Swift Boats), Coast Guard WHECS (Eighty-two foot High Endurance Cutters), WPBs (fifty-five foot Patrol Boats) and the Vietnamese Navy's "Blue Water" ships and the Junk Forces. The purpose of Operation Market Time was to interdict the enemy and prevent him from bringing in supplies from seaward.

Junk Groups were normally assigned a Navy Lieutenant as the senior advisor, a Lieutenant Junior Grade or an Ensign as an assistant and two senior enlisted men. Although I was a full Lieutenant, having been promoted while at Coronado, I was still ordered in as the assistant despite my numerous attempts to change my assignment while in Saigon. I was told that without a doubt an adjustment would be made once I reported in to the Fourth Coastal Zone Commander. Yeah, right!

The next morning at 7 a.m. we got into a Jeep with the same driver as yesterday and headed back to the landing strip. This time, instead of the Beaver, a U. S. Army twin engine DeHavilland Buffalo aircraft awaited us. It was similar to the Beaver and piloted by a young Warrant Officer who seemed hardly out of his teens. He, and his equally young looking co-pilot, appeared absolutely complacent as we climbed aboard. Combs and I sat down and buckled our seatbelts after stowing our gear under the seats.

The pilot taxied his olive drab colored aircraft to the end of the runway and upon turning it around, immediately pushed the throttle forward and lifted off into the clear blue sky that was just beginning to show signs of cloud formations on the horizon. We headed southwest for about twenty minutes over the waters of the Gulf of Thailand until we reached the island of Phu Quoc.

AN THOI, PHU QUOC ISLAND (4TH COASTAL ZONE HQ)

The pilot executed a quick landing on a large airstrip covered in its entirety with 3600 feet of Marston matting. The matting, used initially by the Seabees during WWII in the South Pacific, was composed of perforated sheets of steel linked together atop a smooth dirt base. The reason for the matting was to maintain the usability of the airstrip during the rainy season when the earth became a muddy quagmire.

Once again, a Jeep and driver were waiting to take us to the base. As soon as Combs and I had deplaned with our gear, the pilot turned the plane around and was airborne in a blink of an eye. We drove through an unmanned gate into a barbed wire enclosed compound that housed several Butler buildings. The driver dropped us off in front of a medium sized Quonset hut with a sign hanging over the door that identified it as the Admin Building.

As we entered the office, a Yeoman Third Class motioned us over to his desk and asked for our orders. He then picked up the phone and called the CO of the base, who by the way was also the 4th Coastal Zone Commander.

"Sir, I have two new officers here who just arrived," said the Yeoman into the phone. Listening to the response, he answered "Aye aye sir," and hung up. He pointed to the rear of the building and said, "The CO will see you now; straight back, first door on the right."

A voice called out for us to enter in response to our knock on the door. A tall, well tanned Coast Guard Commander stood up and extended his hand out over his desk to each of us and welcomed us to An Thoi. We learned later that he was facetiously referred to as "Screamin' Beamon." After meeting him, I was somewhat disappointed in that he appeared to be a blank piece of paper, approximately 40 years old and dressed in sharply pressed crisp tropical whites with shorts. He was so laid back that he was almost horizontal. That was my impression.

Not what I expected in one who calls the shots in a combat area. I wondered who back in the world had sponsored him for this billet. It could have been nepotism, but the Navy had been pressured from the beginning into include a Coastie in their command structure. After all, we were utilizing their assets and An Thoi seemed as innocuous a place as any to stick him.

After our meeting, we were given a short tour of the base, which included the Communications Center, the mess hall, the barracks and the best place of all, the bar. It was a small Quonset hut about fifty feet long by twenty wide, with a fifteen foot long bamboo bar at the back end. Six well worn high rattan stools stood guard with a pert Vietnamese girl sitting on the end one folding paper napkins. She was introduced to us as Suzy, the best beer-server around. She smiled demurely at the introduction and said "Hello," as she continued folding napkins. The most noticeable thing about her was that her shiny black hair hung down her back and well below her buttocks. I wondered how long it took her to grow it that long and what patience it must have taken to wash and comb it every day.

A very large mirror was centered on the wall behind the bar giving the impression that the room was much larger than it was. It also gave those who might be sitting at the bar an excellent view of the doorway. I've been told that the practice of placing large mirrors behind the bars in the early Western saloons was to allow the patrons to easily watch their backs as they downed their whiskey.

There were large multi-colored plastic Japanese lanterns hanging on the walls along with the usual collection of naval ship photos and group shots of prior and present military personnel. Two medium wall air conditioning units at each end of the bar hummed quietly while keeping the room goose-pimple cool, while two overhead fans where lazily moving the air around. Upon entering, the sudden drop in temperature from the outside was immediately noticeable and later settling to quite a comfortable drinking atmosphere. To one side, there was a standard sized pool table with a fair assortment of cues hanging on the wall. A genuine Wurlitzer juke box of indeterminate age occupied the opposite side of the room as its colorful lights undulated around its face while the unmistakable strains of Frank Sinatra singing "The Summer Wind" came softly from the speakers. In front of the juke box stood a ping pong table with strategically placed cardboard coasters under two opposing legs for leveling purposes.

We were introduced to a young Coast Guard LTJG named Jim Sutherland from Ohio who was deeply engrossed in an inventory sheet at one of the tables. Jim looked to be about 6 foot tall; carrying about 200 well placed pounds, semi-long brown hair and a tan that enhanced his image. But the most significant feature was his well-tended 1800's style seven inch handlebar mustache. I had to admit, on him it looked good. He had been the Executive Officer of the WPB Point Young and for some unknown reason, had been re-assigned to the Comm Center by the good Commander. In addition, he was also the base Alcohol Inventory Control Officer as a collateral duty. This made him a VIP in my book. After all, he was the honcho in charge of the booze locker and a guy to befriend for future reference.

An Thoi was also the home for a detachment of Navy Swift boats, Coast Guard WPBs and a Vietnamese Junk Group. My first impression of the US side of the base appeared laid back and indifferent, probably mirroring the Zone Commander's personality. This was evident by the total disinterested attitudes of the mama-sans who would shuffle through the head area, (toilets to you landlubbers), as the military occupants downloaded their last meals and drinks into the clean, white stateside type toilets with door-less partitions. The local Vietnamese women were hired as maids to perform the daily janitorial and laundry work for the troops. They worked six and a half days a week and in thinking back now, I wonder how many of them were Viet Cong sympathizers? Oh well!

The men attached to this base, I soon learned, preferred to be out on patrol rather than be ashore and endure the daily regimen of the afternoon volleyball game required by the Commander. This was his idea of providing JFKs for the troops. During President Kennedy's term in office, he initiated a service-wide dictum that the military had to get in shape and the way to do it was by having regular exercise. From then on, these evolutions were referred to as "JFKs." The daily volleyball game was usually played after lunch under a scorching sun on sand that could blister your feet. Having the game played at noon kept the men out of their racks for their usual "nooners", which the Commander felt was primarily responsible for their less-than-optimum physical condition. The only respite from this attempt at providing "recreation" for the troops was the welcome deluge of rain that would inundate the area during the Southwest monsoon season.

I was told that I was to spend the night at An Thoi and be ferried by WPB to Coastal Group 41's base on the island of Poulo Obi early the next morning. At least I wouldn't have to take part in the obligatory volleyball game.

Poulo Obi was the name given to the island by the French as they preferred it to its original name of *Hon Khoai*, which means Sweet Potato in Vietnamese. This island was the southernmost part of Vietnam and had a lighthouse on its highest point. It was located about thirteen and a half kilometers, or eight miles, due south of the Camau peninsula. The entire area of Camau was a "Free Fire" zone and home to many VC and their sympathizers.

ENROUTE POULO OBI

At 0630 the next morning I lugged my gear down the long wooden pier to the end where the WPB Point Banks was moored portside to. Once aboard, I was met on the quarterdeck by the Captain, Coast Guard Lieutenant Bill Shaw, and told to make myself at home. He said the ride to Poulo Obi would take about ten hours and we'd be getting underway immediately now that I was aboard.

As the WPB pulled away from the pier, the sky was clear, but some nasty looking black storm clouds were lying low along the southern horizon. The sea was a dark green with just a hint of small sea wisps scudding along the tops of the long rollers that were coming in from the south.

I descended below deck into the little galley as the WPB started her rhythmic rise and fall into the oncoming swells. The smell of freshly brewed coffee greeted me and one of the Petty Officers seated at the table invited me to sit down and join him in a cup. It seems as if most of the crewmen are always a bit curious about new Navy Advisors coming into country for the first time. They are also quick to offer little bits of advice to the FNG (Fucking New Guy) in order to enhance their old hand status in-country. After downing the hot, black coffee, I went back up to the main deck and headed aft where they had a Boston Whaler secured to the deck. I climbed inside and lay down across the thwarts, getting as comfortable as I could. Now, I've spent quite a bit of time on boats and was not particularly prone to *mal-de-mer*, but knowing that the WPB was a round bottomed turtle, I decided to stay up in the open air, just in case.

Time passed slowly and I had ample opportunity to think about what lay before me. What would it be like living on an island with Vietnamese Junk Force sailors and their dependents? How much combat would I see and when? All these thoughts crossed my mind until a Chief came and interrupted my reverie by inviting me to have some chow. Did I say time passed slowly? Here it was noon already and the sun had started to make itself felt even though there were some serious looking storm clouds to the southeast. I arose stiffly from my cramped position in the Whaler and immediately felt my greens sticking to my back.

Once back down in the galley, the air conditioning made me shiver as the sweat cooled on my back. Grilled cheese sandwiches and grape flavored bug-juice, (the term affectionately applied to Kool-Aid), comprised the lunch menu. For dessert, a pretty fair Brownie with pistachio ice cream rounded out the meal. I figured that I might as well enjoy it while I had the chance, because soon I'd be living on C-rations, fish and rice.

Around 5 that evening, the Captain called me up to the bridge. Fortunately the seas had calmed down quite a bit and negotiating one's way around the boat became a lot easier.

"We're about ten clicks from Obi and we'll send you ashore in the Whaler, so get your gear together and stand by," said the young skipper.

"Roger that" I replied and proceeded to gather my gear and my M-14 rifle. Needless to say I was pretty excited to see what my new home for the next year would be like.

As we came closer to the island, the soft sounds of surf drifted out to us. The Whaler was put over the side and I handed my gear down to a seaman in the bow while a Chief sat in the stern of the boat handling the Evinrude outboard motor. I clambered down and settled on the midship thwart as we pulled away from the WPB. The Chief said that although the base was on the north side of the island, they were putting me ashore on the south side because it was a smooth sandy beach and easy to get in and out of with the Whaler.

"How come you guys can't drop me off on the base side," I asked.

The Chief replied, "Because there are huge boulders in the inlet and the tide is ebbing. We'd never be able to get you in close enough with your gear."

"Why did the Vietnamese build their base on the side with the boulders?" I asked. "That doesn't make sense".

"They didn't originally. The base used to be on the south side until three years ago. From what I hear, when the Junks went out on patrol, they would always lob some mortar or M-79 rounds along the coastline of the Camau Peninsula. They'd also rake the tree line with .50 and .30 caliber machine gun fire since Camau was a free-fire zone. Well, they obviously got 'Charlies' attention. One dark night when most of the Junks were on patrol away from the island, the Viet Cong came across the thirteen kilometer stretch of water and attacked the base. They killed everyone including the dependents, set fire to the buildings and made off with whatever food and ammunition they could lay their hands on.

So the Vietnamese, with the help of the US Navy Sea-bees, rebuilt the base on the north side of the island because they believed there were too many spirits of the former residents occupying the original base."

"Thanks for telling me, you've made my day."

"I wouldn't worry about it too much Lieutenant, the VC were merely making a statement and they've pretty much left them alone since then. That's just about how it goes with Mr. Charles. If you hurt him, you can be damned sure he's going to come back at you to get even sooner rather than later."

The Chief guided the Whaler onto the sandy beach as he tilted the motor inboard so the screw wouldn't get dinged. I dropped over the side and landed in about seven inches of warm water with my rifle and gear in hand managing to make it ashore without any difficulty.

The Chief yelled "Good luck Lieutenant" as he backed down and pointed the Whaler back towards the WPB.

PART THREE

POULO OBI

I stood on the beach and tried to visualize the carnage that had previously taken place here, but it was difficult to imagine with the lush tropical scenery all around me. There was not a hint that a base had ever existed here or the wanton butchery that had ensued. The only disclaimer to that was a ramshackle covered storage hut off to the side containing 55 gallon barrels of diesel oil.

The smooth sandy beach stretched out for about three hundred yards and was seventy yards wide from surf to the tree line. It was bordered by plush jungle greenery that after a few yards inclined upward to the top of the island. Just then, I heard a voice hailing me as two smiling Vietnamese sailors came down out of the dense foliage to greet me.

"We come to bring you to the base *Dai-Uy*," said the taller of the two.

He was about five feet five maybe six inches tall, while the other was slightly shorter. They were both very slight of build and their shiny hair was the color of a crow's feathers. As the two of them hefted my duffel bag and AWOL bag, (gym bag to you), onto their small shoulders, they told me to follow them.

I slung my rifle over my shoulder and eagerly set out behind them. After a few minutes of making our way through the brush, the path angled upward and that's when I realized that we had to go over the friggin' mountain to get to the other side. It took over an hour and a quarter of steady climbing to reach just below the crest where we stopped for a few minutes rest. By now, I was drenched in sweat and puffing like a rutting bull elephant. The Viets, on the other hand, were only mildly perspired. Score one for the skinny guys, I thought. When we resumed the trek and finally made it over the top of the mountain, I could see a beautiful half moon bay with a grouping of metal covered buildings set back against the base of the mountain below us.

"There is the officer's hootch where you will live," said one of the sailors as he pointed down to the right. You *Co-Vans* live on one side of the building and our Commander and Executive Officer share the other.

The descent from the mountain naturally, went much easier and we reached the bottom in less than an hour.

We passed several long buildings on both sides that were divided into individual units that housed the Junk sailor's dependents. They formed a fairly large square area and in the center was a fresh water cement catchment where several children were being bathed by their mothers. All eyes turned to stare inquisitively at the new *Dai-Uy* in his sweat stained greens.

The officer's hootch was about fifty feet wide by thirty feet long and had one centralized entrance facing towards the sea. A pair of swinging doors provided the main entryway and was flanked inside by doors on either side that led to the quarters of the Base Commander and his XO on the right and the Advisors on the left. The entrances were covered by traditional long strips of plastic that is so common in this part of the world. The building had been constructed on a cement slab and stood back about ten feet from the short seawall.

As I approached the building, three Americans came out through the doorway. The first one looked like an Economics grad student, with straw colored hair partially covering his wire-rimmed glasses. He was about my height, perhaps an inch shorter, with dark blue eyes, and a small mole in the center of his left cheek. Later on, whenever I saw John Boy of the Walton's I would be reminded of this guy.

"Hi, I'm Chip Morris, the Assistant Advisor," he said as he extended his hand to me. "I'm sure glad to see my relief finally get here. Lieutenant Graham Edwards is the senior advisor, but he left yesterday on thirty days leave. He's extended his tour for another year and plans on being back here after his leave is up."

I reached for his hand and said "I'm Lieutenant Bob Kay or just plain Greek to my friends."

"If you don't mind my asking, why do they call you Greek?"

"Because I am Greek despite my anglicized name," I replied.

Accepting the explanation, he introduced me to Petty Officer Dewey Angus who was a Gunner's Mate First Class and an African American. His lanky six foot plus frame was topped by well trimmed hair and a razor thin mustache. He wore a Chicago Bear's tee shirt, a pair of khaki shorts and green rubber flip-flops on his size 14 feet. The manner in which he carried himself implied that he was an individual who was in complete control. Although his smile was there, it was minimal. He showed just enough of his white teeth to indicate that he believed in good oral hygiene. Nodding slightly, he shook my hand and stared directly into my eyes and said, "Welcome aboard *Dai-Uy*."

I was then introduced to the other First Class named Rusty Nales. It was obvious that Rusty was so named because of his red hair that was a tad on the long side. He was an Engineman and had spent his Navy time on diesel submarines. The most interesting feature about him was his pale blue eyes that seemed to absorb everything they looked at. Unlike Angus, Rusty had a somewhat wild look about him. His cheeks were covered with freckles and a halfhearted excuse for a mustache struggled under a ruddy, round nose above a thin upper lip. The bottom lip, however, appeared full and petulant which didn't help to enhance his looks. He tossed me a casual salute by touching his ball cap with two fingers like the Brits and said, "Hi Lieutenant."

Just then, two Vietnamese officers came out from the other side of the hootch. They were wearing white tee shirts, khaki shorts and flip-flops. Chip introduced me to LTJG Minh, who was the Commanding Officer and Ensign Le, his Exec. Shaking hands with both of them, it was hard for me to determine how old they were, since most Orientals do not normally show their age early on. I guessed probably around their mid to late twenties. Both men stood about five foot four or five and couldn't have weighed more than one hundred and twenty pounds dripping wet. But Minh's eyes were a different story altogether. Although his mouth was smiling, his jet black eyes really riveted you in place. I could only imagine what they had seen since serving in his war ravaged country.

"Welcome to Poulo Obi *Dai-Uy*, you must be tired after your long trip down here," said Minh.

"Glad to be here and yes I am a bit beat," I said.

"In that case we'll talk in the morning," as he and Le both nodded and went back into their side of the hootch.

Chip picked up my AWOL bag and M-14 and Angus hefted my duffel bag by the handle as we entered the US side of the house.

Angus said over his shoulder, "The Junks ride a helluva lot better than that Coast Guard douche bowl that brought you here Lieutenant."

I could believe that since the WPB tried her damnedest to make me barf several times during the trip. And I used to think that the wave patterns on Lake Michigan were nasty.

There were two metal double-decker standard Navy bunks, complete with mosquito netting located in the back room of the hootch. The room measured about fifteen by twenty and also contained a refrigerator of dubious vintage. A smaller room was partitioned off in the right rear far corner that was used for bathing.

Bathing, I soon found out, consisted of dipping water with an old enamel one quart pot with a handle from a rain barrel that stood outside the back window. The facility was fairly private as it faced onto the side of the mountain. You poured the water over your head and body, repeating the process until you were soap free. A pipe made up of soda cans, with both ends cut out, and taped together end to end, supplied the water from a rain gutter on the roof. All the comforts of home, I thought, but then again, this was war.

"Yours is the bottom one on the right" said Rusty "And I'm topside. Hope you don't mind a little snoring because ol' Angus has one that would cut down Giant Sequoias."

With that, he tossed me a can of Falstaff beer. So far, so good, I thought. But what I really needed now was to hit the sack . . . which I did right after downing the beer. Unpacking would have to wait until tomorrow.

Sometime during the wee hours of the morning, just before the black of night gives way to gray, I snapped awake from a deep coma-like sleep. My instincts apparently had not shut down along with my body and I lay in my bunk quietly trying to figure out what woke me. Then, I heard a noise coming from the trash can. Very slowly, I reached for my flashlight that was hanging from the bedspring above my head. I figured it was only common sense to have some light handy just in case the generator ran out of fuel. I thumbed it on and shined it towards the trash can, where perched on top of the trash, was a huge rat. When the light hit him, he raised his ugly head and stared directly at me. His face looked pinkish in the beam of light and his black beady eyes never wavered.

NO SWEAT! THOSE RATS WILL BE GONE SOON WITH THOSE TRAPS!

About then, Rusty's voice came from the top rack. "Don't pay no mind to our visitor, he's only interested in scraps and likes to lick the soda cans. Besides, he keeps the snakes away. They know better than to tangle with that critter."

With a grunt, I turned off the flashlight, hung it up and went back to sleep.

The next morning I was awakened by the sound of heavy rain pounding on our corrugated tin roof. The wind was blowing through the large window that faced the sea and the plastic strips that hung in the doorways fluttered crazily. I tossed my mosquito net aside and climbed out of the bunk.

Aside from the rat incident, I must have slept the sleep of the dead, and I really felt good. The others were still in their bunks, so I slipped on a pair of khaki shorts and got my feet into my trusty flip-flops. The beer that I had consumed before hitting the sack last night had distended my bladder almost to the bursting point and I could feel my morning constitutional coming on.

About that time, Chip got up on one elbow in the other lower bunk and said "How'd you sleep *Dai-Uy*?"

"Pretty good, all things considered. I guess you didn't hear the rat in the trash can early this morning."

"Nah, we're used to him. In fact, we call him Moon because he only comes out at night."

"Just as long as he doesn't try to get in the sack with me," I replied.

"The second week that I was here, I woke up late one night and found a rat giving birth on top of my mosquito netting. That shook the 'you know what' out of me," said Chip.

"Whew, I hear that. By the way, I need to make a head call, bad."

"The community head is located out front and about seventy yards to the left. Can't miss it, it's that structure built out over the water. If you just have to pump bilges, go behind the rocks over to the right of the hootch and piss in the sea. No one will see you there."

In possession of this information and with my stomach starting to rumble, I decided to head for the duty dumper. I spied the structure sitting some five feet above the water and constructed of thick bamboo poles with a corrugated roof.

"Isn't there someplace closer to take a crap instead of having to go out in that rain," I asked.

"No, all of us have to use the 'penthouse potty'. We have a fresh-water well here on the island that supplies our drinking water and the last thing we want is for some crap to contaminate it."

So, I dug out my poncho, slipped it over my head and started out for the tropical turd locker with a package of C-ration toilet paper in hand. The wind must have been blowing around ten to twelve knots forcing me to walk with my head down and leaning forward about 30 degrees.

This was a new experience for me to say the least. I managed to keep my balance as I climbed the inclined bamboo pole ladder that led to the main platform. It was about fifteen feet long by ten feet wide and was divided down the middle by corrugated metal sheets that separated the women's side from the men's. The advantage went to the guys as our half faced the sea while the women faced inboard towards the village. Each side was further divided into three units. The trick seemed to be to maintain your balance on the poles while getting into a squatting position. Your output would then simply drop between the poles and down into the seawater below. The surging tide provided the required flushing effect.

Having successfully completed my first bowel movement on the island, I carefully made my way back down the ladder and headed for the hootch. That's when I heard some giggling and a female voice said from the ladies' side of the outhouse,

"Good morning *Dai-Uy*, how you today?"

Surprised and embarrassed, I mumbled something unintelligible without looking back. How did I know there were women also using the facilities on the other side? Yes sir, this was going to take some getting used to.

There were one to two patrols out at a time consisting of two Junks each that would go out for about two days. This depended on whether they went into the Gulf of Thailand or into the South China Sea. Our particular patrol area stretched from the Song Ong Doc River on the Gulf of Thailand side to the mouth of the Song Bo De River in the South China Sea. The typical manning of a Junk was one Vietnamese officer, three crew members and a US Advisor with the same complement on the accompanying Junk, without an Advisor and a Chief instead of an officer.

Junks without a commissioned officer were manned by senior Petty Officers since there were only two Vietnamese officers and usually an *Aspirant* assigned to each group. The *Aspirant* was actually an officer apprentice and as a rule, was pretty sharp. Additionally, the Advisors were never all out on patrol at the same time, since at least one had to remain on the base in the event of an emergency where communication with US units was needed.

The Junks would regularly put out to sea without the benefit of any radar or compass. I quickly found out that the Junk sailors navigated by dead reckoning and the stars. At night, the man at the wheel was told to steer with the bow pointing to a particular star or planet. The officer would check his watch and at the appropriate time, point out another celestial body to steer by until we either arrived at our destination or dawn lit up the sky and obscured the constellations. Then it was strictly dead reckoning.

No matter what they had told us back in Coronado, the main purpose of the Advisor was to be able to call in US air support or artillery if the situation required it. This precluded the enemy from calling in any of the above which could prove disastrous. Even the American call-signs used over the radio were comprised of words that an Oriental would have extreme difficulty in pronouncing. These were provided to us by teams of people schooled in the art of linguistics and changed on a monthly basis. For example, the first call-sign I had in the Junks was "Yankee India." Some others that I had later on were "Crazy Racer Eight" and "Thirsty Boats Four." Just think what an Oriental would sound like trying to pronounce those handles unless they were extremely fluent in the English language. Chances were slim that we would run into too many of those guys out here.

The mission of the patrols was to interdict any attempts by the enemy to bring in weapons and supplies by sea. As a rule, most patrols were usually long and boring during the day, since most illicit traffic was undertaken under the cover of darkness. We would take turns catnapping during the day because it was essential that we be alert for any craft moving surreptitiously during the night.

Whenever a vessel was encountered, we would hail them and tell them to heave to so we could go alongside. We would check their papers as well as make a cursory search for any hidden contraband.

Word had come down from An Thoi for us to be extremely alert during these searches. Some incidents had been reported by other Market Time units that hand grenades were being tossed into the boats as they came alongside to inspect a suspicious craft.

MY FIRST PATROL

On my first patrol with my counterpart, Minh positioned me atop the Junk's cabin so that whenever we came alongside a fishing boat for inspection, I would have a good covering vantage point. Whenever we requested to inspect their papers, invariably one of the crew would go into their cabin to get them. From my slightly elevated position, it enabled me to see through their cabin window to prevent any surprises from within, such as grenades or weapons of any kind. My instructions were to shoot if I saw anything suspicious.

I was usually dressed in my greens, black beret, dark sunglasses and a 12 gauge Savage pump shotgun cradled across my knees which gave me an ominous appearance. Once we were tied up alongside, Minh and one of our armed seamen would board the boat and proceed to question the head fisherman as to their point of origin, destination, purpose for being in these waters and demanded to see their papers and ID.

Once all this had transpired, Minh would lower his voice and speak very slowly and deliberately to the fishermen for several seconds. The fishermen would almost always warily cast sidelong glances at me and immediately start nodding their heads up and down rapidly. I found out later that Minh was telling them that if they were caught again in this same area, he would turn the American loose on them, while nodding his head in my direction.

WELL LOOKY HERE, IT'S "CHARLIE"

Since most of these simple fishermen had probably never seen an American up close before, they were naturally intimidated by me. Nice guy! What a way to win the hearts and minds of the people. However, the implied threat was very effective.

On my second patrol, we headed North-North West into the Gulf of Thailand. For some undisclosed reason, we departed around six PM instead of early morning. The wind came up slightly once we passed the tip of Point Camau and the sea worked itself into a moderate chop. I had worn my heavy green cotton shirt with my sleeves rolled up, but quickly unrolled and buttoned them as the temperature dropped. Minh told me to try and get some sleep as it would be some time before we got on station, which turned out to be Cua Bay Hap or Square Bay as we US types had dubbed it. I also buttoned my shirt collar because I was starting to feel a bit uncomfortable. Trying to sleep on a hard wooden cabin top while heading into a northerly breeze with the boat digging it's prow into the oncoming waves, was almost an impossible feat. Every time I managed to doze off, the bow would bury itself into an oncoming wave and toss sea spray all over me. I looked around and saw that the rest of the crew were safely huddled inside the small cabin. With a grunt of disgust, I stretched my aching bones and swung down to join them. They each had a knowing smile on their faces although no words passed between us.

Around first light, we were still making pretty good time and the wind had subsided quite a bit. Minh was using his binoculars and ordered the helmsman to steer towards some running lights off of our starboard bow at about a thousand yards away. He turned to me and said, "It looks like a fishing trawler from Singapore. We will check it because they are a long way from home."

Apparently, the fishing boat must have seen us closing on them because they immediately heaved to and placed some rubber tire fenders over the side awaiting our arrival. I could see that the boat was rigged for long-line fishing by the big rolling chocks on their stern. This form of fishing is done by unreeling a huge length of heavy line with equally spaced horizontal lengths of fishing line with baited hooks connected every ten feet or so along with occasional artificial lures. The depth at which the line is streamed determines the type of fish they are targeting and is controlled by floats attached to the line. Close to the surface is called Pelagic long line and is aimed at Swordfish, Tuna and Sharks, whereas Demersal long line is used along the bottom for Halibut and Cod. This is a very popular method of commercial deep sea fishing around the world

Once alongside, with me in my position atop the cabin and armed with the shotgun, Minh and one of our armed crew boarded the boat which appeared to be about seventy feet in length with an eighteen foot beam. It was definitely a sturdy seagoing vessel. Their papers were examined and a conversation was taking place which I could not hear. Then one of the fishermen pulled back the after hatch cover, reached down inside and came up with two good sized sea Bass that weighed at least fourteen pounds apiece. He handed the fish to our crewmember, smiling

and bowing to Minh while casting nervous glances warily back at me from time to time. Ah, maritime intimidation and international extortion at its finest.

We cast off from the fishing boat, waving amiably at the captain as we headed towards the Regional Force base located on the left bank of the Song Ong Doc river, just a short haul north of Square Bay.

The Junks always made it a point to stop by and see if there was anything of interest going on in that area and touching base with the small US Army Advisory Team assigned there. Sometimes the Junks would even enter the canal-like river and journey up a few clicks to see what shook out, but the VC normally didn't mess with them during daylight hours. But nighttime was something else. Only a darn fool would stick his nose up there after dark, because the saying in the Delta was that the night belonged to "Charlie," and everyone respected that.

Across the river lay the immense dark and brooding Ca Mau peninsula which was the nesting place of the Viet Cong. For that very reason, it was a "Free Fire Zone." However, the inhabitants of the base didn't appreciate our lobbing the occasional M-30 grenades into the brush because inevitably, the Viet Cong would retaliate by mortaring them that night. So this trip, we went along with their wishes and didn't upset the balance of power in the area. Since none of the Advisors were around as we tied up to the dock, the visit was short. I knew from other Advisors that the officers of the Vietnamese Navy didn't much care for the average soldier belonging to the Regional Forces because they were akin to being "wannabes" and looked down on by the military. With nothing noteworthy being learned on our stop, we once again headed out into the Gulf of Thailand and headed South back around the horn.

"Well, it looks like we'll be having fresh fish for supper, eh *Dai-Uy*?"

"Sounds good to me," I replied, especially since I wasn't looking forward to the meager C-rats that I had brought along.

Normally, Advisors would bring a few boxes of C-rations along on patrol. I soon found out that this American fare fell far short of a culinary delight; however, it did wonders for weight control. When it came time for chow on one of these patrols, the Vietnamese would toss a concussion grenade or two into the sea. It usually resulted in several fish being stunned and floating up to the surface. A sailor would jump over the side with a helmet liner into which he collected the catch. Once aboard, the crew pitched in to clean the fish as a fresh pot of rice was already cooking atop a Sterno can. We could save our concussion grenades this time, thanks to the Singaporean fishermen.

Prior to my coming to Vietnam, I was never much of a fish eater, but after being invited to join the crew for their meals while at sea, I quickly learned to appreciate the taste of freshly caught fish. Naturally, we used the pungent *Nuoc Mam* sauce to flavor the food. At first, I was a little hesitant in using the sauce because most of the instructors in Coronado warned us constantly against eating it. But I thought in order to be accepted by the Vietnamese as their Advisor; shouldn't we be expected to share in their customs and food styles?

'SO AT LEAST GET SOME FISH WHILE YOU'RE DOWN THERE!"

I tried it and much to the delight of the crew, found that it enhanced the taste of the fish considerably. Well, so much for bum dope.

Nuoc Mam is derived from the extract of the large Anchovy freshly caught in the South China Sea and the Gulf of Thailand. The fish are placed in huge wooden vats, liberally covered with sea salt and then compressed by turning a huge handle attached to a screw and wooden press. The ensuing fluid drains down into a large container and is then poured back into the vats and pressed one more time. This results in a clear, amber colored liquid resembling fine whiskey.

The *Nuoc Mam* processing plant located on the island of Phu Quoc has the reputation of producing one of the finest fish sauces in all of Southeast Asia. The sauce is the principle ingredient used in Thai, Vietnamese, Laotian and Cambodian cooking. In preparing the *Nuoc Mam* for eating, vinegar, sugar and red chili peppers are added along with the juice of lemons or limes to taste. The fish, meat or vegetables are then dipped into the sauce and eaten. Believe me, it really did wonders for the meal, regardless of the horror stories they told us back in Coronado.

I will admit however, that when *Nuoc Mam* is cooked over a flame, the odor is reminiscent of someone boiling an old homeless person's underwear in a pot of urine. Whew! It brings to mind the old saying, "Once you get past the smell, you've got it licked."

We made it a habit while on patrol to share our C-rations with the Junk crewmen and eagerly partook of their hot rice and fresh fish. The meals were more palatable with this mutual arrangement.

We steamed steadily southward until we made a westward course change to bring us back around the tip of Point Camau. After a few hours of steaming and looking for random fishing vessels, we entered the South China Sea. A small island appeared just to the northeast of us and I asked Minh, "What's that place?"

"It is called 'Bird Island' and we stop there whenever we are in the area. Many sea birds inhabit the island which makes it a good place to gather their eggs."

The Junk eased between two huge boulders on the lee side of the island and three of the crew scampered ashore. Minh had taken over the helm and skillfully kept the bow of the boat away from the rocks. In short order they returned with their sailor hats filled with eggs. Minh edged the bow back in between the boulders and the crewmen nimbly jumped aboard without losing a single egg.

As one of the crew started scaling and cleaning the sea-bass from the Singapore fishermen, another one scooped up a pot of seawater and set it on the engine mount. In no time at all, the water was boiling and the eggs were dropped in. Once they were hardboiled, they were distributed around. I didn't realize how hungry I was as I quickly cracked and peeled the shell of my egg which was the size of a goose egg. With some salt and pepper from my C-rats, I sat on the bulwark and proceeded to enjoy my egg.

The youngest crewman Hiep, who was our engineman, came to sit beside me and offered me another egg. I should have suspected something by the way the others were intently watching us with half smiles on their faces. "Oh what the hell," I said accepting the egg. As I cracked the shell and started to peel it back, a small bird's head poked out taking

"Hey Cookie, how fresh did you say these eggs were?"

me by surprise. Loud guffaws and knee slapping ensued from the crew as they pointed to me in my discomfort. I had heard about these eggs being a delicacy in the Philippines where they were called "Balut," but I didn't realize that they existed here in Vietnam as well.

"I guess you do not enjoy this kind of egg, eh *Dai-Uy*," asked Minh with a grin. Here in Vietnam we call them '*Hot vin lon*.'"

"Not really, *Trung-Uy*," I replied lamely as I handed the egg back to Hiep.

"That's OK," countered Minh. "We cannot expect you to assimilate our culture overnight. Besides, we have other eggs that you can enjoy with our fish and rice tonight for supper."

I was beginning to admire the resourcefulness and the subtle humor of these people and was extremely comfortable with my decision to volunteer for duty over here. Then that familiar axiom crossed my mind, "I wonder what the poor a-holes back in the States are doing right now?" and I silently laughed to myself.

Just for your information, the Balut is usually made from a fertilized duck or chicken egg and is boiled for twenty to thirty minutes only after the embryo is 16 to 18 days old. The finished product is slurped into the mouth from the shell rather quickly before one can consider the options. I'm told that downing the feet, feathers, beak and fluid is a little like eating pretzel sticks in tasteless syrup. I'll pass on that one, thanks.

Our supper on the other hand, was a complete joy and I didn't even have to break out any C-rats to supplement the meal. The fish was cooked to perfection and the meat was sweet and white. I followed suit with the others and placed small pieces of fish atop my bowl of steaming rice and spooned the pungent *Nuoc Mam* over the entire thing. I had a second helping along with another hardboiled egg, and man was that good. My parents would certainly have been proud of me right about now.

All of us slept pretty well that night owing in part to our full stomachs, and the evening passed uneventfully. We had been steadily heading around the tip of Camau during the night towards our new destination, which was the eastern end of the Bo De River. This was the northernmost point of our patrol area in the South China Sea and it was a notorious waterway utilized by the Viet Cong. They transited it across the Camau peninsula to Cua Bay Hap on the western side thereby avoiding the risk of running into any of the Market Time units on patrol.

THE SINGAPORE FISHERMEN RETURN

Just then, the helmsmen called out that the same Singapore fishing trawler was hove-to just outside the mouth of the river. About that time, a thought that had been in my subconscious ever since our first encounter with the trawler made its way into my consciousness.

"Hey Minh," I yelled to get his attention.

Putting his binoculars down, he turned and furrowed his brow as he looked at me curiously.

"How much draft do you think that boat is carrying?"

Turning back to look at the trawler again, he replied, "About nine feet. Why?"

"Assuming that's about right, take out another foot for the bilges and that leaves seven feet of cargo space in the hold. When that crewman opened the hatch cover to get us the fish, he only reached down about a foot, which means that the hold was almost filled to the top with fish and ice. That's a lot of cargo and if that's the case, why didn't he head home to sell it?"

"Good question *Dai-Uy*. Let's go and take another look at this guy." Minh then barked an order for both the .50 and .30 caliber machine guns to be manned as we made our approach to the trawler. I, once again atop the cabin with the shotgun, kept my attention on the trawler's pilothouse. The Singaporean captain dressed in the same dingy khaki shorts from yesterday at least had put on an undershirt, although it was equally as grungy. With a smile of a Cheshire cat pasted on his nut-brown face, he made his way down to the after deck to meet Minh as we again came alongside.

"You want to inspect my papers again?" he asked still smiling affably.

"Yes," replied Minh. "When we boarded you yesterday near Cua Bay Hap, we were under the impression that you had a full load and would be heading back to Singapore."

"Ah," said the captain nodding his head and still smiling. "You would like some more fresh fish for your crew."

"Not really," replied Minh, "I want to inspect your hold.

I thought I detected a slight hesitation on the captain's part, but he maintained his composure and gestured towards the cargo hatch. "Feel free to inspect all you like," he said.

At the captain's command, two of his crew quickly removed the six by eight foot hatch cover revealing the ice-covered fish. Taking out a K-bar knife from a sheath on his belt, Minh knelt down and began probing the point of the knife in and around the fish. When it struck something solid, he looked up at the captain and quietly asked, "What do you think is hiding beneath this layer of ice and fish?"

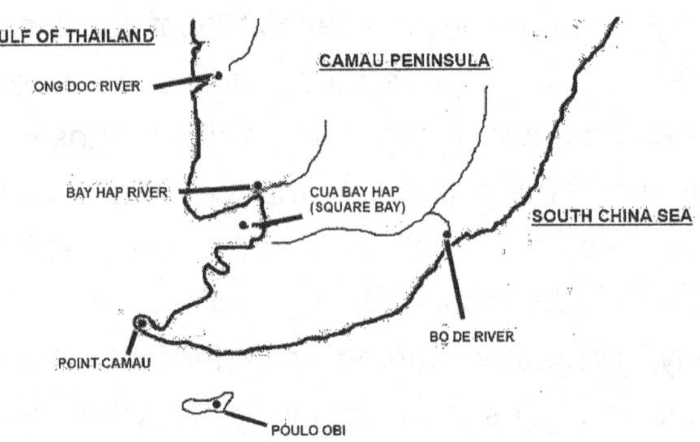

By this time, the captain's face turned a sickly shade of gray and perspiration had broken out on his forehead. "Get the rest of your crew up here on deck, now!" barked Minh straightening up. As he re-sheathed the knife, he pulled out a huge .357 magnum pistol and pointed it squarely at the now very nervous captain's head.

The captain spoke in rapid-fire Chinese ordering the rest of his seven man crew to assemble on the after deck. Minh sent Hiep the engineman, now armed with a .30 caliber carbine, to look for any stragglers. He reported back after completing his search that there was no one else aboard.

The trawler's crew and their captain were ordered to sit down on the deck cross-legged with their hands interlaced behind their heads. It was obvious that the fight was completely out of them, especially with two machine guns and a shotgun to contend with.

Minh then had Hiep dig down through the fish and ice where he discovered a heavy black rubber sheet. Pulling back a corner of the sheet revealed the top of a wooden crate. "Hey *Dai-Uy*," Minh yelled back over his shoulder, "It looks like our friendly fishermen were doing a little smuggling. What do you suppose is in those crates, guns maybe?" Then Minh turned to me and said, "See if you can raise one of the Coast Guard ships to come and give us a hand."

"Will do," I replied as I had the helmsman pass me our PRC-25 radio through the window. I reset the radio dial to the standard US frequency and began calling, "Any US unit afloat on this net, this is Yankee India One, over." It took three tries before I got an answer and it was a Coast Guard unit that responded.

I asked their radioman to inform his Captain of our situation, location and requested assistance.

"Roger that Yankee India One, wait one," came the reply. In short order, he came back on the line and informed us that they would be with us in about an hour and to hold tight. I rogered his transmission and said that we had everything under control.

Minh then ordered the trawlermen to lie face down on the deck head to foot with their arms stretched above their heads for better physical control. This also made it difficult for them to communicate with one another as they had done while sitting.

My respect for this young Vietnamese officer increased considerably as I witnessed the manner in which he was handling the situation. Strangely enough, the time passed rather quickly. Although the sun was at its highest, the skies were devoid of any clouds. Fortunately, there was about a 10 knot breeze blowing out of the southwest which kept us relatively cool.

Suddenly, Minh announced that he had sighted a large white vessel approaching from the east. Looking up, I recognized the ship as being a WHEC (Coast Guard High Endurance Cutter), and it was obvious from her large bow wave that she wasn't wasting any time in getting to us.

In actuality, it took about 25 minutes until she came neatly alongside the trawler. An officer was standing on the cutter's foc'sle and yelled down that he was the Executive Officer and he wanted the US Advisor to come aboard via the Jacob's ladder that had been hung over the side. I acknowledged him with a wave as I made my way across the trawler and climbed up the ladder.

Once aboard the ship's main deck, I threw the XO a salute and said "I'm Lieutenant Bob Kay, Senior Advisor to Coastal Group 41 out of Poulo Obi. We came across these guys twice during our patrol. Once off of Square Bay near the On Doc River and later on the west side near the Bo De River." I explained that our suspicions were aroused when we discovered them the second time in the South China Sea because we had assumed that they were on their way back to Singapore with a full catch. On the second inspection, we discovered large crates under a rubber sheet covered with ice and fish. We figured that these folks were transporting contraband for the VC. Otherwise, why the strange behavior near a known VC waterway?

The XO, who had introduced himself as Lieutenant Commander Julian, relayed the information over a small hand-held radio to the Captain on the bridge. After listening for a few moments, he replied, "Aye, sir." He then told me that they would take charge of the prisoners and see that they were brought to Fourth Coastal Zone Headquarters at An Thoi. Additionally, some of his crew would sail the fishing vessel to An Thoi in company with his ship. Then we'll find out what's in the crates. "Good work Lieutenant and pass that on to your counterpart and men," he said with a smile.

Before I left, I asked the XO if he would send a sit-rep to An Thoi and also have it passed to the Vietnamese side of the house.

"That's not a problem and we'll be more than happy to do it."

I quickly returned to the Junk and explained the Captain's plan to Minh and that a report would be sent to both sides at An Thoi. He grinned and nodded his head happily. He then barked some more orders and had the fishermen climb up the ladder to the WHEC where armed personnel were awaiting them.

Having successfully completed the transfer, we cast off from the fishing boat and headed south. "I think it is time for us to return to base, don't you think *Dai-Uy*?"

My reply was a "thumbs up" with a smirk of satisfaction.

We returned to Poulo Obi some five hours later to a hero's welcome. All the dependents and the advisors were lined up at the water's edge as we approached the beach. Word of our "catch" had spread quickly over the "Bamboo Grapevine" and the grins of joy were infectious all around. We received slaps on the back as we made our way up the sandy beach.

"Boy, look at you," said Rusty. "First time out and you hit the jackpot. I'm not only totally impressed, I'm jealous."

"Hey, we got lucky," I said. "Now all I want to do is take a shower, get out of these salt-encrusted clothes, have a cold beer and hit the sack."

"We heard it from a WPB that was off-shore today and I'm sure everyone in Fourth Coastal Zone is buzzing," said Angus. "It's about time we got a little publicity and credit in this war."

Things settled down once again on the island and life went quietly on. The patrols continued, only this time with a bit more enthusiasm among the crews and perhaps a touch of anticipation hoping that they too might run across some smugglers.

One morning after I had been back on the island for a few days, I was awakened by the loudest caterwauling that I had ever heard. I jumped up out of my bunk as Rusty looked over the side and said, "It's Wednesday, *Dai-Uy*."

"What does that have to do with that terrible sound? It sounds like someone is sticking a hot poker up an elephant's butt."

"You're close, but there's no elephant. It's only Ba Trinh, Chief Mai's wife, dragging her 100 pound boar pig to the water catchment for his weekly bath. She has a hank of rope tied around his front foot and physically has to drag him . . . which he don't like one bit. It's a virtual tug-of-war accompanied by the loudest squealing you'll ever hear. The pig doesn't share Ba Trinh's enthusiasm for the weekly scrubbing. Although I must admit that once the pig gets into the water, the resistance stops and he lets Ba Trinh soap him down. That is one clean pig and you'll get used to it just like we did."

"Great! Just friggin' great! A 100 pound porcine town crier."

That evening after supper, the four of us were sitting around outside the hootch, enjoying some free time off from patrol while the two Vietnamese officers were up in Rach Gia on personal business. For personal business read "getting laid". Since they were both bachelors and came from well to-do families, this was considered standard operating procedure for most Vietnamese Officers. However, it should be understood that as in any other society, the married ones also took an occasional bite from the forbidden apple. Oh really?

A slight breeze was blowing in from the sea that kept the ever-present flies from bothering us. Angus was lying in our only hammock stretched between two palm trees just off the cement slab. Chip and Rusty sat atop the small two foot seawall that kept the surf away from the building, while I was seated on a crude bench with my back against the front of the hootch.

I don't remember how the conversation started, but we somehow wound up lamenting about our lack of erections in the morning.

"It's probably our diet or lack of something nutritional," I said.

"Damn, I hope so," said Rusty. "I was beginning to think that the saltpeter the Navy put in our food during Boot Camp was just starting to kick in."

"That's not true," I said. "The Navy was just screwing around with your mind to keep you focused on the real job at hand rather than on sex, or the lack thereof, during Boot Camp."

It seemed logical to me since we've been subsisting on fish, rice, beer, soda and the ever-popular C-rations, ever since we all came to the island. It was comical in a way for four adult males to admit something as personal as that without being embarrassed.

"You'd think with all the beer ol' Angus consumes that he would wake up with a piss hard-on that would make Cleopatra's Needle look stunted," said Rusty.

"You got that right," agreed Angus as he stuck his big gnarly hand down the front of his shorts and sensuously massaged his pecker while asking, "How're you doing down there big guy?"

"Keep doing that in front of us and I'll have to make a notation in your health record," I said.

"Ha!" he said. "That won't even rate honorable mention after all the Clap Reports I already have in there."

"Now there's a real Fleet Sailor," said Rusty. "If he's had the Clap as many times as he says he did, it's no wonder that his dick doesn't have the stamina to stand up by itself anymore."

"Fuck you and the horse you came in on cherry-boy. You're just jealous because of the lack-o-pussy in your young life."

"Fuck me and my horse pardner and you'll never go back to screwing sheep and bag ladies," sneered Rusty.

Oddly enough, Chip didn't say much during the conversation. I was to learn later that his parents were Missionaries, which would account for his silence during these raunchy dialogues.

Sometime during the early morning hours, I was awakened by a loud gunshot from somewhere on the mountain. As I started to get out of my bunk, which seemed to be becoming a habit of late, Chip said quietly from under his mosquito netting, "Relax, that's just the lighthouse keeper shooting bats. He uses an old Garand M1 rifle and a battle lantern to spot and shoot them."

"What does he shoot them for? Aren't bats supposed to keep the area clear of night flying insects?"

"Yeah, but he also culls the herd, so to speak. He waits until they've finished their feeding and then bags them when they hang upside down high in the trees to sleep."

After a few more shots shattered the island's early morning quiet, I got back under my netting thinking about the bat hunter. I figured it was just another idiosyncrasy of the lighthouse keeper. After all, what else did he have to do up there except maintain the light?

A few hours later when we all were finally up and about, Chip asked me if I'd like to go up to the lighthouse and meet the bat hunter and his family. I quickly accepted since I was not due to go on patrol until the following night.

"What time do you want to go," I asked.

"How about in a half hour? It'll still be fairly cool and we can hang around with him for a couple of hours and come down in the late afternoon."

"Fine with me," I said.

Several times since I had arrived on the island, I had noticed a woman scrabbling up a steep, well worn trail that headed straight up the mountain on the far side of the village. I had assumed that it was the lighthouse keeper's wife heading back up after visiting the other dependents on the base.

When I mentioned it to Chip, he nodded and said that if she was a little on the chunky side, it most likely was her.

"Boy, she must be in good shape the way she beats feet up that dirt trail," I said in admiration.

"Absolutely, her physical appearance is deceiving. She's been doing that for the last twenty years, ever since the French hired her husband to take care of the lighthouse."

"Who pays him now?"

"Beats me," Chip said. "I wouldn't be surprised if nobody did. Just think how many administrators have come and gone in Saigon during the past twenty years. They could have very well forgotten about him."

"You could be right and I'll wager that if someone in the Saigon government got wind of him and could figure out a way to capitalize on the situation, they'd have already sold his job to the highest bidder."

"Sounds about par for the course," Chip replied as he sat down to put on his combat boots. "Better wear these instead of your sneakers; it'll be easier on your feet."

I hadn't been wearing my boots very often since coming to the island because it was more comfortable wearing flip-flops around the base and sneakers out on patrol. But, I heeded Chip's advice and put them on.

THE CLIMB TO THE LIGHTHOUSE

As we started towards the base of the mountain at the rear of the dependent's housing, I noticed that Chip had brought his M-14 rifle along with him.

"What's with the weapon?" I asked. Do you expect to be attacked?

"No," he answered smiling. "I always carry it with me out of habit."

To each his own I thought. I could never recall having read about any Missionaries who carried weapons, so I immediately dismissed it from my mind.

Chip pointed off to the left towards some heavy undergrowth as we reached the end of the dependent's housing.

"I'm taking you up the old road that the French had built. It will take a little longer, but it's a heck of a lot easier than the goat trail that the others use."

As we approached the dense foliage at the base of the mountain, Chip pulled at the hanging vines revealing a five foot wide road that headed upwards at about a thirty degree incline. It consisted of several switchbacks each extending about fifty yards or so, before reversing itself in its upward ascent. He pointed out the thousands of huge rocks that had been piled atop one another to support the base of the road from cascading back down the side of the mountain.

"I'll bet the French must have used mules to haul the rocks up here," I said in wonderment and privately thought to myself that when they were finished, they probably screwed the mules and ate them. Shaking off that depraved thought, I asked, "How come the folks don't use this path to go up and down to the lighthouse?"

"It takes too long, besides I'll show you another reason as we get higher."

Rounding the third switchback, we came upon a massive spider web extending from one side of the road to the other. It was anchored to a vine that had encircled a boulder on the inboard side of the road and the other to a tree that grew out between the supporting rocks on the outer edge.

"Man oh man," I said in astonishment. I've never seen a web as big as that before."

"This is the other reason the people don't like to come this way," He said as he lobbed a small twig into the web.

From out of nowhere, a spider appeared with a body about the size of my hand. It was not only the ugliest spider I had ever seen, but the biggest and scariest one too. Its brown hairy body literally floated across the fine silk like threads until it came to rest in the exact center of the web. It remained absolutely motionless and I was certain that its shiny obsidian eyes were looking directly at me.

"Now what?" I asked.

He laughed and said, "Shoot it. There's more where that came from."

"You're not serious, are you?" I asked trying to decide whether he was pulling my leg or not.

"Yes I am, honest. Unless you want to try and knock him off with a stick so we can get by," Chip said, still smiling.

"Why don't you shoot him?" I asked.

"Because I want you to have the honor of slaying your first dragon on Poulo Obi," he said seriously as he handed me his rifle.

"OK, if you insist," I said as I clicked off the safety, took aim and blew the huge arachnid to hell and gone.

The shot reverberated loudly and I was afraid the base might go to General Quarters. I could have saved myself the trouble of worrying, because nothing out of the ordinary stirred down below. Besides, I'm sure all the dependents were aware that the crazy Advisors were humping up the old French trail to the top of the mountain. There just didn't seem to be any secrets on Obi.

We picked up some fallen branches and proceeded to clear a path through the massive web.

"How many more of these do you think we'll run into?" I asked as I tossed the web entwined branch down on the ground.

"Your guess is as good as mine."

Fortunately, we did not encounter any more webs, save for several smaller ones off to the side of the road.

As we finally crested the top of the mountain, the lighthouse loomed high above us to the right with a modest dun colored cinder block house with a tin roof attached to its base. Several small children rushed out to greet us followed by a wiry, bowlegged Vietnamese male in faded black shorts, bare-chested and smiling from ear to ear.

"*Chao Trung-Uy*," said the man elatedly as he grabbed Chip's hand with both of his and shook it with gusto.

"*Chao Ong Dat*," replied Chip. "This is *Dai-Uy* Kay, the new *Co Van* who will take my place."

Dat continued smiling as he grabbed my hand and repeated the vigorous pumping as he said, "*Chao Dai-Uy*."

As near as I could tell, he looked like he was in his early fifties and lacked the majority of his teeth. Those that remained were stained and yellowed most likely as a result of poor oral hygiene and excessive smoking. His grin however, was genuine and infectious.

"How are you?" asked the keeper of the light in halting English.

"I am fine, thank you," I also answered slowly as I retrieved my hand from his calloused grip.

"Come, come," he said to us as he shooed away his children in rapid fire Vietnamese. They quickly scampered away, laughing as only happy children can do. Dat looked at me and asked, "Do you have children *Dai-Uy*?"

"Yes," I replied. "I was married for awhile and had three daughters, but I am alone now."

He tilted his head to the side as he winced slightly and said, "That too bad. Children bring much joy to family. As you can see, we have seven; three boys and four girls, ages from 18 down to 1 year. After all, I no have television to watch after work is finished . . . and nothing to do but make baby."

I had no answer for that, but I couldn't fault his logic.

He led us into the house through a stout wooden Dutch door that opened up into a spacious kitchen area. The room contained a battered wooden table with eight equally worn wooden and wicker chairs. Although the floor was bare cement, it was surprisingly clean. A brick lined oven, similar to the ones found in old European bakeries and Pizza parlors, occupied one corner of the kitchen. The oven was heated by burning wood or charcoal below in an opening behind a small steel door. It was amazing how much heat efficiency a setup like that could generate. This was immediately evident by the heat that was coming from the oven where a huge black kettle was happily bubbling away and cooking its contents.

I recognized the stout woman who came out from one of the other rooms. She was the same one I had seen heading helter-skelter up the dirt trail to the lighthouse. She nodded as her husband introduced her to us in his broken English.

"This my wy, *Phuc*," he said proudly. It seemed that many Vietnamese who were in the early stages of learning English, dropped word endings, such as wy for wife, how for house, etc.

We both acknowledged the introduction with "*Chao Ba, manh gioi*," and they both smiled at our greeting in their language.

Chip said, "I would like to take *Dai-Uy* Kay to the top of the light," as he pointed upwards with his finger.

Dat nodded in affirmation and said, "OK."

Chip led me to a small alcove at the rear of the kitchen that housed a wrought iron spiral staircase. As we ascended, the very distinct odor of Gauloise cigarettes permeated the air in the stairwell. Gauloise are manufactured in France and once you've been around someone who is smoking them, you'll never forget the strong cloying odor.

"I see you're familiar with French tobacco," Chip said as he saw me wrinkle my nose. "It's amazing how long the smell lingers."

"How come I didn't smell them in the living quarters?"

"His wife won't tolerate his smoking around the children. He can, however, light up when he's topside on the light, or outside the building."

"Where does he get French cigarettes?" I asked.

"He has a brother in Paris who's fairly well off and he sends them to another brother who lives in Rach Gia. Whenever the wife goes up there on a shopping run with one of the Junks, she picks them up from him. Neat, huh?"

Reaching the top of the stairs, I saw a familiar pair of Navy issue 750x50 binoculars hanging by its strap from a nail on the bulkhead and a box on the deck containing a Very pistol and flares.

"Where did Dat get his hands on this stuff?" I asked Chip.

"One of the previous Advisors had given them to him after the original base on the south side of the island was overrun. He probably figured that this was a good vantage point to have a flare gun handy. Dat was instructed to fire off a red flare over the base in the event he saw danger approaching the island. Sort of an early warning system, you might say."

"I'll have to hand it to that advisor, he was a thinker."

We stepped through a narrow doorway that led outside to a three foot wide grilled walkway with a meter high metal railing that completely encircled the glass enclosure. It seemed solid enough to support us and oddly enough, there was little or no rust on the metal. It meant that Dat was doing his preventative maintenance around here when he wasn't making babies.

What a view! From this height, we could see all around the island, including Camau in the distance to the north.

"What powers the light?" I asked after taking in the beautiful panoramic view.

"There's a 500 kilowatt GM diesel generator with a 250 KW backup unit sitting just behind the house in a small shed," said Chip.

"How does he get the fuel up here?"

"He and his wife hump it up in five gallon jerry cans, one in each hand."

"Ouch! My hat's off to them. It's no wonder that no one has come to replace him, not even for free rent."

Chip laughed and said, "Think about them the next time you set your thermostat or turn on the lights when you get back to the States."

We stood and gazed around for a few more minutes and then headed back down the stairs. Just as we reentered the kitchen, Dat came out of one of the bedrooms. He was carrying a young girl in his arms and he gently set her on one of the chairs that had a cushion.

"This my oldest daughter Lien," he said beaming with pride.

She was in her late teens with the most beautiful face that I had seen so far in Vietnam. Her hair was jet black, shoulder length and shiny, framing an unblemished and absolutely angelic face. The almond shaped eyes were black as coal with very thin, arching eyebrows and long eyelashes. Her lips were slightly petulant framing teeth that were white, small and even. Under her plain white cotton shirt, I could see that she possessed a gorgeous, unencumbered set of breasts. Believe me, it was a struggle to keep my eyes elsewhere. From below the hems of her black cotton pajama pants however, two thin and emaciated looking legs protruded.

Chip, following my gaze said softly, "Lien has had Polio since birth and has never been down off this mountain."

I was at a loss for words. What kind of God could create a creature as lovely as this and then afflict her with such a horrible disease? I could only imagine what her life had been like up to now or what the future held for her being tucked away from the rest of the world. But I'll say one thing; she wasn't lacking for any love or attention from her family.

Once Lien was comfortably seated, she looked up shyly into my eyes and said in a soft voice, "How are you today, *Dai-Uy*?"

I was not only surprised at her English pronunciation, but at the clarity of her voice. "I am well, thank you."

"Where did you learn to speak English so well?" I asked.

"With help from *Trung-Uy* Chip," she said, as her eyes drifted over to him. "He has been my teacher for almost a year."

I looked over at Chip and began wondering if I had grossly underestimated this guy. If nothing else, he seemed to have accomplished something worthwhile during his year in Vietnam.

"Will we be able to continue my lessons after he returns home?" she asked looking directly at me.

"I don't see why not," I answered perhaps a bit too quickly. "I must, however, warn you that he is a much more qualified teacher than I am."

"I do not worry; I think you are also a man of great patience and understanding."

There was nothing I could say in response to that, besides I was feeling rather sheepish because of the thoughts that had crossed my mind after seeing her beautiful breasts. Ah, "Once a sailor, always a sailor."

BAT WING SOUP

Dat interrupted my fantasy by saying, "Please sit down and have something to eat with us."

Looking over at Chip, I could see that he was ready to accept by pulling a chair up to the table and noticeably, next to Lien. I sat across the table from them and tried my darndest to appear comfortable, which I was not.

The wife had set bowls of steaming soup in front of us, along with aluminum soup spoons. This was what had been cooking in the large pot when we first arrived and the aroma of the soup was pleasing albeit a little pungent.

"What about the rest of your children?" I asked.

"Oh, they eat later," said Phuc. "They play now."

Dat asked me if I wanted some hot sauce or peppers for my soup.

"I'll let you know after I taste it," I replied. I caught a slight flicker of amusement crinkling the corner of Chip's eyes which made me wonder what was going on. As I dipped the spoon into the thick, steamy soup and brought it warily to my lips, it reminded me of the first time I had eaten Mock Turtle soup. It was greenish grey in color and had a gruel-like texture probably because the rice in the soup was slightly overcooked and mushy.

I had to admit that it was tasty although a bit different from my previous culinary adventures that I've had sampling new foods around the world. After my first couple of spoonfuls, the tension around the table eased and everyone dug in heartily . . . . and no, the soup did not need any hot sauce or peppers.

I decided it wouldn't be polite to ask the host what kind of soup it was and secretly, I didn't want to know. I figured that somewhere along the line, the answer would be revealed to me. The main goal was to survive with dignity, which fortunately I did.

After the plates were cleared away, Dat got up and brought a small bottle containing a clear liquid to the table. As soon as he did that, Phuc came over and picked Lien up effortlessly in her arms and carried her away from the table.

"Time for man talk and man drink," she said over her shoulder as she set her daughter gently on a rice mat near the fireplace.

"Do you drink *Ba Xi De* before, *Dai Uy*?" asked Dat.

"No, I don't believe I have," I answered looking from Dat to Chip. Neither of their faces gave a clue as to what was being asked of me, so I calmly played along with them.

Chip finally broke the silence by saying, "It's the local moonshine here in Vietnam and it is rice wine with a kick."

I watched as Dat carefully poured the clear liquid into three small shot glasses. The three of us clinked glasses as we said the traditional "*Chin Chin,*" and as I lifted the glass to my lips, the aroma of kerosene immediately assailed my nostrils. I would have set the drink back down, but I noticed that the other two men had tossed the liquid down quickly. I had no intentions of being the lone chicken of the group, so I knocked mine back in true sailor-like fashion.

What followed next was classic. My eyes instantly watered as the liquid passed over my tongue, down my esophagus and into my stomach, leaving a taste of JP-5 Jet fuel in my mouth. Wow, I had never had anything so potent since my first taste of Ouzo with my maternal Grandfather. Both men sat looking at me and smiling.

"How you like, *Dai-Uy*?" asked Dat grinning from ear to ear.

"Whooeee," I finally managed to gasp. "What octane rating does this stuff have?"

"It gets easier to handle as you go along," piped in Chip. "You'll find after awhile, that it's not too bad."

"I'll bet. Sure hope my taste buds are salvageable."

"No problem *Dai-Uy*," said Dat as he proceeded to refill our glasses again.

"Oh, the things that I do for my country," I said as I reached for my glass. "Here's looking at you, kid," and down went the second drink.

True to Chip's word, it did go down a lot easier than the first one. Now I thought, if I could only hold on until I got back into my rack down below.

As Dat prepared to refill our glasses a third time, his wife said something very sternly to her husband in a voice that left no doubt as to who the boss was up here. Dat reluctantly put the cork back into the bottle and surrendered it to her.

"Sometime, he drink too much and fall down," said Phuc.

I nodded twice affirmatively, while secretly being elated that I didn't have to endure another drink. One more of those liquid Semtex Sizzlers and I would probably have done a half gainer off the top of the lighthouse rather than attempt the walk back down.

The cessation of drinking, thankfully, had signaled the end of our visit. Chip and I both stood and thanked Dat and his wife for their gracious hospitality, to which they both bowed in reply. I went over to the fireplace and took Lien's slender hand in mine and said that I would return shortly to help with her lessons. She cast her eyes downward as she bowed her head to me.

Retracing our steps down the old French road was much easier than the ascent, but I'm sure it had to do with our senses being numbed by the *Ba Xi De*. I was certain that neither Chip nor I would want to eat anything else tonight once we returned to the hootch. All in all, I felt pretty good despite the constant buzzing in my ears.

As we started down the trail, there was a little bit of an offshore breeze rustling through the palm fronds and it carried a hint of approaching rain in the air.

After a few minutes, Chip asked, "What did you think?"

"About what, the family?"

"The whole deal up there: I figured you'd be surprised not only at the lifestyle, but of Lien too."

"You can say that again." I had never heard much about them before and least of all, about a daughter with Polio. It's a damned shame."

"Too true, like it's almost embarrassing to talk about it."

"Do you realize that she has no idea whatsoever of what life is all about except what she sees in that old lighthouse?"

"Like you said, it's a shame. That's probably why I took it upon myself to try and teach her English. At least it gives her something to keep her mind occupied and gives me a little bit of self satisfaction."

"You're all right Chip; I see your point."

"By the way," he replied with a devilish grin on his face, "How did you like the Bat Wing soup?"

"What wing soup?" I stammered.

"Bat Wing," said Chip as he crossed his hands pressing the thumbs together and wagging his fingers while making a kissing sound. He was obviously enjoying my discomfort. "That's why he hunts the bats, for the wings. Apparently the French taught him the fine art of preparing the soup, and it's also reputed to be a strong aphrodisiac. It must be true; after all he's managed to pump out seven kids up there."

"What else has he got to do except diddle Phuc once the generators are running and the light is working?"

For the rest of the way down, I kept imagining that my stomach was getting ready to regurgitate the soup and listened intently for any rumbling sounds with apprehension. Luckily, the rice wine must have put a lid on it.

By the time we reached the hootch, we found Rusty and Angus sitting on the seawall each holding a can of beer.

"How'd the visit go?" inquired Angus.

"Pretty good," said Chip, "and the good *Dai-Uy* here, got his first taste of Bat Wing soup."

"What did you think of it?" asked Rusty crinkling his eyes.

"Admittedly, not bad, but the *Ba Xi De* was something else.

"Don't tell me ol' Dat made you drink that drain cleaner," asked Angus, making a wry face.

"Yep, and he probably would have done me in if his old lady hadn't made it 'Last Call' after the second one."

"Did you get to meet Lien?" asked Rusty grinning lewdly.

"Yes, I did, and it breaks my heart to see a beautiful girl like that have to exist the way she does."

"But she doesn't know any other way," said Chip. "Can you imagine what it would be like if she had lived in the city before being isolated up there?"

"You know, I have a buddy in Sweden who married a Vietnamese girl and she had an older sister who also had Polio like Lien. Once he managed to get all his in-laws out of Vietnam and over to Sweden, his best friend Bendt married the sister. It's a good thing that Bendt was a big strapping, easy-going Swede, because he carried his new bride everywhere. In fact, they had two kids the last I heard. So, I'm sure Lien could do the same thing if she ever gets lucky enough to meet a guy like Bendt."

"Fat chance," said Angus. "From what I've seen of these Viets, the big majority of them only think with their dicks."

"That's not totally true," said Rusty. "I think for the most part that they have good family values. Although, I'll agree, there are some bad actors that I wouldn't let get within sniffing distance of my sisters."

"Look at the pot calling the kettle black," said Angus throwing a pebble at Rusty. "That horny bastard humps up the hill at least twice a month, saying that he's going to do preventive maintenance on the generators. You know he's only doing it to be around Lien."

"Stow that shit," said Rusty angrily. "Besides, old Dat would blow my sweet Irish ass away if he even suspected that I had designs on his daughter."

"I can believe that," I said as I thought about my willingness to teach her English. "They don't give Purple Hearts for wounds received from an overly protective father, do they?"

We all decided at that point to call it a day and hit the sack. I was asleep before my head hit the pillow and didn't so much as move until the sounds of activity woke me up the next morning. Slowly easing my eyelids open, I saw Rusty trying quietly to gather his gear. It looked like he was fixing to go on patrol.

"Sorry if I woke you Boss, but duty calls. Aspirant Tam caught me as I was making a head call this morning and said he was taking out a patrol. I told him that I was in the jump seat and I'd go with him."

"That's OK. Take care and call if you need us," I said to his back as he went out the door.

Getting back to sleep was impossible now that I was awake and the sun was lighting up the front room. My mouth tasted like a hundred lizards held an orgy in there. Yuk! Ptui! So, I slowly got my body up and headed for my toothbrush, paste and Listerine. After about ten minutes of vigorous scrubbing and rinsing, I felt my mouth was finally ready for some hot coffee.

Good old Rusty had thoughtfully put on a fresh pot before he left. I made a mental note to myself to inch his evaluations up a skoshe when the time came. I poured myself a mug of the hot, aromatic liquid, dumped in some sugar and carried it outside to enjoy the beginning of a new day. Just as I came through the door, I saw a Coast Guard WPB come around the point and heave to about a hundred yards off the beach. I hustled back into the hootch without spilling a drop and fired up the radio.

A voice answered me and said that they had orders to pick up LTJG Morris and ferry him back to An Thoi. Although I knew that Chip was to be relieved to return Stateside, I didn't expect it so soon since LT Edwards was still on leave. The voice then asked if there was anything we needed before they made their return to Phu Quoc.

Angus' voice croaked back from his rack with, "Tell them we'd like some bread and a big can of peanut butter. The crap that comes in the C-rats ain't worth a shit." He also told me to ask them if they had any pussy to spare, which I naturally ignored.

I relayed the request and added "If you have an extra block of American cheese, we'd appreciate that too."

"No problem," crackled the voice over the radio. "We'll be over in about thirty minutes."

Having heard the conversation, Chip jumped up eagerly and said, "I'll be packed and ready by the time they get in."

True to their word, a Whaler, with a Chief at the helm and a seaman in the bow, worked its way in through the surf. Since it was high tide, the boat was able to make it easily through the boulders and land on the beach. Angus and I were eager to get our "care package", so we helped pull the boat up onto the dry sand.

"Two fresh loaves of bread, a #10 can of Peanut Butter and a five pound block of American cheese already sliced by the cooks," said the Chief as he handed me a cardboard box. "You guys planning on having a party are ya?"

"No Chief, it's just something we decided was missing from our diet. Mr. Morris is gathering his gear now," I said just as Chip ambled down to the water's edge all decked out in his black beret, greens, boots, duffel bag and rifle.

"Man, that's the fastest packing I've seen yet," I said.

"Hey, I've been getting my gear together since you got here. After all, transportation opportunities off this island are few and far between, and I wasn't about to miss this one."

"I hear you," I agreed.

"Well guys, it's been fun, but it's time for me to go home. I'll be heading for Destroyer School after my leave is up. I'll think of you guys here on this tropical island paradise while I try to endure the Rhode Island scene. Keep in touch and stay well. Say goodbye to Rusty and the Viets for me."

With that, we shook hands as he slapped me on the back saying, "It's all yours now *Dai-Uy.* Take good care of our two juvenile delinquents and keep clean thoughts."

We smiled as he handed his gear to the seaman and clambered into the Whaler.

"Many thanks for the goodies. You've made our day," I said to the Chief.

"Glad to be of help," he replied. "That's part of our job description."

We helped push the boat off the beach and with a wave from the two Coast Guardsmen and Chip, the boat backed around and headed for the WPB. We went back into the hootch a little slowly feeling somehow that we had just lost a family member.

In order to break the spell, I said, "Are you hungry?"

"And horny, as always," retorted Angus.

With that, we proceeded to make peanut butter and cheese sandwiches. Man, did they hit the spot. Believe it or not, they even tasted good being washed down with beer.

Rusty's patrol returned early the following day because of engine trouble. When I told him about Mr. Morris's departure and the care package from the Coast Guard, he immediately went for the bread, peanut butter and cheese. It took him longer to make the two monstrous sandwiches, than it did to devour them. Ah youth, I thought rather enviously.

About three days later a loud yell from the other bunk fractured the morning silence. I leaped from my rack again not knowing what to expect and quickly looked around the room. I finally determined that the sound had come from Angus. He was lying on his back with a smile on his face that would make a reclining Buddha jealous.

"Looka here *Dai-Uy*, ain't this the prettiest hard-on you've ever seen?"

Well, not having made a practice of looking at other guy's penises in my life, I was a little embarrassed. But the thought behind it spurred my curiosity.

"I had one last night," mumbled Rusty softly as he grinned down from atop his bunk.

What's happening here? I wondered. Then I remembered getting up to take a leak during the night. I thought it had merely been a piss hard-on, but now I wasn't so sure.

"We've got to look at this phenomenon scientifically" I said.

"How's that?" asked Rusty.

"What's changed in our diet that would resurrect the dead?"

"We only had peanut butter, bread and cheese aside from our regular fish, vegetables, rice, soda and beer," said Angus.

"Well, it's got to be the bread, cheese or peanut butter, since I'm sure it wasn't the other stuff," I surmised.

We all seemed to agree on that point, but what should we do about it?

"Tell you what guys, I'll keep eating the bread, Rusty the cheese and Angus the peanut butter and let's see what happens.

"How the hell do you expect me to eat peanut butter without bread," growled Angus.

"The same way that I'm eating bread without cheese or peanut butter," I growled back.

"This is the only way we can isolate the source. Who knows, we may be on the verge of a big discovery for men."

"Screw the other guys in the world," laughed Rusty. "I just want my 'bone' back."

Less than two days after we started this pseudo-scientific experiment, it was evident that the peanut butter contained the magic ingredient, since only Angus continued to enjoy tumescence of his "bone."

"Do you think we should write to the company and tell them about this?" asked Rusty. "I'll bet they'd send us a case or two of peanut butter."

"Yeah, and we'll tell them that we found out it contains Vitamin 'E' for Erection," said Angus, laughing at his own joke.

"On the other hand, we can keep this secret to ourselves; otherwise there'll be a run on peanut butter in Southeast Asia. Then we won't get any at all and we'll be right back where we started," I added.

"Good by me," said Rusty.

"Me too," agreed Angus, with a big grin on his face as he once again went back to massaging his genitals.

The Vietnamese officers returned from their brief R&R and were obviously sexually satisfied for another four weeks or so. Our patrols resumed and nothing out of the ordinary happened with the exception that our beer and soda supply became critically low.

"Time to make a booze run to An Thoi," said Angus seriously one evening over fish, rice and vegetables.

"Why don't you make this one *Dai-Uy*?" said Rusty. "I'm sure you can use a break since you haven't done anything but patrol and sit around this island since you got here."

"You neglected to mention his weekly trek up the mountain to tutor Lien," chimed in Angus with a leer on his face.

"Do I detect a bit of jealousy in that remark?" I asked Angus. "If so, feel free to alternate tutoring sessions with me."

"Nah boss, I'm pulling your leg. Besides, it ain't Kosher for me to be near her as long as the peanut butter is still working."

"In that case, I nominate Rusty for the job. He can alternate with me and check out the generators at the same time. It will take some wear and tear off of my aging bones. "As for the beer run, that's a good idea. I'll talk to Minh and see when the next patrol to Phu Quoc is scheduled."

BEER RUN

As fate would have it, a few days later I was called on the radio by the local CIA type who resided in Camau. The head honcho in that encampment was a likable ex-Marine fighter jock by the name of Tex Childress. He had crash-landed in North Korean territory during that police action after his plane had been hit by ground fire. Miraculously, after successfully ejecting out of his damaged jet, he managed to make his way out after twelve harrowing days. That feat alone should give you an idea of the makeup of this gent.

He made it a habit to touch base with us every so often to find out if we had run across anything interesting during our patrols. Since I had nothing of value for him, I mentioned that I was planning a trip up to An Thoi as soon as I could get a ride.

"Oh, oh," he said. "Sounds like you're trying to bum a ride at the expense of our good taxpayers. Tired of riding those worm-ridden boats of yours already, Squid?"

"Not exactly, but this is a very important mission and I could use a faster mode of transportation. After all, the guys are depending on me to replenish our beer and soda supply because we're about dry."

"Well, in that case, I just might consider giving you a lift providing you don't start telling me any friggin' sea stories."

"I promise, honest."

"We'll be at your location around 0700 and I'll have a thermos of good hot coffee to wake you up," Tex said.

With that good piece of news, I signed off and started to pack some gear for an overnighter in An Thoi. I was looking forward to some U. S. type food, a hot shower and maybe a decent movie to watch.

The next morning, exactly at 0700 and true to his word, the sound of a helicopter's rotor whup-whupping broke the island silence. The white Air America helo came in low over the water, flared out smartly and landed gently on the sandy beach just off to the right of the hootch.

Minh and Le came out of their side rubbing the sleep from their eyes, while Rusty and Angus were already up and having coffee. I should correct that and say Rusty was having coffee. Angus was drinking his usual cup of hot, sweet chocolate because he said it helped maintain his complexion.

The pilot nodded to me and remained aboard the helo with the rotors idling as Tex climbed down. He stood an inch over six feet tall with a slightly receding blonde-gray buzz cut, a massive chest, nineteen inch neck and a thirty six inch waist. His curly hair covered arms resembled Louisville Slugger baseball bats and ended in hands that could squeeze the air out of a football. All in all, he presented a very imposing figure even though he didn't look like Hollywood's version of a spy. He was in his mid-forties with washed out brown eyes that took in everything.

Typical of most American civilians in-country, he wore a light tan colored bush jacket with short sleeves that failed to cover the globe and anchor tattoo of the Marine's emblem on his right bicep. The wrinkled khaki pants were cuff-less and terminated about an inch above an expensive pair of snake skin cowboy boots.

Casually approaching the hootch, he acknowledged the two Vietnamese officers with a jaunty salute and a beaming smile.

"How's everybody here on the best kept secret of this here war?" He asked.

Both men smiled and returned his greeting.

"We are fine so long as the Viet Cong do not decide to pay us a visit again," said Minh.

"Well if they do," Tex said, "all you have to do is give me a holler and me and my Nungs will come over and give you a hand." "That's a promise, hear?"

All CIA compounds in-country were guarded by Nung tribesmen who were contracted to provide base security. They hated the Viet Cong with a passion because they looked down on the Nung people. They considered them inferior to the Vietnamese and subjected them to extreme fratricide.

"We've come to give your Squid counterpart a lift to An Thoi," said Tex, "If that's OK with you *Trung-Uy*."

It was a neat bit of diplomacy seeing as this was a Vietnamese Base and Minh was the CO.

"No problem, as long as he brings back a case of *Nuoc Mam* for us from Phu Quoc," said Minh with a sly grin.

"That's do-able," said Tex as he grabbed me by the arm and pushed me towards the waiting helo.

"Don't forget the mail," Yelled Rusty from inside the hootch.

As I buckled myself into the rear seat, the pitch of the rotors increased until the vibrating craft slowly lifted off the beach. Once we were clear of the palm trees, the pilot angled us northward into a gray overcast sky.

PART FOUR

AN THOI NAVAL BASE, PHU QUOC

The trip to the island of Phu Quoc was pleasantly normal until Tex turned around from his right front seat and asked, "Did you hear about the Army chopper that was downed by ground fire just outside of Can Tho last week? It was up around four thousand feet when somebody opened up and riddled them with a .51 caliber machine gun."

As he said that, my eyes automatically went to the altimeter and noted that we too were at four thousand feet. Just then, I heard this whack, whack, whack against metal and my stomach did a reflexive lurch. My fear must have been obvious from my facial expression because Tex and the pilot started guffawing loudly. Evidently this was a standard joke with these guys to scare the crap out of the newbie by making him think we were being shot at. In reality, it was Tex banging the bowl of his pipe on the helo console. Some joke I thought. Good thing that I had made a head call before we left, otherwise I'd be in need of a skivvy change.

"AREN'T YOU FLYING A LITTLE BIT LOW ANDY?"

The rest of the trip passed uneventfully with minimal chatter until after a little over an hour's flight, we landed at An Thoi.

Tex opened his door and said, "We're heading on over to the Special Forces Base at Ha Tien so we'll pick you up tomorrow a little after noon. Will that give you enough time to finish your business?"

"That'll be great," I said. "Sure appreciated the lift even though you guys really tested the watertight integrity of my sphincter up there."

Again, they both laughed good naturedly and waved as I got clear of the helo. It lifted off and headed towards Ha Tien which lay east-north-east on the Vietnamese Cambodian border.

I made my way to the main building and really had to make a serious visit to the nearest head. I was relieved that my fear didn't cause me to soil myself, even though I had brought a clean change of clothes and skivvies. Some days you're the cat and others you're the canary. Finished with the head call, I set out to find my Coast Guard buddy, Jim Sutherland. If you'll recall, he was also the Liquor Locker Custodian of the base along with being in the Comm Center.

I found him stretched out on his bunk listening to a tape from his mother back in Ohio. He motioned me to sit down and said, "You've got to hear this new tape of dirty jokes my Mom sent me."

It was one of the funniest tapes I had ever heard and my sides started to hurt from laughing at the jokes.

"How about giving out with some of your jokes for her and Dad to hear? I'll bet you know some that they haven't heard before."

Never being shy when it came to telling jokes, I proceeded to tell some of my better stories for his folks back home. Now that's the way a family should be, spreading humor rather than lamenting about their poor son being in Vietnam, etc., etc.

When we finished with the tape, Jim sat up in his bunk and said, "How's life down on that island paradise of yours?"

"Not bad, but we're down to the last of our beer and soda."

"Well, we're almost in the same shape here," he said grimacing. "A couple of the guys are in Saigon as we speak, to replenish our stock. They should be back in the morning."

"That's good. I got a lift from the 'Air Whiskey' folks, (that's how the Viets referred to Air America), and they're picking me up tomorrow noon on their way back from Ha Tien. Not to be outdone, however, we gringos retaliated by referring to "Air Vietnam" as "Air Nuoc Mam." I guess we were all just big jerk-off kids at heart.

"They must have some special ops going with the Green Berets," he said. "It must be nice to have your own special airlines at your beckoned call."

"Hey, beats bouncing around at sea in a wooden Junk for thirty hours. Why not? Besides, the Special Forces people are there to react quickly to any nasty situation and if they had to plod through the red tape to get transportation, they might as well have stayed home."

"That's why they get to wear the green beanie, Squid," said Jim jokingly. "After all, you get to wear a black beret like the French Fags and have all those comfortable Junks at your disposal to dally around on the briny."

"Funny, but I'm not amused," I replied. So what's left to drink until the supplies come in?"

"There's some Carling Black Label beer left in the club but the rum, gin, vodka, bourbon, rye, scotch and wine are all gone."

"If I drink any of that Black Label, it'll give me a dose of the Ho Chi Minhs for sure." (This refers to the trots, the Hershey Squirts or simply diarrhea of the worst kind, which I had already experienced since coming to Vietnam).

"Do you have any suggestions?"

Jim furrowed his brow and said, "Let me check the locker."

He walked into the passageway where a stout wooden door with a massive lock protected the hard liquor storage. The beer supplies were kept in a huge walk-in cooler next to the mess hall freezers and were also protected by a fist sized lock.

Jim came out of the liquor locker shaking his head and holding a quart bottle of Crème de Menthe in his hand.

"This is it Boobala," he said with a frown.

"Well, it's going to have to do, if you're game," I said.

"It's okay by me too, what the hell?"

"Put it on my tab and we'll hit her a lick later."

"I've got the 1600-2000 Commo watch tonight, but we can muster on the beach after that, if you can hold out that long."

"Sits good with me, but I'd better eat some chow to prepare my stomach against the Green Death. What's on the menu tonight?"

"Yankee Pot Roast, oven browned potatoes, fresh corn on the cob, mixed greens salad and Jell-O for dessert."

"Oh Lordy, I've died and gone to the great mess hall in the sky," I said as my salivary glands kicked in. This was really something to look forward to after the rice, fish and C-rat regimen that had been sustaining me since I landed on Poulo Obi.

Jim had to eat early chow so he could relieve the watch in the Comm Center, so I went to my bunk in the transient's room and flopped back to wait for regular chow call.

If it wasn't that I was anticipating a good hot stateside meal, I probably would have dozed off. Instead, I lay there enjoying the cool evening breeze wafting in through the screens.

I wondered what the poor guys were doing back aboard my old ship. They were probably facing another day of endless paperwork, drills and monotonous watches after having visited all those lush South American ports on the Unitas Cruise. Well, since I had volunteered for this, it didn't really matter.

The evening meal had met all my expectations. After washing it down with a cold glass of fresh milk, I went over to the galley window and let the cooks know what a great meal it was. What the hell, compliments never cost anything and I'm sure they were appreciative to get even one in this mess hall.

I meandered over to the bar where the TV was playing. Bobbie the Weather Girl for the Armed Forces Radio Network based in Saigon filled the screen. She was a fairly attractive young blonde whose primary work was as a secretary for United States Aid In development (USAID), but volunteered her time to AFVN. Her mellifluous tones caressed the ears of her many viewers all over South Vietnam as she reported the local weather nightly.

Following the news and weather, everyone's favorite TV show in-country was "Combat," starring Vic Morrow and Rick Jason. Even the Vietnamese liked the show. I loved to hear them roll the r's when they pronounced the name of Vic Morrrrow. Ah, WW II. That was a war, when you could tell the enemy by the uniforms and their distinctive helmets. Not so here in Vietnam where they all looked alike. However, in time, I came to believe that one could distinguish a VC from a friendly simply by looking in their eyes. Early Greeks believed that the eyes were the windows to the soul and thus, it was hard for the VC to hide their hatred for us.

The show was just ending when Jim got off watch and joined me at the bar.

"Watching the boob tube *Dai-Uy*?" he asked.

"Better than listening to some of the shit kicking music playing in the barracks," I said.

"Hey, don't knock Country Western cousin," he feigned his displeasure with a wry lopsided grin.

"I'm not," I said, "It's just that the songs are all about lost love and broken hearts. I listen to music to cheer me up, not pull me down.

Give me George Shearing, Count Basie and the Four Freshmen anytime."

"To each his own Bubba, but I also like the Four Freshmen and they sing plenty of love songs too, you know."

"Yeah, you're right, but too much of that self-pity crap isn't good for you. Another thing that bothers me with the CW scene is their 'Line Dancing.' Having traveled through Alabama, Louisiana, Mississippi and Texas, I can understand why they line dance."

"Why's that," Jim inquired.

"If you've ever seen the size of those big-butted buffarillas down there, you can see that this form of dancing was made for fat people. No way could they dance close together because their arms would be too short to get around their partner's waist."

"Never thought of it in that light, but it does make sense once you think about it," he said with a smirk.

"Did I ever tell you about the time my car conked out while I was visiting the "then" in-laws in Rochester, Minnesota? It was a February evening in '58 and I was in a garage just on the outskirts of town. It was colder than a witch's tit with ice and snow all over the ground. The local mechanic was replacing my pitted distributor points while I sat next to the hot air heater in the corner of the garage. A van pulled up, obviously also in need of some minor repairs and five men entered the garage. One of them asked the mechanic if he'd be able to look at their van when he had a minute.

"No problem," said the mechanic, "I'm almost finished."

Meanwhile, their leader, a slim, curly headed guy, came over to me by the heater and said, "Hi, I'm Roy Acuff."

I stood up and as we shook hands, I told him that I was Bob Kay and was pleased to meet him. He stared at me for a few seconds and with a puzzled look on his face, smiled slightly, turned and walked back to his companions.

The mechanic whispered from behind me, "Son, don't you recognize Roy Acuff, the great Country Western singer?"

I said, "Nope, never heard of him. I'm sure my failure to recognize him might have hurt his feelings, but I didn't mean any disrespect."

"It figures, you Navy types weren't taught any couth," said Jim. "Well, are we going to drink to the woes of the world or not?" he asked as he got the bottle of Green Death from his locker and a couple of cans of salted Planters peanuts. "I can't drink seriously unless I have something to munch on."

That reminded me of the many times back in Coronado, when a bunch of us would sit in the Green Anchor, and drink rum cokes with Queen Anne olives in them. The Green Anchor was the BOQ bar on the second deck and had large green tinted window panels. The bar was "L" shaped and with the existing chairs and tables could accommodate about sixty people. The bar was appropriately named because of its location on the Amphibious Base. The congenial enlisted Filipino bartender always obliged us with two olives in each drink because he knew we also liked to eat while we drank.

One occasion in particular stuck out in my mind just a few weeks before graduation on a Friday night. Most of us had just returned from our showers after the daily physical workout and sought the coolness of the bar. That evening, the place was packed to over capacity and the liquor flowed freely. Suddenly, the bartender reached up and clanged the ship's bell behind the bar signifying that someone had entered the bar with his hat on.

In the Navy, such an affront results in the guilty party buying everyone in the house a drink. The perpetrator in this instance was obviously a Reserve Officer and I say obviously because his hair was way too long and almost covered his ears. Ernesto the bartender informed the officer that a round of drinks was on him and naturally everyone switched from beer to hard liquor. The officer's face reddened and he immediately retreated out the door.

It turned out that the guilty party was a Lieutenant Commander dentist who was here for two weeks of annual active duty from New York. He was surprised when he later received a call at the BOQ from the Executive Officer of the base informing him that he expected a check for $165 on his desk the next morning to cover his bill or else a disciplinary report would be sent to his Reserve Unit's Commanding Officer. Don't you just love it?

Ah, what memories! I then said, "Lead on Captain, I'm following in your wake sir."

We went down near the water's edge and sat with our backs against two huge coconut trees, bare feet burrowed into the sand and facing the South China Sea. The night sky was clear of clouds and all the constellations stood out brightly amid the other far off stars and planets of the universe. A soft breeze blew in off the sea and some unidentifiable music was playing in the bar. This was a perfect atmosphere for imbibing and reflecting philosophically.

"You know Jimbo, this kind of quiet night reminds me of my first cruise to the Mediterranean aboard a Navy Tanker when I was a kid. As Quartermaster of the watch, I was on the port wing of the bridge taking an alidade bearing on the Island of Stromboli some ten miles in the distance. It was a little after Taps and the crew was settling in for the night. The volcano on the island was erupting slightly spewing flames up into the pitch black sky.

All of a sudden, sounds of murmuring came from the forward deck fifty feet below as both the Officer of the Deck and the duty Boatswains Mate came out of the pilothouse to investigate. As the three of us peered down over the splinter shield, we could just barely distinguish four crewmembers in their skivvy shorts. They were standing on deck facing the island and holding their crotches chanting "Ingrid, Ingrid."

"Sure glad I wasn't on that cruise. Sounds like you had some terminal cases aboard," remarked Jim.

"Not really. That was just after Ingrid Bergman and the Italian director Roberto Rossellini got it on making the picture 'Stromboli' on the island. Morals were more stringent in those days and the scandalous affair that resulted in her becoming pregnant, hit all the front pages. I never imagined that those deck apes could even read. Go figure!"

"Sounds to me like you squids need more time ashore with other human beings," he replied.

What could I say to that, I wondered? Then again, life at sea can cause rather deviate behavior in some folks.

Feeling completely at peace with the world, I chanced to look up at the sturdy palm tree whose fronds were gently swaying above us in the evening breeze.

"Hey, what happens if one of those coconuts comes crashing down on our skulls?" I asked faking a genuine concern.

"Never happen GI. The ripe ones have already been harvested by the Junk sailors. They carry them out on patrol in case they get hungry or thirsty. The coconut makes a satisfying snack and the milk is sweet, as you will find out if you don't already know."

He screwed off the cap, held out the bottle, and told me to do the honors.

"May the last Chinaman be bent over," I said as I lifted the bottle to my lips and took a healthy slug of the syrupy liquid.

"Where in hell did you hear that?" he asked me as he reached for the bottle.

"It's an old-time Turkish Sailor's toast, or so I was told,"

"Well, I've heard that you Greeks have a reputation for anal attraction, so I would have assumed that it had originated from your part of the Mediterranean."

"That bit of mythological history dates all the way back to the Peloponnesian Wars. The Greeks had young boys accompany the troops in the field where they served as spear and sword carriers during battle. At night they performed the function of surrogate wives. But that practice ended a long, long time ago. Alas, the stigma still thrives. The truth is that the Turks are really into butt buggering, and I'm not saying that just because the Greeks and Turks historically do not get along with each other."

"Hmmm, interesting bit of Mediterranean lore my friend, but I will still keep a wary eye on you because I've heard that a true Greek never leaves his friend's behind . . . . and I am your friend." Jim said jokingly.

By now, I was feeling the liquor warming my stomach. "At least this stuff will help digest the chow that I had so wolfishly put away for supper."

"You ate that much?" he asked.

"Damned right I did," I replied. "Although it was great, it wasn't better than getting laid; I can assure you."

"Amen to that Matey." He said somberly as he passed me back the bottle. "By the way, have you ever been to the 'Grass Shack' in Rach Gia yet?" he asked after a pause.

"No, what's the Grass Shack?"

"It's the local whorehouse in Rach Gia that caters strictly to us GIs. Whenever you get over there, ask anyone at the BOQ and they'll direct you. They've got one horny honey there that is a little on the portly side, but pretty as a picture. We call her the Chunky Donkey."

"Chunky Donkey, I get it, a fat piece of ass," I said shaking my head in amusement.

"Yep, and she's clean and cheap too."

Now I know many of you reading this probably can't imagine two adults deliberately getting wasted on Crème de Menthe. Perhaps it was the time and place, being on the opposite side of the world from the places we knew, or whatever. But, it indeed happened. Little else is remembered of that episode, except to say that we later both slept like babies once the bottle was empty.

The next morning, I awoke in my bunk, poncho liner on the deck and the grandmother of all hangovers squeezing my skull in a vise. How I got from the beach to my bunk remains a mystery to this day, but I'll never forget that horrible fur-clad piece of meat that was my tongue dripping drool all over my pillow. Why did people do this to themselves? Did we deliberately try to fill our experience locker with the nastiest memories so that every ensuing action would appear better by comparison? Who knows? Did you ever wake up next to an ugly old, naked woman? Oh well, whatever floats your boat. Ugh!

After a few scalding cups of regulation black coffee served in an oversized Navy ceramic mug in the mess hall, I began to feel almost human. The normal chow-hall chatter from the other diners felt like someone was drilling core samples in my brain. I got the impression that everyone there was aware of my surfside binge, when in reality no one paid me the least attention. Must be the normal paranoia that accompanies a happy drunk, I thought. At least I hadn't become obnoxious, abusive or uncivilized; otherwise I would have been sporting some bumps and bruises. We were merely two buddies partaking of the same hemlock, unlike Socrates who drank alone.

In retrospect, I must admit that Jim survived the evening much better than I did as he entered the mess hall all clean-shaven and in good spirits. After all, he was the keeper of the alcohol on An Thoi, and it wouldn't have looked good if he was hung over. How'd he do that, I wondered?

Spotting me, he came over and sat down across from me and said with a grin, "How goes the head?"

"I told you that one of those friggin' coconuts would fall and hit us, didn't I?"

"Nah, you're just not used to the hard stuff anymore. You'd have been better off if your Navy ships were allowed to carry rum onboard like the Brits. Then maybe you could have built up a tolerance to the grog and wouldn't be such a candy-ass."

"Nice talk, I don't see where the Coast Guard allows any booze on their boats either," I retorted. "Well, that should tell you something. By the way, how come you hooked up with the Guard instead of going Navy?"

"Since my Dad had a marine salvage business on the Great Lakes, I was naturally around boats and water all the time. After high school, I opted for an appointment to the Coast Guard Academy. I just figured that I had a better chance to get command of some type of boat in the Guard quicker than plodding through the lower echelons of the Navy to reach the same objective."

"Sounds reasonable," I said. "But you missed out on traveling to all the exotic ports around the world that the Navy visits. Instead, you get to serve in the lighthouse off of Coney Island, on a lightship bobbing at anchor off each coast or waiting for distress calls from some idiot boater off the Florida Keys. Man, how exciting!"

"Well, I figure that I was just not cut out to be a soldier of fortune,"

"Neither was I, but getting to see how other people live and visiting the places that up to then I had only read about in books, piqued my interest early on. Well, I'm going to go take a douche, if there's any hot water left," I said as I slowly got to my feet and stretched out the kinks.

"Good idea." He said as he wrinkled his nose and playfully sniffed the air around me.

Back in the barracks with a towel wrapped around my waist and my leather toilet kit in hand, I headed for the showers. It would be the last hot shower that I'd have for a while, so I turned the water on as hot as I could stand it and let it sluice over my body. The effects were almost immediate in that I felt all my muscles relax and then slowly revive. I followed it with cold water to close my pores and help my bodily juices continue to flow. After shaving, I packed my gear and sat on my stripped bunk to wait for the two aspirins to kick in.

The maids had obviously already come through and collected the laundry from the barracks. Jim appeared in the doorway and said that the supply plane had returned from Saigon and that he had already filled out my order and placed it in a corner of the liquor locker. I asked him what I owed and he told me fifty bucks. Not bad for six cases of beer and five cases of soda.

"I'll spring for the Crème de Menthe since there wasn't anything better to offer you," he said with a grin.

"Okay, but you don't have to do that," I said as I peeled off fifty dollars worth of military funny money to cover the tab.

"No sweat *Dai-Uy*, it was good seeing you. Let's do this again sometime, but with something better to drink, OK?"

"Roger that," I replied. "I could sure go for a bottle of Bacardi Dark Rum and pineapple juice next time. Did you know that it helps keep you from getting malaria?"

"How do you figure that?" he asked.

"Simple, I haven't gotten malaria yet since I've been drinking the stuff."

"Get off my island and have a safe trip; I have to get back on watch. I'll have one of the seamen load your booze on the chopper when it arrives along with the case of *Nuoc Mam* you bought, ugh!"

With that, we shook hands and he disappeared into the darkened Comm shack. I moseyed out into the passageway just as Commander Beamon came out of his office. As usual, he was immaculate in his Tropical Whites complete with knee high white socks. I had to admit, he was definitely poster material for Coast Guard Recruitment.

"How are things down in Poulo Obi," he asked offhandedly.

"Pretty quiet sir," I replied. It was merely idle chatter on his part because as Fourth Coastal Zone Commander, he was the recipient of all the weekly sitreps from the field. "I hitched a ride up with Air America to get some soda and stuff. They're picking me up around noon."

"Good, let me know if you need anything else."

"Yes sir, will do." I said as I went outside to wait for the chopper, realizing that I had been politely patronized.

True to his word, the Air America helicopter landed a few minutes before noon. Tex jumped down and ambled over to where I was standing in the shade of an overhang.

"Did you get everything you needed," he asked.

"Yep, and a couple of hot showers and some good chow to boot," I said.

"How was your trip," I asked.

"Classified, I'm afraid," he answered slowly. "The VC are really acting up along the Cambodian border and making a real pain in the ass of themselves; other than that, same-o, same-o. Well, ready to go home?"

"Might as well, no dancing girls here," I replied as I watched my beer and soda being loaded onto the chopper.

THE RETURN TO POULO OBI

The trip back to Poulo Obi was uneventful and quiet due to Tex having dozed off just after we departed An Thoi. I could have easily followed suit, but I was too taken in with the view of the dark blue-green water below. It was a rare cloudless morning and the sun brought everything into a bright, vivid perspective. We passed over many fishing vessels powered by engines and sails, plying their way in search of fish that would supplement their owners' livelihood. I wondered how many of those innocent looking boats were actually carrying arms and ammunition to the enemy. From up here, I got an idea of what a massive undertaking the people at MACV in Saigon had put upon those of us assigned to Operation Market Time. We were tasked with finding and interdicting any and all such waterborne traffic along the entire 1200 mile coastline of South Vietnam.

We landed on the beach near the hootch, but no one came out to greet us. Some of the dependents waved at us from in front of their homes, but other than that, it was quiet. Rusty and Angus were most likely out on patrol knowing that I would be returning today. Tex helped me offload the beer and soda from the chopper to the hootch while the pilot kept the engine idling slowly.

"I really appreciate the lift Tex," I said.

"Don't mention it pardner, we round-eyes have to stick together . . . . and don't forget to keep me informed of anything you think is out of the ordinary."

"Will do, and thanks again."

With a firm handshake, he was back aboard the chopper as the rotors increased in speed and lifted the craft up off the beach.

Sometime later as I sat around the front room looking over the message log, I felt the urge to have a bowel movement. Oh, how I disliked the trek to the Poulo Obi Hilton on these occasions. That's the new name I conferred upon our outhouse in the sky. At least at sea, all you had to do was drop your trousers and hang your butt over the stern of the Junk. You also had to be darn careful to hold on to something solid so you wouldn't fall overboard with your pants at half-mast. Naturally, a fairly calm sea was preferred for this maneuver. Gravity would take over and some lucky fish would enjoy a warm meal. It's a good thing that fish have such an excellent filtration system otherwise I would never be able to eat seafood again.

Moving rather quickly over to the Hilton, I made it up the poled ramp without mishap. I could hear some ladies using the facilities on the other side of the structure this time and as I squatted easily over the poles, I felt a cool breeze caress my bare bottom. Could it get any better than this, I thought.

Just then, a large burst of gas escaped my rectum followed by numerous decent sized turds splashing into the water. I heard snickering coming from the ladies on the other side, but hell, this was a toilet wasn't it? A few minutes passed and then I urinated through the poles into the seawater below. This indicated that my bowels were devoid of all matter, so I performed the obligatory wiping until I was certain that it was relatively clean. Not easy to do considering the small sheets of toilet paper that come in the C-ration packs. Standing up very carefully, I pulled up my underwear and shorts and proceeded to leave.

A woman's voice came very softly from the other side asking me if I were ill. Puzzled by the question, I happened to glance down and saw the most God-awful Kelly green colored turds floating in the seawater below. It had to be all that Crème de Menthe that I had consumed with Jim. No wonder the women had been snickering. They probably had never seen anything like that before.

"Khong phai, toi khoe," I replied in Vietnamese, which meant I was OK. But if I could have seen their faces, I would have known that they didn't believe me.

Later on that evening, I had another head call to make. Only this time, there were a bunch of dependents, along with their kids, following me to the Hilton. Apparently, word of this afternoon's green droppings had made the rounds of the dependents and they wanted to see it for themselves. They were disappointed. The minuscule deposit that I dropped into the sea this time was a common everyday brown colored turdlet. With this, they turned and shuffled back to their huts, chattering among themselves.

The next day when both Rusty and Angus returned, I related the story to them and they split their sides laughing.

"Hey, look at the *Dai-Uy* shitting green turds," mimicked Angus. "Man, you've just become a living legend among the Junkies with that performance."

"I guess so, but let that be a lesson to you guys. Stay away from Crème de Menthe. It's a good thing that I didn't drink Grenadine instead, otherwise they would have thought that I was hemorrhaging to death through my poop-chute."

"Is this a fucked up place, or not?" asked Rusty laughing.

"By the way, have either of you guys been to the Grass Shack in Rach Gia?"

"I have," said Angus, "But the snipe here won't go because he heard that last year some VC hung a Claymore mine on the front gate. He was hoping to get some simple Americans entering the establishment, but luckily, a passing National Policeman saw it and disabled it before it could be detonated."

"That's true," said Rusty, "But tell *Dai-Uy* what happened to you the last time you went there for an oil change."

"Ah, that was no big thing. I was in the room lying on the bed waiting for the Chunky Donkey to come in to service me, when the Mammasan stuck her head in the room and said that Phuong was 'ver busy.' I figured that Phuong was the Donkey's name, so I nodded my head and said "OK." She asked me if I would rather go a round with her instead of waiting, but I backed off because she looked pretty shopworn. Mammasan gave me a pout, shook her head and said she'd have someone else come to do me.

A few minutes later, in walks this skinny female carrying one of those Vietnamese brooms. Since she looked about 50 years old and flat-chested, I thought it was the maid coming in to sweep the room. But faster than greased lightning, she dropped her pajama bottoms, jumped up on the bed and straddled me all the while grinning from ear to ear with her betel nut stained teeth.

Before I had a chance to react, she had a hold of my limp Waldo and proceeded to stuff it into her snatch. Even though it felt like a catcher's mitt, the damned thing got hard and she started doing squat thrusts like you wouldn't believe. She kept grinning down at me until I finally blew tubes, 1, 2, 3 and 4. Then she was off me in a flash, hoisted her pants, grabbed her broom and was gone before my dick had as chance to shrivel up.

As I walked out of there feeling stupid, I saw the old gal sweeping the leaves in the courtyard, and that's when I knew the Mammasan had pulled a fast one on me."

"Did you ever go back," I asked.

"Sure, in fact the next time I went there, I strapped on the Mammasan just for drill. And guess what? She not only was a good fuck, but she didn't charge me either. I guess in her mind she was grateful just to be competitive again. But she did say one thing that sort of bothered me."

"What was that?"

"She said she liked my '*chim*' because it was purple and that was her favorite color."

"Whatever keeps her skiff afloat," I remarked wryly.

"I was told in the Navy that a ship had to blow the carbon from its boiler tubes at least once every four hours for economical steaming," mused Angus.

"Yeah, but bending on the Mammasan will shut you down from the other girls whenever you go there again," I said.

"So what *Dai-Uy*, pussy is pussy, especially when it's free."

There was nothing left to say after that.

THE SHOOTING

A couple of uneventful weeks followed the outhouse episode, but that's not to say that it had died down in the minds of the island inhabitants. After all, how much diversion can occur in an isolated environment such as Poulo Obi? Whenever I happened to pass one of the dependents during our everyday functions, they would invariably smile as they averted looking me in the eyes. I wouldn't have been a bit surprised if they began referring to me as "*Dai-Uy* Green Turds" among themselves.

Finally, one overcast morning as I was finishing my shower, a shot rang out from the area where the armory was located. I quickly donned a pair of shorts and ran out dripping wet to investigate. Rusty and Angus were still out on patrol along with the two Vietnamese officers, so this fell into my lap as SOP (Senior Officer Present).

I ran towards a gathering group of dependents and sailors in front of the armory where we stored weapons and ammunition. Chief Petty Officer Tai was in charge of the armory and a highly capable and conscientious veteran who had fought alongside the French against the Viet Minh. He had married a Cambodian woman and had two children, a 14 year old girl and a 4 year old son. Both children were extremely well behaved and had the dusky hued café-au-lait skin inherited from their mother.

Chief Tai had been routinely cleaning some .45 caliber automatics with the help of his daughter Mong, when one of the guns discharged as she was handing it to her father. The supposedly empty automatic sent a bullet tearing into the girl's right upper thigh and passed completely through her buttock. The screaming caused all hell to break loose on the island.

I pushed my way into the armory just as Chief Tai was placing his daughter on a cleared-off work bench. The blood was flowing profusely and Mong appeared to be going into shock. In fact for a minute, I thought Chief Tai would faint himself as the blood drained from his face leaving him with a pale, helpless look. I grabbed the First Aid kit that was hanging on the wall as reality returned to the Chief. He tore the black pajama pants from the wounded girl's leg and I applied sterile gauze pads to the entrance and exit wounds. He helped me tie a pressure bandage around the thigh, but we had to tape her buttock separately in order to stem the flow of blood.

The worst part was that one of our unit's Hospital Corpsmen was on leave in Sa Dec visiting his ailing father while the other one was on patrol with Rusty. This left just me and my Merk's Manual to handle the situation. I had watched enough programs of Dr. Marcus Wellby, MD with Robert Young, that I was moderately confident. I gave her a squib of morphine to dull the pain that would surely come after the initial shock wore off.

The Chief then gently lifted his daughter off the bench and carried her through the still gathered dependents to his house. The mother was no help at all as she once again went into a wailing fit of hysteria. Several of the women tried to console her by saying that this was not a fatal wound and that Mong was more than young and strong enough to survive it. Maybe I should have also given the mother a shot of morphine to shut her up, but I thought it was a natural mother's instinct and she would eventually get over it.

Once Mong was comfortably settled in her bed and her mother slowly regained her composure, I went back to my hootch and fired up the PRC-25 radio.

I was fortunate in raising the Half Moon, a Coast Guard High Endurance Cutter that was patrolling in the vicinity. I explained the nature of my emergency and knowing that these ships carried a Doctor, asked for their assistance. I was told to hold while their CO was informed. In less than five minutes, the voice of the Captain came on and asked if we could possibly transport the wounded girl to a rendezvous with the ship. They were about thirty miles away and could not approach the island too closely because of its fairly shallow waters and highly suspect maritime charts. When the CO gave me his compass heading from Poulo Obi, I agreed to head towards his ship and deliver the girl to them.

Mong was gently carried over the rocks in a stretcher and loaded aboard the waiting Junk. I also managed to clamber aboard without too much effort and the Cox'n then backed out into open water. I gave him a general course to the Southeast as soon as we rounded the eastern side of the island. The Cox'n pushed the 371 diesel engine all ahead full as we headed for our rendezvous.

I looked in on Mong whom we had placed in the small cabin of the Junk. She was lying on a thin mattress and was trying to look brave, but it was evident she was one frightened young lady. I tried to reassure her by saying over and over, "Mong OK, Mong OK." It seemed to have some effect as she appeared to relax slightly, but her apprehension still remained. I returned to the outside deck and fortunately the seas were fairly calm and following allowing the Junk to ride comfortably. About a half hour later, one of the crew pointed ahead on the horizon and said the ship was in sight. Once the WHEC heaved to and was dead in the water, we made our approach on her leeward side.

In short order, we were tied up alongside and ready to make the transfer. Since it would have been difficult to bring the girl up an accommodation ladder in a stretcher, the Chief Boatswain's Mate on the ship had rigged a J-bar davit on the main deck. With this, they quickly lowered a Stokes stretcher down to us on the Junk. My crew of pirates gently carried her out of the cabin and secured her onto the stretcher while assuring her that there was nothing to fear. Meanwhile, an aluminum Jacobs Ladder was lowered over the side for me to come aboard the ship.

The Captain, along with his Executive Officer and the ship's doctor, met me on deck and we shook hands as we introduced ourselves to each other.

Commander Morse, who was the CO, looked every bit the mariner. He was average in height, but stocky like a linebacker and I would have bet he had a crew cut under his ball cap. His blue eyes were steady and crinkled on the sides from too much exposure to wind and sun. His accent was unmistakably New England as he introduced his XO as Lieutenant Commander Tim Ball and the ship's doctor, Lieutenant Commander Laine. The XO was somewhere in his late thirties, tall and had the look of most people who are up to their eyeballs in paperwork. Somebody has to be the administrator and that chore falls to Executive Officers. It's one of the tickets that has to be punched while aspiring for command at sea.

Doctors aboard these vessels, on the other hand, belong to the U. S. Public Health Service and are not in the Coast Guard. He was a cherub of a man about 5 feet 8 inches in height, late thirty's with thinning blonde hair and light brown eyes. His most prominent feature was his bushy eyebrows that resembled two fat, yellow caterpillars.

He took Mong's hand and spoke softly to her. Through LTJG Tran, a Vietnamese Navy Liaison Officer assigned to the Half Moon, he welcomed her to the ship and assured her that she would receive the very best of care. I was told by the Captain that they would keep her aboard for awhile to ensure no infection or other complications set in before they returned her to us. I agreed and asked the interpreter to explain this to Mong and that we would be back to get her as soon as she was released by the doctor. She raised her eyes to me and softly answered "*Dung roi, Dai Uy*" which means all right. With that, the Captain said he would keep in touch to apprise us of her condition and advise me when and where we could rendezvous to pick her up.

As I was climbing down to the Junk, the Captain leaned over the side and said, "Don't worry Lieutenant, she'll be well looked after. My crew certainly can use this opportunity to focus on something other than our everyday patrol boredom."

I nodded my thanks and threw a salute as we cast off our lines and headed back to Poulo Obi.

As our island's southern shore came into view over the horizon, we saw a civilian freighter making its way westward towards the Gulf of Thailand. The ship was doing about 7 knots and was obviously loaded down because we could barely discern her waterline. Minh was staring hard at the ship and remarked that he couldn't make out what flag she was flying. He then ordered the Cox'n to increase speed and steer a course that would close the distance between us. I could see from the angle we had taken and our relative speeds that we would not get any closer and I said so to Minh. Ignoring that, he ran up forward, uncovered the .50 caliber machine gun, jacked back the bolt and commenced firing rounds towards their stern. Thankfully, the ship was too far away from us to be hit, but our efforts did not go unnoticed. A belch of black smoke soon erupted from the ship's stack as it picked up speed and increased the size of its bow wave. Her Captain must have concluded that we were no threat to over-take her and too far away to hit her with our bullets, so he prudently kicked his ship in the ass and beat feet. I could only imagine what he was thinking. It served him right though because he paid the price for trying to cut across sovereign Vietnamese waters in order to reduce his transit time around the country.

Minh reluctantly stopped firing when he realized the impotency of his effort to stop the vessel. His face was flushed and he was all perspired as he sat down sullenly on the deckhouse. I knew better than to question his reasoning and remained silent until he decided to speak.

After uttering some Vietnamese epithets that I recognized, he finally said in English, "It was probably a Chinese chicken-shit ship and that is why they would not heave-to when I fired on her." Then he looked up at me and smiled broadly and added; "Now I have something of substance to include in my weekly report to the Coastal Zone Commander."

I nodded and smiled in understanding while my mind was envisioning a black fly trying to crawl up a water buffalo's ass with the intent of rape.

With our little adventure behind us we got back to the island where the word was passed around that Mong was in good hands. She had seemed a lot more relaxed when I left the ship, considering the fact that she had never before been away from her family. Now there she was, a bullet wound in the leg and left aboard a ship full of strangers with only one person who could speak her language. But youth compensated for these things, and I felt that she would do just fine with some 150 red-blooded American males competing for her attention.

About a week and a half went by until we finally received word from the Half Moon that Mong was ready to be returned to us. Arrangements were made as to where we could rendezvous and after signing off, went next door to inform Minh. He was eager to go along, so he gathered the crew of his best Junk and made preparations to depart in a half hour. This gave him time to put on a clean uniform in place of his baggy khaki shorts, T-shirt and flip-flops.

The ride out to the Half Moon took about 35 minutes because the ship was closing us on a reciprocal course. During the trip out, the young Gunners Mate Quan asked me if it would be all right for him to talk to the Gunners Mates aboard the Half Moon.

"What's the problem Quan?"

"We need a new firing pin assembly for our .50 caliber machine gun. I checked with Chief Tai yesterday, and he said he didn't have any."

Knowing that these Vietnamese sailors were expert cumshaw artists, I saw no reason why he couldn't give it a go with the Coasties. I was sure that they would help Quan out if they could. "Hands across the sea" and all that crap. One thing I had learned since being in-country with regards to the Vietnamese Navy Supply people was that if you were in need of a particular part of which they had only two left on the shelf, you'd be disappointed. The reasoning behind the standard reply of "Not in stock" was that if they gave you one, there would only be one left . . . and this would not look good on their weekly inventory reports to the VNN Supply Center in Saigon. Go figure!

We tied up alongside and this time they had rigged out their accommodation ladder for us. The CO and the Doctor were standing on the quarterdeck where they met us as I saluted and introduced my counterpart, LTJG Minh and Gunner's Mate Quan. I asked the CO if it would be OK if Quan could talk to his Gunners Mates.

"No problem," said CDR Morse. He turned and told one of his seamen to escort Quan to the Weapons shack and introduce him to the Senior Chief. With a smile as big as Texas, Quan eagerly followed the sailor.

"How about some coffee and fresh hot cinnamon buns in the Ward Room?" asked the Captain? "We have a great baker aboard and today is pastry day. I think you'd enjoy them."

"Sounds good to me," I said as Minh nodded in agreement. I have yet to see any Vietnamese turn down an offer of food since

I've been here. We followed along behind the Captain into the cool Ward Room which was empty except for one of the Filipino Steward's Mates. He was setting the table with a huge plate of buns. Boy, did they smell good. Minh and I waited for the Captain to sit in his chair at the head of the table before we sat. Fresh cups of coffee were placed in front of us as the Captain asked Minh if he would rather have tea.

Minh said, "No, I would prefer to have coffee. I acquired a taste for it during my training in the States, and Vietnamese coffee, unfortunately, does not compare."

I took one of the warm buns after the Captain took his and placed it on my plate. My saliva was already building up as I took my first bite. If the Captain hadn't been there, I'd have dunked that bun into my coffee. A throwback to my youth, I'm afraid. Yeah, there are some things that one really misses being away from home. I was three quarters finished with my bun when there was a knock on the Ward Room door. A seaman entered and informed us that the girl was ready to be put aboard the Junk. I quickly stuffed the remainder of the bun into my mouth and washed it down with the last of my coffee. Now I was more than ready to face the rest of the day.

When we came out on deck, Mong was already waiting on the quarterdeck dressed up in new dungarees folded up at the ankles, a white T-shirt and a ship's ball cap on her head. She was supported by a beautiful pair of aluminum crutches that were obviously made in the ship's machine shop. Mong was surrounded by no less than ten crewmen who were falling all over themselves trying to help her get accustomed to the crutches. The Captain smiled knowingly and said, "Are these kids great or what?"

"You'll get no argument from me on that Skipper," as we both shook his hand and descended the accommodation ladder to the waiting Junk. Several of the crewmen carefully helped Mong down the ladder behind me just like a brood of mother hens. One of them also carried a small duffle bag that I learned later was full of the ship's tee-shirts, ball caps with the ship's logo and more dungarees. I noticed that Quan the Gunners Mate, was already aboard and smiling like the cat that had eaten the canary.

"By the way," the Captain said to me from the top of the ladder, "How about my resident Doc and his team doing a MEDCAP for your people next weekend? They can use the practice and it'll look good on my PSYOPS report to Saigon.

"That'll be greatly appreciated Captain. Please call me and let me know when you'd like to send them ashore and I'll make all the preparations."

The lines were cast off and we pulled away from the ship. The rails above were lined with fresh-faced sailors waving their good-byes to Mong oblivious to the rest of us. After all, she was a damned sight prettier than we were. Ah youth, what a glorious time in one's life.

As we were making our way back to Obi with Mong comfortably sitting atop the cabin, a ship's siren suddenly cut through the air. Looking astern, I could make out the Half Moon flashing her signal light trying to get our attention. I could also see the high bow wave of the ship which meant that she was coming on like all get-out. Minh immediately ordered the helmsman to come about and steer for the cutter. Almost instantaneously, Gunner's Mate Quan blurted out excitedly to Minh in rapid fire Vietnamese that he had helped himself to an additional firing pin assembly above and beyond the one that they had given him. I thought Minh was going to pull out his revolver and shoot the terrified sailor right then and there.

We hove to and waited until the WHEC approached and slowed to a stop. Minh ordered the Cox'n to come back alongside the ship. The Half Moon's Chief Gunner's Mate was glaring down at us with a vengeance as he pointed an accusing finger towards Quan and bellowed, "That sneaky little SOB swiped another assembly from the gun shack and I want it back before I climb down there and toss his skinny little ass into the sea."

"Sorry about that Chief," I replied, "My counterpart and I weren't aware of it until just now and we'll be glad to return it to you with our sincerest apologies."

With that, the guilty Quan sheepishly produced the extra firing pin assembly and handed it to Minh. A line was lowered with a bucket attached and Minh placed the part into it. With a knowing wink, the XO on the wing of the bridge gave us a friendly wave as we once again cast off. The Chief, on the other hand, just stormed back to his lair probably believing that all Vietnamese were thieves. What an embarrassing experience and talk about shooting one's self in the foot . . . . damn!

As we resumed our journey back to Obi, my Counterpart Minh was aft and really reaming Quan a new asshole. He was red-faced and shaking his fist in the embarrassed sailor's face. I wouldn't want to be in Quan's shoes for awhile after that stunt.

"Well Minh," I said after the tirade was over, "I guess sailors are the same the world over."

"That may be, however losing face like that makes me angry. Besides, I'm not upset because he stole the assembly after they were good enough to give us one. I was angry because he got caught and that is unacceptable."

That gave me a whole new insight as to how the Oriental mind reasons. Oh boy, this whole Advisor thing was going to be a lot harder than I thought.

We finally made it back to Obi and pulled alongside the big rocks on the starboard side of the island. Several sailors and dependents, along with Mong's father Chief Tai, were already there waiting for us. The process of getting Mong off of the Junk and safely onto the rocks went surprisingly well. Everyone else on the

Junk got off except the Cox'n and Quan. They would beach the Junk further down the coast where it would be readily accessible.

Mong's mother and a host of neighbors came running down the path to greet her daughter and after much embracing, said that Mong appeared to have put on some weight. There was no doubt in my mind that she did, because of all the personal attention she received from the young crew of the Half Moon.

I made it back to our hootch and found Angus sweeping the floor.

"How'd it go Boss?" he asked.

"Real good," I replied, "except for the incident of Gunner Quan and the firing pin."

"What did that conniving little shit pull this time?" Angus said as he stopped sweeping and leaned on the broom.

"Quan had asked me if he could talk to the ship's Gunners Mates once we were aboard about getting a firing pin assembly for the .50 caliber on the Command Junk. I told him it was OK with me as long as the CO of the ship agreed . . . which he did. We cast off to return to Obi once we had Mong back aboard and comfortable.

"How did the Half Moon's skipper react to that little bit of unauthorized larceny?" asked Angus.

"Not bad actually, but the Chief Gunners Mate was ready to do bodily harm to Quan, The Captain had a previous tour in Vietnam and was well aware of the logistical procurement idiosyncrasies that the Vietnamese have almost perfected to a science. However, I don't believe they've quite reached the level of expertise that our own Chief Petty Officers have acquired."

"Rusty has been on a supply run to Rach Gia with Ensign Le since yesterday noon. Otherwise, it's been pretty quiet around here."

"The Captain asked if we'd like to have his medical people conduct a MEDCAP for the dependents. Minh naturally agreed, so we'll have to pass the word and have the dependents ready with their ailments once the 'Pecker-Checkers' come ashore. The ship will call us and set the time and date."

The next afternoon when it was usually siesta time on the island, Petty Officer Quan was running around a twenty five foot circle in his dungarees carrying a twenty pound rock in his arms. Master-at-Arms Chief Van was sitting in the shade of a palm tree and softly counting cadence for Quan. Whenever Chief Van yelled "*Di xuong*," Quan would drop to the ground holding the rock up against his chest.

This went on for an hour over the course of three days and was the punishment awarded by Minh for Quan's stupidity. Who said the Vietnamese didn't learn anything from the French?

PART FIVE

MEDCAP

As promised, the ship raised us on the radio three days later and said they would like to come ashore the following Saturday morning around 0900. I rogered up and said we'd be ready

From that day on until the weekend arrived, the main topic of conversation among the Poulo Obi dependents was the coming of the American *Bac Si*, as the doctor is known in Vietnamese.

Buddha must have been pleased with the world that Saturday morning as the sun made its way high into an extremely clear blue sky. There was a moderate breeze blowing, just enough to keep the palm fronds undulating happily and the humidity at a comfortable level. The Half Moon lay-to about two hundred yards offshore when they launched her motor whaleboat with the Medical crew aboard. From there, it was about a fifteen minute ride into the beach, where fortunately, it was high tide. This enabled the whaleboat to run straight in over the rocks and discharge the passengers onto the sandy beach.

Rusty and Angus helped bring the medical supplies ashore, while trying very hard to suppress their laughter. The focus of their glee was the sight of the Doctor, LCDR Laine. He was decked out in a flak jacket and helmet with a bright red cross painted on it. As he stepped ashore, his eyes furtively swept the island and we could see immediately that he was a little apprehensive. I extended my hand and welcomed him to Coastal Group 41 and added quickly that the island was perfectly secure with nothing to fear. He breathed a deep sigh of relief as he removed his helmet and flak jacket. He appeared a bit embarrassed at the picture he had initially presented to us. Fortunately, the Vietnamese managed to conceal their smiles and commenced to enthusiastically applaud his arrival. This helped to relieve his earlier tension.

We had set up three tables in the shade under the palm trees. The first one was manned by a First Class Corpsman from the ship and was designated as the triage post for prescreening each patient. From there, the patient would proceed directly to the Doctor if the ailment was serious enough, or be diverted to the third table manned by the ship's Chief Corpsman. He would in turn, provide the necessary treatment and/or medication required. Each table had an English speaking Vietnamese sailor to act as interpreters for the Coast Guardsmen and Doctor.

In most cases it was treating skin sores, simple abrasions and bandaging. The Doctor was presented with a multitude of problems, either imaginary or real, ranging from diarrhea to migraines, Tuberculosis to constipation. For the tubercular patients, he administered a white horse pill of undetermined origin. I had a suspicion that it was probably a placebo. Other cases involved the lancing of boils, which seemed extensive, especially among the children.

Once the evolution started, it seemed to go fairly smooth. The only sound that broke the island silence was the occasional baby or youngster letting out a howl when their boils were lanced. The Coasties had been farsighted enough to bring bags of M & M candy to placate the startled kids and that took care of that problem.

It was a little before noon and the lines had pretty much dwindled down. However I wouldn't have been surprised if some patients had come back around again with an additional malady. LTJG Minh came over to me and said that he would like to invite us, along with the Doctor and his medics to a simple lunch in his quarters. By this time, the Medics were ready for a break and eagerly accepted the invitation. Since there wasn't enough room to accommodate us all around their tiny table, the place settings were laid out on woven fiber matting on the floor. Minh said that eating on the floor informally was not unusual in Vietnam, especially when relatives would visit and share a meal with the family. The average kitchen table in Vietnam was not designed to accommodate large numbers of people unless they were in the homes of the upper class in the cities.

The meal was simple, as American standards go. Large bowls of clear consommé, garnished with scallions, cilantro, clear noodles and strips of sweet white meat fish. The aroma was delightful and the soup delicious. For drinking purposes, Angus had brought in cold cans of coke and orange soda from our side of the hootch. For some reason, I noticed that the Vietnamese always seemed to prefer orange soda over coke.

The meal was served by a sailor named Truc and prepared by his wife Thuy. She was also the lady that we had hired to cook one meal a day for us at the exorbitant sum of ten dollars a month. Most of the meals consisted of fish, rice and vegetables and were perfectly suitable for us. Naturally, we supplemented this fare with US type food purchased monthly from the Army at Rach Gia. The only drawback to that was by the time we managed to get up there, the food was pretty much picked over by the other Advisory Teams. But, we managed to survive OK.

As the meal was winding down, the cook's husband came over and whispered in my ear that his wife was having some problems. He wanted to know if the *Bac Si* could possibly examine her. I passed on the request to Doctor Laine and he said he'd be only too happy to oblige for the women who had prepared such a fine lunch. Wow, Mississippi gentry at its finest, I thought. Laine motioned me to accompany him outside where the cook was shyly waiting.

"Ask her what's wrong," he said.

By that time the cook's husband joined us and I asked him what the problem was.

"She trow up *beaucoup* and say her stomach hurt," he said as he opened his mouth and made a roar as he bent over at the waist.

"When did this start?" asked Laine.

"Maybe three days now and she no sleep good either," answered Truc.

The Doctor sat her down on one of the chairs under the palm tree and listened to her chest and back with his stethoscope. He then took her blood pressure and checked her eyes, throat, pulse and temperature.

"Probably a slight case of stomach flu; I understand that there's a lot of this going around lately. Her lungs and heart appear normal and her eyes and throat are clear. Her pulse is slightly elevated, but that's to be expected. We call it the 'White Coat Syndrome'. I'll give her some All-Purpose Capsules, which was the military's idea of a universal cure-all and something to ease her stomach discomfort."

He gave her a bottle of white liquid that looked suspiciously like Keopectate and a small container of pills after which she bowed several times in thanks.

"Tell her to take a tablespoon of the liquid every evening before bed and one pill every morning when she gets up. You guys check on her every day for a while. Make sure she takes the meds and it wouldn't be a bad idea if you took her temperature too."

"No problem there Doc," I said. "We can handle that easy."

The rest of the day went by smoothly with nothing major to speak of. We helped the Doctor and his crew gather up their equipment while the Vietnamese sailors returned the tables and chairs to their owners. Minh and Le shook hands with Laine and thanked him on behalf of the Coastal Group for the generous service that he had so thoughtfully provided to them. By this time, their boat had come in to retrieve them and Doc Laine gave a sheepish grin as Angus handed him his helmet and flak jacket.

"Many thanks for coming over Doc and give my respects to the CO and Exec for making it happen," I said as I shook his hand.

"Hearts and minds of the people and all that stuff," said Laine as he clambered aboard the waiting boat. "See you around."

The Whaler backed down, turned and skillfully made its way through the surf to the awaiting cutter lying just offshore.

"Well, that seemed to have gone pretty good," said Rusty. "At least the small stuff's been taken care of with the dependents, but what was that all about with Cooky?"

"Oh, she was complaining about throwing up and having stomach pains. Maybe she's eating too much of her own cooking," I said with a grin. "Anyway, the Doc wants us to keep an eye on her and take her temperature daily for awhile in case it's something more serious. I'll start tomorrow and we'll rotate depending on who's here, OK?"

"Can do *Dai-Uy*," said Angus rolling his eyes skyward.

DOCTOR KAY, OB/GYN

The following morning, I headed for our Advisor's office with a mug of my instant coffee in hand. The office was one of three little twelve by ten rooms in a low building situated just to the rear and left of our hootch. The other two were the CO's office and the Sick Bay. Our office contained a battered desk, two metal chairs, a filing cabinet and a slim five foot table against the far wall for laying out maps and charts. The large corkboard hanging on the wall covered with missives from headquarters along with a small US flag, gave the place a more official air.

I left the door open as I sat at the desk and prepared to read some of the paperwork that had piled up. Among which, was the monthly report to the Senior Naval Advisor in Saigon on my counterpart's performance. All senior advisors in the field had to submit these reports as a CYA (cover your ass) function in the event somebody screwed up.

A soft knock came from the doorframe and standing there shyly was Cooky. Her name was really Thuy and she was between twenty-five and thirty years old. Her jet black hair was economically cut "bowl style" and it framed a small oval face with thin lips and fairly even white teeth. She stood about four foot ten in her rubber flip-flops and weighed about ninety pounds soaking wet.

Thuy was clad in the standard white cotton shirt over black cotton pajama pants. Her eyes were obsidian black and always cast downwards whenever she was in the presence of us Advisors. When she did look up on rare occasions, one could see that she had a lazy left eye whose lid sat slightly lower than the right one. Perhaps for this reason, she avoided looking directly at us.

"Come in Thuy," I said. "What can I do for you?"

She entered timidly and sat down in the chair in front of the desk and folded her hands in her lap.

"I here for checkup like *Bac Si My* say yesterday." (Bac Si My meant American Doctor.)

"OK, go over and sit on the table and I'll be right with you."

I opened the bottom drawer of the file cabinet and took out the standard issue stethoscope, blood pressure kit, thermometers and our trusty Merck's Manual that was given to all the Advisors in the field. As I took hold of her wrist to feel her pulse, I found that although it was slightly fast, it was extremely strong. That's when I noticed the heavy throbbing in the hollow at the base of her throat just above the collarbone. Then it hit me. A long time ago, my grandmother had told me that you could always spot a pregnant woman by the heavy pulse beating in that hollow. Yes, I thought to myself. That would account for the throwing up in the morning and the stomach pains.

"Thuy, are you having a baby-san?" I asked softly.

"Yes *Dai-Uy*, I tree months now."

"In that case, I want you to stop taking the white medicine and the pills that we gave you, OK?"

"OK, I no take yet today. What I do with bottle and pills?"

"Keep it for when your husband has a stomach ache," I said smiling.

"You still check me *Dai-Uy*?" she asked looking at me almost imploringly in the eyes for the first time.

"Of course Thuy, we want this baby to be number one, right?"

It was then I remembered that our cook already had a young boy around two years old and I asked her, "Where did you have your last baby?"

"Me and my husband were at Kien An base near Rach Gia."

"Did you have the baby with a *Bac Si* in Rach Gia?" I asked.

"No, only Vietnamese *Y-Ta* (Corpsman) and one woman friend help be-bee come."

I figured it was probably a mid-wife that had delivered her baby therefore making any prenatal care non-existent. Well, at least here on Obi, we could hopefully provide a little better than that.

I took a clipboard off the wall and started a sheet entitled "Cooky's Stats." Then I proceeded to take her blood pressure and all the while, her eyes never left my face. I recorded the reading on the sheet and then took the stethoscope and placed the head on her back in several areas. When I went to listen to her chest, from the outside of her shirt of course, she unbuttoned her top three buttons giving me free access to her skin. I couldn't help but notice that she had small but perfectly formed breasts with huge purple hued aureoles and nipples. When I placed the head of the stethoscope under the right breast, I saw that her nipples were standing erect.

Oh God, what's happening here? I thought. Having finished listening to her heart and lungs, I told her to button up her shirt as I placed an oral thermometer under her tongue. While her temperature was being taken, she still kept looking at me. Needless to say, I was becoming a bit uncomfortable. I noted her temperature on the sheet and said "OK, that's it. See you again tomorrow, same time."

Instead of getting off the table, Thuy turned and lay down, raised her hips and deftly pulled down her pajama bottoms. My eyes were naturally drawn to the wispy fine hair that covered her pubic area and I just stood there absolutely speechless.

"Now you know I have be-bee, you check like *Bac-Si*," she said.

The first thing that crossed my mind was to shut the door before someone looked in and got the wrong idea. I hurriedly pulled the door closed while my mind was racing wildly about this situation. The only idea I could come up with was to grab a rectal thermometer, gingerly open the lips of her vagina with my left thumb and forefinger and slowly inserted it in part way. I then proceeded to feel the sides of her throat and under her chin like my doctor used to do. From there, I lightly felt her breasts as if examining for lumps and said that I was checking for *sua* (milk). She nodded slightly and had a half smile on her face. Naturally I had to keep feeling gently around the stomach just above the pubic area. As in all things, Mr. Murphy of "Murphy's Law" popped up in the guise of Angus coming through the door. \

Talk about a pregnant pause. We were all a bit embarrassed, but nowhere as much as Angus seeing me with our cook bare-assed on the table and a thermometer sticking out of her vagina.

"Uh, sorry *Dai-Uy*, I didn't know you were busy," he stammered.

"No big deal Angus, in fact I'm glad you're here. Cooky here is three months pregnant and it behooves us to check her out every day. I've made up a chart for her and we'll take turns recording her vital signs. How does that sound?" I asked raising my eyebrows while maintaining an innocent look on my face.

"Uh, that's OK with me and I'm sure Rusty won't mind either."

"I'll bring him up to speed on the procedure to follow when he gets back from patrol," I said, hopefully in an off-hand manner, "And I'll fill you in later."

I turned to Thuy and said as I gently removed the thermometer and made as if I were reading it, "You and baby good. Tomorrow, you come back same time," because I thought that the rest of the base would be taking their noontime siestas and give us some sort of privacy. "Angus will check you out and Rusty the day after. Is that OK with you?"

"OK," she said as she quickly got down off the table, pulled up her pants, bowed to me and Angus and headed for the door completely happy.

"What the fuck was that, *Dai-Uy?*" asked Angus scratching his head after she had gone.

"Hey, it was her idea for a bottom sounding," I answered. "Once I asked her if she was pregnant, she dumped her shyness over the side and the only thing I could think up after taking the usual vital signs, was taking the temperature of her snatch and giving her a standard touch exam. I didn't want to give her a friggin' pelvic exam for God's sake."

"And what did you learn from that, *Dai-Uy*?"

"I learned for some odd reason smartass, that the temperature in her snatch was two degrees warmer than that of her mouth."

"Well, if I was her old man, I'd sure keep my dick in her pussy where it's warmer than in her mouth. Besides, if I was getting a blowjob from her, one look at that lazy eye looking up at me would make my cock limp."

"I'll bet. Nothing will make your dick limp short of an earthquake or some incoming."

That evening when Rusty returned from patrol, Angus couldn't wait to relate the events of the day to him. Rusty sat there in disbelief listening to the tale being spun out.

"Hey *Dai-Uy*, do you suppose she wanted a little bit from the big white and handsome *Bac Si?*" snickered Rusty.

"Beats the shit out of me, but she sure took me by surprise."

"Let me get this straight boss, that me and Angus here get to take our turns playing Doctor Kildare to Cooky too?"

"That's it, but let's not let our libido override our good sense because this island is too small to have a jealous husband with access to weapons get pissed-off at us. Do you read me?"

They both nodded, but I could almost hear the wheels of possibilities turning in their heads. Young horny males, bah!

The next few weeks passed by uneventfully. Our patrols were still going out on a fairly regular basis and the "caring" of Cooky proceeded unabated seven days a week without a single problem. Apparently, no one else on the base was privy to our temperature taking routine and I for one, was extremely happy to keep it that way. How the hell could I ever explain it to Minh, Le and her husband?

Finally, one evening as I was lying in the hammock in front of our hootch, Rusty came over and sat on a rock by the edge of the water.

"How's it going?" I asked just to make conversation.

"OK boss, but Cooky's husband came in just after I took the thermometer out of her snatch."

I sat up quickly in the hammock with my stomach muscles tightening, as I asked, "Did he see anything?"

"Nah, the moment the door started to open, she had her drawers up faster than greased lightning." Thuy's husband didn't seem upset at all seeing her on the table. In fact he came to see us because he was having a terrible headache. Since I was still holding the thermometer in my hand, I made him sit down and I stuck it under his tongue. Thuy almost had a cat as she started laughing and holding her stomach. The husband had no idea what all the fuss was about and gave her a look that made her regain her composure. Hey, the more I know her, the more I respect her. She's quite a lady."

"And don't you forget it," I added with a grin. "Angus will get a kick out of that one when he returns. It's apparent that she hasn't told her husband anything about our daily routine. Yeah, she's quite a lady at that."

The vitals taking continued for another two weeks, and when the novelty started to wear off, we decided it was time to cut her loose. The chore fell to me, naturally, so at the end of my last "exam" I said "Thuy, everything is going well for you and baby-san and we do not have to check you anymore."

I thought for a minute that she was going to break out in tears, but she succeeded in holding them back. Slowly, she got off the table and took my hand in both of hers and softly placed a kiss on it. Still holding my hand, she looked up at me and said "Thank you ver' much *Dai-Uy*, and I feel I must tell you this. When you all take care of me, I ver' happy and know you 'Mericans have good hearts. No one try touch me like they do to Snack Bar Girl and I no fraid. Many time, I think what it be like to have 'Merican make love to me. I no can do Angus because he black and I no want black be-bee. I no can do Rusty because maybe my be-bee have red hair like he. So, I think only you *Dai-Uy* no change be-bee too much. If you want Thuy, Thuy do with you.

I was dumbfounded and embarrassed by her sincerity. Her hands were still clutching mine as I looked alternately from one of her eyes to the other and said, "Thank you very, very much, Thuy. I would like to make love to you, but we do not want to hurt your husband. Maybe, some other time or place, but not here on Poulo Obi, OK?"

With that, she quickly let go of my hands and left the office without another word. For some reason, the office now seemed awfully deserted.

It was obvious to us that Thuy had not told anyone on the base about the "treatment" she was receiving at the hands of the Advisors. I guess she wanted to keep us all to herself, which was OK as far as we were concerned. Could you imagine trying to explain our actions to anyone up at Fourth Coastal Zone, like Mister Screamin' Beamon for example? Not hardly.

BIZARRE EVENTS ON THE ISLAND

A week or so later, one of the patrols brought back a "VC" sampan that they had captured at the mouth of the Bo De River. They had spotted two men in the sampan trying to hide under a nipa palm along the shore when they decided to check their papers. The two occupants bailed out when they saw the Junk bearing down on them and disappeared into the undergrowth leaving the sampan. Upon inspecting the boat, it was loaded down with three huge bags of rice and several bottles of *Nuoc Mam*. Apparently, they had been making a market run when they had been discovered by the patrol.

Since "finder's keepers, loser's weepers," the spoils were hoisted aboard the Junk and brought back to Obi. The happy sailors brought the sampan to the officer's hootch and presented it to us as their gift. Now we had a play toy to occupy our time when we weren't out on patrol. The sampan was turned upside down on the small seawall just in front of the hootch.

In case I had not mentioned it before, we also had an unofficial Advisor's mascot in the form of a white mongrel bitch that someone had named Obi. We would have much preferred one of the legendary Phu Quoc dogs, but they were scarce. Phu Quoc dogs were easily identified by the ridge of fur along their backbones going in the opposite direction, from tail to head. Legend has it that back in the early history of Vietnam; one of these dogs protected the King against his enemies. Out of gratitude, he placed his sword on the back of the dog as if bestowing Knighthood, and thus, caused the anomaly in the dog's fur.

In actuality, the dog is believed to be an offshoot of the Thai Ridgeback that was brought to Phu Quoc by early traders. Anyway, Obi was a far cry from that breed. She would hang around the outside of the hootch patiently waiting for some tasty (?) morsel of C-rations or a friendly scratch under the chin from someone. During the heat of the afternoon, she found a cool resting place under the sampan where she could watch for any scraps of food from us. She turned out to be a good watchdog for us because she would let out a low grumbling growl whenever a non-American came near our hootch.

On one particular afternoon while going for her noontime siesta under the boat, she was surprised by a Pit Viper that had also sought the cool shade. The snake struck Obi just above her nose, and by the time we came out to investigate the yelp, the viper was heading for the rocks. Obi had crawled completely under the boat and never uttered a sound. We didn't have a clue as what to do for snakebite on a dog. Do you try to suck the venom out of an animal? Where could we have applied a tourniquet to stem the poison, around her neck? All we could do was leave her alone and hope that somehow she could fight off the venom. By that evening, she still lay lethargically under the sampan. But now, her nose had swollen considerably and she was the spitting image of Snoopy in the comic strips.

"Doesn't look too good for the old gal," offered Rusty. "Damn, I wish we could do something for her."

"Do what?" asked Angus. "We'll just have to let nature take its course and hope for the best."

The next day, we awoke to find Obi dead. Rusty said that he would take care of burying the dog halfway up the mountain overlooking the base. As far as I know, that was the last Advisor's mascot to ever be on the island except for the 100 pound pig that belonged to Chief Tai's wife.

One interesting piece of information that I picked up, was that the cement catch basin was constructed totally by detainees. For detainees, read "suspected" VC who were brought to the island for interrogation. Although it was against Vietnamese Navy policy that detainees were not to be subjected to forced labor, the folks on Poulo Obi turned a blind eye and took advantage of the situation to better their lifestyle. No big deal.

One day, the unthinkable happened. Our refrigerator suddenly stopped working. Rusty did his utmost to try and fix it, but found out that the old compressor had finally given out. It was shot. So I put a call into Barbados, which was the Fourth Coastal Zone's call sign, and reported that we needed a new refrigerator ASAP. To say that the powers that be were extremely sensitive to the needs of their Advisors in the field would be sacrilege. It seemed that unless we were on the verge of instant destruction by the enemy, lip-service not priority were pretty much the norm. This caused most of us Boonie Rats to once again fend for ourselves and cumshaw to the best of our ability. The tale of our dead refrigerator was a good case in point.

After a week and a half of no response to our request, we started looking for alternatives. Maybe we were a bit spoiled up to now, but no one should be expected to drink piss warm beer and soda. Angus had been on a run to Rach Gia with Ensign Le aboard the Command Junk. It was wider and longer than the standard narrower hulled Kien Giang Junk and rode considerably better at sea. When he checked in by radio one morning, I told him that An Thoi had still not responded to our request and that we had to do something. Angus said that he had an idea and would talk to Le about it.

"I'll keep you posted," his voice came through faintly as the atmospheric gremlins started to mess with his transmission.

"Roger that," I said into the microphone and signed off. I had the utmost confidence that Angus and his devious mentality would come up with some solution to our dilemma.

Sure enough, my trust in him was not misplaced. He called in the next day to say that our problems were temporarily over, but he didn't get a chance to elaborate as his signal faded and the radio went silent.

Three days later, the *Chu Luc* returned to Obi. Angus was waving from the boat as they neared the shore to let him and Le debark on one of the huge boulders that we used for that purpose. Rusty and I hustled over the rocks to find out what Angus was waving about. Sitting on the deck was an aluminum coffin that he pointed to proudly as he gave us his broadest grin.

"Just what in the hell is that supposed to be?" I asked as I caught the bowline tossed to me by a crewman.

"It's our temporary refrigerator," he said. "We went up to the Special Forces base at Ha Tien and I explained our problem to a Staff Sergeant. He said we could have one of the coffins and fill it with ice to keep the beer cold. He also said that it should hold us until those dorky squid supply types at An Thoi got off their fat asses and delivered us a new refrigerator."

"Where are we going to get the ice to fill it with?"

"No sweat *Dai-Uy*. Remember going alongside to check the papers of those fishing boats from Singapore? Their holds are always packed with tons of ice and they cover it with sawdust to keep it from melting."

"Yeah, so?"

"Well, one of those boats agreed to give us all the ice we needed as long as we lightened up on them. I figured there's more than enough fish in the South China Sea and no fear of the place being fished out. Besides, they agreed to also give us some fresh fish too. Is that OK with you?"

"For a cold drink right now, I'd agree to about anything. Good thinking."

Rusty had been standing off to the side with his hands on his hips all the while Angus and I were having our conversation. When I looked over at him, he said somewhat sarcastically,

"Are we going to stand here all day and shoot the shit, or are we going to get this meat locker off-loaded and cool the beer?"

With that, we all laughed and the three of us mule-hauled the ice-filled coffin off the Junk and over the rocks to the hootch. Ensign Le, with his ever present smile, said as he trailed us over the rocks, "You could have used our refrigerator. How come you did not ask, *Dai-Uy*?"

Rusty piped up before I could answer and said, "We didn't want to bother you and *Trung-Uy* Minh. Besides, it wouldn't have been polite for us to be going in and out of your quarters like that."

What he really meant was that he didn't trust them to keep their paws off our beer and soda. Apparently, Le was satisfied with Rusty's answer and headed off to his side of the house eager to tell Minh about the crazy Americans next door.

Angus and Rusty dug a shallow grave-like hole under some palm trees that grew a few yards away from our side of the hootch and buried the ice-filled coffin up to its lid. After loading the "reefer" with our beer and soda, they went down to the water's edge and rinsed themselves off. In the meantime, I had gathered some palm fronds and covered the top of the coffin to further insulate the ice from the heat of the day. Having done all this, we retired to the shade of the trees in anticipation of our first cold drink in what seemed an eternity.

As it so happened that weekend, Minh did not schedule any patrols to go out due to a Vietnamese religious holiday. That left the three of us with time on our hands, so I decided it was a good opportunity for us to perform a much needed field day on our hootch. Neither one of the guys put up any argument and pitched right in to square the place away. I found that neatness of one's surroundings was more prevalent among senior petty officers in the Navy than the junior ones. It seems that the "Field Day" mentality that was drummed into them at Boot Camp, never really left them. It just lay dormant in their minds until leadership responsibility got to play a part in their lives.

HAVE A COOL ONE

We had just finished putting the final touches on the place, when the sound of a helicopter's rotors filled the air. I went to the front window just in time to see a Navy chopper landing in the open area on the beach. To my surprise, the first person out of the bird was Commander Beamon, resplendent in his starched, sharply creased greens. Right behind him was the Command Master Chief of An Thoi, Tom Briggs. The Master Chief was well into his early fifties, but his physical shape belied his years. Rumor had it that he did five hundred pushups and sit-ups every other day and religiously ran five miles daily around the compound. He was hands down a great example to represent the Command and right in line with Commander Beamon's focus on fitness.

Putting on my beret, I hustled out to meet them, threw the Commander a smart salute and welcomed him to Poulo Obi. Unlike the Army, Navy folks never saluted without a hat on. Besides, it made a better impression on Beamon to show him some semblance of military bearing, regardless of the surroundings. I'm sure he thought that the majority of the Advisors in the field had gone completely native once they were away from the normal military routine. That much I had already surmised about the man.

As he and the Master Chief entered the hootch, Angus yelled "Attention on Deck", while he and Rusty stood at rigid attention. This was customary in the Navy whenever a senior Officer entered a room too and I was happy to see the Commander's reaction.

"As you were," Beamon said in acknowledgement.

"Have a seat Commander, Master Chief," I said. "What brings you gentlemen to our island paradise?"

"It's just a courtesy visit to see how you men were getting along. I like to make the rounds of our Advisors occasionally just to keep my hand in, so to speak."

I nodded with a bland look on my face as I thought, Yeah so you can justify the Combat 'V' that you are going to put on your end of tour Bronze Star along with the customary Legion of Merit for O-5s and above. What a load of crap, besides who cares?

Angus politely asked them if they would like a cold drink.

The Commander said, "I could do with a soda, if you've got one."

"Same for me," replied the Master Chief.

With that, Angus went outside to get the soda from our makeshift reefer. The Commander turned in his seat with a perplexed look on his face as his eyes followed Angus passing by the open front window.

"Where's he going?" asked Beamon.

"Out to get the soda, Commander,"

"You keep the soda outside instead of in your refrigerator?"

"Yes sir, we've had to make other arrangements to keep our food and drinks cold ever since our refrigerator died several weeks ago. We sent a request for a replacement to An Thoi right after we tried unsuccessfully to repair it, but never got a response."

"What the hell are you talking about, what request?" said Beamon, raising his voice.

By now, his neck and face were turning scarlet and the Master Chief began fidgeting in his seat.

"Show me where you keep the soda," ordered Beamon as he stood up and headed for the door.

I quickly followed him out and as he turned the corner, he spied Angus replacing the palm fronds after taking out the cans of soda.

"Jesus Christ in the foothills," yelled Beamon as he kicked aside the fronds with his spit shined combat boots. "This is a goddamned coffin for Chrissakes."

"It was the best we could do under the circumstances," I mumbled. "The Special Forces at Ha Tien gave us the idea and the coffin when they learned about our problem, sir."

"Just great, now they'll have a good laugh on our account and we'll look like first class jerk-offs to the Army." he said as he rolled his eyes skyward.

"Those Green Berets aren't like that Commander. They're good people and we try to help each other out whenever we can."

Turning his angry glare at me, he said, "I want you to get rid of this tin box as soon as I get you a replacement reefer and I don't want a word of this to get out to anyone . . . . anyone. Is that understood Lieutenant?"

"Yes sir," replied, while inside me there was pure elation. I could guarantee that some puke Supply Officer's head would roll when Beamon got back to An Thoi.

He turned to the Master Chief who was trying hard not to smile and said, "Get on the horn and call the base right now. Tell them I want a new refrigerator flown down here immediately. If they don't have one in the warehouse, take the one from the Supply Office. They can damn well do without until a new one can be delivered down here and swapped back for theirs."

"Yes sir, right away sir," said Briggs as he turned and winked at me. "Can I use your radio, Lieutenant?"

"It's all yours, Master Chief. Be my guest."

"In all my years of service, I haven't run across anything as bizarre as this, although I must admit, it does keep the soda cold," said Beamon having calmed down somewhat.

I could see Rusty through the window, smiling and holding his thumb up in a gesture of victory. I returned the thumb to him out of the Commander's view.

The Master Chief, having passed the word to An Thoi over the radio, said, "Supply's on it Commander."

"They'd damned well better be and I want an investigation as to just whose in-box the original request is pigeonholed in."

"I'm sure it'll get tossed as soon as Supply gets the word. No one will want to own up to this sir," said the Master Chief.

"I suppose you're right as always Master Chief, but it'll tighten up their sphincters a skoshe. Damn, I hate Staff indifference. It doesn't sit well with me."

With that, Beamon put out his hand and said, "Let me know immediately if that damned refrigerator doesn't get here within the week and when it does, get rid of that abominable coffin."

I shook his hand and replied, "Yes sir, and thank you. We really appreciate it."

The crew of the helo had been dozing in the sun and jumped up immediately when they saw the Commander and the Master Chief heading towards them. Once everyone was aboard, the Commander looked over and waved as the chopper lifted smoothly off the sandy beach. The Master Chief just sat there smiling at us behind his dark sun glasses as the pilot dipped the helicopter's nose down and quickly banked northwards over the water towards home.

I had to revise my opinion upwards with regards to the good Commander and somehow, it gave me a lift to know that someone was looking out for our interests back at Headquarters.

The very next day, which was Sunday, another US Navy chopper touched down on Obi and two crewmen offloaded a brand new refrigerator that was still in its carton. Don't you just love it when a plan comes together like that?

As we were busily removing the brand new appliance from its carton, a small group of children arrived to watch us set up our newest possession. The kids had practically made it a habit to visit us whenever the mood struck them. They would stand in front of the hootch looking in through our big window and make subdued comments to each other. I often wondered what they were saying and which one of us they were talking about. Since they presented no bother, we welcomed their visits to help break up the monotony of life on Obi.

The group consisted of six children between the ages of 12 and 2. The oldest was Tan and we had never seen her without her infant brother Be Nam, whom she held contentedly on her hip. As is customary in most Asian countries, the oldest daughter takes on the roll of babysitter for the youngest sibling, giving the mother a much needed break to carry out her other chores.

Next in line of progression was Dao. She was 6 years old and her hair was raven wing's black and cut in what I like to call a "Soup Bowl Special." She loved the hard "John Wayne" crackers and peanut butter packets from our C-rations.

The fourth child was 5 year old Dau and she was the quietest of the bunch. Her gamin-like face was framed by scraggly sun streaked brown hair. Very rarely did we ever hear her speak unless she was asked a specific question that required an answer. She never seemed to initiate conversation with anyone, which was strange for a young girl. Her most prominent feature was that she was missing her top two front baby teeth. When she smiled, which was often, you could just see the white tips of her new teeth starting to emerge.

Next in line was Xuan, also 5 years old and who was destined to grow up to be a genuine heartbreaker. Whenever you looked at her directly she would flash a coquettish smile which would instantly disappear when eye contact was broken. She was the epitome of shyness. She too, sported the "Soup Bowl Special."

The last and final member of the group was Muon. He was the four year old brother of Mong and the youngest son of Chief Gunner's Mate Tai. Muon existed in a state of perpetual nudity and according to the collective memories of the Advisors; he had never been seen wearing any kind of apparel whatsoever. His little nut brown colored body inherited from his Cambodian mother, was in constant motion. This caused his penile appendage to undulate freely that naturally everyone but us guys ignored. Unlike children from other cultures, they never begged for anything, even when we were drinking soda. Occasionally we would give them a half finished can and watch as they unselfishly passed it around among themselves. Where else would you expect to see that?

At this point, I should also mention one of our other frequent visitors. Tan was one of the dependents and the wife of a young sailor named Son. She had just turned twenty and her athletic body and ready smile turned heads wherever she went. Son was a meek but likeable individual with clean cut features and a quiet demeanor. Son was madly in love with his wife, but was way over his head in their marriage. She was just too much for him to handle even when they were growing up. She had completed two years at the university majoring in Economics, whereas Son could only boast a high school diploma. However, he had no choice in the matter because it was an arranged marriage. His family owned a considerable tract of land on the outskirts of Hue and Tan's family had almost as much acreage adjacent to theirs. It was only logical that a union be forged so that eventually the young couple would inherit the vast property and the families would continue to prosper. But fate stepped in and the young groom found himself called into service. Fortunately, the prominence of both families assured him acceptance into the Navy rather than going into the ARVN as potential cannon fodder.

Upon finishing recruit training, he was assigned to Coastal Group 41 on Poulo Obi. Tan, with grandiose visions of an island paradise, eagerly begged her husband to let her accompany him.

After less than a month, the adventure became a suffocating existence for her with one monotonous day dragging hopelessly into the next. Outside of the normal everyday household chores, Tan had nothing to do and no place to go which caused tension between them. The other wives noticing the body language dropped subtle and sometimes not so subtle hints that perhaps a baby would brighten their world. But Tan was not about to be tied down; just the opposite in fact. She began looking for a way to escape her dreary life-style.

Tan started looking forward to the days that her husband was away on patrol so that she could be alone with her thoughts and not feel guilt about her lack of feeling for him. She eventually came up with the idea of perhaps attaching herself to one of the advisors. With her growing boredom, she never once considered an affair with any of the Vietnamese men on the island; because society would ostracize her. Running off with an American however was understandable since it happened frequently throughout Vietnam. Yes, an American could be her ticket off of Obi and who knows, maybe to the States if she was lucky. Unfortunately, although the advisors would have happily accommodated her, they also knew the consequences from being on a small island with a jealous husband with access to weapons.

So Tan would fritter away the hours sitting in front of the hootch on a lawn chair whenever her husband was on patrol, hoping to spring her trap. She firmly believed that Americans were strong healthy men with normal sex drives and who certainly were not getting laid on Obi. But alas, no one did more than carry on short innocent conversations with her, which was hard because of her limited English and the obvious temptation being flaunted.

It was shortly before Lieutenant Edwards went on leave that Tan had started her flirtatious vigil in front of the hootch. She soon realized that the *Dai-Uy* was deliberately rebuffing her attempts to fraternize with his troops and abject embarrassment began setting in as she sat alone.

Once I arrived on the scene, Tan again began to appear with her chair out front in order to test my resolve. Since the guys had already informed me about her, I decided to take the bull by the horns.

I casually approached the open window and leaned on its bottom ledge as I looked out and said, "*Chao Ba*."

At the sound of my voice she straightened her back so that her breasts strained against her lightweight cotton shirt.

"Good morning *Dai-Uy*," she said almost in a whisper. "My name is Tan and you are ver' handsome."

"Thank you very much," I replied. "I hear your husband Son is very handsome too."

That brought her up short, so I continued by telling her in a menacing tone that if she didn't get her ass back to her husband, I was going to tell *Trung-Uy* Minh and let him deal with her.

She might not have completely understood what I said, but my tone and the mention of the CO's name convinced her to pick up her chair and head for her house.

Angus and Rusty had been eavesdropping and when I turned to them, Rusty said, "Damn *Dai-Uy*, there goes another lost piece of ass."

"I grant you that, but the pussy wouldn't be worth a grenade being lobbed in on us as we slept." Letting out a breath of exasperation, I then remarked, "God almighty, she was gorgeous."

The three of us then cracked open some beer and sat piously in silence with our own private thoughts of what could have been.

PROVING A POINT

Another week passed by routinely with no more visits from Tan. On the eve of the weekend, Ensign Le knocked on our door and announced that he and the CO were heading for a meeting with the Regional Force people at Song Ong Doc. The Province Chief of Camau, Lieutenant Colonel Tao, would also be attending. Apparently, the meeting was to plan a joint operation against the local VC who were probably getting a bit too rambunctious against the "Ruff Puffs" in his Province.

It was common knowledge that the position of Province Chief was a political appointment by whoever currently resided in the Presidential Palace in Saigon. In this way, old debts were paid, favors culled and the administration could be fairly certain that their policies would be carried out throughout the country. The unwritten law, however, was that each of the Chiefs was to uphold the party line and everything over that, was personal gravy. I'm sure that they were advised to be as discreet as possible when it came to lining their own pockets during their tenure.

"You have the Conn *Dai-Uy*," said Minh using U.S. Navy terminology smilingly as he stuck his head through our entryway. He and Le then headed for the Command Junk waiting for them near the rocks. They were dressed in starched and pressed uniforms and both of them shone like brand new copper pennies.

Normally, an Advisor would accompany his counterpart to any operational planning meeting, but for some reason, we weren't invited this time. Maybe they wanted to express their feeling of independence, but just as long as they didn't wind up getting us in the middle of something that we couldn't get out of.

Since the three of us were to be left to our own devices, it was like having "Rope Yarn Sunday." That was the name given to a day off at sea in the early navy where the crew traditionally used the time to mend and repair their clothes. It was only natural that we would conjure up some sort of mischief solely for entertainment purposes.

"Hey Angus, remember when I asked the CO about base security, considering what had happened to the old base when the VC decided to get even? He had sort of sloughed me off by saying that our security couldn't be any better, especially at night."

"Yeah, I remember that conversation. If he was referring to the one guy assigned to stand watch at night in the gazebo down at the far end of the base, his idea of security and mine are one hundred and eighty degrees out of phase. Besides, whoever has the all-night watch has his hammock and portable radio with him. As soon as it gets dark enough, up goes the hammock and down goes the sentry."

"I've been mulling an idea over in my mind about how we can correct that problem," I said conspiratorially.

"Oh, oh," said Rusty, "It sounds like we're about to be put in harm's way with the Vietnamese."

"Ah, where's your sense of adventure? Have I ever steered you wrong," I said with a sardonic laugh.

"If I answer that truthfully, you'll only lower my evals."

"You know that I'm not that kind of officer, besides, we'll all be in it together."

"That's what I'm afraid of," piped in Angus.

"Here's the drill. We'll wait until it gets dark plus an hour or so, to give the watch time to settle in for the night. Then the three of us will hug the waterline and come up from behind. We'll jump him, hog-tie and gag him securely in his hammock. In the morning when the base wakes up, they'll find him trussed up like a Christmas Turkey."

"What's that going to prove?" asked Rusty.

"It will show the CO that his security blanket has a hole in it, and just maybe, he will beef up the watch and let us all sleep better at night."

So, with our plan laid out, all we had to do was wait until nightfall before the CO and XO returned from their meeting with the Province Chief.

The Command Junk arrived with the two officers late the following afternoon. They came directly to their hootch with just a casual greeting to us through the window, obviously pooped out from their trip to the mainland.

Rusty, Angus and I sat around the main room quietly going over our plan. As darkness spread its black cape over the South China Sea and we were sure that the sentry had enough time to relax in his hammock, we stealthily moved out. The three of us sprinted quietly to the rocks so we could hug the shoreline and approach the gazebo unseen.

When we were finally in position and sure that the sentry was asleep, we made our move by leaping over the low railing of the gazebo. I grabbed the sentry pinning his arms to his side while Rusty put his hand over his mouth to prevent him from crying out. Angus took the coil of six thread manila line that he had tucked into the back of his shorts and proceeded to tie the startled sentry into his hammock. Rusty replaced his hand with a red checkered bandana tied securely across the sentry's mouth and around his head.

Following the uncomprehending look on the man's face with eyes as big as silver dollars, he released some sudden noxious fumes of flatulence, no doubt brought on by sheer fright. He was tied up securely and resembled a pupa larva in its cocoon. I had to reassure the young seaman that no harm would befall him and that we were merely trying to bring home a point to his CO. Of course, this did little to allay his fears as to what fate awaited him come the dawn.

The next morning, the three of us got up before the two officers started their ritual morning exercise, which was a version of Tai Chi. Rusty lay in the duty hammock, while Angus and I sat on two folding chairs propped against the front of the hootch beneath our window. As the two officers came out shirtless in their shorts to start their routine, they were surprised to see the three of us already up and about.

"Good morning gentlemen," I said. "I hope your trip went well with the Province Chief."

"Good morning to you," said Minh, while Le had on his usual toothy grin. "What brings you out so early in the morning?"

"Well, to be honest, we were discussing the attack on the former base and the chance of another one ever happening again."

"And what were your conclusions?" asked Minh warily.

"We figured that a similar attack could happen, especially during the night when we are the most vulnerable."

"Ah," said Minh. It seems as if our security is in question once again. The last time you and I spoke of this matter, I indicated that our constant alertness, especially at night, was all the protection we needed. Besides, the lighthouse keeper and his family are also providing daytime security from their vantage point. They will signal us immediately if they see any suspicious craft approaching the island. What more could you want?"

"I just don't have that warm and fuzzy feeling when there's only one sentry posted at night. Besides, they bed down as soon as it gets dark while they listen to music on their radio."

With that last remark, we could see that Minh was becoming not only angry, but annoyed and exasperated. He turned his back to me and gazed out towards the gazebo. When he couldn't see any sentry present, he turned around and looked at me accusingly.

"Just what happened that brings this matter to my attention again?"

"Sorry *Trung-Uy,* it was time to prove a point. If you and *Thieu-Uy* Le will accompany me to the gazebo, the facts will speak for themselves."

Minh, with Le and me close on his heels, set off at a double quick pace towards the gazebo. All the while, Minh was mumbling to himself. He was most likely cursing his fate for saddling him with this hard-headed American and wishing that Lieutenant Edwards would return and put an end to this misery.

When we neared the gazebo and could see over the sidewalls, Minh stopped in his tracks. His whole upper body turned beet red and a cry ripped from his throat as he ran to the hapless sentry trussed in the hammock. He started raining blows to the sentry's head and body until Le and I restrained him.

"It's not the sentry's fault Minh. He was only doing what the other sentries did before him. That's why we decided last night to test his vigilance and this is the result. We took turns staying up during the night with our binoculars and basically stood the watch for him. We meant no harm to anyone, but we were just trying to drive my point home to you. This security system is unsatisfactory and really needs rethinking."

Minh finally regained his composure as he leaned against the side of the gazebo. "Do you have any recommendations to remedy this situation?" he asked softly through clenched teeth.

"I do *Trung-Uy*, but first allow me to let the sentry loose. He's suffered enough, first with our aggressive sneak attack and then fearing your reaction all the while he was tied up. I would suggest that an additional sentry be placed on the eastern point of land on the rocks so he can see around the corner of the island. When I was atop the lighthouse, I noticed that this area is a blind spot from up there. You can bet that the VC are also aware of that, so it behooves us to cover that avenue of approach as well. Additionally, we should bring a few more dogs to the island. I'm sure the dependents would be willing to take care of them. They would provide a good early warning system in the event that the VC decides to attack us by coming over the mountain from the south side of the island."

Nodding his head in agreement, Minh said that this could be done. He turned to Le and said in guttural Vietnamese, "See that it gets done."

"One more favor. Please don't hold the sentry accountable for what we did last night. Besides, our radio reception from Saigon wasn't too good and we had nothing else to do."

"OK, OK," said Minh as he extended his hand to me, one military man to another.

That matter having been resolved, we returned to our hootch where Angus and Rusty tried hard not to show their apprehension as to what had transpired. Once Minh and Le entered their side of the house, I filled the guys in quietly with a blow-by-blow accounting and they were surprised at the final outcome.

"I thought for sure that Minh would be on the horn to VNN Headquarters in Saigon requesting that the three of us get thrown out on our respective asses," said Angus.

"It could have gone that way, but Minh has been in the military long enough to understand that he doesn't have all the answers and that's what we're here for."

"What made you suggest the dogs?" asked Rusty.

"I figured I had pushed the envelope with him and it would be easier than asking for an additional sentry at night to watch our back door."

"Good thinking boss, now I know why you get the big bucks," chimed in Angus.

"Yeah right, lots of *pesos* for the college guy," I retorted sarcastically as I headed in to take a much needed shower.

"Besides," added Rusty to my back as I was leaving, "if they don't work out as watchdogs, the dependents can always use them for an entree at a Luau."

POP GO THE WINDOWS

The next few days passed by uneventfully. Nothing was said to us by the Vietnamese about their meeting with the Province Chief and this was about par for the course. Didn't anyone tell them that we were on their side? What a way to fight a war.

It was obvious that a course in avoiding frustration should also be included in the Counter Insurgency curriculum to better prepare future Advisors in handling their Oriental counterparts.

I could see that this was also eating at Rusty and Angus, although they never mentioned it to me. I decided that I would keep quiet about the subject and see if Minh would eventually pass the word down to us. I could have waited until the Polar Ice cap melted and tried very hard not to let it influence our relationship.

It would, however, be included in my monthly report to the Fourth Coastal Zone Commander under the "Counterpart's Evaluation" section. It would describe him as a Mushroom Farmer, which is better translated to mean that he keeps us in the dark and covers us in manure.

This was the "Cover Your Ass" part of the report in the event something went wrong at the base. Not every Advisor and his Vietnamese Counterpart were compatible and the Senior Naval Advisor in Saigon wanted to know what was actually happening in the field and why.

Up to now, Minh had been given good evaluations, but then again, I was told that Minh and Lieutenant Edwards were of a same mind. Apparently he did not completely intend to open up to me since I was only here temporarily and holding the fort until Edwards returned from leave. Hard to figure, but then again as Rudyard Kipling observed, "*Only a fool tries to hustle the east.*"

A few days later on patrol off of Song Ong Doc; the WPB Point Comfort hailed us and came alongside. LT Ted Ryerson, the skipper leaned down from the bridge and yelled that he wanted to talk to me. I nodded to Minh as I made my way aboard the WPB. Maybe this was my chance to show Minh that two could play the "need to know" bullshit game.

"Have I got something for you to sink your teeth into," Ryerson said as he reached out to shake my hand. His short sun bleached blonde hair accentuated his tanned stubbled features and a pair of aviator's dark glasses hid his eyes, giving him a Hollywood mystique. He was a mustang Coastie and a former Gunners Mate First Class who hailed from Pascagoula, Mississippi. His youthfulness and thicker than molasses drawl, belied the fact that he had a law degree and planned on becoming a "Lynching Judge" in his home state once he returned to civilian life. Well, better him than me, I thought. I had enough mosquitoes growing up as a boy in New

Jersey, but the swamps of Mississippi bred some big suckers, I was told.

"What's up?" I asked as I braced my back against the bulkhead of the yawing bridge. The ground swells were long and about two feet in height which caused the WPB to roll like a drunk on Saturday night. The Junk had lain off some thirty yards away to avoid damage to either craft.

"While we were in Ha Tien socializing with the Green Beanies the other day, one of the officers offered to trade us a 97 mm recoilless rifle with 20 projectiles for a couple gallons of ice cream. How could I refuse an offer like that?"

"Super! What did you have in mind?" I asked warming to the possibilities.

"Well, we've been getting reports that several of the recon flights over Camau have been receiving considerable ground fire and since it's a free-fire zone, I thought we could add our two cents worth using the recoilless."

"I don't see why not, but I'll have to run it by my counterpart first."

"I have about four more days on station in this area before getting relieved, so you'll have to get back to me pretty soon, OK?"

I waved the Junk back alongside and disembarked the WPB, then went aft to talk to Minh. At first, he seemed receptive to the idea, but he finally said that he was not authorized to undertake such an operation without specific authorization from his boss at Fourth Coastal Zone Headquarters and Saigon. In fact, he was certain that his superiors would definitely not support such a plan until they contacted the Province Chief of Camau.

"But, Camau has been declared a free-fire zone, which to me means that he has already agreed to our shooting at targets of opportunity," I said.

"True," said Minh, "but you have to understand the politics that are involved here." After a few moments he said that he personally wouldn't have any objections if the Advisors alone collaborated with the WPB in this scheme as long as he and his officers were not involved.

"Fair enough," I replied, "However we'll still need the use of one of the Junks with a Cox'n and a seaman to provide transport."

"That much I can do for you, but remember, you do this on your own if any repercussions come down from the north, OK?"

"Roger that *Trung-Uy,"* I replied.

With that having been resolved, I contacted the WPB over the PRC-25 radio on a preselected frequency to eliminate "Barbados" from monitoring our conversation and told Ryerson that we'd meet at first light tomorrow just off the coast of Point Camau. He rogered and signed off.

On the way back to Poulo Obi, I kept wondering why Minh wanted to avoid our proposed soiree and it finally hit me that he didn't want to cross swords with the Province Chief. Well, that was OK by me because I wasn't going to let any petty politics distort my objectivity when it came to inflicting damage to the bad guys.

In the early dark of the following day, Angus, Rusty and I boarded the assigned Junk that was already waiting for us next to the rocks. At least Minh provided us with two good crewmembers who were proven fighters and one of the better boats. As we made our way to the rendezvous point, there was no sound except for the steady rumble of the diesel engine and the susurration of the water going past the shark's mouth freshly painted on our bow.

Finally, we spied the WPB and I told the Cox'n to come up alongside. As we neared the craft, I noticed that most of the windows in the pilothouse were gone.

"What happened to your windows?" I yelled up to Ryerson.

"We tried testing the recoilless rifle last night off of Bird Island and the back blast blew out some of our friggin windows."

"How're you going to explain that to Beamon?" I asked.

"Beats me, but hopefully I'll come up with something."

"Well, how about transferring the weapon to us and put your Boston Whaler over the side. Rusty and I will use the Whaler to get in close to shore as possible where we can lob in some M-79 grenades. We'll also be able to direct Angus by radio where to aim the recoilless rifle."

Because of the shallow water around the Camau Peninsula, the WPB had to stay out about 1,500 yards; the Junk was 75 yards out and we in the Whaler, maneuvered to within 25 feet of the shore. Rusty was having some difficulty being in that close because the outboard motor was starting to suck in silt from the bottom.

"Boy, we could really use one of those long shaft motors about now," he said as he eyed the muddy water roiling up around the stern of the boat.

I agreed, but there was nothing we could do about that now. However, it's something we would have to think about the next time we planned one of these ops, I thought to myself.

Rusty and I were both armed with M-79 grenade launchers with roughly 20 rounds apiece and I had also brought along my trusty M-14, just in case. Once we got in as far as we could safely go, I gave the command to commence firing. I told Rusty to keep us moving parallel to the coast because I didn't want to be a sitting target in case we received hostile fire from the shore.

We both started popping grenades into and over the tree line as fast as we could reload our weapons. Once you fire an M-79, you have to break it open like a shotgun, remove the expended casing, insert another round and close the breech. Then she's ready to fire again. Rusty, while steering the boat, was busier than a one-armed paperhanger with the crabs as he fired, reloaded and fired again.

Our firing was the signal for Angus to commence shooting the recoilless at maximum range towards the general area of our targets. The resounding boom reached us across the water as the first round left the Junk and sailed well back behind the trees. His orders were to keep firing until I waved to him to stop. On the fourth round from the recoilless, there was a horrendous, loud secondary explosion from beyond the tree line.

"Wow," said Rusty, "Sounds like we hit a cache of ammo."

I had to agree because there was nothing else that would result in an explosion like that. Hopefully, we might have even taken out some of the VC that took potshots at our helicopters.

Finally, with all our M-79 and recoilless rounds expended, I told Rusty to head back to the Junk. As we clambered aboard and tied off the whaler for towing, I noticed Angus and the two sailors looking a bit sheepish. I had expected a much different reaction, especially since they nailed something of importance.

"What's up?" I asked Angus.

With consternation etched all over his face, he pointed to the starboard gunnel of the Junk. It was split from the bow to just forward of the cabin.

It was obvious that the back blast from the recoilless caused the damage when they elevated it for maximum range. Fortunately, it did not impair the Junk's seaworthiness, but now we would have to face Minh upon or return.

"Don't worry," I said to the Cox'n, trying to sound confident. "The damage is not that bad and it can easily be fixed at An Thoi. I'm sure Minh will understand and treat it as acceptable battle damage. After all, you boys hit the target dead on."

"I hope so *Dai-Uy,* but you please help me explain to *Trung-Uy* Minh," implored the Cox'n.

"Can do," I replied as I patted him on the back like a big brother, quelling some of his apprehension for a while at least.

We had already come alongside the WPB and the crew quickly began hauling the Boston Whaler aboard. Ryerson leaned out from the top of the WPB's pilot house and said, "Looks like a good day's work to me considering my windows."

"Take a look at the starboard gunnel of the Junk," I yelled back. "Looks like someone drove a giant rail-splitter into it."

"Wow, what's Minh going to say?" he asked as he wiped the perspiration from his brow with a raggedy old faded green towel.

"Probably something along the same lines as Beamon is going to lay on you, I would assume. Hopefully, we can repair the damage without the fuss-budgets in Saigon hearing about it and getting all bent out of shape."

"Yeah, I suppose. But there's no way I can sneak this by Beamon. He'll have to be advised. Hopefully our sitrep about the secondary explosion alleviates his mood and he can figure out a way to make points towards with the Head-Shed in Saigon."

That being said, we cast off from alongside and pointed our bow back towards Poulo Obi and the potential wrath of LTJG Minh.

As we approached the island, Minh and Le were standing in front of the hootch shading their eyes from the setting sun and watched our approach to the landing rock. We debarked without incident, leaving the Junk crew to back away and bring the boat around to the other side of the island for mooring. As we neared the hootch, Minh and Le were all smiles as Minh said, "Looks like the trip was a success, eh *Dai-Uy*?"

"I'd say so because we had a secondary explosion, but it came at a price. The starboard gunnel of the Junk was damaged by the back blast from the recoilless rifle and the Cox'n is fearful of what your reaction will be. It wasn't his fault Minh."

"We will look at the damage and see if we can get it repaired without having to tell Commander Chau at Fourth Coastal Zone. Sometimes what he doesn't know won't hurt us," he said letting his words trail off. I knew exactly what he meant.

"That's what I would have done," I said as I followed the other guys into our side of the hootch. I was sure that Minh was satisfied that I agreed with his decision, and it was now time for a dip in the ocean, a fresh water shower and a cold beer . . . in that order.

The next morning, I found Minh sitting just inside the window on the VN side of the hootch. He looked up and said "I looked at the damaged Junk when it was brought around this morning and believe that it can be repaired by some of the villagers at Son Ong Doc. Of course, I may have to come up with a 55 gallon drum of diesel fuel, but that should be no problem."

"That's good," I replied. The staff weenies at Phu Quoc will be more than happy to hear that we suffered no damage to our boats, but Commander Beamon will be another problem when he sees the pilothouse windows of the WPB."

"Ah yes, your Commander Beamon appears to be quite difficult at times. I know that Commander Chau is not too pleased with him since he got along so well with Beamon's predecessor. At least Commander Wade tried to speak some Vietnamese during his tour and he actually enjoyed our food, whereas, Beamon shows a distinct dislike for both."

"I've heard that from others and from what I observed when I first met him, I'm glad he's in the Coast Guard and not the Navy. Well, let me know if there's anything we can do to help *Trung-Uy,* and we'll be glad to do it."

I came back into the hootch just as Rusty and Angus were making up their bunks. Some things never change once you've been through Boot Camp, I thought. I told them what Minh's reaction was to the damaged Junk and they both smiled and nodded their heads in approval.

"That's the way things should be done out here in the boonies instead of the chicken-shit paper shuffling and bitching," exclaimed Angus.

"Amen to that," mumbled Rusty into a cup of coffee.

Later that evening just before sundown, Minh knocked quietly on our door.

"Come in *Trung-Uy,"* I said rising up from my wicker chair where I had been busily trying to work on some reports.

As Minh entered, he took a seat next to Angus who had been deeply engrossed in studying for his upcoming Chief's exam. Settling back and nonchalantly crossing his legs, Minh said, "I've been meaning to bring you up to date on my meeting with the Province Chief the other day. I thought that this would be a good time since the three of you are all here together."

Rusty joined us after his shower, wearing a towel around his shoulders, khaki shorts, flip-flops and wet red hair plastered to his head. He casually perched a haunch on a corner of the desk where I had been writing as Minh now had our full attention.

"First of all, I would like to inform you gentlemen that Lieutenant Colonel Tao, the Province Chief of Camau, is my uncle. He is my mother's eldest brother and looks upon me as a son since his only son was killed in Quang Tri in 1964. My cousin was an infantry officer whose unit was ambushed by the Viet Cong during a routine patrol. He died instantly when a grenade exploded at his feet as they entered the kill zone. So there is no love lost between the Colonel and the VC."

I had heard that there was a great deal of nepotism within the government and military branches of South Vietnam, so this did not come as any great surprise to me.

"One of the items we discussed during our meeting," Minh continued, "was ways in which we of Coastal Group 41 could assist in harassing the local VC that are provoking all the hard working people in his province. Colonel Tao contacted me by radio this morning and said that he has received word through his extensive intelligence resources that the VC have harvested several hundred kilos of shrimp, and that they are still in the nets at the eastern mouth of the Bo De River. I propose that we take three Junks, each with an Advisor aboard, slip into the Bo De under cover of darkness and relieve them of their catch."

The three of us looked at each other and as one nodded our approval to Minh. "It's about time we put a good hurt on old Charlie," said Rusty. "Besides, it would be nice to have some shrimp to eat for a change with our rice."

"I'll say, it will definitely put a hurt on the VC, not only to their stomachs but to their pride as well," I chipped in.

"When is this party going to take place *Trung-Uy*?" asked Angus as he quietly set his study material aside.

"I would like to get underway later this evening, say around 2230 hours. It is about a two and a half hour run to the mouth of the Bo De where it empties into the South China Sea and there is a new moon tonight which will favor us greatly. Additionally, since the tide will be flooding, we will not need our engines once we position ourselves offshore. Two of the Junks will drift in and silently haul in the nets while I, aboard the Command Junk with *Dai-Uy* Kay, will provide security in the event we awaken the hive. Our information is that they are not guarding the shrimp since its existence is not general knowledge, so our task will be much easier."

It sounds like the old Province Chief has an insider working among the VC to get this kind of information, I thought to myself. After tossing random ideas around for about another half hour, Minh stood up, stretched his thin but well muscled body and looking directly at me said rather facetiously, "Time for me to make a short tour of the base before turning in. Besides, I want to ensure that the posted watch standers are awake and alert."

I knew immediately that this was for my benefit, especially since our sneak attack upon his guard in the gazebo. "If you don't mind *Trung-Uy*, I'll accompany you, if nothing else to work the kinks out of my legs." I might have been mistaken, but I could have sworn that he was smiling after he nodded and left.

"I'll see you outside in a few minutes," he threw over his shoulder as he disappeared into his side of the hootch.

When he reappeared, he was carrying a flashlight and an 18 inch rubber baton. As he lifted the baton deftly in front of me, he said, "This is one idea left over from the French and it is called the 'punisher' because it provides emphasis to a Commanding Officer's words when directed towards a non-vigilant watchstander. Best of all, its bite leaves no mark."

"Gotcha *Trung-Uy*, I sure could have used a motivational tool like that once in awhile aboard ship, but unfortunately my Navy frowns on physical abuse of any kind."

As fate would have it, the "punisher" was not to be unleashed this night as all the sentries were awake and alert. Since arriving in Vietnam, I've learned that the French were overly strict colonizers and freely applied harsh discipline akin to that meted out to their own Foreign Legion. It obviously worked because the Legionnaires were a well trained and formidable force to be reckoned with in battle.

Returning from our rounds a short while later, Minh and I said our goodnights and headed for our respective sides of the hootch. Although I was physically tired, I knew that sleep would not come easily. In the other bunks, Angus was already snorkeling quietly and Rusty was curled up in a fetal position beneath his mosquito net. I stripped down to my shorts and lay down atop my poncho liner, pulling the mosquito net close around me. Nighttime was no place to be unprotected from the constant assault from the pesky mosquito brigades. You could not have any part of your body touching the net lest the ever-present mosquitoes could draw your blood even through the net.

I didn't think that any of us would sleep this night because of the real possibility of engaging the Viet Cong tomorrow, but I was wrong. Preparing for our normal patrols was slightly less than enchanting and caused little or no apprehension, but this was different. We were going right into Charlie's backyard in an attempt to steal his property. Somewhere during this train of thought, I dropped off into a dreamless sleep.

When Rusty nudged me awake around 2300 hours, I felt as if I hadn't had any sleep at all. Despite that, I rolled out and quickly dressed. By 2330, the three of us were ready to embark, each carrying our M-14 rifles and several bandoliers of ammo.

Minh and Le came out a few moments later as Minh said, "*Aspirant* Tam will take us aboard his Junk by the rocks. From there we can each transfer to our respective boats out in deeper water where the other Junks will be waiting." The unmistakable rumble of the diesel engine reached out to us over the sound of the incoming surf that was gently slapping against the rocks.

ANYONE FOR SHRIMP?

We quickly clambered aboard and the Junk reversed itself into deeper water. Once we were about seventy five yards off-shore, Minh and I transferred to the Command Junk, Angus and Le then boarded their Junk and Rusty remained aboard with Tam. The Command Junk took the lead heading North-North-East with the other two Junks trailing astern of us in single file.

Our broad bow dug itself into the dark green waters as the big GM671 engine propelled us through the South China Sea towards our destination. We couldn't have asked for a better night with favorable sea conditions ensuring a comfortable passage. As I sat quietly on the wooden deckhouse, I gazed out over the tranquil sea and I thought about the thousands of my other shipmates around the world monotonously responding to "This is a drill, this is a drill, General Quarters, General Quarters. All hands man your battle stations." The majority of them will never get to see actual combat, but the redundant training aboard ship is a constant reminder that it could someday happen and preparedness is half the battle.

Now here I was at my GQ station without any fanfare, claxon alarms or racing against a stopwatch held by an Executive Officer timing the evolution. This was more to my liking and undoubtedly, I thought, a throwback to my Spartan heritage.

The Command Junk plowed effortlessly through the dark, almost flat surface of the water. There was a new moon that ensured total darkness that enveloped everything around us. The myriad of stars forming a canopy overhead from horizon to horizon, shed no light on us and for this, we were extremely grateful.

We made our way easily with our running lights extinguished and only the phosphorescence of our bow waves and the muted deep rumbling sounds of the diesels giving testimony to anything alien on the slightly undulating sea.

As previously estimated by Minh, about two and a half hours later our trio of Junks idled their engines about one hundred yards offshore from the mouth of the Bo De River. We were slightly to the northeast of our target in order to take advantage of the tide that would help carry us soundlessly to our objective. Once again I was amazed at the unerring celestial navigation ability exhibited by these Vietnamese seafarers in getting us to our destination without the use of modern radar.

The silence of the night was broken only by the sounds of night birds calling to each other from the trees. As we let the current pull our crafts towards the mouth of the river, the familiar smell of charcoal fires permeated the night air. It's an experience normally reserved for mariners approaching the coast of a distant land to first smell the distinct aroma coming from the shore. My first time as a young sailor aboard a naval tanker making its way to Golfe Juan on the French Riviera, I experienced the subtle essence of perfume titillating my senses. Whereas, later on in the cruise making landfall off the coast of Bone, Algeria, the extreme heat contained strong hints of dusty, dry and heavy air. Naples, Italy, on the other hand, was a rough combination of the two with a hint of raw sewage thrown in and depending on where along the coastline you approached.

The crews aboard the Junks began using long paddles and poles that had been previously loaded aboard and with the aid of the flooding tide, managed to maneuver the boats stern first into the mouth of the river. The mangrove trees and foliage on either side of the river in this area extended to the water's very edge.

"So far, so good", I thought. It looked as if our intelligence might be right for a change, since there was no sign of anyone raising an alarm at our clandestine approach. Fifty feet of one and a half inch manila line connected the bow of the first Junk to the stern of the second, and another two hundred feet of line went from the second Junk's bow to the broad stern of the Command Junk. In this way, the Command Junk with its larger engine could tow the other two boats out bow first towards the open sea where they could start their own engines. Once inside the dark brooding mouth of the river, the crew of the lead Junks propelled their boats with the long poles. They stayed close to the northern side of the river in order to blend in with the shadows of the heavy foliage. On the Command Junk, Minh ordered the anchor dropped silently about fifty yards outside of the river's mouth in order to provide security for the other two craft.

The two Junks made their way stealthily up the river to where the nets were said to be located, however, there were no nets strung across the river. Instead, they were already empty and hanging from the trees on the southern embankment to dry out. Fortunately, Le did not panic and after a hurried conversation with his crew and Angus, he decided to put two men over the side to reconnoiter the shore.

What must have seemed like ages to Le, but in fact was merely a few minutes, the two sailors waded back to the Junk and whispered that they had located the cache of shrimp. The VC had unloaded the shrimp and placed them into five large finely meshed sacks that were sitting in the water and secured to the bases of nearby trees. The sacks measured about five feet long by four feet wide and were filled to the brim with shrimp. Obviously the Viet Cong were not yet ready to distribute such a large catch, and rather than risk spoilage, submerged them in the river.

Le clicked the microphone of the PRC-25's radio twice to let Minh know that the two boats were in position and starting to load the shrimp. Minh clicked his microphone three times in acknowledgement. Turning to me in the darkness, he flashed me a thumbs up with a nod of his head and a grin.

Le and Tam worked their crews quickly and silently. The two sailors that were already in the water untied the ropes from around the trees and passed them to the waiting boat crews. Each crew managed to position a sack on either side of their boat where they retied them securely through the chocks and around the gunwales. The fifth sack was strung out astern of the last Junk. This kept the tops just below the beading around the hull and permitted the shrimp to still be in the water. The Junks took on the appearance of loaded pack mules with the sacks tied on either side of their hulls like saddlebags.

On the bow of each Junk, the forward .30 caliber machine guns had been temporarily replaced for this incursion with heavier .50

caliber guns manned by Minh's most capable Gunners. Now came the crucial part of the operation, the successful extraction of the two Junks with their booty of shrimp safely in our possession.

When all the shrimp-laden sacks were securely tied to the Junks, Le clicked his microphone four times rapidly to signal Minh that the boats were ready to be hauled out. Minh quickly acknowledged with a single click and quietly issued an order to commence taking in the anchor.

The deep growl of the Command Junk's big engine rumbled into life at the touch of the starter. Since our bow was already facing the open sea due to the set of the anchor, it made it easier to gain momentum until there was a good strain on the tow rope. Once it was pulled taut above the water, Minh had the Cox'n push the throttle ahead for all it was worth and started pulling the shrimp-laden Junks out of the Bo De into the safety of the South China Sea. The Gods must have been smiling down on us this night for a slight breeze appeared from the Northwest carrying our engine sounds out to sea and away from the darkened shore.

All the while the operation was in progress, the normal night sounds continued unabated in the brush and no sign of the VC was ever detected. Apparently, the Viet Cong were feeling so secure that they left the shrimp unattended while they were most likely elsewhere harassing the local inhabitants.

Once we were well clear of the river's mouth, the trailing boats started their engines with a puff of black smoke from their exhausts. We had assumed at the outset that we would have to continue to tow the boats back to Poulo Obi because of the added drag of the shrimp laden nets. However, the mesh sacks offered no problem to the smaller engine Yabutas and they managed to maintain a respectful speed without the tow. Despite the slower passage through the water by the trailing Junks, the return trip proved to be uneventful. The relief of a well executed and successful operation was shared by all concerned and a gentle feeling of euphoria engulfed the homeward bound craft and crew.

The eastern sky was rapidly starting to change hues from a deep rosy pink to a whitish cerulean blue. Nowhere else in the world does the sun rise as brightly as in the Far East and it was beginning to look like a sailor's morning. There was just a slight hint of chop on the sea's surface and schools of flying fish were leaping out of the water by the hundreds. This was a good indication that a larger predator fish was out to get some breakfast early and the smaller fish were in a panic mode. Some of them even landed aboard the deck of the boats. Although we were going at a slower pace because of the drag of the fully loaded sacks, we still managed to make relatively good time.

Le and Minh were jabbering steadily over the radio and it was obvious that fatigue was starting to set in. Le was saying that it appeared to be around four hundred kilos of shrimp that had been appropriated. In Yankee terms, this equated to about one thousand pounds. Not a bad night's haul, I mused. We could only hope that the Viet Cong, upon noticing the missing shrimp, would be in the dark about who was to blame for the theft. I was sure that we would be among the suspects, but there were many others in the surrounding area who were equally capable of committing such a dastardly crime.

If they knew positively that we to blame, there is no doubt in anyone's mind that we could expect some form of retaliation; only time would tell and extreme vigilance would have to be maintained from here on in.

Minh planned to address the entire base's complement and their dependents with a warning not to spread any word whatsoever of our involvement, if and when they ventured off the island. The incredible speed with which rumor and innuendo spread via the bamboo grapevine was notorious here in

Southeast Asia. Only through the strict observance of absolute silence about the matter could we avoid or at least delay any repercussions by the VC. This was going to be a good test of our people's resolve, because the Vietnamese by nature are a highly talkative society.

I managed somehow to raise "Barbados" on our radio as we cleared Point Camau and headed to our base and made a concise oral report about our raid on the VC. I recommended that the word be passed to all friendly units in the area to avoid the eastern end of the Bo De River mouth for awhile because the VC would certainly be on high alert for anyone approaching that location. They rogered and said the word would be disseminated immediately.

Almost four hours had elapsed since we had cleared the mouth of the Bo De River and arrived at Poulo Obi. It looked as if all the inhabitants had come down to the shoreline to greet us. Once we were within hailing distance, Minh shouted in a voice that cracked with emotion and louder than I had ever heard him yell, that we were very successful and that everyone would be eating shrimp tonight. This was followed by loud cheers and applause from the joyous on-lookers as the children splashed merrily into the surf. Man, this is what it's all about I thought, getting caught up in the excitement of the moment. Right now, I could use a good shower and a cold can of beer as I am sure Angus and Rusty would agree.

We three Advisors, along with our counterparts, disembarked onto the rocks and headed towards the hootch. The Yabuta Junks in turn nosed into the rocks where the sacks were untied and manhandled ashore by the eager sailors. The joviality on the base was infectious as the sacks were carried down to the fresh water catch basin where the shrimp would be washed, beheaded and liberally doled out to the individual families. As the sacks were being emptied, the superb workmanship that went into their manufacture became evident and we had a chance to examine them closer. We could not help but be impressed at the skill that went into their construction.

A NAVAL ADVISOR USES NATURAL RESOURCES JUST LIKE "CHARLIE" DOES.

Minh later announced that the five sacks would be put to good use as "punishment" containers for any of his sailors that required temporary confinement in the future. This he said with a twinkle in his eye and I found it intriguing once I learned about using the sacks for punitive purposes by hanging them from a tree. That thought had never entered my mind, but then again, the Vietnamese, who were involved in this war for such a long time, took advantage of every opportunity that presented itself . . . and why not?

Back in our side of the hootch, Rusty said, "Boy oh boy, I could really go for some Shrimp Scampi or better yet, a huge bowl of Creole Shrimp and rice."

"So could we all," Angus replied, "But I think we'll wind up with boiled shrimp in noodle soup. At least it'll be a change from our usual fish and boiled rice menu."

Two days later, after having consumed our fair share of the delicious shrimp, it was time to go back to work. Rusty had already departed on patrol with Aspirant Tam and they had strict orders to avoid going anywhere near the Bo De River. It didn't take a rocket scientist to know that the VC would be watching diligently for the shrimp pirates and they'd be willing to put a hurt on anyone that even remotely filled the bill. With that thought uppermost in their minds, Tam and Rusty put out to sea.

Since it was close to the end of the month, Angus, with Le in command, set out for the standard supply run to our Advisory Team base in Rach Gia. It was usually an exercise in futility because all the good foodstuffs would already have been picked through by the Advisors in and around Rach Gia. There were three Junk Force bases located nearby in Kien An, and that meant twelve hungry American Advisors loading up before we could get there. Food purchases were made in military script that each of us kicked into the kitty monthly. This was above and beyond the local meals that we paid our cook to provide. If we were lucky, there would still be some borderline stale bread and jars of non-descript jelly available. Allotments of C-rations, on the other hand, were free from the military and were always the second choice. From there, it was a PX run for soda and beer. It was Lieutenant Edward's decision that the enlisted men would make these runs, most likely figuring that the sailors would visit the Grass Shack to address their libido. I don't recall reading anywhere in my commissioning contract with the navy that I had to remain celibate, but since I was only holding the fort temporarily until his return, the rule would stand.

That afternoon the Coast Guard WPB Point Grey paid us a visit. It was transporting a navy Electronics Technician First Class by the name of Paul Dillon. Naturally everyone called him Marshal Dillon in honor of "Gunsmoke's" James Arness. I had met the "Marshall" previously at VNN Headquarters in Saigon where the ET twidgets had their own little cubbyhole of an office. There were six techs assigned and their sole function was to keep the men in the field up to speed where radio communications were concerned.

I came out of the hootch to greet the tech as he and a Coastie seaman were offloading equipment from the Boston Whaler. "How's it going Marshall? What brings you to our fair island?"

"I'm going to install two new AN/VRC-46 30 watt transceivers for you and your counterpart so that 4th Coastal Zone HQ can raise you guys once in awhile. This mountain backdrop of yours may be the cause of your PRC-10 and PRC-25 communication problems and the general consensus is that the 46 will do the job. I have to string more antenna wires to your existing towers, realign the sets and you should be in business."

"Can't say that I miss talking to 'Barbados' much, but if an emergency should arise, it would be nice to be able to ask Big Bubba for help."

"You're exactly right, *Dai Uy*. I hear through the grapevine that Lieutenant Edwards will be returning from leave soon. Are they going to leave you here or reassign you someplace else?"

"It beats me. You've been in long enough to know that you can't predict what the paper-shufflers will do, so I'll just have to wait and see."

"By the way," said Dillon, "I came across some C-4 plastique blocks and pencil detonators and figured that you may be able to put them to good use. They're in this .30 caliber ammo box."

"Yes indeed I can use them and I don't want to know how you got them either. Now maybe I can blow some of these huge boulders out of the water and clear a channel to bring the Junks in to the beach. For that, you've earned yourself a beer. Come in and stow your equipment in the hootch," I said over my shoulder as I lovingly carried the C-4 in myself.

Just then, Minh came out of his side of the hootch. "Hello Dillon," he said with his usual boyish grin. "I hear you have some new radios for us."

"That's a fact *Trung-Uy*. You don't know how good it feels to get out of Saigon. The Captain is planning a personnel inspection for all the Headquarters people and rumor has it that he wants the officers in their service dress whites with choke collars."

"That's a crock," I said disbelievingly, "because none of us even brought our service dress whites over here. I guess he must have some idle time on his hands and he's dreaming up a 'to-do' list to keep busy. And the worst part is that I might be back in Saigon after Mister Edwards get back. Oh shit!"

Minh said quietly, "I hope Captain Chon doesn't want to do the same with a similar inspection of his own."

"I don't think so, *Trung-Uy.* Chon is much more levelheaded than that and he knows that a personnel inspection during wartime would be a morale buster for sure," I remarked solemnly. "By the way, Dillon brought some C-4 down with him and I'd like your permission to try a clear out some of those boulders so we can beach the Junks occasionally."

"That would be good if you can do *Dai-Uy*. Do you need help?"

"No, it's a one man job because once I pull the detonator ring, I'll have 15 minutes to clear out and I don't want to have to worry about someone else in the water with me."

"When do you want to start?" asked Minh.

"Probably tomorrow morning; everyone will be awake and it will give you time to spread the word so that no one panics when they hear the first charge go off. Is that OK with you?"

"OK, OK," said Minh nodding his head. "But be careful, I don't want to lose an Advisor. There's too much paperwork to fill out."

The next morning I checked the weather and it was another sultry day in this part of the world, so I donned my bathing suit and prepared for the job ahead. I carried the ammo box of C-4 and the detonators outside and placed them at the base of the larger of the two palm trees in front of the hootch. My plan was to start with the largest boulder out and work my way in towards the beach, setting the C-4 so that the explosive force would be to seaward.

Holding a single block of C-4 and a detonator, I waded out into the cool morning water until I identified the largest boulder that lay in my proposed pathway to the beach. It was located about thirty yards out and I estimated it to weigh about five hundred pounds. Fortunately, all the pencil detonator fuses had been set with fifteen minute lengths so I didn't have to calculate and cut each one individually. I pushed the metal tip of the fuse into the quarter pound block of C-4, dove underwater and placed it beneath the beachside of the monster rock. Once I pulled the ring on the other end of the detonator, I turned and swam quickly for the beach. When my feet hit the sandy bottom, I stood up and splashed through the shallow surf towards the shelter of the hootch. It's amazing how long fifteen minutes can be when one waits for it to pass, whereas, when time is of no consequence, it flies by.

The ensuing boom of the explosion ripped through the serene morning air sending a gusher of water high into the sky and shards of broken rock out to sea. With the initial blast, the dependents, although forewarned by Minh, still rushed to their doorways with curiosity, while they unceremoniously dragged their animated children back indoors. When they saw me appear from my doorway, they rewarded me with applause and yelled encouragements to me. Over the course of the morning, I repeated the process five more times. Coincidentally, after the first explosion, no one bothered to come out for the rest of them except Minh. He appeared out of his hootch just as the last explosion ripped through the air.

"What do you think, *Dai-Uy?* Is the way clear enough to beach a Yabuta?"

"Actually, I think we can even bring in the *Chu-Luc*," I replied confidently.

"Good work, my friend," he said with a smile as he gave me a pat on the back before going back into the hootch.

It's a good feeling to know that you alone have accomplished something for someone and that the effort will most likely be remembered long after you're gone. With that thought in mind, I collected the remaining blocks of C-4 and detonators and brought them into our side of the hootch. One could never tell when the rest of the blocks would come in handy.

There is one thing however, and that is after finishing clearing what I felt were the obstacle boulders, I decided to blow one more that was off to the side. I am publically admitting that I have never revealed this to a soul since then, and that is that the last detonator didn't work. No boom and that put a scary feeling in my mind because now I was wondering whether the detonator was faulty or not. I waited for thirty minutes just in case, because I knew that this was another item manufactured for the government by the lowest bidder.

I spent the rest of the afternoon in the hammock under the palm trees and luxuriated in the cool breeze that was blowing gently in from seaward. With a fresh cup of coffee in my hands, I could watch the efforts of Marshall Dillon and two of the young Vietnamese radiomen stringing new antenna wire. Man, I thought to myself, I could not think of any place on earth that I would rather be than here in this hammock, on this island with these people. It made me all the more aware of the world that I would someday have to return to; the steel grey ships, the endless drills, the paperwork and constant responsibility that goes with running these ships. I knew that eventually I would have to accept the decision to go back to that world and continue my chosen career. But could I in all honesty, after practically being on independent duty, devoid of all the Mickey Mouse crap, go back as if nothing had happened? That immediately brought to mind the impending Captain's Inspection that would probably find me in Saigon and an unwilling participant. I would have to call home and have my service dress whites sent to me if my mother could find them. No sense in worrying about that now, I'd just let it play out and see what happens. Maybe I could plead ignorance about the inspection since I had been in the field.

FILL 'ER UP

Later that evening after supper and the radio work had been completed and tested; Minh came into our side where Dillon and I were sitting lazily around the front room. He said, "I just received word on our new radio that our monthly diesel fuel allowance would not arrive for another two weeks. It seems that the LSSL that normally delivers the fuel has had an engine malfunction."

"Hell, they have other ships that can haul the stuff down here in their place, don't they?" I asked.

"Unfortunately, my navy doesn't run like yours, *Dai-Uy*. The Captain of the refueling LSSL jealously guards his assignment and no one else can replace him without much loss of face."

"That doesn't make sense," chimed in Dillon.

"So what are we supposed to do in the meantime?" I asked. "How much fuel do we have left?"

"I sent one of my men to the other side of the island where the fuel is stored to count the barrels."

The replenishing LSSL normally beaches on the southern side of the island where the 55 gallon drums are unloaded from the ship's lowered bow ramp and then rolled to a small shelter under the trees. That was our fuel depot and when the Junks needed refueling, they would steam around to the other side of the island and pump the diesel from the drums directly into the boat's tanks. Unfortunately, the skipper of the LSSL would only replace the fuel on a one-for-one basis. In other words, say we were authorized 110 barrels or 6,050 gallons of fuel a month; if we only had one hundred empty barrels—that was it. The Captain of the LSSL would literally "pocket" ten full barrels that he could dispose of any way he saw fit. And that is why no other ship could take its place. It's a helluva way to fight a war, but it was their country and our money. But my devious mind already had a solution and that was for us to get our hands on some empty 55 gallon drums and use them to get some more fuel from the LSSL. I'd have to pass that on to Minh so we could act on it. In the meantime, I had to find a way to scrounge up more fuel ASAP.

Then the thought hit me—I'd get on my brand new radio and try to contact the Coast Guard WHEC Half Moon. I was sure that they'd still be on station in our vicinity and the Captain had told me if we needed anything, not to hesitate to call him. It only took about ten minutes and the Half Moon answered up. I asked to be patched through to the CO or the XO. A few moments later, a strong voice came on the line saying, "Captain Morse."

"Good evening sir," I said. "I hate to bother you again, but the Vietnamese resupply vessel has been delayed in Saigon and they can't give us a delivery date. We're running on fumes and without some diesel, our patrol commitments will seriously be impaired. Is there any way that you can spare some fuel, at least enough to keep some of our boats going?"

"How much fuel do you need?"

"I figure about a thousand gallons should do it."

"That's no problem Lieutenant. Can you rendezvous with us tomorrow in the same location where you brought the wounded girl and how is she by the way?"

"She's better than before skipper and that location will be fine. I'll pass the word on to my counterpart and we're deeply indebted to you. I don't know what we'd do without you," I said.

"Hey, that's what we're here for and it'll look good on our monthly sitrep under 'Viet Assist.' Just head on out in that general direction and we'll close with you once we spot you on radar. See you tomorrow around 0900."

"Roger that and many thanks. This is Yankee India, out."

I went next door to pass the good news to Minh and there was no doubt that he was ecstatic and relieved. He said that we would get underway at 0700 in the morning and he'd have his crew load the empty barrels on board by then.

It was almost six-thirty the next morning when I awoke after a pretty good night's sleep. I could hear Minh moving around his side of the hootch, so it must have been time to get up and get ready for the trip out to the Half Moon. Dillon was still cutting Z's in his rack and after the hard work he put in getting the radios on line, I figured he deserved all the sleep he could get. I was dressed and standing out front in fifteen minutes when Minh came out and joined me.

"Too bad it is still low tide, otherwise we could bring the Command Junk into the beach through your new channel," he said. "I instructed the cox'n to pick us up at the big rock as before."

As if on cue, the *Chu-Luc* was just coming around the eastern end of the island and making its way to the pickup point. Minh and I nimbly negotiated the large rocks as if we had been doing it all our lives. By the time we reached the big boulder, the Junk's Cox'n had already eased her bow up against it and holding her steady for us to board. We both made the short jump down to the deck only to find it loaded with eighteen empty 55 gallon drums. It didn't leave much room on deck for us to make our way aft to the deckhouse as the big diesel engine roared mightily as she backed out into the ebbing tide. Once the Junk's bow was turned seaward, the cox'n headed back around the eastern end of the island and steered a course towards the Half Moon.

The sun was just a few degrees above the horizon but it already seemed to indicate that today would be a scorcher. The reason I say that is because by this time of the morning, there would usually be a breeze of some kind wafting down on the island. Today, however, there were no tell-tale white caps once we hit the open sea and the only movement of air was that caused by our passage through the flat sea. As we headed out leaving the island in our wake, Minh broke out two large thermos bottles from the small gym bag that he had carried aboard. When he pulled the cork out of the first one, the delicious aroma of hot French Roasted coffee reached my nostrils and my stomach immediately began to rumble. To my further surprise, Minh also produced a loaf of French bread from his bag. "The baggette may be a little stale, but we can always dip it into the coffee," said Minh with a little smile.

Let me tell you something; even a stale loaf of bread and fresh hot coffee consumed with salty sea air in your face is unforgettable. Once again I thought how fortunate I was in being able to experience all these moments.

It was just a short time after we finished our impromptu breakfast that the Half Moon made her appearance from the southwest. We closed the distance rapidly and the larger ship heaved-to as we made our approach to her starboard side and secured our lines fore and aft.

The captain leaned out over the wing of the bridge and casually returned my salute. "Glad you could make it Lieutenant, but unfortunately we won't be giving out any Green Stamps for this evolution."

"That won't be a problem skipper, besides there's no local redemption center to turn them in to," I floated back up to him.

"Let me know when your crew is ready for us to begin pumping so we can get this show on the road," he retorted businesslike.

Once the hose was lowered down to us from the main deck, two of the Viet crewmen mule hauled it over to the first barrel and gave me the thumbs up. I, in turn, looked up, waved at the Captain and replied loudly, "Ready to receive sir."

The fueling, although slower than I would have liked, was making steady progress. I was perched on the top of the Junk's deckhouse watching the proceedings just as the unmistakable sound of another diesel engine reached my ears. Craning my neck to see behind me, I saw the last thing that I could have wished for at that moment. One of our Yabuta Junks had arrived and her decks were covered with empty 55 gal drums. I jumped down to the deck, quickly turned around and glared at Minh trying with all my might to control my anger. He immediately saw that I was pissed and gave me the typical Vietnamese smile that is so common when they are caught in an embarrassing situation. I was really angry at being made to look like a smacked ass. It was the same old story of giving someone an inch and them taking a yard. I looked up to catch the Captain's reaction to the additional boat and was surprised to see him grin and casually wave his hand as he turned and disappeared into the pilot house.

The crew aboard the cutter had hung a Jacob's ladder over the side and after throwing another nasty look towards Minh, who by now had dropped his smile, I clambered up to the main deck. From there, I quickly made it up the inclined ladder leading to the bridge where I found the CO sitting relaxed in his Captain's chair. As I started to offer my apologies for apparently having taken advantage of his generosity, the Captain held up his hand and said, "It's OK Lieutenant. As I've said before, this is not my first tour here and I'm accustomed to the idiosyncrasies of our allies. I can't promise to fill all the barrels, but we will try to do as much as we can during the time that I have allotted out of our schedule."

The CO recognized my discomfort as I softly tendered my sincerest apologies and thanked him for his understanding.

"We all have our jobs to do out here Lieutenant and for some, more difficult than others. I personally admire you Advisors in the field that have to constantly temper any advice given to your counterparts diplomatically while being militarily sound and culturally correct. It can't be easy."

"You're right skipper. It's not always easy, but I honestly can't think of any job that I'd rather be doing than this one."

"Then you're a fortunate individual Lieutenant and you should make the most of your opportunity. Don't be too hard on your counterpart. Dollars to donuts are that you would have done the same if you were in his place, right?"

"Since you put it like that, yes I would have. But I wouldn't keep that silly smirk on my face whenever I got caught with my hand in the cookie jar."

"I hear you. Just for the record though, I can only stick around and pump oil for about three hours and then we'll have to wrap it up. I don't think that we can fill all your drums, but you'll have enough to carry you through till you're resupplied."

"I'll pass that on to Minh and once again thanks for bailing us out. Please let me know if there's anything we can do for you in return." With that having been said, I saluted and left the pilot house feeling a lot better than I did before.

Once back aboard the Junk, I purposely avoided looking at Minh who was still standing on the stern overseeing the work. The filling of the barrels continued steadily and at the end of the allotted time, the barrels on the Command Junk were topped off and all but seven of the ones on the Yabuta.

As the lines were cast off and both Junks pulled away, crewmembers from the ship waved at us from the main deck while the CO and the Executive Officer stood stoically on the wing of the bridge. Both Minh and I tossed a salute to them and they waved in return.

Heavily ladened with the barrels of oil, both Junks wallowed deeply in the dark green water as we set our course back home.

Minh edged his way slowly along the deckhouse where I was once again seated and softly put his hand on my shoulder. "I know you are displeased with me for bringing two boats, but I have learned to be an opportunist where command is concerned. We do not have many chances to turn a negative into a positive and when the occasion presents itself, one must act accordingly. Please try to understand. I consider you my friend as well as my counterpart and I have not always been so lucky with my advisors. Although I regard *Dai-Uy* Edwards in high esteem, I also feel that towards you. In the short time that you have been on Obi, you have shown a deep personal affection for my crew and their dependents. This has not gone unnoticed. I know that you will be leaving us when *Dai-Uy* Edwards returns and I want you to understand that you will be sorely missed. So please, let this little disagreement fade into the past so that we may enjoy each other's company in the time remaining."

What could I say in response to that? Minh was so open with his apology that it would have been callow of me to rebut him, so I shrugged and said, "No sweat *Trung-Uy,* I understand."

With the air between us cleared, he asked me if I wanted any more coffee from the second thermos. I had my sights set on a cold beer back at the base instead, so I replied, "No thank you. I'm good." With that, Minh returned to the shelter of the helmsman's station leaving me alone with my thoughts. The most prevalent one being centered on what I had just learned about dealing with the

Vietnamese and hopefully that it would make me a better person and a more astute advisor in the future.

We arrived at the southern coast of Obi and found another Yabuta Junk hove-to off shore obviously awaiting our arrival. There were ten sailors gathered on her deck and as we came alongside, Minh motioned for me to go aboard. As he and I stepped down to the smaller craft he said, "This boat will bring us back around the island and let us off. The other sailors will unload the barrels and stow them under the shelter."

"That sounds good to me, because I'm sure looking forward to a shower," I replied as I leaned up against the cabin and held on to the handrail. In less than a half hour, we had been offloaded onto the boulder and back in our respective sides of the hootch.

I found Petty Officer Dillon industriously working over a shortwave radio that belonged to the advisors and had never worked worth a damn. He looked up and asked me earnestly, "How did the refueling effort go *Dai-Uy*?"

"Oh, we managed to get all of the barrels on the Command Junk filled and almost half of the ones on the Yabuta."

"What Yabuta?" he asked raising his eyebrows.

"The one that Minh conveniently had follow us discreetly so that I wouldn't notice. Then he plied me with hot coffee and French bread to hold my attention."

"Boy, these guys have a set of balls on them, don't they?"

"I'll have to agree on that, but they sure expose them when it comes to a firefight."

"That I couldn't tell you since I've been fortunate enough not to find myself in that situation. We twidgets usually don't aspire to heroic deeds, if you know what I mean."

"Gotcha, Marshal. I'm in need of a general douching, so if you'll excuse me, I'm heading for the rain barrel."

"OK. By the way, Rusty called in and said that they'd be back tonight and I guess Angus may still be getting it on at the old Grass Shack."

"That figures," I replied as I went to the rear of the hootch where our "rain locker" was situated. I quickly stripped off my clothes that were reeking of diesel oil fumes and threw them on the floor. The rain barrel just outside the open window was nearly full, so I grabbed the handle of the pot and began scooping up the tepid water. I worked up a rich lather all over my head, face and body with the duty bar of soap, rinsed off and repeated it again. I wanted to be rid of that diesel smell.

It was time to shave my three day stubble after finishing my shower. I tried to shave every day in order to present a good appearance to the Vietnamese, but island life sometime got the best of me and I became lax in that department. After all, why I was trying to impress the Vietnamese whose men generally didn't produce much facial hair making whiskers a non-problem?

When I finished, I donned clean shorts and a skivvy shirt and was pleasantly surprised to find a bowl of hot rice, veggies and a fried fish filet awaiting me. Dillon was already chowing down with gusto as he said around a mouth full of rice, "Man, it must be the fresh air down here that stimulates my appetite. Your cook just delivered it and I wasn't sure how much longer you'd be, so I decided to start while the food was hot. By the way, is she pregnant?"

"Yes she is," I replied without going into any details. I was glad that I was in the shower when she brought the chow because it had been about three days since any of us "checked her out" and I knew she must be a little apprehensive by now.

Later on that evening, Rusty came back in from an uneventful patrol. When I related the fueling episode to him, all he could do was shake his head. "Well, you managed to keep us afloat awhile longer anyway *Dai-Uy*. Hey Dillon, are these new radios as good as they say they are?"

"Would I bring you guys anything less than outstanding considering how hospitable you've been to me?"

"Just wanted to make sure because you know how the Navy always says, 'Nothing's too good for our boys in blue.'"

"I hear you," he said laughing, "But this one you'll like and by the way, I fixed that piece of crap shortwave radio you guys had gathering dust. It was just a few loose connections."

"Gee thanks," said Rusty. "Now we'll be able to hear who's appearing at the USO for the friggin' Saigon Warriors."

"Beats choking your Willy for entertainment, I'd imagine."

"Maybe, but not by much," said Rusty lasciviously. "When's Angus coming back from the supply run? Does anyone know?"

"I figure tomorrow is as good a guess as any," I replied.

The rest of the evening was spent leisurely hanging out and working on what was left of our beer supply. It at least gave us an incentive to sleep soundly through the night.

The next morning as we were up and about, each with our coffee cups in hand, we heard Angus hailing us through the front window. The Junk was nosed in to the beach and he was standing on the bow yelling for some assistance.

"Hey *Dai-Uy*—you did a good job blowing open this channel. We heard about it from Minh on the radio to Le. It'll save some heavy humping over those old rocks."

"I did it just for you in celebration of your losing your cherry at the Grass Shack," I said with a grin.

"You bet your life I lost it again because the thing damn near had grown over since my last trip up there," he replied.

We all started carrying the supplies that he was handing down from the boat. As expected, there was predominantly more beer and soda than there was foodstuffs, if you discounted the twenty cases of assorted C-rats. When we were done, Angus jumped nimbly off the boat and landed lightly on the sand. With a wave of his hand to the crew, the Junk backed off and headed around to the other side of the island.

Minh stuck his head in our window as we were stowing our food away and said, "I'm sending a patrol out towards Song Ong Doc at 1000 hours. Who will be going with me?" he asked.

I quickly replied, "It's my turn since I was the first one back. I'll be ready *Trung-Uy.*"

SONG ONG DOC RUFF-PUFF BASE

We were underway once again and the seas were as calm as yesterday. When the water gets feisty, the Yabutas have a tendency to ride rough, not like the wider beamed Command Junks. Since there was only one *Chu-Luk* assigned to each Junk Group, utilization depended on the particular occasion and this occasion didn't warrant it.

We arrived at Song Ong Doc without sighting any boats to be inspected and that seemed a little odd because there was always marine traffic of some sort in these waters.

Once we debarked and entered the small base, it was obvious that something had happened. The base was situated on about two acres of land and was surrounded by four foot high dirt mounds similar to the levees in New Orleans, with the exception that the mounds were topped by razor sharp concertina wire. The base defenders consisted of a small contingent of Regional Force—Popular Force personnel known as Ruff-Puffs, which are somewhat like our own National Guard. The personnel however, are mainly older men who fell outside of the regular military recruiting parameters and in the majority of cases, were local inhabitants.

Since there were no large cities in the area, it was safe to say that most of the men were from rural backgrounds. These paramilitary units normally had two US Army advisors assigned, one officer and one senior noncom.

Striding out to meet us was a hatless lanky six footer with corn yellow hair buzzed down to the scalp in an extreme military cut. His tiger striped uniform was hanging on his spare frame as if he had slept in them and was in dire need of laundering. He stuck out his hand in greeting with a somber expression on his face saying, "Captain Frank Newcombe, but you can call me Newk."

I introduced Minh and myself, then explained where we were from and asked what the situation was.

"We got hit early this morning while we were busy eating breakfast. A couple of VC sappers infiltrated into the base and tried to hit our ammo storage but fortunately one of our roving patrols saw them and started shooting. A couple of mortars rained down on us along with some small arms fire from across the canal. We smoked the two sappers before they could do any damage, but unfortunately we lost one of our guys. The whole thing couldn't have lasted more than fifteen minutes and then they packed up and left."

"No wonder we didn't see any boats on our way here," I said.

"News travels fast down here in Camau," replied Newk.

"Is there anything we can do for you?" asked Minh quietly.

"Nothing thanks *Trung Uy*, but I appreciate your asking. Why don't you follow me to the hootch where I can at least offer you some coffee? That is if you don't mind the mess because we have our fatality in there where my medic was trying to save him."

Minh and I followed Newk into the darkened hootch where we were invited to sit down at a small table on the left side of the room. Adjacent to us against the wall, was a body of a dead soldier lying morbidly on a stretcher. A slim older Vietnamese officer quietly entered the room and was introduced as *Trung Uy* Phap, his counterpart and CO of the base.

As Minh and Phap conversed in subdued Vietnamese, I couldn't take my eyes off the fallen soldier. He was hatless with no apparent signs of trauma. His forehead, which blended into a receding hairline of fine black hair, was tight and shiny. The eyes weren't completely closed but slightly open as when a person is trying to feign sleep. Although his mouth was closed, his prominent buck teeth were plainly visible as they overhung his lower lip. He also had high pronounced cheekbones that were a physical characteristic of people from North Vietnam. It was difficult to even guess at his age which is common among the majority of Vietnamese, but the thing that drew my attention was the slim golden wedding band he wore on his brown and coarsened finger. My thoughts went to the simple peasant mother of his children that would very shortly be informed that she was now a widow. It brought reality to me as well as a deep sadness for the pain that she would soon be enduring. Her husband's pain, on the other hand, was over.

Newk noticed me staring intently at the body and said that the Province Chief had already been notified and that someone would be dispatched to return the body to his home. "This is the part of war that I hate the most," he said quietly. "I don't mind seeing dead bad guys, but losing people that soldiered alongside me sticks in my craw."

After finishing my cup of coffee and Minh's conversation obviously at an end, it was time to go. We bid our farewells and quickly strode across the compound to our waiting Junk.

Once aboard and heading back out into the Gulf of Thailand, Minh said "I apologize for not telling you sooner, but I had been told about the attack on the base early this morning over the radio. You see, *Trung Uy* Phap is my brother-in-law and he was just assigned to Song Ong Doc a week ago. I owed it to my sister to check on his well-being."

"I understand. It wouldn't have made a difference to me either way you know that, but I'm glad that he's OK."

We made a half-hearted attempt to look for any suspicious sampans once out in the open water, but since our bow was pointed back to Poulo Obi, the interest just wasn't there.

The wind had shifted and was now blowing from the northwest at about seven knots which resulted in our having a following sea. The sturdy diesel engine easily propelled us through the water assisted by the low slow rollers that swelled under us from astern and gently surged us forward. With the lulling motion of the boat, I thought about that dead soldier and felt heaviness in my heart. How many more like him would I see before my tour of duty was up? It brought about a distinct sense of reality when one sees the result of mayhem and destruction up close and personal. I marveled at the endurance and fortitude of these people after so many years of being lackeys to the French and as they watched their nation being ripped apart by conflict. Sure, we went through that in the States during our country's infancy, but there was no guarantee that the Vietnamese would have the same staying power and physical resolve necessary to attain a peaceful and agreeable settlement to their conflict.

Thus was the trend of my thoughts and it surprised me in a way because I didn't consider myself a philosophical individual. Was it possible that the Far East was maturing me in ways yet unknown to me?

After what seemed an eternity of quiet sailing, we arrived at Obi and although night had fallen, the cox'n maneuvered the Junk unerringly to our usual drop-off point guided by the small searchlight located at his station. Minh and I lightly jumped over to the big boulder and made our way back to the hootch without conversation. There were lights coming from both sides which meant that everyone was still up and awaiting our return.

We both said our "Good Nights" politely as we entered our respective sides. Rusty, Angus and Dillon were lounging casually in what passed for our sitting room listening to music playing softly from the newly repaired shortwave radio.

"Boy, you guys have got the life," I grumbled with a smile as I flopped down on the only other vacant chair.

"How was the trip, boss?" asked Rusty.

"Dull as dirt, that is if you don't count sitting around an Advisor's hootch in Song Ong Doc with a dead soldier lying at your feet. They were hit this morning and suffered only one KIA, but they nailed the two sappers that tried to get their ammo storage. The Viet CO is Minh's brother-in-law, so when he heard about the attack over the radio he had to go up and check it out for himself.

"I wouldn't care one bit to be stuck on that shitty piece of real estate knowing that all your neighbors are closet Viet Cong that come out at night with a vengeance," remarked Angus dryly.

"That's for damn sure," said Rusty. "Besides every swinging dick outside that encampment is just champing at the bit to overrun that base and hang them all upside down with their genitals stuffed in their mouths."

"Man, that's nasty. What makes them so screwed up in the head to do things like that?" asked Dillon.

"Beats me,' I said. "Most likely it's a way to strike fear into their enemies the way Genghis Khan used to do."

"Do you believe all that crap that Sun Tzu wrote about warfare?" asked Rusty.

"I certainly do. I read his book while I was chasing my Anthropology degree and you would be amazed at the foresight that guy had. So much in fact that some of the world's most successful generals have read him too and apply his principles into their tactics."

"Then why don't our top brass follow suit?" asked Angus.

"Probably because they know that Ho Chi Minh and his General Giap have also studied it, so it's a stand-off of sorts. I'm going to have a beer and then I'm hitting the sack, if you guys don't mind and that music must be coming from Bangkok, I'll bet"

"Better than static," said Dillon with a grin on his face.

The next morning, we were all up and sitting around with cups of hot freshly made coffee in our hands. The conversation had been centered on my trip to Song Ong Doc and Rusty was busy questioning the effectiveness of the Ruff-Puffs.

"Just what do they do to aid the war effort?" he asked.

"I'm not too sure myself, but I would imagine that by having some form of armed local militia in the area, it cancels out the need to have the regular armed forces in every nook and cranny of the country. There's no way the ARVN could cover every place where the VC reside because it would stretch them too thin."

"Well like Angus said last night, I wouldn't like to be stationed in a rat hole like that. No sir," said Rusty.

Just then, the radio crackled and an operator from An Thoi was calling us. Angus quickly answered and the voice on the other end informed us that Yankee India One (LT Edwards), was back from leave and would be arriving at Poulo Obi along with a new assistant in the morning. I and Petty Officer Dillon were ordered to board the chopper with all our gear and return to An Thoi for further transport to Saigon. It would appear that the powers that be in Saigon decided that two Lieutenants on Poulo Obi would be considered over-kill and therefore a junior officer was being assigned to replace me.

The message was acknowledged and the previous air of exuberance that had been experienced quickly turned to despair and disappointment. Dillon's departure had been expected but mine was a kick in the ass.

"Just when things were right where we wanted them," said Angus grumpily.

"Goddamned pencil-necked paper pushers," Rusty added.

"We all knew this day was coming," I said, "but no one could foresee that I would be relieved and jerked off the island after only a month."

"Well, at least there's still enough war going on for all of us," said Rusty softly.

I was genuinely taken aback at the sincerity in his voice and felt that I was being forcibly removed from my family and sent to an orphanage. But, I should be used to the idiosyncrasies of the Navy by now and decided to accept my fate like a true officer by thinking "it's the same old bullshit."

A little while later, *Ha Si* Truc, our cook's husband, came in bearing a tray with four heaping bowls of steamed rice, a huge platter of shrimp that had been stir-fried generously with garlic and chili peppers and a large bowl of mixed greens and onions laced with lime juice, coarse sea salt and black pepper. Word must have somehow gotten around about my impending departure and this was our cook's way of thanking me for the medical attention we had been bestowing on her and her unborn baby. Looking at the sincere sadness in the eyes of Truc, I realized that I was really going to miss these people.

That evening after we finished devouring all the food that had been so deliciously prepared, the four of us sat around sort of languishing lazily after the larger than normal meal. Our lazy conversation became slightly subdued and about absolutely nothing in particular, which coincided nicely with the ice cold cans of beer that we were consuming. Finally I said, "As soon as I find out where they're going to send me, I'll get word back to you guys. It's not the end of the world and it is a small navy, so our paths are bound to cross again."

"Right on," said Angus saluting me with his beer, while Rusty just sat and gently nodded his head. It became very evident that these guys were going to miss me as much as I was going to miss them.

The quiet dialogue soon ran its course and it was time for me to pack my gear. It's funny how man will procrastinate when it comes time to do something that is objectionable . . . and so it was with me this night. Fortunately, our laundry had been done the day before by our maid, so there were only the clothes that I had worn today to pack separately. It took about fifteen minutes to quietly collect and pack my belongings. The others had already reluctantly turned in for the night. I decided to leave my three bandoliers of M-14 ammunition for the guys since I knew that I could obtain more at An Thoi tomorrow. Besides, they could use the extra ammo here where it was needed. With nothing else left to do, I turned in for my last night's sleep on Poulo Obi. Oddly enough, I dropped off immediately despite my disappointment and my pending departure in the morning.

ROOSTER'S REQUIEM

There were two roosters belonging to one of our neighbors who resided behind our hootch that unfailingly announced each new morning's arrival. One had the standard "Cock-a-doodle-do" that was always crisp and clear, while the second one was discordant and highly offensive to the ears. When I had first arrived, the combined raucous cries would pierce the morning stillness and painfully served as our resident alarm clock.

In discussing this situation one day, we decide to draw straws to see which one of us would covertly put the strident bird out of its misery. Rusty drew the short one and he was elated. Having formulated a plan of attack, he prepared to put it into effect later that evening. He executed the deed admirably in the dark of night as he had surreptitiously stalked and ambushed the poor unsuspecting rooster inside the neighbor's enclosure. He made short work of the bird by deftly twisting its neck before it could let out an alarm. Hopping the low fence behind our hootch with the dead bird safely tucked under his shirt, he came in smiling from ear to ear.

"What do you think guys? Care to help me pluck and gut this bird so we can boil him in a pot of water and make hot rooster sandwiches tomorrow?"

"Sounds good to me," I replied and immediately pitched in to de-feather the has-been harbinger of dawn. All this had to be done in complete secrecy lest the neighbors learn of our hastening the demise of their rooster.

The next morning, with our bird already boiled and wrapped in tin foil in our refrigerator, the surviving rooster threw out his chest, stretched his neck upward and let fly his grating cry into the face of the breaking dawn.

"Oh shit," said Angus, "You grabbed the wrong friggin' bird, asshole. You're a typical goddamned below-decks dickhead."

"Screw you, at least I tried," Rusty replied chagrined.

"Well, I wouldn't have made that mistake because us black folks know all about chickens," retorted Angus.

At least we'll have a couple of days of fine dining at our neighbor's expense as we all laughed under our mosquito nets.

All this came back to me as the last cacophonous sounds shattered the morning air. I tossed back my netting and headed for the rain barrel to shower one last time on Poulo Obi. The water retained the coolness of the past evening and raised goose bumps all over my body. While I was showering and shaving, Angus was putting on a pot of coffee and the aroma permeated the hootch. I put on a pair of skivvies, slipped into my flip-flops and with a towel around my neck, sat down to have some coffee. The four of us sat quietly around the table, enjoying each other's company.

Finally, Rusty broke the silence by saying, "Are you all packed *Dai-Uy*?"

"All set," I replied: "Nothing to do now but wait for the chopper."

After I finished my last cup of coffee on Poulo Obi, I went back inside the sleeping area to finish getting dressed. As I was lacing up my combat boots, there was a soft knock on the side of our doorway. Minh entered with Le close behind.

"*Dai-Uy*," he said softly. Le and I wanted to see you before you left us. We are very sorry to see you go and I would have preferred if both you and *Dai-Uy* Edwards were working together with us, but I know how Saigon views these matters. The desires of the individuals seem to have no place in time of war."

"Thank you Minh, there's nothing I'd like more, but unfortunately, my bosses up in Saigon appear to have other plans for me."

"Well, we just wanted you to know that we enjoyed having you here as an advisor, even if it was for such a short time."

"And I enjoyed the privilege of being here too, *Trung-Uy*. I hope we get to meet again someday."

I had no sooner finished my last words when the unmistakable sound of an approaching helicopter filled the air. Looking out through the front window, Angus remarked quietly that my government taxi had arrived.

Once the blades of the Huey were cut back to an idle, the sand and flying debris settled down. A Naval officer jumped out, and I assumed it was Lieutenant Edwards returning from leave. He was about five feet ten and probably weighed about one hundred and sixty pounds, although it was difficult to be certain because of the baggy, faded green fatigues that he was wearing. For some reason, I had pictured him as being much taller. His average appearance was deceiving after having heard of his exploits against the VC. Just goes to show you that you can't judge a book by its cover. One could see that he was extremely happy at being back on the island by the enormous grin that lit up his boyish face. Immediately, Rusty, Angus, Minh and Le, warmly greeted Edwards and it was Rusty who introduced me to him as I emerged from the hootch with my gear in hand.

"This is Lieutenant Kay, *Dai-Uy*. He held down the fort while you were gone," said Rusty.

Edwards extended his hand to me and said, "Word has it in Saigon and An Thoi that you guys have been pretty active lately."

"Well, it sure beats sitting around and letting the war pass us by."

"Amen to that," he said. "I guess that I still don't have an assistant down here because LTJG Lowenstein, who was supposed to come with me, is now in the 3rd Field Hospital in Saigon. He hurt his back this morning on the tarmac as he tried to lift his gear out of the back of the Jeep. He was in some kind of pain and who knows how long he'll be laid up. I thought that Saigon would have kept you down here until he was ready for duty, but I guess not."

"I think they obviously have a problem with allowing two full Lieutenants assigned to the same base," I remarked sullenly.

"Do you have any idea where they're going to assign you?"

"Not a clue, but I'm sure they'll tell me soon enough since I've been told to report directly to the Senior Naval Advisor."

"Good luck with that," said Edwards. "I hear that he recently graduated from the Harvard Business School before being assigned here and plans to revamp and improve the whole program."

"That scares me. Book learning can never totally prepare a military man for this type of warfare because we've never encountered anything like it before," I offered.

"I agree with you," said Edwards. "Maybe you can put a bug in his ear as to what it's really like out here in the field."

"I'll try," I said then shook hands with everyone and climbed into the Huey where Dillon was already strapped in snugly. Rusty and Angus handed me my bags and rifle without looking me in the eyes. It was apparent to me and Lieutenant Edwards by their body language, that a strong rapport had been forged among the three of us during the short time that we had been together.

The pilot looked back to check if we were all clear and then quickly lifted the craft smoothly into the blue sky over the bay. As Poulo Obi grew smaller as we climbed to cruising altitude, I experienced a feeling of remorse and regret in leaving. One thought that crossed my mind was what would the guys tell Lieutenant Edwards about the daily “examination” of our cook? Chances are he would disapprove of our involvement, but then again, he might just put himself into the rotation. Although I personally would have been satisfied to remain assigned there for the rest of my tour, I knew in my heart that everything in this life seems to happen for a reason. The Navy had certainly proved that to me so far.

With the island slowly fading away behind us, my mind ruffled through thoughts of the guys, the lighthouse keeper and his family, his daughter Lien, who would be looking for her English lessons; Chief Tai’s daughter Mong, the kids of Obi and last but not least, Thuy, our cook. I wondered how her baby would turn out after our ministrations. It had been an experience not soon forgotten to have been on the island with the inhabitants who were brought together in time of war. Yes, I sure had compiled a lot of memories in such a short period of time.

PART SIX

RETURN TO SAIGON

The ride to An Thoi was uncomfortable as the aircraft vibrated like a terrier trying to shake a pitch pit out of its butt. Both side gunners leaned over their M-60 machine guns looking bored since no danger was expected while over the water. The rushing wind made conversation impossible and since Dillon and I weren't wearing headsets, we were forced to remain silent. I sat back on the hard canvas seat and gazed down into the blue green waters of the South China Sea. A few fishing trawlers dotted the surface along with a Swift Boat and some Junks on patrol.

Finally, after what seemed ages of body shaking and wind blast, we made our approach to the landing pad at An Thoi. I immediately noticed an Army NU-1B DeHavilland Otter sitting off to one side on the strip with its engine idling. Upon touching down, the pilot of the Otter waved to me as I disembarked the chopper with my gear. I turned and threw a "thank you" wave to the Huey pilot and nodded to the door gunners as I headed for the Otter. Dillon had orders to report to the Comm Center on An Thoi, so we shook hands as he said, "I'll probably see you in Saigon."

The pilot signaled for me to get aboard once he recognized that I was Lieutenant Kay.

"I've got orders to bring you up to Saigon Lieutenant," he yelled through his window, "So if you'll get aboard and strap in, we'll be on our way."

With a quick nod, I clambered through the door tossing my gear in first. I saw a lanky Negro sergeant slouched in the rear row with his long legs draped over the seat in front of him. A Green Beret was worn low over his left eye as he appeared to be dozing.

I stowed my gear under the seats and buckled in, giving a thumbs up to the co-pilot as he looked over his shoulder into the compartment. The engine increased its power as the plane vibrated and began its bumpy ride to the end of the air strip. Without a stop, the pilot made his turn and increased the throttle to full power, sending the plane hurtling down the strip. Reaching the proper speed, we easily became airborne and on our way.

I was a little disappointed that I did not get a chance to visit my Coast Guard buddy Jim Sutherland before heading to Saigon. Oh well, perhaps we'd get another chance to lift a few cool ones somewhere down the line.

As the plane climbed to gain altitude, I noticed quite a few monstrous thunderclouds directly in our path. If there's anything I dislike more about flying, it's going through one of those. It's something like stepping into an open elevator shaft and visions of calamity suddenly appeared in my mind.

The pilot, who was a young Army Warrant Officer, juked and jinxed his way around the huge grey-white clouds whose heads soared unbelievably skyward. Just as it appeared that we would be spared the discomfort of flying through these huge mountainous clouds, we found ourselves heading directly into one. There was no way around it and the pilot increased engine power to provide positive forward momentum.

A few minutes into it, the bottom dropped out suddenly and the plane was caught in a horrendous downdraft. My rectal orifice immediately seemed to rise up into my esophagus as my body strained against the safety belt that I had fortunately cinched tighter upon first seeing the huge clouds. I heard a yelp from the rear of the plane as the sleeping Green Beret Sergeant was catapulted upward against the overhead and then slammed back down into the aisle when the aircraft regained control. Obviously, he hadn't strapped himself in and the whites of his frightened eyes were enormous. Luckily, he only had the wind knocked out of him. He frantically climbed back into his seat and this time he fastened his seat belt.

I thought I detected the aroma of released rectal gas from the rear of the plane and rightly so. I wouldn't have been a bit surprised if the trooper had soiled his pants after being so rudely and violently awakened. It was then that I noticed that the pilot was descending and assuming a glide path for landing. I thought that we were heading non-stop for Saigon from An Thoi, but it was apparent that this was not the case.

We landed on a small dirt strip that I identified as Camau from a faded sign on a lone Quonset hut. Once the engine was shut down, the co-pilot looked back and said we were stopping to check for any damage because we had dropped almost seven hundred feet in that downdraft. The Special Forces Sergeant quickly followed me off the plane and was carrying his gear with him.

When the pilot saw him deplaning with his baggage, he said, "This is Camau and you're scheduled all the way to Saigon."

"Screw that brother. I know a sign when I get one. I ain't going no further with you guys and I'm staying here until I can get another ride."

"Suit yourself, but you'll only be wasting your time and it may be several days before another hop is available."

"Don't matter, besides I have to change my undershorts."

"I could think of much better places to wait for a ride than Camau, because this is definitely Indian country," I said,

About that time I noticed the co-pilot trying to light a cigarette with hands that were shaking uncontrollably. If he was affected so much by that experience, shouldn't I have been too, I thought?

Finally after about a half hour, the pilot and his co-pilot finished their inspection of the olive drab colored aircraft. The pilot motioned to me as I sat on an old crate in the shade alongside the hut and said that we were ready to resume our flight to Saigon. The Green Beret was nowhere to be found, so we got aboard and continued our journey with no further mishaps.

There was a faint odor of crap in the rear of the compartment and I made a mental note to myself to always, always strap myself down securely in the future.

As we made our approach over Saigon into Tan Son Nhut, it brought back memories of my first sight of the capitol when we arrived from Stateside. Although it was only a little over a month and a half ago, it seemed like ages. The thoroughfares were still congested with vehicles, motorbikes and pedestrian traffic that quite frankly resembled a colony of ants from above. Gone were the lush greens and subdued hues of the Delta, replaced by the dun colored streets and drab surroundings of a city at war.

The former Pearl of the Orient, as Saigon was once known during the French occupation, now resembled an aging, jaded lady who was frantically trying to appease her pimp that she was still marketable. It brought a sort of sadness to me when I thought back to everything I had read about this once proud city.

The French colonizers had built her up to their standards only to methodically rape her consistently of her virtue. It's no wonder that Ho Chi Minh rallied his forces to rid the country of their cruel and self-indulging masters.

With this thought in mind, one could ponder as to just whose side we were on. Granted, when Ho chose to ally himself with the Communists after being ignored by the West, what other choice did he have? No matter, I decided that these thoughts of mine had to remain personal lest I be considered a Communist sympathizer.

Never in my wildest dreams would I ever go against the flag and country that I had sworn to serve and defend when I received my Navy commission. There was undoubtedly much more to this war than was let on to the general public. The South Vietnamese knew, but they were definitely caught between a rock and a hard place.

The Otter came to a rolling stop on the military side of the terminal after a somewhat bumpy landing. Climbing down from the aircraft with my gear, I turned and waved to the two pilots, each nodding their heads in return. A Navy Jeep was parked in the shade of the building and as I approached, the driver looked up and asked if I was Lieutenant Kay. I nodded and he said, "Hop aboard Lieutenant, I've been instructed to bring you to VNN Headquarters to see the Boss." The Boss, I learned was the newly arrived Senior Naval Advisor, Captain P. A. Bjorkman. Stories of his command ideology had already caused ripples through the Advisory community and not in the least bit complimentary. The troops had started referring to him as "Bjorkman the Dorkman."

The driver quickly exited Tan Son Nhut past the ARVN checkpoint and we proceeded down Cach Mang which was a fairly wide thoroughfare. It eventually narrowed down to two lanes which became Cong Ly Street and would bring us downtown.

Like all other US drivers that have been in-country awhile, my driver took on the air of a NASCAR wannabe as we careened down the crowded street. He deftly guided the Jeep around cyclos, motorbikes, ancient Renault taxis and the ever-present multitude of bicycles. It was amazing to see a family of four riding on a 50 cc Honda motorcycle. In this particular case, the man was driving with a young boy of two or three years of age nestled in front of him between his arms. Behind him, a woman was perched sidesaddle, holding an umbrella to ward off the sun in one hand and a baby in her other. These people must have an exceptional sense of balance, I thought to myself.

We passed Dinh Doc Lap or Independence Palace, on the right hand side of the street where the President resided. Built in 1966 on the site of the former French Governor's Headquarters, its perimeter was completely enclosed by a high black iron fence. As would be expected, the gates were guarded by Vietnamese paratroopers who warily eyeballed the passing traffic. Experience had taught them that a grenade could easily be tossed at them even from a speeding motorcycle.

On the left directly in front of the Palace, Thong Nhat Street intersected Cong Ly where two blocks over stood Nha Tho Duc Ba or the Catholic Cathedral of Our Lady. Her large twin red brick spires rose over the city and were a familiar landmark.

From there, it was only a few more blocks until we came to the intersection where we made a left turn at the traffic light. This was Le Loi and led to the center of Saigon. I was informed by my driver that traffic lights had been installed throughout the city after the French had been ousted. I could just imagine what chaos existed at these busy intersections prior to that. I knew that the European solution to dangerous intersections was to replace them with circles that would allow the traffic to flow easily around them. A person entering one of these could dart into the flow of traffic as long as he did not make eye contact with the driver whom he was cutting off. Making eye contact with a driver already in the circle flow acknowledged acceptance to his right of way. It was therefore incumbent upon the driver making the incursion to always yield.

I could visualize where a couple of intoxicated drivers would undoubtedly screw up the grand scheme of traffic etiquette. On the other hand, the lights provided only a modicum of traffic control since most motorists, especially the motorcyclists, tended to view the yellow caution light as a signal to speed up and go on through regardless of where they were located near the intersection.

Another noticeable trait of the motorcycle crowd was to weave through the stopped vehicles at a red light and settle directly in front of them, even if they wound up over the line and precariously in the way of the crossing traffic. I had always thought that patience was a virtue that originated in the east, but somehow this did not hold true where Vietnamese city traffic was concerned.

After proceeding on Le Loi for one block, we came to a circle that occupied the center of downtown Saigon and turned right onto Nguyen Hue.

Nguyen Hue was a wide boulevard that ran east and west for about four blocks containing two parallel islands constructed on either side about ten feet from each curb. The islands mirrored the length of each block so that cross traffic could enter the main thoroughfare from the cross streets. Many kiosks of flower sellers that gave Nguyen Hue the alternate name of the "Street of Flowers" were located on these islands.

The USO, the International House that was managed by the US Embassy and the McCarthy Bachelor Officer's Quarters, were located on the right hand side of the street within two blocks of the circle. It was easy to recognize the USO because of its canopied entrance and the constant stream of servicemen entering and leaving. The International House further down had a tall, rotund black bearded Sikh attired entirely in white with the traditional turban, performing doorman duties. His main function was to deny admittance to anyone who did not conform to Embassy standards which was civilian attired westerners or military. Vietnamese females were allowed to enter only if they were employees of the embassy and escorted by members.

Nguyen Hue terminated four blocks later at Ben Bach Dang, which ran parallel to the Saigon River. The next block over on the left was Tu Do Street and the one after that opened to a circle that contained a large statue of General Tran Hung Dao, the legendary ancient warrior.

In the 1300s, he amassed a guerrilla army that went on to defeat the fearful Mongol, Kublai Khan, who was intent on invading what is now Vietnam. The imposing fifteen foot high statue stood atop a thirty foot concrete pedestal facing the Saigon River. His right arm was extended with his index finger pointing across the river as if to indicate the line of attack to his troops. The standard joke about the statue among the American forces was that it obviously was not to scale, because his pointing finger was too big to fit in his nose. In actuality, the fact that he was wearing gloves never figured into the equation. It merely provided fodder for ridiculing a much revered ancestor of our Asian allies.

As the driver bore counter-clockwise around the circle, we found ourselves in front of the Vietnamese Naval Headquarters compound on the left. We drove through the main entrance whose two large iron gates were surprisingly open and unguarded. The compound consisted of three white-washed buildings whose window shutters and doors were trimmed in faded light blue paint.

The main building was four stories high and faced the main gate. The buildings on either side, however, appeared to be afterthoughts additions because they lacked the typical French colonial architectural style that featured veranda-like exteriors with the offices set back about five feet. The building on the left was also four stories high but only windows with open shutters faced the inner courtyard. The unattached building on the right was a single storied affair and was most likely the latest addition to the complex, obviously constructed by the Vietnamese.

NAVAL ADVISORY GROUP HEADQUARTERS

My driver pulled up in front of a doorway at the extreme far end of the building on the right. This housed the office of the Senior Naval Advisor.

"Just go in that door, Lieutenant and I'll keep a watch on your gear until you come out," said the driver as he slumped in his seat

I got out of the vehicle and went up the four concrete steps to the door that had a painted sign that indicated this to be the office of the Senior Naval Advisor. Opening the door and stepping inside, I found myself in a rather small office that contained two gray government issued desks. The one on the right was empty and facing the wall, while the one on the left was positioned in the corner facing the center of the room. This one was occupied by a very big US Navy Commander with a receding hairline. The nameplate on his desk identified him as Commander M. Selfridge, Assistant Senior Naval Advisor.

"Good morning Commander. I'm Lieutenant Kay reporting as ordered from Coastal Group 41," I announced as I removed my cap.

"Ah yes Lieutenant, we've been expecting you," he said in a deep voice as he leaned his ample body back in his chair. "The Captain said to send you

right in as soon as you arrive," he said as he indicated the closed door to his left with a nod of his head.

"Aye sir," and with my hat in hand, I knocked on the door.

"Enter," boomed a strong voice from within.

Sitting behind an enormous walnut desk, the Captain gave me the immediate impression of a Chief Executive Officer of a large corporation. He was sitting upright in his starched, neatly pressed work khakis and he appeared to be somewhere in his early to mid-fifties. He had close cropped black curly hair that was just showing signs of gray at the temples and it was difficult to make out whether his eyes were black or dark brown.

He stood up and extended his hand beckoning me to sit down in one of the chairs fronting his ample desk. Once seated, it became apparent to me that the guest's chairs had somewhat shorter rear legs than the front ones because I found myself looking slightly upwards towards him. Later on, this was confirmed when I learned that Captain Bjorkman had served in the Navy's nuclear program. He undoubtedly had copied this little management technique from Admiral Hyman Rickover, the Father of the Nuclear Navy.

As rumors had it, when Admiral Rickover created and assumed command of the Navy's nuclear program, he insisted on personally interviewing all prospective applicants. He had the back legs of the chairs shortened by one inch so as to create an atmosphere of subservience to his exalted being. The officers that appeared undaunted by the experience were almost guaranteed acceptance into the fold.

Good psychological ploy, I thought, and a good way to keep a new guy off balance.

He sat back down behind the desk and leaned his chair back. This allowed him to cross one leg over the other, thus giving the interview an air of informality. I sat up ramrod straight and tried to present an attentive attitude for whatever was coming.

"Welcome to Saigon," said the Captain. "I'm sure you'll find being assigned here at Staff more to your liking than being out in the boonies."

"On the contrary Captain, I was very much at home in the field and I had hoped to be reassigned to another Junk Base."

"Unfortunately, that's not what I have in mind for you at the moment. Besides, word of your 'John Wayne' actions down there was not in keeping with Advisory protocols. Operating independently without direction from the Fourth Coastal Zone Commander presents a problem in that it does not set a good example for the rest of the Advisors in the field, or to our Vietnamese counterparts, I'm afraid. You were assigned duties as an Advisor to the Vietnamese Navy at an isolated forward base, but it did not give you a blank check to run amuck on unscheduled and unauthorized operations. Fortunately, we suffered no casualties except for some material losses aboard the WPB."

"But we did get secondary explosions exactly where the Province Chief of Camau said the enemy was overly active."

"Be that as it may, the operation was not sanctioned by either the Fourth Coastal Zone or Saigon," he said lowering his voice and riveting me with his eyes as only a Captain can do.

Right then, I realized that the fid was being applied to my stern sheets and I decided to ride out whatever was coming next. After all, this was the man who held my naval career in his hands at the moment. The fid, by the way to the uninformed, is a smooth tapered piece of wood about eight inches long and is used to splice manila line by separating the strands with the narrow end.

"I suppose you're wondering what's in store for you for the rest of your tour in-country," he said with a sardonic grin on his face. It was obvious that he and I had gotten off on the wrong foot and it behooved me to remain frustratingly silent. "Well it so happens that I have a billet here on my Staff for a sharp, energetic, self-starter like you. I want you to create and publish a monthly Advisor's Newsletter so that we can keep our men in the field up to speed on what is happening within our community and the latest word from Headquarters."

"But I'm not a Journalism Major, sir; I have a Bachelor's degree in Anthropology and a BSME in Mechanical Engineering."

"I can appreciate that fact Lieutenant, but since you are a university graduate, you should be able to handle this assignment without too much effort. I am assigning you a staff Yeoman by the name of Hardin, who will do all your required typing. The rest of it will be up to you. Your office is on the top deck of the central building and is shared by several other Advisors.

See Commander Selfridge on your way out and he'll let you know where you will be billeted."

With that said, it was clear that no further discussion was necessary or required and that the interview was over. I stood up and said "Aye sir," and quickly exited his office. What a self-righteous prick, I thought to myself.

The XO was sitting in much the same position except that he was engrossed in working the crossword puzzle in the Stars and Stripes newspaper and happily munching an untoasted Pop Tart.

"How did your meet with the Captain go?" he asked between bites of the Pop Tart.

"I've had better", I replied unenthusiastically. He said that you'd tell me where I am to be billeted."

"That's affirmative. You've been assigned to the McCarthy BOQ just off the circle at Nguyen Hue and Le Loi. The Petty Officer who picked you up at the airport is waiting outside and will drive you there. We start work at 0700 and work till 1800 with an hour off for lunch, seven days a week; any questions?"

"None Commander, would it be OK if I started work tomorrow so I can get settled in at the BOQ?"

"That will be fine," he said as he brushed crumbs from his crossword puzzle.

Boy, this place really sucks; I thought as I exited into the glaring sunlight and dejectedly climbed back into the Jeep.

"Home James," I mumbled to the driver.

"Not too impressed with the Head Shed, eh Lieutenant?"

"I was slightly less than thrilled, I'm afraid, but it was better than a sharp stick in the eye," I said dispassionately. I certainly didn't envision anything like this while I was going through all the pre-deployment training at Coronado. Anything I detested more in the military was paper pushing, and here I was about to become a recalcitrant participant.

The McCarthy BOQ was just an old hotel that was leased by the military to provide housing for both officers and civilians assigned to the Saigon area.

The dark entryway was located about thirty yards from the southwest corner of Nguyen Hue and Le Loi and set back some fifty feet from the street. It was flanked by another building on the left that also provided housing and a wing of the McCarthy on the right.

Inside the entrance on the immediate left was the bar where I would probably be spending most of my spare time whenever I could escape at Headquarters. It was a long bar and was tended by a sharp featured Oriental named Anna whose raven black hair hung down well past her slim buttocks. It was obvious that she had not cut her hair in several years since the average person's hair grows from 3/8ths to 1/2 an inch a month and her hair was at least three and a half feet long. I'd have to get to know her better just out of curiosity.

The front desk was separated off to the right of the entrance and it was tended by two young Vietnamese females in their traditional all white Ao Dais. I said that I was Lieutenant Kay and that I was to be billeted here. I got the standard once over from the girls and the taller of the two, who by the way, was the better looking said, "Hello, my name is Catherine," with a smile through remarkably picture-perfect teeth. "We have been notified of your intended arrival," she said in crisp and precise English. "May I have a copy of your orders please?"

I took my orders out of my pocket and presented them to the demure and interesting Catherine.

"We hope you will be comfortable here with us," said the second girl, whose nametag identified her as Michelle. Ah yes, another throwback from the former French influence. She was a bit shorter than Catherine and her body was Rubenesque with large rounded breasts. Her eyes, however, were something else in that they were a light green. They were probably gene-pooled down from a Frenchman who had frolicked somewhere in her family tree.

Catherine interjected by handing me a key and saying, "Your room is number 200, the first door on the right, two flights up."

The floor actually turned out to be the third floor, since the rest of the world, excluding America, did not consider the ground floor as the first floor. What we normally consider the second floor in the United States, was actually their first floor, and by protocol, was reserved for Field Grade Officers, Lieutenant Colonels, Majors, Commanders and Lieutenant Commanders. Ranks higher than that were assigned to private residences in the city in order to preserve the old military cliché that "Rank has its privileges." Second floor and above housed us junior officers.

My room measured 20 by 20 feet and contained three single beds, three wardrobes and three dressers. The only drawback was that the two lone windows in the room overlooked the BOQ's main entrance and the huge diesel generator that thumped noisily twenty four hours a day supplying electrical power to the building. Well, I could live with that as long as it kept working and provided the much needed air conditioning to the room. Since I did not expect to be spending much time other than sleeping here, the noise was inconsequential.

I learned later that there were two other officers also assigned to these Spartan accommodations with me. An American Army Captain named Martin Tolliver, who was a big portly Negro from St. Louis. He was a shade over six feet tall and worked in Army Supply at MACV Headquarters. The other officer was a Korean Army Captain named Han Kim Pak. He was slightly built and medium height, but anyone could see by the way he carried himself that he was no one to trifle with. It was amazing how the younger generation of the South Korean male population had bulked up in size and body strength since the Korean War. This most likely was due to the introduction of American foodstuffs which greatly enhanced their growth potential. In any event, I wouldn't care to take them on in a hand-to-hand combat situation. This was true especially in Han's case. Even though he was on the thin side and wiry, his calloused hands bore witness to the endless hours spent in Taekwondo training.

After stowing my gear and taking a quick shower, I headed down to the bar in hopes of seeing the long-haired bartender up close. I found a vacant stool at the far end and was pleasantly surprised when she placed a napkin in front of me and asked in a low modulated voice, "What is your pleasure, Lieutenant?"

"A cold beer with a glass," I replied. She immediately placed a cold can of Budweiser and a glass on the napkin.

"Cheers," she said as she swept up the proffered script money that I had placed on the bar.

Boy did that beer hit the spot, as did the several other ensuing ones that I had. In fact, with the lack of food in my stomach, it hadn't taken me very long to feel that numbness buzzing inside my head and the rubbery sensation that affected my lower extremities. I can honestly say that I had a limited recollection of departing the bar and making it up to my room without any serious consequences. Somehow, I made it to my bed, undressed and slipped under the poncho liner that served as my coverlet without any mishaps.

Someone once said that God looked out for fools and drunks, or is that redundant? My two room-mates were already asleep and both gently snoring, which masked any noise that I might have made getting into bed. In no time at all I fell into a deep, fitful sleep wrapped in the gentle arms of Morpheus. Just as an aside, was Morpheus male or female? Screw it. It didn't matter anyway.

I awoke the next morning feeling actually refreshed around 0630. Some semblance of daylight managed to filter diagonally in through the windows as I threw back my poncho liner. My two roommates had already departed, so I had the bathroom all to myself. Standing under the cascading tepid shower, I could feel my spirits being elevated despite the setback of my present tour of duty. I learned long ago that events in one's life seemed to happen for a definite reason and I decided not to let my current situation drag me down.

After stepping out of the shower, I wrapped my towel around my waist and proceeded to shave and brush my teeth. Just as I came out of the bathroom, the front door opened and a startled maid stood there in the open doorway. She was in her middle forties with a beige pajama top over the usual black cotton pants and slightly on the chubby side. Her round face gave the appearance of puffiness usually attributed to someone who has just woken up from a deep sleep. It was obvious that she was embarrassed by catching the new occupant standing there equally embarrassed in just a towel.

"My name Ba Tu," she said trying to overcome her discomfort in a tremulous voice.

"Hello Ba Tu, I am *Dai-Uy* Kay."

"*Chao Dai-Uy*," she said with a large grin now splitting her face. "You just come now Viet Nam?"

"No, I was on Poulo Obi, an island off the coast of Camau."

"Ver bad place Camau, many VC," she said, obviously never having heard of Poulo Obi.

"I will be working on Ben Bach Dang at *Hai Quan Cong Sung*," I added, and from the look on her face, that didn't seem to ring a bell either. Apparently, Naval Headquarters was not part of her frame of reference.

"You bring me Tide soap so I wash your clothes every morning," she said in a no nonsense manner.

"I'll stop by the PX and pick some up today for you, OK?"

"OK," she said over her shoulder as she proceeded to make up the beds.

I decided that I had better gather my things and get dressed in the bathroom otherwise Ba Tu would probably get a bad first impression of me. Little did I know how our relationship would develop in the future.

Having dressed rather hastily, I exited from the bathroom and headed for the door.

"No forget Tide soap," she said while busily sweeping the floor with her traditional Vietnamese broom. Unlike the standard American broom, it was roughly a meter long and consisted of wheat-like stalks bound together by strands of the same material over half its length. The bottom flared out in feathery wisps and appeared to be ideal for gathering dust from the tiled floors.

I went down to the lobby and located the cafeteria by easily following the sound of clattering dishes and the buzz of low conversations. The cafeteria was a rather large room containing many tables and an empty stainless steel serving line at the far end. The place was over fifty percent occupied by BOQ occupants, mostly in military uniforms of the various services. Interspersed with them were several civilians whose men seemed to prefer the popular "bush jacket" imported from Bangkok, Hong Kong and Singapore.

The most bizarre thing about this room was a huge framed portrait of General Westmoreland hanging on the far wall. He was the present Military Commander of all the American Forces in Vietnam and the picture was done in a three dimensional effect that had the General's eyes following you no matter where you sat in the room. Great, just what one needed while trying to eat a meal . . . Big Brother sternly staring at you from under those big bushy eyebrows.

Several young Vietnamese girls in starched blue uniforms with white aprons sauntered between the tables and the kitchen. They were all moving at the same slow pace as if they had all the time in the world. The other thing they had in common was that they all appeared to be in their early twenties. This said something about the Mess Sergeant who ran the facility. Obviously, he showed a penchant for hiring only young, fairly attractive girls to staff his messing facility while the older women were hired to do kitchen and custodial work. I found that not only interesting but admirable.

My waitress, who evidently had never seen me before, appeared a little shy when she approached me for my order.

"Good morning *Dai-Uy*," she said softly. "What you like for breakfast?"

Not seeing a wedding band on her finger, I replied, "*Chao Co.* I would like two fried eggs, over easy with toast, ham and a cup of coffee."

Without writing it down on her pad, she nodded once and headed back to the kitchen. I was really beginning to admire this trait of shyness among young Vietnamese women. Boy could some of the girls back home benefit from that trait, or is that being a male chauvinist? Oh well, it was just a random thought.

Less than fifteen minutes had elapsed before my waitress appeared with my food deftly balanced on a tray. It looked and smelled great, probably because I couldn't remember when I had last eaten since my arrival in Saigon. She reappeared with an insulated pitcher of coffee and topped off my cup. Looks like the Mess Sergeant trained his staff well, I thought. As I looked up to thank her, she pointed to the little plastic nametag on her apron over her left breast and said, "My name Quyen."

"Pleased to meet you Quyen," I replied looking her directly in the eyes, which brought a little color to her cheeks. With that, she turned rather hastily to service her other customers. I finished my meal quickly, which was a habit shared by anyone who has ever served aboard ship. One had to eat fast in order to relieve a hungry shipmate who was on watch, so he could also get to eat before the messhall shut down.

After paying my bill, I headed out of the BOQ into the already busy Street of Flowers. The weather seemed to be excessively hot and humid, especially since I had just emerged from the air-conditioning. I crossed Nguyen Hue, which contained two wide concrete islands that ran its length on either side of the thoroughfare from Le Loi down to the waterfront. On these twelve foot wide islands, the many kiosks of the flower sellers were already open in anticipation of the day's business. I wondered just how long the many freshly cut flowers could survive in the noxious air that polluted the city once the vehicular traffic took to the streets.

On the other side of *Nguyen Hue*, there were many shops, bars and restaurants with apartment buildings rising from three to four stories above them. I took the first short cross street that brought me to Rue Catinat, whose name was later changed to Tu Do Street when France lost control of its colony in 1954. Tu Do meant Freedom in Vietnamese, but believe me, there was nothing free on that street.

From one end of the street to the other on both sides, there were bars and the lovely ladies who unashamedly solicited "Saigon Tea" from the foreign civilian customers and GIs who frequented these establishments. Even at this early hour, many of the bars were open for business and had their doors ajar rather than boost their operating expenses by turning on the air conditioning. Although the interiors were somewhat dim, I could make out several die-hard Caucasian romantics bellied up to the bar trying to seduce the current love of their lives. Most of the girls working this early were probably the ones who couldn't compete with the more glamorous and experienced late shift employees. They were sort of the "Apprentice" group, who within a very short time, would hopefully graduate to the night shift where there were more opportunities to increase their take-home pay.

There was another short cross street diagonally from the one from which I had emerged onto Tu Do Street and it led to Hai Ba Trung Street that paralleled Tu Do down to the river. This was another bar-studded street named after two legendary sisters named Trung who had led the Vietnamese to victory over the Chinese from 39 to 43 AD. This street was considered by some to be a cut below the Tu Do establishment standards; although from the outside they all looked alike. I suppose the point of view depended on which bar the opinion-giver's girlfriend worked in.

At the end of the street on the left hand side was the local ice factory. It was a long, grimy grey two story building with loading bays taking up much of the ground floor. The area was bustling with people going in and out with all manner of carts loaded with ice.

Somewhere during one of my early indoctrination classes, we were strongly cautioned not to drink the water in Vietnam. This being the case, it was also brought to our attention that if the water was not deemed potable, then by all means, avoid any ice in your drinks other than those served in our billets or US run facilities. What reminded me of that fact was seeing a huge block of ice being dragged over the sidewalk to a local bar. I would hope that upon its arrival, someone wouldn't rinse it off with non-potable water. Oh well, what some people didn't know, wouldn't hurt them . . . unless of course they later came down with a case of the Ho Chi Minhs, dysentery or diarrhea to be precise.

The street also ended at the Ben Bach Dang circle where I turned left until I arrived at Vietnamese Naval Headquarters where I passed a small empty cement sentry booth. From there I entered through the main gate that was once again unattended, and proceeded straight towards the main building. This structure, as I stated before, was definitely constructed in the French style. It consisted of two identical buildings with a center passageway through the center from front to rear. A wide stairwell with black wrought iron railings provided access to the upper floors and covered balconies ran around each of the two sections on all floors. The outer wall of the balcony was about four feet high, so that with the office doors open, a breeze from the river could run completely unabated through the building.

I quickly climbed the stairs to my office that was on the top deck of the middle building. As I entered through an open double door, I found myself in a large office that was occupied by two Vietnamese females sitting behind their desks on either side of the spacious room. Behind each desk there was a filing cabinet of indeterminate age against the wall and a solitary paddle fan that hung motionless from the center of the fifteen foot high ceiling.

Four large twin fluorescent light units also hung from the ceiling that illuminated the otherwise austere office space.

The secretary on the left was slight of build, in her early thirties and wearing a pale blue Ao Dai with white pants. Her black hair was cut to her shoulders making her look slimmer than she actually was. The other girl was wearing a very western one piece striped miniskirt or mini-Jeep as they were called. She was somewhere in her early twenties, stood about five foot three and weighed about 125 ponds. She was well proportioned and had all the necessary curves, but her facial complexion was marred by a slight redness called Rosacea. As for her figure, it was obvious that she had a push-up bra to enhance the little she had in the boob category. To top it off, she wore her hair cut short, just above the shoulder, which I thought detracted from her overall appearance. Her hair was short coming to just below the ears and framed her round face. The body wasn't that hot, but you couldn't blame her for trying.

The secretary in the Ao Dai, who was obviously the senior of the two, quickly stood up and asked in a soft voice if she could be of any assistance.

"I am *Dai-Uy* Kay and have been assigned to this office," I said.

"Welcome *Dai-Uy*," she replied with a smile. "I am Ba Lan and that is Co Mai. We are Secretary/Translators for your office in the next room," she said as she pointed to the wide entryway at the rear of the room.

Thanking her, I entered an office that was the exact duplicate of the one with the secretaries, with the exception that it contained six desks. There were three on one side facing the three on the other and standard Navy gray filing cabinets behind each. Four officers were sitting at their respective desks, while one, who turned out to be an Army Major, stood studying a map of Vietnam propped on an easel. I introduced myself to a Commander who sat at the first desk on the right as he stood up and offered me his hand.

"I'm Commander Tod Johnson," he said sitting down again. "I dabble in Ops and Plans." A Lieutenant Commander occupied the second desk and as I extended my hand, he stood and said, "Hi,

I'm Fred Klamath. The Army token over there is Major Bill Towson and he and I are masquerading as Base Defense experts."

Across the aisle closest to the rear door, a young Navy Lieutenant with a crew cut stood up and announced in a very distinct New York City accent that he was George Morrow, the Advisory Group Historian. He indicated the center desk to his right and said, "I guess this will be your workbench."

Behind the last desk sat a good sized Lieutenant Commander who introduced himself as Ed Rogers. He was the Advisor to the River Boat Force Commanding Officer, who was a Lieutenant Commander in the Vietnamese Navy although they came under the jurisdiction of the Vietnamese Army. Boy, I could only imagine the organizational and administrative nightmares involved in that organization.

Lieutenant Commander Rogers asked me if I had just arrived in-country and I replied that I had previously been assigned to Coastal Group 41 on Poulo Obi. I explained about the screw-up in administration that had assigned me as the Assistant Advisor to that group when the billet called for a junior officer.

"Figures," murmured Commander Johnson from under his half-glasses. He had the typical long-faced Scandinavian countenance complete with frown lines that bore out his Norwegian ancestry.

"Have you met the Captain yet?" asked Lieutenant Commander Klamath with an inquiring wry smile.

"I did yesterday and he wants me to produce a monthly newsletter for the Advisory Group. He's also assigned me a Petty Officer named Hardin as my Yeoman."

"His name should be 'Hard-on' instead of Hardin," said Major Towson with a chuckle. "He can't keep his snake in his pants and spends most of his time at Sick Call trying to get rid of some venereal disease that he picked up in the bars.

"Great, that's just what I needed."

"By the way," Commander Johnson said, "Every Monday morning at 0745, except when it rains, a platoon from the Advisors has to dress in tropical whites and muster on the street out in front. The senior officer of each group, and that is me in this office, selects someone to represent the US side of the house. This is a weekly ritual and the entire Headquarters contingent lines up in ranks to hear the Vietnamese Navy's Chief of Naval Operations, Captain Chon speak following the morning colors ceremony. He stands at a podium with his back to the Saigon River and delivers short motivational speeches to the troops. It usually lasts about a half hour and I'd recommend that you wear sunglasses because you'll be facing into the sun. You can figure on being in the barrel every fifth week."

Commander Johnson added, as he removed his glasses and gave me his best avuncular look, "If you need help from any of us, don't hesitate to ask. We're a pretty congenial bunch up here."

"Thanks," I replied. "First I have to figure out exactly what the CO wants and how to go about doing it." Boy, was that an understatement.

The next few weeks were spent trying to find out just how in hell I was supposed to give birth to a newsletter. It came to me that a good place to start would be the JUSPAO Office in the Rex Building on the corner of Nguyen Hue and Le Loi. The Joint US Public Affairs Office issues all the daily releases from MACV to the press. This official function was locally referred to as "The Five O'clock Follies," and it was where all the journalists in Saigon interrupted their drinking in order to gather information for their next report to the people that were paying their per diem. Upon conclusion of the press briefing, most of them would quickly make their way diagonally across the street to the Press Club where they could call in their "Latest breaking news from the front," even though the majority of correspondents cynically considered the offerings jaded to some extent. Others would return to the Rex rooftop where they would sit around the tables with their drink of choice and discuss their newly acquired information with other journalists. In this way, they could embellish the data so their editors back home were satisfied that their money was still being well spent.

I wandered over to the Rex Building that morning around 10 o'clock and entered the lobby of JUSPAO. I approached the Information Desk and asked if I could see Mr. Barry Zorthian, who was the head of JUSPAO in Vietnam. The young Vietnamese receptionist informed me that she did not know if the Director was available, but that I could check with his secretary whose office was located down the hallway. Following her directions, I found the office and entered. The Director's secretary, who was a pleasant, middle-aged Caucasian, looked up and asked if she could help me.

I explained who I was and what I was trying to accomplish. She nodded her well coiffed gray streaked head, picked up her phone and buzzed the inner office. After speaking a few words, she listened and once again nodded her head as she hung up the phone. Surprisingly, she said that Mr. Zorthian was available for a few minutes and that I could go right in. It seems that my luck was holding out so far.

I entered a large paneled office with no windows and the gentleman sitting behind a cherry wood desk motioned me to sit down in one of the leather chairs fronting him.

"What can I do for you Lieutenant?" he asked, as his eyes wandered over my uniform for any identifying unit patches.

"My name is Lieutenant Bob Kay and I have been assigned to the Naval Advisory Group to produce a monthly newsletter for our men in the field. Since I don't hold a Journalism degree, I hoped that I could get some pointers from your organization as to how to get started, since you are the professionals."

Thinking a few moments, he pursed his lips and said, "I don't see why not. Let me have you meet Captain Meehan. He's my Public Affairs Officer liaison and I'm sure he can point you in the right direction." With that, he buzzed his secretary and asked her to summon the Captain to his office.

While we waited for the officer to arrive, Mr. Zorthian and I made small talk about my career in the Navy, my home town and what college I attended. I had the feeling that I was filling out a resume and to be sure, certain agencies of the US government find potential employees this way. However, at this point, I was not in the market for a new job.

A knock on the door preceded the entrance of Captain Meehan. He was of medium height, sandy colored hair with brown eyes and about 160 pounds. The beginning of a spare tire was visible around his mid-section that I attributed to desk work.

"Come on in John," said the Director. "This is Lieutenant Bob Kay from the Naval Advisory Group and he needs some advice on starting a newsletter for his group. I figured you're the best man to show him the ropes, OK?"

"No problem," said the Captain as he reached out to shake my hand. "Glad to be of service and please call me John. With your permission sir, I'll give him a tour of our facilities," he said.

I thanked Mr. Zorthian for his time and assistance and exited the office with the Captain. As I followed him down the hallway, he asked me several questions regarding the size of my staff, print capabilities and what the intended publication size and the duration between each issue. I answered these questions and when I was finished, he chuckled and said, "Who did you piss off?"

"Oh, the Senior Naval Advisor thought I was playing John Wayne in the boonies, but in reality, he was covering up for an admin screw-up. They assigned two Lieutenants to the same Junk Base instead of one Lieutenant and one Lieutenant Junior Grade or Ensign. Originally, I was assigned as the Assistant Advisor to Coastal Group 45 in Kien An, but when they discovered that I was a Lieutenant, they reassigned me to Poulo Obi. They didn't tell me that the Advisor there had extended his tour for another year and was preparing to go on thirty days leave. When he returned with a new assistant in tow, it made me surplus and I got the hook and the rest is history."

We spent the next hour going through the various offices where the USIS materials were written, edited and finally reproduced for distribution. I counted some twenty personnel, both American and Vietnamese involved in the process and thought that my task was practically impossible for two people, especially with one being a sex addict.

John said, "How about grabbing some lunch topside and we'll go into the mechanics of editing when we come back?"

"Sounds good to me, I'm feeling a little like David going up against Goliath without stones for my slingshot," I replied.

Slapping me gently on the back, John said, "It's no big deal once you get it off the ground, it will run on automatic."

After a quick lunch on the rooftop, we returned to his office that was a quarter the size of the Director's. He patiently walked me through the steps to take and kept reassuring me that I could always reach out to him whenever I got in a bind. I started to feel a little bit better about the job that lay before me.

Two hours later, we parted with the shaking of hands and my promise to let him know of my progress. In fact, he requested that he be included on the distribution list of my newsletter each month in order to monitor my progress and be able to provide any suggestions along the way. I left there in a much better frame of mind than I had this morning. Hey, I can do this, I thought to myself as I started back to my BOQ. After all, it was quitting time and a Bloody Mary would definitely hit the spot.

GETTING ORGANIZED

The next couple of weeks found me requesting inputs of all items of interest from the Advisors in the field on a monthly basis. I also managed to solicit help from First Class Petty Officer Bill DeVries who ran the NAVFORV Reproduction Office to help me print the newsletter.

One big setback occurred when Yeoman Hardin was Med-Evac'd to the Naval Hospital in Yokosuka. He had contracted some form of Venereal Disease that had completely stumped the local witch doctors. Previously, Captain Bjorkman had ordered the people at Sick Bay to keep a daily log of people with VD related problems. He was bound and determined to raise the morals of the Advisory Group by personally admonishing the offenders. Since this was Hardin's third episode with Gonorrhea after the Captain's enactment of the "Daily Clap Report," he was being shit-canned back to the States for instant reassignment to sea duty.

It looked like I'd be typing the Newsletter myself, but no big loss because he had typed out three items for me and I wound up having to retype the articles myself. How he had made First Class was beyond me. I intended to let the XO know that no replacement for Hardin was required and that I could go it alone. He'd love that because it would be one less chore for him to do.

Three examples for the masthead were sketched for me by an artist at JUSPAO and I chose the one that I thought was the most appropriate. Additionally, I had listed the staff box on the inside of the first page which was kind of unique in that it had listed Captain Bjorkman, Senior Naval Advisor and Lieutenant Bob Kay, Editor-in-Chief, period.

Fortunately, I had taken copious notes of the many suggestions that Captain Meehan had given me and aside from having lost my Yeoman, I still thought that I could manage. But it wasn't going to be easy because the front office said that I could not use the services of Ba Lan and Co Mai because they were there strictly to work for the operational advisors . . . or whatever that meant.

The tricky part of preparing inputs for the Newsletter was that I was forced with my hunt and peck style of typing, to justify each paragraph manually by counting letters and adding spaces between words. Justifying meant that each paragraph started with a word and ended in a word forming nice even block margins required for printing. I got past this by first typing a rough draft and then editing with pencil marks where spaces had to be added to produce the desired effects. Not very time effective, but then again, what else did I have to do ten hours a day, seven days a week? Anyway, a linotype machine would have done that automatically but there was none in my immediate future. I thought about trying to locate one in the Saigon area and perhaps conning the owners into letting me use it. But then it was too much of an effort and I didn't feel like being indebted to anyone. Besides, I got to be pretty good at it.

Information from the field was practically nonexistent for the first issue that was due to come out in one week and needless to say, a good deal of creativity on my part was necessary. By the way, for creativity, substitute "Bullshit."

I took the final typed pages over to NAVFORV where each page was reproduced onto a magnetic mat and then transferred to the printer.

We initially ran off 500 copies of a six page Newsletter and delivered them next door to the NAVFORV Post Office for distribution. By direction, I had to include a copy also to MACV and to CHINFO (Chief of Naval Information) in Washington, DC. Here goes, I thought to myself as I headed back to my office.

The next morning, I was summoned down to the Captain's office. He was holding a copy of the newsletter and proceeded to critique my initial effort.

"It's OK as far as it goes," he said, "but there's not enough information from the field."

I explained that there wasn't a big response to our request for feedback.

"Well I'll take care of that and you can be sure that every advisor of mine will comply . . . or else," he said sternly. "Additionally, there's not enough white space between stories and it tends to tire out a reader seeing paragraphs running one on top of another. Better see if you can come up with some symbols for insertion between stories that will whiten the page up some."

"Aye sir, I'll get right on it for the next issue. How would you feel about a cartoon or two?" I asked.

"That'll be OK, but no Playboy stuff, understand?"

"Aye sir."

With that, I was dismissed. Well what did he expect for a first attempt, a Pulitzer Prize candidate?

True to his word, the Captain sent out an "All Hands" memo to the field directing them to submit items of interest again, by the middle of each month. It was also to be noted that a record would be maintained of these submissions and passed on to the Captain. This left no doubt as to the seriousness of his latest "rocket" to the guys.

Back in my BOQ room, I began noticing a strange pattern developing. Every two weeks, just like clockwork, two burley Korean Army Non-Coms would come to our room and remove the Captain's footlocker and replace it with an empty one. Captain Han was apparently stockpiling canned goods from the Commissary and sending it home aboard a Korean freighter docked at Saigon Port. The groceries were most likely being used to supplement his family's dietary needs or eventually find their way into the Korean Black Market, which in turn generated additional income for him.

Another ploy used by the Koreans, I learned, was that a group of three or four of them would enter the PX Package Store that sold beer, wine and liquor. They would split off from each other and appear to be casually shopping the various aisles. Each of them would have a hidden brown paper shopping bag from previous purchases from the store with the register receipt still stapled to the top of the bag. They would take the identical liquor item indicated on the receipt, place it into the empty bag and reseal it by refastening the original staple. With the seemingly already paid for bags in their shopping cart, they were able to safely exit past the clerk at the door. This practice continued unhindered for several months until an inventory uncovered the huge amount of missing merchandise.

Close scrutiny by the PX security eventually pinpointed the Koreans as the perpetrators. To prevent future pilferage, the clerk stationed at each exit inspected all outgoing parcels and matched the items with the receipt stapled to the bag. They would then affix a large 'X' with red marker on both the stapled receipt and the bag, which prevented the reuse of either for this type of scam. No arrests were made, and Uncle Sam looked the other way in order to maintain good relations with our allies. Can you imagine what would happen if a US type was caught doing this? Right!

Events such as this caused me to start looking at every civilian working in Vietnam with a jaundiced eye, regardless of nationality. I concluded that some of them were simply trying to "make a buck" by any means available, but by and large, this was not the case for the overall majority. It's amazing how a person's judgment can become skewed with all the widespread corruption occurring throughout Vietnam.

Another strange event occurred one day involving our maid, Ba Tu. Since, as I stated before, both my roommates left for work very early, I would take advantage of this by lying in bed a little longer. Thus, I could start each day with peace and quiet, with the exception of course, of the huge generator's constant clamor below our windows.

One morning before I could roll out of bed, Ba Tu rushed in, grabbed hold of my poncho liner and whipped it off me saying, "Get up *Dai-Uy*, time go work and make Vietnam safe."

I couldn't help but notice that she said this with a lascivious grin on her round face. Another thing I noticed was that when she peeled my cover off, her eyes immediately went to my shorts. Hmmm! I'll fix this gal, I thought as I headed to the shower.

A plan was hatched and the next morning I put it into action. I set my alarm that night to wake me when my roommates departed. Once alone, I quickly shed my shorts and proceeded to work up an erection into a significant "woody," I then tied a large red bow around it and held him flat against my abdomen.

With my covers securely pulled up to my neck, I lay on my back feigning sleep while softly squeezing my erection to maintain its rigidity. Sure enough, in came Ba Tu and true to form, she grabbed the corner of my covers and whipped them off me. I let my erection snap forward and as I laid there stark naked with an upright penis decorated with a red ribbon, she never got to say her usual greeting as her voice temporarily froze in her throat.

You've all heard the saying, "A picture is worth a thousand words." Well, I wish I could have captured her expression on film, it was unbelievable. She was caught between fear, surprise and I think a little admiration at the sight that lay smiling naked on the bed before her. She spun around quickly, letting out a low howl as she took off for the door and slammed it shut behind her. I lay in my rack, doubled up with laughter and since I hadn't had my morning piss, I came close to doing it in the bed. Needless to say, the ritual morning unveiling ceased and Ba Tu managed to avoid me for the next couple of weeks.

Inputs began pouring in from the field in response to the veiled threats issued by the Captain. I received information as to who had newly arrived aboard, their last duty station, who was leaving and where he was heading, several anecdotes and some superfluous gobble-de-gook that I eventually tossed into the round file or trash-can if you prefer.

The one thing that all of the submissions had in common were that I had to rewrite everything so that it was readable to all hands. This editorializing occupied a good deal of my time and I was beginning to enjoy the experience as the days progressed.

During one of the lull periods when I didn't have to do any rewriting, LCDR Rogers looked over at me and asked, "Hey Bob, what do you do with your time after work each day?"

"Oh, I usually, wind up at the bar in the McCarthy BOQ where I toss back a few beers and tease the bartenders and waitresses. Then, after a quick shower and change of clothes, I wander up to the roof of the Rex. Once in awhile they have some entertainment and the food is usually palatable. After that, it's only a hop, skip and a stumble back across to the McCarthy and my rack. That's about it in a nutshell," I explained. "Not much to write home about."

"Sounds like you haven't made the rounds of the local bars yet," he said.

"No, with all the pressure of trying to put out the Dorkman's newsletter on time, my carnal urges haven't come into play yet. But I'll get around to them eventually. Am I missing something?"

"Well, I've been frequenting this little place on Cong Ly just up from Le Loi. It's called the Golden Dragon Restaurant and it's kind of quiet, not like the Tu Do bars. I thought you might like to go with me some night."

"Sure. I really don't like walking into any of the bars cold-turkey. At least I'll still have someone to talk to over a couple of beers if I don't see any girl that piques my interest."

"As it so happens, I plan on going there tonight after work. How's about I pick you up around 1930?"

"OK by me," I replied.

In the Naval Advisory Group, Lieutenant Commanders and above were issued their own Jeeps, while junior officers were relegated to getting around town with local transportation and at their own expense. Conversely, the Airborne, ARVN, Ranger and Marine Advisors, O-4 and above, not only had their own vehicles, but Vietnamese military drivers as well. Now why is that, I thought?

My early impression of LCDR Rogers was that he did not appear to be your standard bar habitué. He was a very quiet individual, slightly over six feet tall with a big boned body and bulldog jaw. His walk was slow and ambling and I initially placed his accent as being from the upper mid-west. This was confirmed when I learned that he hailed from Anoka, Minnesota—the Pumpkin Capitol of the World, located just a few miles north of the Minneapolis suburb of Coon Rapids.

One Monday when LCDR Rogers had the dubious distinction of being picked to represent our office at the morning colors ceremony, I noticed that among his ribbons, he wore a Navy Good Conduct Medal. This indicated that he had been enlisted and therefore must be a man of experience. For this reason, I had no qualms about accepting his offer to accompany him on "Liberty."

He arrived promptly at 1930 just as I was emerging from the McCarthy. I climbed into his Jeep, which was the older Toyota model assigned to the Vietnamese and Advisors. The M151A Jeep, which would have been preferable, was only used by the US military. The Toyota was the taller and narrower of the two, but its ride was significantly harder. Many Vietnamese removed one or two leafs from the spring suspensions giving them a softer ride, but definitely impacting its stability. Oh well, as long as they drove on pavement and not country roads, it seemed to work OK.

We drove down to the first cross street and made a right turn. Three short blocks brought us to Pasteur, which was one way heading north, where we made another right. Then across Le Loi Boulevard and up one more block where we turned left into *Le Thanh Ton* street. After another short block, it intersected Cong Ly that was one way heading south. We took a left, went halfway down the block and parked on the left side of the street with our two left wheels on the curb in front of the Golden Dragon. This was acceptable in Vietnam wherever the streets were narrow.

THE GOLDEN DRAGON

The exterior of the restaurant was more subdued than many of the other establishments in town. In fact, it was extremely ordinary with the exception of a large vertical sign that hung over the entrance. Big yellow and red neon letters proclaimed that the "Golden Dragon" was directly below as indicated by a flashing arrow. The door through which we entered was a large black painted portal adorned with polished brass fittings.

Once inside, we found ourselves in a small alcove that separated the entryway from the main room. I followed Ed through a beaded curtain and just as we entered the main room, a stunning Vietnamese woman approached us dressed in a black Ao Dai with a white flower embroidered from just over her breast to her waist.

She said in a low, slightly accented voice, "Hello Commander, I see you brought a friend with you. Good. Won't you please follow me?" as she showed us to a table near the bar. The center of the room held ten tables covered with crisp white tablecloths and napkins, while plush booths with round tables adorned three of the walls. Two of the center tables were occupied with couples quietly talking and several of the booths were also occupied. The bar was adjacent to the entrance and two swinging doors in the rear left hand corner of the room, led to the kitchen.

Before we were even seated, a young Vietnamese waiter appeared on cue to take our order. He was one of four waiters dressed in black pants and white shirts with black bow ties who tended the customers. I noticed that most of the men in the booths were Vietnamese and dressed in somber business suits. Next to each man, a pretty Vietnamese girl sat listening in rapt attention to their every word. These, I assumed were the "Hostesses" who were there to provide companionship. The tables in the center of the room were occupied by a mixture of Caucasian men and a few round-eyed women, who seemed to be enjoying themselves over dinner.

As we were being seated, Ed said, "Marie this is Lieutenant Kay. He just arrived from down south and is now working with me."

I acknowledged the introduction with "It's my pleasure Marie," as I gently shook her offered hand.

"Kay," Marie said as she gave me the once over. "You must be from the Mediterranean."

"Yes, I am actually of Greek descent," I answered quizzically

"You have those soft dark brown eyes that spell intrigue and your ears are well developed and classically Greek. I've known several Greek gentlemen in Paris, and they were most charming. Are you also charming?" she asked me flirtatiously.

"Runs in the blood, I'm afraid."

"Mmmm, that's good," she murmured as she let her hand softly trail over my shoulder as she left our table. "I'll come back in a little while."

I was quick to notice that she had the standard oriental cast to her eyes, but the color was a pale hazel with dark flecks of brown in them. This confirmed my original impression that she might have had a bit of French admixture among her ancestors. I had also detected the fine scars that remained after the surgery to trim the epicanthic folds of her upper eyelids. As I continued to eye her figure as she walked away, I could see that she was much more full bodied than the average Vietnamese woman. I would not be the least bit surprised that she had also had her breasts augmented toot. All in all, she looked like one hell of a woman.

The young waiter brought us each an ice cold "33" beer with a frosted glass and said in a low conspiratorial voice, "These are on the house from Marie."

We both raised our glasses in a salute towards Marie who rewarded us with an impish smile and a delicate wave of the hand.

"Well, what do you think about this place?" asked Ed as he sipped his beer contentedly.

"So far, so good," I replied. The place is really classy. I don't care to drink in a place that is either too bright or too dark but this place is just right."

"You're right, they both have their drawbacks."

"So, my friend, is Marie the reason you like to come here?"

"As a matter of fact no; can you see that round-eyed guy that's behind the bar talking to the bartender?" That's Henri, and right now he's the one who goes home with her every night."

I glanced at the fairly tall, solidly built man with a blue and white striped tie-less shirt. He appeared to be in his early to mid forties, with close cropped salt and pepper hair that peaked slightly in front. A pencil thin mustache of the same color grew below a nose that was definitely Gallic, as were his petulant lips. The jaw looked as if it had been carved from granite and his eyes were a lifeless blue. All in all, he looked as if he had served in the French Foreign Legion at one time. The cuffs of his shirt-sleeves were turned under and a bluish tattoo on his right forearm was partly visible.

His breed was all too common in places that France had colonized and eventually lost.

Now I understood why I had subconsciously noticed him giving me the evil eye from behind the bar when Marie had played feely-touchy with me. That's all I needed was a jealous Frog boyfriend zeroing in on me when I hadn't made any moves on his lady. He obviously was insecure in his relationship with Marie since it probably was her assets rather than his that funded their union.

Ed said that there were rumors about Marie also having some very senior Vietnamese Naval Officers cavorting from time to time between her sheets, which would account for Henri's jealousy.

Just then, a lovely young Vietnamese girl appeared at our table from out of nowhere and sat down.

"Hello Ed, have you been here long," she asked in fairly good English.

By the immediate flush of Ed's face, I knew that this was the magnet that drew him to the Dragon. She was dressed in a dark blue Ao Dai with white pants and her hair, black and long, hung over the front of her pert breasts and down to her waist. She had a fairly solid body, but nowhere near Marie's caliber. Her teeth were white and even when she smiled upon being introduced to me. "Bob, this is Lan. Lan this is Bob; he works with me," Ed said overcoming his initial shyness.

Wow I thought, I could see why Ed might be serious about this one.

After I answered the usual questions from Lan of "How long you be in Vietnam, do you have wife, Vietnamese girlfriend?" etc., etc., she turned her attention back to Ed. During the Q and A session, Ed had managed to signal the waiter to bring her a "Saigon Tea," which would placate Marie for the time her hostess spent with us.

"If you like," said Lan after taking a sip of her drink, "I will introduce you to my friend Tuyet, but she not work tonight."

"Sure," I replied trying to act nonchalant. My affirmative answer seemed to go over well with Ed, since he would now have a willing partner for future visits to the Golden Dragon.

After two hours of light conversation and three or four more "Saigon Teas" to cover the hostess rental, we decided that it was time to take our leave. Apparently, our quiet demeanor fell well within the bounds of conduct expected by Marie of her patrons, especially since the drink consumption rate was acceptable. We settled up our bill, which wasn't exorbitant and as we stood to say our goodbyes to Lan, Marie came gliding over to bid us *adieu*.

"I hope to see you again and soon," she said as she touched each of us on the arm familiarly.

With that send-off, we got into the Jeep, which fortunately was still intact and Ed dropped me off at the McCarthy.

The next day in the office, I proceeded to sketch out a small cartoon for the Newsletter. Using our last night's visit to the Dragon, I depicted a sailor sitting in a booth with a pretty Viet hostess. She was holding a stemmed glass in a salute to her companion and the caption read "To your wealth." The illustration was entitled "Saigon Tea-Sers," which I thought was a good play on words and apropos under the circumstances. It would also open the door for more follow-on cartoons.

However, and much to my chagrin, I found myself summoned to the Captain's office the day after the second edition of the Newsletter hit the street.

"Just what in the hell do you think you're doing?" he said angrily as he waved the cartoon in front of my face.

"I thought it was in line with what our people run into here in-country," I said defensively.

"Horse manure!" he replied. "Didn't I tell you none of that Playboy cartoon humor just last month?"

All I could do was stand there looking him in the eyes as he continued his tirade. He was one pissed-off gent. After what seemed an eternity, he finished venting his wrath by asking, "How do I explain this crap to my wife?"

"I wasn't aware that you were going to send this home sir," I replied meekly.

"Well now you know. Besides that's irrelevant and I'm not sure how the CHINFO Office is going to view this." he grumped.

"I also didn't think that it would be offensive to CHINFO," I added to an already weak defense.

"Of course since CHINFO gets a copy, he'll see this piece of trash. He gets every publication that is generated in the Navy and Marines," he added calming down a bit while putting his hands into his pockets.

"I'll make sure it doesn't happen again Captain."

"See to it that you don't," he said as he sat down and summarily dismissed me.

The next morning, I went over to the Naval Support Activity, or NAVSUPPACT as it was known. The four story building was painted a creamy white and was across the street from COMNAVFORV. I was there to follow up on a lead about an artist attached to the staff who was an Aerographers Mate First Class by the name of Jim Hummel. I humped up the three flights to his office and found him at his desk with his fist wrapped around a coffee cup.

"What can I do for you Lieutenant?" he asked me half-heartedly as I stood in front of his paper strewn desk.

I went into my pitch explaining the whys and wherefores of my visit and showed him a copy of the cartoon.

"What's so freakin' bad about that?" he asked as he tilted his seat back against the wall.

"I didn't think anything was wrong with it, but Captain Bjorkman had other views, unfortunately."

"Well, what do you need from me?" he asked unenthusiastically.

"I would like your help in getting at least two cartoons a month from you. I'd provide the ideas and themes of what I want and you'll get full recognition for your efforts."

"I guess I can do that," he said as he stood up and shook my hand. "When do you need the first ones?"

"Not for another three weeks," I replied. "I'll get the info over to you by the day after tomorrow." I went down the stairs very relieved to have garnered another collaborator in my effort to publish the Dorkman's newsletter.

The following week whizzed by rapidly because of my full and undivided attention in preparing for the next edition. I dropped off two cartoon ideas for Hummel and I continued to edit the inputs that started pouring in at a pretty good rate from the field. Rogers seeing that I was totally engrossed with my work surmised that any invitation for a foray to the Dragon would not be received affirmatively and therefore remained silent. I did ask him one day how things were there and he mumbled, "OK. By the way, both Lan and Tuyet send their regards."

I thanked him and continued on with the grind at hand. Just then my phone rang. It was the Captain's Yeoman informing me that my presence was requested in the head office ASAP. Now what the hell did I do, I thought grabbing my hat and going out the door.

I entered the Senior Naval Advisor's office and greeted the XO who was still slumped behind his desk with the Stars and Stripes crossword puzzle and munching another untoasted Pop Tart. The Captain's Yeoman, Petty Officer First Class Norman, was at the copying machine. Turning to me, he said, "Mornin' Lieutenant, the Captain's waiting for you, g'wan in."

"Thanks," I replied as I knocked on the door.

"Enter," said the voice of my master. "Have a seat."

Before I could say anything, he slid a folder across his desk and said, "Coastal Group 16 was overrun yesterday and the Senior Advisor was killed. Since you were in the Junk Force, Did you run run across a Lieutenant William C. Fitzgerald?"

"No sir, was he the Advisor at 16?"

"Yes he was. The initial report from the 1st Coastal Zone Commander is in that folder. Read it carefully and keep it strictly confidential because tomorrow morning you are going to accompany Captain Chon to the site. I consider you my unofficial Public Affairs Officer and since you are familiar with a Junk base, I want you to find out and report what actually happened there not what the Vietnamese want us to know. Understand?"

"Aye sir," I replied, a little taken aback by the Captain's frankness and at the same time spiritually uplifted because of the confidence he was placing in me.

"Get in touch with Captain Chon's office and they'll provide you with the itinerary. They've already been apprised of your participation, so keep your eyes open and your head down."

I left the office with my mind racing at a hundred miles an hour and I don't think I said a word to the XO as I departed. It didn't matter anyway, because he was still busy brushing Pop Tart crumbs off of his puzzle. Ah, war in Saigon can indeed be hell.

A young female Ensign in Captain Chon's admin office with the name Chao on her nametag informed me that we would depart from the heliport on *Vo Thanh* Street at 0630 tomorrow. Just then, the Captain came out of his office. He was my height, with a slight paunch that added some poundage. His hair was cut close on the sides and the two inch long hairs on top stood straight up and gave the impression that he never combed it. His traditional Colt .357 Magnum was holstered on his right hip and a crumpled white handkerchief was sticking out of his left hand pants pocket of his working blue uniform.

Upon seeing me said, "Ah, Lieutenant Kay, I hear you will be joining us on tomorrow's trip. It was a very unfortunate incident and I deeply regret the loss of your Lieutenant Fitzgerald. We also lost the base commander, *Trung-Uy* Thong and fourteen of his men along with twenty civilian dependents. Thirty five wounded Vietnamese sailors are being treated at the Naval Hospital in Quang Ngai and I plan on visiting them before returning to Saigon. Although I do not foresee any danger, I strongly suggest that you bring a weapon."

"Yes sir, I'll look forward to accompanying you tomorrow."

Since it was nearly lunchtime, I decided to get something substantial in my stomach before tomorrow's journey. There was a neat little Corsican restaurant located on Nguyen Hue and diagonally across the street from the McCarthy that I had found by accident one evening as I was returning late from the office. A sudden downpour had forced me to take refuge inside as I was passing the place. There was a drawing depicting the Island of Corsica painted on the big plate glass window and the name above it announced that this was "*Le Corse*."

The establishment was owned and operated by two Corsican expatriates named Francois and Milo who had served in the French Foreign Legion. Having spent a considerable part of their Legion time in and around Indo-China, they chose to remain after the fall and the humiliation of the French at Dien Bien Phu. Both men passionately believed that the intense, smoldering hatred that arose between France and the United States began when America refused their plea for help in their fight with the Viet Minh. It wasn't until the Americans got involved in South Vietnam that France figured that we had back-doored them. There was nothing that we could ever say or do that would convince them we did not want Vietnam for ourselves or for any future development of her resources. That made sense and would explain the veiled animosity encountered when dealing with the local French expatriates here.

Francois and Milo were sitting at the end of the bar and greeted me with familiarity even though I had only been in there that one time. A very tall Eurasian female in her early twenties was behind the bar and I had no doubts that she was already spoken for by one of the owners.

There were five double tables on the left side and the bar ran halfway down the length of the room on the right. A large lithograph picture of Napoleon hung next to the mirror behind the bar and as usual, the artist had the little Emperor staring off into the distance. I always imagined a possible caption attached to these as asking, "What the hell just happened at Waterloo?"

Napoleon had been the home town boy who made good for the Corsicans just after France purchased the island from the Genoans. His defeat at Waterloo however must have really pissed off the French because they exiled him to the island of Elba off the coast of Italy rather than to his home of record, Corsica.

During my initial visit to Le Corse, I had tried their *biftek and pomme frittes*. I decided to have the steak and French fries again since they were very good the last time. I knew from my many trips to Greece that French fries cooked in pure olive oil are unequaled for flavor. A cold glass of "33" beer over a few ice cubes complemented the meal and a shot of Pernod on the rocks rounded out the meal nicely. Pernod, along with Pastisse and Ricard, are the French cousins of Greek Ouzo. All anise-based liqueurs turn milky when poured over ice or splashed with cold water. If the drink remains clear, it's because the bottle is old and the alcohol content has degraded, so a gentle word to the bartender would then be in order.

As I sat back languishing after my delicious meal, I decided to look over the report on Coastal Group 16 while I sipped my Pernod. I turned my chair slightly so that my back was angled towards the wall preventing anyone from looking over my shoulder, and proceeded to read.

The report was fairly short and to the point in accordance with standard naval reporting procedures and read as follows:

"In the early morning hours of 7 August, 1967, a large enemy force attacked and overran Coastal Group 16, located on the banks of the Song Tra Khuc River about seventy miles southeast of Da Nang. Several Market Time units responded to the urgent calls for assistance from the Senior US Naval Advisor Lieutenant William C. Fitzgerald. However, despite the combined firepower of the US and Vietnamese Navy vessels along with a Helicopter Gunship, they failed to keep the base from being overrun.

Lieutenant Fitzgerald was killed during the ensuing action along with the Base Commander LTJG Nguyen M. Thong, fourteen Vietnamese Navy personnel and twenty civilians who had been on the compound. Thirty five wounded Coastal Group 16 sailors were moved to a Vietnamese medical facility in Quang Ngai and the three remaining US Advisors managed to escape with only minor wounds.

The attack and been so well coordinated, vicious and swift, that the defenders were taken completely by surprise.

An investigation team from Saigon is being dispatched to the area."

The report said a lot and yet said nothing. I could see why Captain Bjorkman wanted me to accompany the Vietnamese CNO in trying to piece together what actually happened. There were too many unanswered questions as I reread the report a second time. I hoped that I would be able to come up with something significant.

Closing the folder, I finished my Pernod, which by now had become tepid, paid my bill and walked pensively back to the BOQ. Tomorrow morning would come soon enough and I could only hope that my mind would let me have a dreamless sleep.

PART SEVEN

COASTAL GROUP 16

Early the next morning, I got into a taxi parked just off the entrance to my hotel. The driver was dozing in the front seat and jerked awake as I opened the rear squeaking door of his antique yellow cream and blue Renault taxi. He relaxed immediately when he recognized that I was a US military man and not some young rowdy street cowboy trying to relieve him of his cash. After telling him my destination, we left in a cloud of black smoke.

Along the way, I had him stop by an early morning street vendor and bought two egg sandwiches on French bread wrapped in newspaper. He was genuinely surprised when I handed him one and the happy expression on his weathered face said it all. Besides, how could I possibly sit in the rear of his cab eating a hot egg sandwich whose tantalizing aroma filled the entire vehicle? Who knows, maybe I'll ride in his cab again someday. At least hopefully he'll remember me as the not-so-ugly American.

We arrived at the heliport with both of us having devoured our sandwiches on the fly. As I paid him, he reached out and took my hand in both of his and thanked me in Vietnamese, all the while smiling and bobbing his head. Perhaps I might have unconsciously been trying to appease the gods of fate by being generous and hoping for a successful outcome to this morning's trip north.

I entered the compound and returned the salute of the ARVN guard at the main gate. The compound consisted of hard packed dirt that was oil and fuel soaked to the point where you could see purplish blue and red rainbows on the ground. A Vietnamese Huey helicopter was sitting on one of the three concrete pads with its rotors turning slowly. Captain Chon, still dressed in his faded blue working uniform with his ever-present .357 caliber Colt pistol on his hip, stood by its open starboard door. Next to him, stood the same female Ensign from yesterday and his Flag Lieutenant, *Dai-Uy* Toan. Now here was a guy I instinctively took a dislike to. He had never done anything to warrant animosity from me, but somehow he gave me the impression of being a wise-ass. His physique was the same cookie-stamp model as the majority of Vietnamese men, standing about five foot six or seven and one hundred thirty pounds with zero fat. His jet black hair that was uncharacteristic of the military touched the top of his collar. The one aspect that differentiated him from the others was that his eyes always appeared to be half closed as if cigarette smoke was blowing into them. Maybe he had seen too many Humphrey Bogart films and tried to pattern his image after the actor. Regardless, he was a poor knock-off if that was his intention.

Seeing me as I passed through the main gate, Captain Chon smiled and waved me over. "Good morning Lieutenant Kay. Are you ready for our trip?" he asked.

"Yes sir," I replied patting the obvious Colt .45 holstered on my hip. I never mentioned the five shot, snub nosed S&W .38 that I wore under my fatigue jacket at all times. I had bought the gun off of a Coastie when his WPB made a routine stop at Poulo Obi. He said his time was almost up in Vietnam and he didn't want to try to sneak the weapon out of country. So, for fifty dollars US, I obtained my security blanket. From then on, it accompanied me wherever I went in Vietnam since it was too damned hard to tell the good guys from the bad.

The Captain checked his silver Seiko watch whose band was a tad too big for his wrist, ordered everyone aboard the chopper. "*Chung ta di*," he yelled up to the pilot and pointed his finger in the air which literally meant let's get this show on the road.

The trip took about an hour and a half, during which time the canvas seats proved very uncomfortable and the noise blasting through the open doors prevented any conversation whatsoever. Finally the helo made a slow low pass over the Junk Base in preparation for landing and the scene down below wasn't very encouraging. Devastation was everywhere and there was only one individual standing near the center of the compound. The pilot quickly descended and deftly landed the helo just outside the main entrance to the ravaged base and in front of what used to be the dependent's housing.

Our party disembarked and as we made our way through the entrance, the individual whom we had seen in the compound came forward to greet us. He pulled up, executed a crisp military salute while announcing that he was *Dai-Uy* Phan from the First Coastal Zone Commander's Staff. He said that he had been assigned to provide the Captain with information and assist in any way possible. I stood in the background taking this all in and thinking that the Coastal Zone Commander should have been here himself rather than sending an emissary. On the other hand, wasn't that exactly what Bjorkman had done with me here?

Han took us around the compound speaking in rapid fire Vietnamese as he described the events that had taken place. Not being able to follow his conversation, I broke off from the group and went off on my own just as an Air America helicopter landed close to the Huey that brought us. A US Naval Officer and a civilian jumped out and headed towards the Captain's group. They must have asked for me because they all turned towards me as the Captain pointed my way and resumed his tour. One of the newcomers was Navy Lieutenant Chad Taylor, who introduced himself as the resident NILO (Naval Intelligence Officer) out of Da Nang. The other civilian was simply introduced to me by Taylor as Mr. Cal Fields. Since they had arrived on "Spook Airways" and no further identification or affiliation was given concerning the civilian, I had to assume that he was a local CIA type.

As the three of us surveyed the area, there were empty metal ammunition containers lying all around the bullet riddled ground, but the weapons had obviously been carried off by the enemy. Also evident, were the many dark stains in the hard compacted earth where the fallen had bled.

Lieutenant Taylor proceeded to give me his background info on the attack. It seemed that the local VC had become annoyed by the Junk Group's stepped up offensive against them over the last few months. Many notices had been surreptitiously tacked up on trees in and around the nearby village of Co Luy warning everyone that an attack on the base was imminent.

Obviously, the base occupants ignored the warnings and continued their nightly ambushes and supply route interdiction along the river. The day before the assault, the VC infiltrated the village and quietly killed all the dogs to prevent them from barking prior to their attack.

Just before dawn on Monday, the 7th of August 1967, two battalions of Viet Cong stormed the base in a frontal assault. From numerous sites along the river bank adjacent to the base, automatic weapons fire and mortars poured onto the compound. For some reason, the defenders seemed to have been taken completely by surprise. All four advisors were asleep in their bunks and only two Junks were out on patrol.

As the attack commenced, the base personnel awoke and wildly rushed to their designated defensive positions. At some point early in the attack, a large enemy group of three hundred men managed to penetrate the northern minefield that protected the base. Hunkered down in their bunker which was the last area of resistance, the advisors feverishly fired through the shooting ports at the enemy while Lieutenant Fitzgerald tried frantically to radio for help.

An American Swift Boat PCF-20, received the call while they were patrolling in a nearby area and promptly relayed it to other Market Time Units. Jamming the throttles ahead at flank speed, the CO of the Swift Boat headed for the besieged base and arrived about twenty minutes later. They immediately commenced firing on the enemy mortar and automatic weapons firing positions along the adjacent bank of the river.

During the ensuing battle, another US Swift Boat, PCF-75 and the Vietnamese Navy's PCE-10 arrived on the scene and commenced firing at the entrenched enemy positions. However, they were unable to stem the advance of the attackers for fear that they would kill any of the defenders.

The Junk Force CO, *Dai-Uy* Thong, sought refuge in the concrete base of the old French tower situated in the center of the base and barricaded himself inside. The Viet Cong blew open the steel door with a satchel charge followed by another one thrown inside the small enclosure instantly turning Thong into spaghetti sauce.

Lieutenant Fitzgerald seeing that the enemy had succeeded in breaching the perimeter and overrunning the base recognized that their position was untenable. He ordered the three advisors to escape through a rear opening that faced the river as he called for immediate artillery support and an air strike directly onto the base itself.

As the three Americans managed to scuttle out of the bunker and into the water safely, Lieutenant Fitzgerald had finished transmitting and was bringing up the rear. As he squirmed through the opening, a Viet Cong had climbed atop the bunker and seeing the advisor halfway out of the opening, shot him through the back of the head killing him instantly.

By this time, USS Gallup (PG-85), USS Camp (DER-251), PCFs 15 and 54 and a USAF "Dragon Ship" arrived and commenced inundating the base and the adjacent bank of the river with withering fire. The battle raged on for several hours until one US and two Vietnamese infantry units arrived and launched a counterattack on the surviving enemy inside the wire. This battle lasted for about a half an hour before the base was once again safe and secure.

The ground was littered with empty .30 caliber and .50 caliber ammo boxes attesting to the urgency of the beleaguered defenders. The area reminded me of an empty field after a county fair had packed up and departed, leaving only bits of debris scattered haphazardly all around.

All of the original buildings on the base but one had been destroyed during the attack. Approximately forty Vietnamese survivors were pulled out of the river by the USS Camp and fifteen of the more seriously wounded were helicoptered to the Vietnamese hospital in *Quang Ngai*. The final total was fourteen Vietnamese sailors killed, thirty five wounded and twenty dead civilian dependents at the end of the day.

Naturally, no Viet Cong bodies were found since they always took their dead and wounded with them. The thirty five VC suspects that had previously been detained for interrogation in the compound before the attack, all escaped into the countryside with their comrades. It should be noted that the two Coastal Group 16 Junks that were out on patrol during the attack, oddly enough failed to answer the frantic calls for help.

Captain Chon was going to have a lot to say to his officers and staff concerning this incident. My own personal feelings were that the boats would have definitely responded had an advisor been aboard. But that is just hindsight and therefore a moot point. However, I would make sure that this lapse of response on the part of the two Junk crews would be included in my report to Captain Bjorkman stressing the fact that no advisors were aboard.

Lieutenant Taylor said that according to his information, the three advisors that managed to escape from the bunker were picked up by the Swift Boat. The assistant advisor suffered temporary blindness, the Chief Engineman had a flesh wound and the other enlisted man was unscathed.

He continued with his narration by saying that the PCE-10 had been ordered by VNN Headquarters to remain anchored in the area in the event that the Viet Cong returned. Their .40 mm gun could easily cover the compound from the mouth of the Song Tra Khuc River. The US PCF-45 had also been ordered to remain on station to provide additional security. As evening approached, the Swift Boat CO and the PCE-10's skipper along with his Naval Advisor discussed and coordinated their plan for the rest of the night.

During the ensuing hours of darkness, sporadic harassing gunfire erupted from the sandbar just to the east of the compound. The Swift Boat immediately returned suppressing fire with their .50 caliber machine guns as the gunners on the PCE-10 joined the fray. But in the darkness, they could not distinguish the Swift Boat's silhouette up close to the shore and took it under fire.

Fortunately, none of the .40 mm rounds hit the Swift and the firing was discontinued only after the VNN liaison aboard the Swift Boat made a frantic radio call to the PCE screaming to cease fire. This friendly fire was the result of jittery nerves, a lack of discipline and the total darkness that prevented the gunners from identifying the low profile of the Swift Boat.

As the three of us wandered around the base taking in the aftermath of the battle, I said to Lieutenant Taylor, "I understand from the preliminary reports that the breach occurred from the northernmost side of the base."

"That's the word that we got too."

"Then that would be at one apex of the triangle, so let's check it out."

The triangular layout of these bases was considered by the French to be the most defendable configuration for the locale in Vietnam, but the scene spread before us seemed to disprove that theory.

Approaching the far end of the base, we could see where a .50 caliber machine gun emplacement had been positioned. Although the stand remained in place, the gun was missing. The barbed wire fronting the position had been pulled down and trampled into the dirt and there was no doubt that this was where the VC entered the compound.

The most damaging bit of evidence was a length of blackened wire that was tied off at one end of the concertina wire support and stretched across the minefield to the outer wire barricade that was also downtrodden. This indicated that the VC had help from inside the base. Chon was really going to love this, I thought to myself.

Just then, the Captain and his group made their way over to us when they noticed us crouching down near the gun emplacement.

"Have you discovered something of interest?" he asked.

"It looks like someone rigged this wire as a guide through the minefield," said Lieutenant Taylor.

The look of despondency that crossed the Captain's face was only momentary as absolute rage soon turned his features blood red. He started a tirade in rapid Vietnamese that caused all of us around him to back up a few paces. I've never seen anyone so damned angry and the impotency of the moment was totally understandable. He turned on his heel and growled, "We go!"

As I shook hands with Taylor he said, "One other thing for your information. The VC somehow always know who the new Advisors are in-country and they immediately put a price on their heads." "Thanks for the tip," I said as I went to shake hands with Mr. Fields, who up to this point had not uttered a word. I was sure that he had taken in everything that he needed to see. Talk about conservation of effort.

VN NAVY HOSPITAL, QUANG NGAI

The helicopter ride to Quang Ngai was devoid of conversation. No one wanted to be the first person to break the uncomfortable silence that hung over our group. Captain Chon's ire was almost a living entity, and interrupting that would have been tantamount to being thrown bodily into an alligator pit.

We landed on a sparsely grassed area adjacent to the Medical Facility in Quang Ngai. Once out of the helo, we followed the Captain into the building where the medical staff immediately performed the obligatory ass-kissing procedure. A bespectacled Doctor, complete with the ever-present stethoscope hanging around his neck, escorted our party to the ward where the wounded from Coastal Group 16 had been isolated.

Captain Chon entered the ward and stopped just inside the double doors. The rest of us stood quietly behind him as he stood with his hands on his hips and surveyed the two rows of beds occupied by the survivors. After a few moments, he approached the first bed. The sailor's head was completely swathed in bandages and some blood was still seeping through on one side. As Chon stood quietly looking down at the young sailor who was nervously staring back at him through eyeholes cut in the gauze, the female Ensign extracted a white envelope from her briefcase and handed it to the Captain.

It is the custom in the Vietnamese Navy to present a wounded man with a conciliatory crisp, brand new five hundred piaster bill. At the present currency exchange rate, that came to about five US dollars. The solemn presentation with the murmured words of consolation and appreciation was repeated until all the wounded had received their envelopes. The ceremony concluded, our small group headed quietly back to the helicopter.

On the trip back, I thought cynically to myself, "Thank you very much for your sacrifice, get well soon and get your asses back to the job ASAP." Five whole dollars, big friggin deal!

When we finally landed at the helo-pad in Saigon, dusk was just turning to darkness over the city. Once on the hardstand, handshakes were proffered all around. The Captain asked if I would like a ride in his vehicle back downtown, but I thanked him and said that I would be heading in a different direction. I wouldn't have minded going along with the Ensign, but I couldn't bear to spend any more time with the second rate Oriental "Bogey" than I had to. Once the Captain's vehicle headed off down the street, I hailed a passing taxi and told him to take me downtown and drop me off at the McCarthy.

I barely remember the ride into town because my thoughts were still revolving around what I had witnessed today. It was only a matter of time before the base would be repaired and re-manned. I didn't envy the new quartet of American Advisors who would be assigned there. I would hope that the brain trust at headquarters would select some seasoned advisors from other bases rather than assigning four FNGs (Fucking New Guys) just in from the States. Not what I'd consider a choice assignment right off the bat, because LT Fitzgerald was the third American Naval Advisor to be killed at Coastal Group 16 up to this point. LTJG Phil Robinson was the first to die on 25 March 1966, then LT John Chapman on 2 April 1967. Well, time and fate would ultimately provide the answer, but just for the record, an Assistant Advisor, LTJG Doug Vaughn would also die from wounds received there on 20 May 1969.

Arriving finally at the BOQ, I quickly paid the driver and headed for the entrance. I decided to sprint up the stairs rather than confront anyone in the elevators. My luck was still with me as my two roomies were already in bed and fast asleep. It made me wonder why these two Saigon Warriors were so bushed at the end of the day that made them turn in so early every evening. Oh well, better off that I didn't know. There were other matters pressing me at the moment and all I could hope was that sleep would come to me as easily as it had found them. It did.

The next morning I awoke, thankfully, refreshed and dreamless. My roommates again had already departed so that left the bathroom free for me. I turned my radio on to the Armed Forces Radio Network just in time to hear the morning benediction. Oddly enough it was Captain David Cohen, an Army Chaplain and Rabbi who also resided here at the McCarthy. I jumped into the shower halfway through his sermon because I had heard rumors that he was also fond of the Tu Do Street ladies and I didn't think he could honestly offer me any form of salvation with those credentials. To be fair to the good Rabbi, he was single. Now whether or not this worked in his favor, I had no idea not being familiar with the Judaic principle concerning these matters.

I decided to grab a quick breakfast down in the cafeteria and lo and behold, there was Captain Cohen sitting alone at a table. I went over and asked if I could join him, to which he replied by merely nodding.

"I heard your inspirational offering this morning on AFVN."

"Did it help you any?" he asked as he looked at me over his coffee cup with intense dark brown eyes.

"Not really, because I'm still a virgin at heart," I replied.

"Fat chance! You Greeks are notorious philanderers. Check the history books under Helen of Troy."

"Big deal, that's only one case, even though it did start the Trojan War. By the way, did you ever think that if Jesus wasn't born a Hebrew he might have been Greek?"

"If he was, then he would have been bent over the cross instead of being crucified upright. Then you and the rest of the Christians would have wound up kissing his butt on Sunday. How would that grab you?"

"OK, OK. It was just a thought for which I deeply apologize. You win Padre."

"I always win in the end and next time, pay attention to the sermon. You most definitely need guidance," he said piously.

A waitress came over and asked for my order, which was simply an English muffin and coffee. I looked around but didn't see Quyen anywhere in the room. However, this waitress was attractive and a good bit taller than her. I couldn't help but notice that she had an appealing sensual way about her, especially when she walked. Her nametag proclaimed to all, that her name was Dawn. Now that was different because I would have expected to see that name in Japan or Korea, not Vietnam.

Captain Cohen noticed my appraising once over of the waitress and matter-of-factly said, "Someday, I would like to wake up by the crack of Dawn."

The play on words didn't escape me and I said with a grin, "Sir, you are a lecher without peers, but I couldn't agree with you more."

His reply was a wink and a wicked leer as he arose from the table and walked away with a slight swagger.

Having finished breakfast, I headed for Headquarters by the shortest route, even though I wasn't looking forward to making my preliminary report to the Captain. On the way, I was rehearsing exactly what I had planned to say, but nothing seemed to sound right to me. So, I decided to play it by ear and would try to not be intimidated by his Lordship.

Entering the Senior Naval Advisor's outer office, it was almost like de-ja-vu. Commander Selfridge was hunkered behind his desk still scarfing down the freebee Pop Tarts and drinking coffee from an ugly brown stained mug. I could only imagine what would happen if Admiral Veth, COMNAVFORV himself wandered in here unannounced. Boy, would there be some instant wedgies.

In between bites he asked, "Well how was life in the boonies?"

"A little bit different from Poulo Obi, Commander, because everyone down there is still alive."

"Captain's waiting for you," he said dourly as he wiped a crumb from his lower lip.

The Captain responded to my knock with his usual at-sea command voice that said, "Enter."

He was sitting behind his desk in freshly starched Greens with the sleeves rolled up in four inch wide folds. He gave me the once-over and indicated for me to take a seat.

"Well, what did you find out on your trip?"

I proceeded to tell him who was along from the Vietnamese side of the house and about the NILO from Da Nang and his CIA companion. This caused him to raise his eyebrows a bit. "Wasn't the First Coastal Zone Commander or his counterpart LCDR Cummings there to meet the Captain?"

"No, he had sent *Dai-Uy* Phan from his Staff," I replied.

"Boy, you can lead these horses to water but you can't get them to drink," he said with exasperation. "That wouldn't fly in our Navy, that's for damned sure."

I laughed inwardly at that and then came the sticky part: When I mentioned that all four advisors had been on the base while two Junks were out on patrol, it didn't register with him. Standard operating procedure was that at least one advisor should have been on patrol in order to prevent the lack of immediate response to the attack But all he said was, "They were lucky that they all didn't get killed."

I went on to describe how we found the guide wire that was strung through the outer perimeter minefield and made sure he understood Captain Chon's pain and anger when he saw it. I finished up by relating our trip to the Vietnamese Naval Hospital in *Quang Ngai* and the bit about the new 500 piaster bills that were distributed in white envelopes to the wounded.

"Damn! What does that get them, a bowl of noodle soup from a sidewalk seller?"

"It's purely symbolic," I said. "But it's just a neophyte Navy that was created by the French. So what can you expect?"

"Well I suppose that's true, but in any event, I want your report in writing and on my desk by the close of business today."

I stood up and said, "Aye Aye sir," then quickly took my leave and hustled out the front door before the Commander had a chance to engage me in any further conversation.

LT Morrow was sitting at his desk dutifully composing yesterday's historical entry for the record. Other than that, the only other people in the office were the two lady translators trying their darndest to appear busy. LT Morrow said a little wistfully that everyone was out in the field and under his breath I could swear I heard him say, "Lucky bastards." I really felt sorry for him because he was a Naval Academy graduate and his anguish at being relegated to spend his tour in Vietnam as a desk jockey was painfully evident. But then again, so was I, but I had plans to correct that as soon as an opportunity presented itself.

My desk was covered with the latest Newsletter inputs from the field, so that this month's work was cut out for me. You can imagine the various levels of writing that I received with regards to grammar, context and relevance. I was fast learning the art of being an editor. By rewriting all the articles myself, I had hoped to give the reader a smoother Newsletter to read instead of a hodge-podge of writing similar to Letters to the Editor columns favored by many newspapers. So far, the "Dorkman" hadn't voiced any complaints in that area.

TEDIUM

The rest of the month went by rather quickly as I spent the better part of my days chasing down the finished cartoons from Hummel and arranging for the printing and delivery of the next edition by the NAVFORV Print Shop. My office-mates had all returned from their sanctioned individual forays into the field and things were back to normal once more. One evening after work, I decided to visit the Dragon Bar alone. I wasn't in the mood for military company and the time was appropriate because LCDR Rogers was on bed-rest with a mild case of stomach flu.

The ever-sexy Marie was gracious as ever as she warmly greeted me upon my arrival. Upon seeing that I was alone, she inquired as to LCDR Rogers whereabouts. I told her he was not feeling well and was ordered to stay in bed.

Monsieur Henri was standing at the far corner of the bar and when he spied me, he took on a supercilious, aloof attitude as only a Frenchman can do. Apparently he did not consider me a serious rival for his paramour and was therefore summarily ignoring my repartee with Marie.

Rumor had it however, that Marie had recently taken on another very senior Vietnamese Navy Captain as a lover whenever he came down to Saigon from his post in Nha Trang. I surmised that Marie was definitely obtainable if the right situation presented itself and Henri's position wasn't too stable if I read their body language correctly. Theirs seemed a very tumultuous and strained relationship because I had no doubt that Henri was dipping his wick into some of the hostesses on the side. It was just a matter of time before Marie ditched him because she didn't need a Frog, who was actually a "Horny Toad," making her lose face among her employees. The Golden Dragon was her exclusive property as well as the girls who worked for her and she wasn't the type to be cuckolded by this "Misanthrope from Marseilles."

As she showed me to a small table, she informed me that both Lan and Tuyet were not working that evening. Lan had called in sick while Tuyet, unfortunately, had received word that her ARVN husband had been reported killed somewhere near the Cambodian border. To make matters worse, Tuyet had just recently discovered that she was pregnant with her second child. This was becoming an all too common occurrence in this war-torn country. After hearing that bit of news, I lost the desire that had brought me here, so I had one beer and quietly took my leave.

Somehow the atmosphere in the Dragon had changed and I decided to go elsewhere. The most logical place was the bar at the McCarthy BOQ. In the event that I would drink too much, I would only have to go topside to bed.

They were standing two deep at the bar when I arrived and I managed to elbow my way in between a couple of well-sloshed and gregarious civilians to order my beer. With the cold can of Carling's Black Label securely in my hand, I re-elbowed myself away from the bar and took an empty seat in the corner. After a few minutes of having my ears bombarded by the incessant drone of the conversations going on around me and the cloying cigarette smoke that threatened imminent emphysema, I quickly finished my beer and headed for bed.

The next morning found me mercifully with no hangover since I had only consumed two beers. I skipped breakfast and opted to have a cup of coffee in the office. When I arrived, I found several pieces of personal mail on my desk. One of them was a greeting card from a buddy of mine in the States which triggered an extraordinary coincidence. The card had the classic picture of a uniformed Napoleon staring off into the distance with his right hand tucked inside his tunic. The large lapel that covered his hand was folded over and upon opening it, there was his hand firmly gripping an upright enormous pink penis. I immediately thought about the owners of Le Corse Cafe and wondered whether they would be offended if I gave them the card. I decided to give it a little thought first. Was this weird or what?

Everyone was back in the office again and I brought LCDR Rogers up to speed about Tuyet. He took it in his usual mid-west style by raising his brows and softly saying, "That's too bad."

A flyer from the Captain was passed around the staff announcing that the bi-annual Advisor's Meeting was scheduled for next week at the MACV compound auditorium. This event assembled all the Senior Advisors throughout Vietnam to meet with Captain Bjorkman, his entire staff of officers and Rear Admiral Veth, who was COMNAVFORV.

Two days later, I had made my decision to bring the Napoleon card to Le Corse after work. Just as I entered the restaurant, a nasty bolt of lightning followed by a horrendous clap of thunder split the evening air. For a moment I thought someone had thrown a satchel charge into the street, but was relieved to see that it was only nature acting up.

The torrential downpour of rain that ensued made me thankful that I was under cover. Only Milo was behind the bar as I took a seat and ordered a beer.

"It would seem that you were fortunate to arrive when you did my friend," he said as he worried an unlit small black Italian Parodi cheroot in the side of his mouth.

"Ah, but of course," I tried to mimic with my best French-English movie accent. "By the way, I have something that I'd like to give to you and Francois. A friend of mine recently sent it to me and I immediately thought of you two." I handed over the card that I retrieved from my briefcase and handed it to him. He stared at it thoughtfully and then realized that the tunic flap opened. Upon doing so, his face reddened and he let out the loudest guffaw that I'd ever heard. Still holding the card, he bent over the bar pounding it with his fist as tears ran down his face. Combined fits of laughter and a smoker's coughing launched his cheroot over the bar and onto the floor.

WHAT MAKES YOU THINK SHE'S PART FRENCH?

"Where did you get this?" he asked as he tried to control himself. "It is *tres magnifique*."

"From a good friend in the States," I replied.

"Wait till Francois and my other compatriots see this," he said as he placed it on the mirror behind the bar for all to see. "Your drinks this evening are on the house," he announced as he vigorously shook my hand. "Do you know how badly the miserable French treated Napoleon after all the victories he provided for them? They exiled him to the island of Elba rather than to his beloved birthplace of la belle Corsica and the bastards have not changed to this day, *merde*."

"Have you heard that your lovable French are also trying to purchase the Rock of Gibralter from England at this very moment because they want to rename it DeGaulle Stone?" I asked.

"What do you expect from people who fight with their feet and fuck with their faces," he said derisively with a scowl.

I managed to have another beer to accompany my Italian Tuna plate, sliced tomatoes and hard boiled eggs quartered on crisp Romaine lettuce. Then I used the French baguette to soak up the olive oil on the bottom of the plate. A final glass of cognac rounded out the evening. As I headed across the street to the McCarthy, the rain had stopped, leaving the air fresh as it would ever be in Saigon.

The day of the Advisor's meeting had arrived and the uniform of the day was wash khakis. I rode along with Ed in his Jeep to the MACV compound and found a space in its ample parking lot.

As we entered the auditorium, we were surprised to see that everyone had arrived early. Usually, there were stragglers wandering in well after the event had started, but for some reason, today was different. It could very well be that the Advisors had been made aware of the Dorkman's displeasure with their past tardiness.

Seated on the stage were Admiral Veth, his deputy Captain Behrens and Captain Bjorkman. The hubbub in the room died down as Captain Bjorkman rose and approached the standing microphone. He proceeded with his opening remarks by welcoming the Admiral and his deputy to the Advisors meeting. Then he looked directly at me and said, "Will Lieutenant Kay please come up to the stage?"

It took me completely by surprise as I struggled to get out of my seat. Lucky for me that I had been sitting on the aisle, so I didn't have to tramp on anyone's toes getting out. On the short walk to the front, my mind was racing to recall what I had done wrong to merit this attention. I made it up the four small steps and tried my best to look military as I approached the Captain.

"For those of you who aren't familiar with Lieutenant Kay, he's the reluctant tiger on my staff. When he was reassigned here from

Coastal Group 41, I informed him that he was to produce a monthly Advisor's newsletter. He commenced to enumerate all the reasons why he wasn't qualified to undertake such a task, but those of you who know me can appreciate my obstinacy when my mind is made up."

A small trickle of laughter rose up from the audience and even the Admiral cracked a small smile. "However, after much arduous work on his part and the many man-hours he expended getting the publication up and running, I am pleased to announce that he has been awarded the CHINFO Award for the best Navy-Marine Corps Newsletter of the last quarter." A hearty round of applause broke out in the auditorium as I stepped forward to receive the award from the Admiral. A photographer snapped our picture and then I shook hands with his Deputy and Captain Bjorkman.

The Admiral stepped up to the mike and said, "This award is by no means a minor accomplishment because your editor here went up against all the newsletters produced by the Navy and the Marine Corps around the world. And he came out on top. How he did it in three short months with no background in journalism, is indeed a feat. Not to mention the fact that most of the other newsletters are produced in well equipped printing shops staffed with all sorts of support personnel. Kay has done it all by enlisting the help of Petty Officer Jim Hummel, a cartoonist from the NAVSUPPAC Staff, Saigon and the NAVFORV print shop manager Petty Officer Bill DeVries; A hearty 'Well Done' Lieutenant."

I tried to look as humble as I could, while inside I wanted to jump up and down and wave my arms as if I had just won the Irish Sweepstakes. I made it back to my seat as Ed said, "Atta boy kiddo, maybe this'll keep the Dorkman off your ass now."

The rest of the meeting was a carbon copy of last quarter's in that it droned on about what great strides we had been making. I'm sure all this was for future reference when it came time for Captain

Bjorkman's end of tour Legion of Merit award. Cynical yes, but right on the money, I would wager.

Lieutenant Morrow joined Ed and me in the Jeep as we headed towards Tan Son Nhut air base where we had decided to try their newly opened Mexican restaurant. On the way over, George asked if we had heard about the NILO from My Tho.

"Isn't that Lieutenant Jerry Palmer?" I asked. "He lived next door to me at Coronado. What happened?"

"They said he took his Jeep and headed south out of My Tho down Highway 4 sometime after midnight the day before yesterday. When they discovered he was missing, an all-out search was started. They finally found him asleep in his Jeep beside a rice paddy in Camau and from all reports; he was stone sober, although totally incoherent. They brought him to the medical facility in Can Tho where they have him under observation."

"Man, he must have flipped out to drive by himself into VC country after dark. I wonder what triggered that?" said Ed.

"Got me," answered George. "How well did you know him Bob?"

"Hardly saw him at all during our time in Coronado, except at physical training. In fact, I had the impression that he was shacked up on the beach since he wasn't in his room much. He was a loner who didn't hang around the base after classes, but he could have had a wife or girlfriend on the outside."

"Well, it takes all kinds," said Ed philosophically in his mid-western way as we arrived at the restaurant.

The meal was so-so, considering that all the cooks were Vietnamese. We'd have been better off getting a bowl of *Pho* from a street vendor rather than incur a case of *agida* from the spicy pseudo-burritos. On the way back to the BOQ, I'm sure all three of us were anticipating a severe case of the "squirts" after indulging in our ill-advised trip to the "Mexican" restaurant.

I awoke the next morning surprisingly without any ill effects, but to be on the safe side, I decided to forgo any breakfast and opt for a cup of Navy coffee at the office.

Ed and George were already at their desks and fortunately, both reported no digestive problems from the previous evening. My telephone rang just as I was pouring my much awaited cup of coffee. It was the Captain's Yeoman telling me that my presence was required immediately by the Captain.

"Damn! What did I do now?" I said under my breath as I put the cup on my desk, grabbed my hat and headed below as requested.

As I crossed the compound from the main building, I saw Captain Bjorkman standing on the top of the three cement steps leading to his office. He was hatless and dressed in starched greens with a large manila envelope under his arm. Upon seeing me, he came down the steps and met me halfway.

"I want you to follow me to Captain Chon's office," he said.

Wow, I must be in deeper trouble than I imagined was the thought that went through my mind. I couldn't get a read on the Captain's demeanor so I decided to let it play out. I would find out soon enough.

We entered the main building and made our way up to the second deck where the head of the Vietnamese Navy had his offices. The outer office was sparsely furnished with two desks, one of which belonged to Ensign Chao, the female aide and the other to the Administration Yeoman. Chao, who looked pristine in her uniform and pretty as a picture, escorted us into the Captain's office. As we entered, Chon got up quickly from behind his desk and came forward to greet us.

"It's a pleasure to see you Captain Bjorkman," he said with a perfunctory shake of hands. Turning to me, he said, "It is also a pleasure to see you again Lieutenant Kay. I suspect that you have no idea of why I summoned you here," he said with an impish grin on his face. The look of bewilderment on my face was all he needed to corroborate his assessment. "Captain Bjorkman, would you care to make the first presentation?"

The Captain cleared his throat and turned to face me as Chon and the Ensign stepped slightly to the rear of him. Bjorkman had taken a blue folder out of the envelope and proceeded to open it and read the enclosed citation. It described my part in the interdiction of a Singaporean fishing trawler in the act of weapons smuggling to the enemy. Moreover, my instinct and keen observation of the boat's activities plus realizing that the hold had been full upon the first inspection, led to the ultimate seizure of a considerable amount of contraband. For this accomplishment, the Secretary of the Navy was proud to award me the Navy Commendation Medal with Combat "V".

As the Captain proceeded to pin the medal on my jacket, I was dumfounded and all I could manage to mumble was, "Thank you sir," as he shook my hand. Bjorkman then stepped back as Captain Chon stepped forward. Ensign Chao held out a rose colored pillow that held another medal. Captain Chon proceeded to read a citation that pretty much repeated the previous one and ended with the pinning of the Vietnamese Cross of Gallantry with a silver palm next to my Commendation Medal.

Captain Chon then congratulated me heartily and gave my hand a strong handshake. "Now it's customary to celebrate with a cup of tea for our new warrior," he said patting me on the shoulder. I could see out of the corner of my eye that Bjorkman was feeling a little uncomfortable over the attention I was receiving and inwardly it made me feel good.

At the conclusion of the ceremony and the small talk that followed during the drinking of tea, Captain Bjorkman and I bade our goodbyes as we made our way to the door. On the way out, I caught a slight wink from Ensign Chao and I made a mental note to explore this possibility in the future.

Going down the stairs, Bjorkman asked me gruffly why I hadn't apprised him of that little feat when he welcomed me to Staff and berated me about my "John Wayne" antics with the Junks.

"The event happened before you assumed command of the Advisory Group and I didn't think at that time that you were interested in hearing any rebuttals from your subordinates, sir."

With a gruff "Harrumph," he reached the courtyard and said, "Carry on," over his shoulder as he strode back to his office.

I climbed back up the stairs to my office carrying both citations and the medals still pinned on my greens thinking to myself that the Dorkman appeared a little embarrassed by the awards. As soon as I entered, catcalls and whistles greeted me from my office-mates. "We've got a real live hero in our midst," said Commander Johnson grinning from ear to ear,

"Shucks pa, tweren't nothing," I said adapting a sheepish grin. The citations were passed around the room and a warm feeling engulfed me as I thought that things didn't get any better than this.

BOAT FORCE HEADQUARTERS

After that, one week ran into another and all of us in the office were starting to get tired of looking at each other. It appeared that I was the only one next to George, who always had paperwork to do. The pressure to maintain a high standard with each ensuing newsletter was starting to get me down.

Then one Saturday morning, Ed came in and asked if I would like to accompany him to visit his counterpart at the Boat Force Headquarters. They were having a party for no particular reason and Ed wanted me along for company. I jumped at the chance to break the monotonous daily routine.

"Do I have to bring anything, beer, soda, whiskey?"

"No, I've already taken care of that. The parties are like drinking marathons and as you'll see, they can't hold their liquor too well. By the way, they'll try their damndest to get us drunk, so be ready."

"I've been through that drill with the Junk Force boys. I'm beginning to think that it's a national custom trying to see who the last one standing is."

"Well, the odds are in our favor since we're physically larger and have a bigger capacity for alcoholic intake. Wear your wash khakis and spread on the cologne because there'll be *beaucoup* females there too. I'll pick you up outside the McCarthy at 1800," he said on his way out to get a haircut.

At precisely 1800, Ed pulled up in front of the BOQ.

It's amazing, that those of us who were or are in the military, punctuality is not only a trait of pride but a habit borne of the respect for others. I cannot remember any instances where I was relieved late for watch or I was late relieving a shipmate. The Vietnamese, on the other hand, placed little importance on time when it came to keeping appointments. As long as they showed up, the specified time was inconsequential and their obligation was considered fulfilled.

We drove down to the waterfront and turned right until we reached the bridge by the famous My Canh Floating Restaurant. The My Canh was a large ferry boat that had been converted into a popular eatery that is until a VC sapper exploded a claymore mine directly across from the gangway and killed several people. This happened before my initial arrival in Saigon, but word had already reached Coronado. Needless to say that business had dropped off dramatically until only recently when the patrons began to timidly return.

Once you crossed the bridge, you had the Khanh Hoi section on the right and Thi Nghe on the left. The Boat Force compound was on the Thi Nghe side and was located almost directly across the river from Vietnamese Naval Headquarters. Now I would have a reference point if I ever had to stand Monday morning formations again listening to Captain Chon exhort the troops.

As I had mentioned before, the Commanding Officer of the River Boat Force was a VNN Lieutenant Commander, whereas the rest of the officers and men were in the ARVN. I found this intra-service configuration a little strange, wondering why army personnel were used to man their boats instead of sailors. Perhaps that was another throwback from the French.

Ed introduced me to his counterpart, Lieutenant Commander Khanh, who immediately congratulated me for having received the medals from Poulo Obi. I was a little taken aback until I realized that Ed must have told Khanh beforehand that I would be coming with him and about my awards. We shook hands amiably as I thanked him for having me at the party.

Khanh seemed a little older than usual for his rank which made me think that this may have had something to do with his current assignment at the Boat Force. In our Navy, we refer to this as a Twilight Tour. Other than his age, his most notable feature was his hair. It was black, untouched by gray, about two inches long on top and stood straight up from his head. I guess they hadn't heard about hair gel or pomade in these parts yet.

Next, I was introduced to his second in command, ARVN Captain Cat. Now here was a slick looking individual, not in a physical sense, but in his affectation. He wore narrow, black wraparound sunglasses at all times and had a suave way of conversing with strangers, giving him the air of sophistication. His face was smooth and slightly angular and the only physical drawback seemed to be his teeth; they were badly discolored from his constant smoking habit. I was informed however, that he always dealt with his subordinates in a no-nonsense military manner. Apparently, he was the CO's enforcer and obviously a good one. I could see why Ed referred to him as "Ninh the Cat."

After more introductions to the remaining officers and senior noncoms present, we settled ourselves around a long table that was set with individual glasses and chop-sticks. Innumerable bowls heaped with steaming boiled rice were brought out and several pots of vinegar were busily bubbling away over small hibachis. Platters arrived covered with lime slices, mint leaves, cilantro, bean sprouts and several other types of green leafed vegetables with which I wasn't familiar. The larger platters held thin strips of raw beef and small bowls of Nuoc Mam with more than the usual amount of small, thinly sliced red chili peppers added, sat in front of each person.

Lastly, several large galvanized tubs of ice containing bottles of frosted "33" beer were placed on the floor behind the table. I thought to myself as I saw Ed broadly smiling at me from across the table, that this had all the earmarks of one damned good party.

"Have you ever eaten *Thit Bo Nhun Giam*?" asked Khanh as he picked up several slices of beef with his chopsticks and placed them into the boiling vinegar.

"No, I haven't, but I'm looking forward to trying it," I replied as I too placed a few strips into the pot.

"The trick is not to let the meat overcook," said Ed, as he too added a piece into the boiling vinegar.

I watched Khanh as he took the cooked slices and placed them onto a narrow lettuce leaf, added various greens and bean sprouts and deftly rolled it up. He then dipped the roll into the Nuoc Mam and took a healthy bite out of it. Following Khanh's lead, I managed to roll a decent combination on my first try and then dipped and ate. Wow, was that good. I looked across at Ed and saw that he too was enjoying the meal immensely.

This is better than any of the tailgate parties I used to go to at Soldier Field and Yankee Stadium," I said to Ed.

Ninh the Cat looked a little puzzled at my remark so I had to explain what a tailgate party was, where and when they were held and what we ate there. He smiled at my explanation and said smoothly that it sounded like fun.

We worked on the main course for about an hour during which the beer supply had to be replenished several times. As I looked down along the length of our table, the faces of many of the men were noticeably crimson and creased with broad-toothed grins.

With the main course finished, large bowls of mixed tropical fruits were placed on the table. The Vietnamese seemed to favor the big oranges which had to be imported and could only be bought on the black market. Since Thi Nghe contained several deep water piers, obtaining fresh fruit was easy because the huge freighters berthed close by to offload their cargo. As in any port in the world, produce and material goods mysteriously had a way of going astray and disappearing before they reached the warehouses.

To complement the fruit, several liter bottles of a clear liquid were brought to the table.

"Ah, here is the Ba Xi De," announced Khanh, whose face was also tinged with red. Directing his question to me, he asked, "*Dai-Uy*, have you ever had Ba Xi De?"

"FIRST TIME YOU DRINK BA-XI-DE LIEUTENANT?"

"Yes I have, but I still am not sure what it's made of."

"Good! In that case, please join us. It is a very popular wine made from rice and most commonly made and drank throughout the Vietnamese countryside."

Khanh poured me a small glass of the clear fluid and as I raised it to my lips, I again got the faint aroma of kerosene or JP-5 jet fuel. Not wanting to offend my hosts, who at this point all had their eyes on me, I downed the liquid quickly. It was a good thing that I had sampled this liquid nitro before up in the lighthouse on Poulo Obi. The difference however, was that this stuff had been iced down and was much more palatable than that served by Dat, the bat-slayer. It was assuredly an acquired taste so I bravely pushed my glass forward for a refill. This brought applause of approval from everyone, including Ed, whose face was also starting to color up nicely.

At this point in the festivities, two young Vietnamese men with long hair and amplified guitars appeared on the small stage in the front of the room. As they tuned their instruments, a lovely petite young lady in a pale green Ao Di with white pants glided delicately to the microphone. At first, a hush fell over the group, quickly followed by enthusiastic whistles and applause. Cat leaned over to me and said that this was Co Thanh, one of South Vietnam's favorite singers.

Shyly acknowledging her reception, she thanked the audience in a diminutive voice that I had a hard time hearing. She then nodded back to her accompaniment and quickly launched into a ballad which was familiar to me. Co Thanh exhibited good stage presence, despite her soft speaking and her tonal range was amazing, almost effortless.

The rice wine had put me in a relaxed mood and the melodies flowed easily from one song to another. When Co Thanh's performance ended, an exuberant round of applause erupted as she introduced another vocalist who was mounting the stage. This one was in her mid thirties and wore a black Ao Di adorned with a golden flower and green leaves down the bodice. The flower accented the fullness of her body and the size of her breasts had more than likely been the work of a plastic surgeon. Cat again leaned over and said, "This is Xuan Ha. She has sung for a long time and her husband who plays piano, has written many of the love songs that she sings."

Her delivery was slow, low and throaty which helped peak the alcohol soaked libido of the men in the room. Glancing over at Ed, he seemed caught up in the moment as he listened raptly to the singer. I could see that the rice wine was helping to transport him to a higher plateau as evidenced by the fixed lopsided grin on his face. He caught me looking at him and clumsily raised his glass in a gesture of camaraderie.

Xuan Ha finished her three song set, gracefully bowed and thanked everyone sincerely for their appreciative applause. Before leaving the stage, she announced the next act introducing them as the Three Sisters.

The men were on their feet applauding and whistling as the three lovely young girls stepped onto the stage.

The three of them were dressed in tight white denim jeans with multi-colored tank tops that failed to hide the fact that they were braless. Each girl had her hair pulled up and back in a pony tail and their feet were clad in sockless white sneakers. They introduced each other as Chi Hai, Chi Ba and Chi Tu, which translated meant number two, number three and number four sister. This was the standard method of identifying female siblings in Vietnamese society. They brought an energy to the party that up to now had been somewhat subdued by the traditional songs offered by the previous singers. The girls were extremely talented and animated as they performed "Cherish," "I'm Feeling Blue," and finishing with a lively rendition of Nancy Sinatra's "These Boots Were Made for Walking."

The place was liquor and male hormone induced pandemonium as the girls retreated from the stage to resounding applause from the appreciative audience. *Dai-Uy* Cat had slipped up to the side of the stage, whispered something to the three women, who in turn looked at each other and nodded in the affirmative. With that, he led them to our table. Three chairs appeared magically as he seated Chi Hai, the oldest next to me, Chi Ba, the least attractive next to Ed and the cutest, Chi Tu next to him . . . . naturally.

None of the girls opted for the rice wine, but settled for cans of orange soda. Clean plates were placed before them so they could partake of whatever food and fruit remained. It's funny how you can tell when a party should come to an end. People stop drinking and quietly sit back in their chairs and stare with a glazed look on their faces. Such was the case here.

Khanh looked more than ready to hit the sack as he unsteadily got to his feet. Raising his arms for attention, he said that he hoped everyone had enjoyed themselves and thanked Ed and me for attending. "You are most welcomed here any time," he said as he looked at us through red bleary eyes.

Cat, in the meantime, had been in an urgent conversation with Chi Tu. He got up and whispered something in Ed's ear that I could not make out from where I sat. Ed looked up at me and then back to Cat as he told him that it wouldn't be a problem.

"What's up?" I asked getting Ed's attention.

"Cat asked me if we could drive the other two sisters home, since it's getting close to curfew and taxis are scarce, especially out here at this time of night."

"I go along with that." It was obvious that Cat had other plans for the younger sister, poor girl. And sure enough, as we were leaving, I looked over my shoulder just in time to see Cat corralling Chi Tu into his personal sleeping quarters.

We loaded the two remaining sisters into the back of Ed's Jeep and I jumped in front.

"Where to?" Ed asked trying to act more sober than he was.

"You know where Phan Dinh Phung and Le Van Duyet is?" asked Chi Hai softly.

"Sure do," he said as he proceeded to steer a sinuous course back across the bridge towards downtown Saigon.

Once we arrived at the location, Chi Hai pointed to a large green metal double gate beneath the sprawling branches of a huge chestnut tree.

"Stop here and I will open the gate so you can park inside," Chi Hai said as she squeezed out of the Jeep.

Ed and I threw a quick glance at each other, instantly realizing that we were being invited to stay. The two girls led us into a two story brick building that Chi Ba said belonged to them. Their widowed mother and three smaller siblings still lived near Tay Ninh, close to the Cambodian border. The two older sisters had been married, but Chi Ba's husband deserted her for another girl and Chi Hai's had been killed serving with the Vietnamese Rangers two years ago. Only Chi Tu was still unwed, but I surmised, not a virgin either.

Since I was raised not to demean my sexual partners by volunteering to graphically describe the events that took place between the sheets, positions, frequency or quality of the previous night's encounter, I will only say, "Ooya!"

Ed, on the other hand, honestly confided that he had suffered from early fallout on his first two attempts which prompted Chi Ba to refuse a third trip to the well of joy. His failure most likely could be attributed to the copious amounts of alcohol that he had consumed at the party. I would have liked to have been in the walls as the sisters critiqued our performances after we left. Oh well, it should all be fun when the job's well done.

PAYING THE PIPER

My smugness and self-satisfaction stemming from that one incredible evening with Chi Hai came to a screeching halt with the first signs of itching in my urethral canal followed by a burning sensation when I urinated. In a state of denial and disbelief that Chi Hai's oasis of love's waters had been tainted, I hurried off to see the duty Hospital Corpsman at Sick Bay.

Hospitalman First Class Murphy was just finishing up Sick Call as I came through the door on the ground floor of the compound. His little office was tucked away in the rear and he treated all the usual maladies that affect sailors since time immemorial.

He looked up and said, "What can I do for you Lieutenant?"

"Think I've contracted a case of 'Old Joe,' probably from that dirty toilet seat at the Rex last night," I said off-handedly.

"Did you now? And you an officer and a gentleman," he said with a pseudo Irish brogue and an air of humor in his eyes. "I'll need a smear sample so I can ID whatever little bug you've picked up. Then we'll know what medication to give you to clear it up. I hope for your sake that it's not one of those resistant strains."

"Me too," I said as I gently milked down my penis to get some fluid onto the slide that he gave me. "To be honest with you I was an officer and a gentleman, but obviously it didn't matter."

After examining the slide under the microscope, he looked up and said, "You lucked out this time Lieutenant because you've got the standard garden variety of bacteria known as *Neisseria Gonorrhoeae*, so I can highly recommend the quick 'Kill or Cure' treatment. You'll take ten Tetracycline pills now, ten more in four hours and ten more after another six hours. It usually does the trick, especially since we're getting an early jump on it. By the way, I'll make sure this doesn't get into your medical file." Two years later, I was to learn that the Upjohn Pharmaceutical people had come up with a single injection in your buttocks called "Trobicin." Its main attribute was that it cleared up the infection in 24 hours. Oh, what a relief it is!

Taking the small white envelope with the pills, I thanked him from the bottom of my heart (and my urethra) as I poured myself a cup of water from the cooler to wash down the first dose.

As I returned to my office and plopped down in my chair, Ed looked up and said, "Why so glum, chum?"

"To put it plainly old buddy, those three sisters last night got the applause but I got the Clap."

"Are you shittin' me?" he asked as he straightened upright from his usual slouched relaxed position.

"Yup. I just got back from Sick Bay with enough Tetracycline to immunize me from leprosy for life."

"Oh man, that means I'd better get checked out myself," he said with furrowed brow.

"Only if you think you got in deep enough," I answered flippantly and I immediately regretted having said that.

He looked up sharply and noticing my discomfort said with a wry smile, "I don't think anyone's ever plumbed Chi Ba's depths. Aside from your companion being the conveyor of VD, how was she otherwise?"

"Well, since you asked, she had one of the tightest mousetraps that I have ever encountered in my life. She had so much muscular control of her vaginal walls that once you were up against the stops; it felt like you were stuck in an automatic milker on a dairy farm that was preset for six quarts."

All Ed could do was look at me forlornly and shake his head.

"Well," I continued, still trying to take my foot out of my mouth, "It's only the second time that I've had the 'Social Disease.' I picked that up on my first trip to Naples, Italy."

So, as the days went on and the medication did its job, I noticed however that I had a slight yellowing around the whites of my eyes and my appetite had diminished a little. But that too went away and life returned to normal.

Finally, the end of the month rolled around, bringing payday and another edition of the Newsletter was ready for distribution. My telephone rang and it was Norman, the Captain's Yeoman informing me that the old man wanted to see me on the double.

"What's it about?" I asked.

His only reply was, "Dunno," followed by a short chuckle just before the line went dead.

The reason for the Yeoman's cynicism became clear as I found myself, along with seven other sailors, standing at attention before the Captain's desk.

"Do you people know what this paper is in my hand?" he growled as his angry eyes washed over each of us.

Since no one replied, he continued, "It's the monthly VD Report that I have been getting from the Medical Department. And guess whose names made the hit parade this month?" he snarled with a glare that would burn asbestos. "Are your morals so lax that you have to engage in illicit sex? I know that some of you must have wives and girlfriends at home. How would you feel if they betrayed you like that? Navy men should pride themselves in being able to keep it in their trousers. We're a cut above the other services because their camp followers are always close by, whereas the harlots can't tempt us when we're at sea. Especially you Mister Kay, I would have expected more from you as an officer and a leader. What have you to say for yourselves?" he asked as he sat back heavily in his chair.

"Well Captain," I said, deciding to take the bull by the horns. "The eight of us here had spent an hour at most getting treated at Sick Bay. That's a sum total of eight lost man-hours, whereas there were six reported cases of flu among Headquarters personnel that required three days bed rest for each man. Their incapacitation resulted in eighteen lost work days."

"So what's your point?"

"My point is, that comparing a loss of a mere eight man-hours against eighteen man days, I venture to say that contracting a venereal infection is more beneficial for the Navy than being bedridden with the flu. Besides, if any of us had a choice, we would choose the sexually transmitted disease because it is more enjoyable to get and with less discomfort than the flu, sir."

The row of sailors started to fidget uneasily as they tried hard to suppress the laughter that was threatening to explode from their grinning faces. The Captain, not quite believing what he had just heard, almost had an apoplectic fit. He bolted up from his chair, face blood red, pointed to the door and shouted for us to get the hell out of his office.

As our group of sinners erupted from the Captain's office heading for the outer door, the XO and Yeoman Norman were taken by surprise. Commander Selfridge flew out from behind his desk and ran into the Captain's office fearing the worst. He pulled up short when he saw the Captain leaning forward with both hands on the desk and taking deep breaths. Regaining his composure, the Captain sat down, leaned back in his chair and calmly crossed his legs. He looked up at Selfridge and said in a low modulated voice, "Everything's under control. Please shut the door behind you as you leave."

By this time I was thinking that this encounter with the Dorkman would make me a living legend within the Advisory Group because what had just transpired would spread like wildfire.

I managed to avoid any further contact with the Captain for the next few weeks, and for that I was extremely grateful.

A few days later, two scruffy men wearing floppy bush hats, wrinkled greens and boots covered with red clay, noisily entered our office. I recognized them despite their disheveled appearance as Lieutenant John Kelleher and his assistant Senior Chief Gunner's Mate Shipp. They were the RAG 27 advisors out of Cat Lai and we had gone through Coronado together. Kelleher had been in my language class and on several occasions, tossed back a few beers with me in the Green Anchors. I remembered the Senior Chief because he brought a Montagnard spear and a bow to show us that he had carried back from a previous tour in Vietnam. Other than that, he remained pretty much invisible because when PT was over at the end of the day, he would head home to San Diego where he had a standard issue wife and family.

Kelleher's previous duty station before being assigned to Vietnam was as Chief Engineer on a destroyer. Coincidentally, LCDR Klamath, sitting across from me, had been his XO.

"Gunner and I came into town to get some clean clothes and decided as long as we were in the area we'd stop by for a visit."

"Good to see you again John," Klamath said as he came around the desk to shake hands with him. "It's been awhile. I hear you guys have been busy down in the Rung Sat."

"Yeah, you know how it is. Most of the time, Charlie's already taken off by the time we get there. They gotta have someone in VNN Ops tipping them off, I'm convinced of that."

"You got that right," mumbled the Chief bitterly as he sat leaning back in the empty chair next to my desk.

"Hey, Lieutenant, I read your article in the Newsletter about your trip to Coastal Group 16. That must have been pretty grim I'll bet," remarked Gunner.

"That it was Senior Chief. There's a lot of frustration when it comes to fighting the VC. Some of the guys swear by the Vietnamese units they're assigned to and others swear at them."

"I know exactly what you mean. Me and the *Dai-Uy* here are pretty lucky in RAG 27. Rach the CO, is a tornado when it comes to tangling with Charlie and he expects no less from his men."

"That's a fact," added Kelleher, "And I'd bet he'd shoot any of his crew personally if they chickened out in a firefight."

"Sounds like a good man," I said.

"He is," added Gunner. "And two more out of that same mold are Minh of RAG 30 and Gia of RAG 24."

Kelleher said to me, "I seem to recall that you had orders to the Junk Force before we left Coronado. What happened?"

"It's a long story involving internal politics. I'll tell you all about it over a case of beer some time."

"Hey, since he sent you to Coastal Group 16, do you think the old man would let you ride downriver with us? You could write a story about how us 'real' advisors operate," he said laughing.

"I'd love it. Anything to get away from this place and these REMFs that I have to put with in this office," I said jokingly. "I'll try and clear it with the Captain. How do I get in touch with you?"

"We'll be in town for the next two days and then we're heading down to Ben Luc. I'm in the McCarthy, so you can reach me there."

"I'm there too. I'll let you know, and thanks for the offer."

With that, both men waved and left.

When they were clear of the office, Klamath leaned back in his chair and said, "Kelleher's a good officer, a damned good Chief Engineer and a hard charging SOB. But he plays as hard as he works and I haven't met anyone yet that he couldn't drink under the table.

One night while we were in port, we lost the electrical load which left the ship in total darkness. Even the emergency lights failed to come on. I knew John didn't have the duty, but I felt as Chief Engineer, he should be informed. His stateroom was close to mine, so I decided to go wake him up.

As I entered his pitch black room, the acrid smell of stale cigarettes, sweat and sour beer almost gagged me. Apparently, he had been on the beach and somehow got back aboard ship without breaking his neck staggering up the brow or down the ladder to his bunk. I could hear his heavy breathing in the dark, so I inched forward with hands outstretched feeling for his body.

When I finally managed to find him, I tried to shake him out of his stupor by telling him that we had lost the load. He jumped out of the bunk, eyes as big as a lemur's and yelled for someone to turn on the friggin' lights so he could find his shoes. It was at that point that I realized he was in no condition to tackle the problem, so I gently pushed him back onto the bunk and left. He was snoring before I managed to grope my way back out into the passageway."

"Wow, I hope he doesn't get like that before he goes out on the river," I said.

"He won't, that's not his nature."

The next morning, I went down to the head office to speak to the Captain. The XO was not in his customary chair, most likely out trying to scrounge up some free Pop Tarts for breakfast. The pussy-faced, constipated Yeoman however, was there and I told him to see if the Captain was available. I seemed to have a problem with this puke ever since day-one for some reason or other.

He got up sullenly from behind his desk, knocked on the door twice and stuck his head in the Captain's office. I couldn't hear what was said, but he turned around and mumbled that the Captain would see me. During the entire encounter, the twit avoided direct eye contact with me. He must have just missed getting into the WAVES by virtue of having a small penis, I thought.

"Good morning Bob," the Captain said amiably. "What can I do for you?"

"Well Captain, since this month's edition is already being distributed, I was thinking that perhaps you could authorize me to strap-hang with one of the RAG units for a few days. I would like to familiarize myself with the scope of their day-to-day operations and perhaps even accompany them on a patrol. That way, I could get some real-time information for the Newsletter."

Momentarily digesting my request he said, "That's a darn good idea. Now you're getting the hang of it. Do you have any specific unit in mind?"

"Yes sir, RAG 27 out of Cat Lai. Lieutenant Kelleher asked me yesterday if I'd be interested in a trip downriver and I told him that I'd have to clear it with you first.

"Where are they going?"

"Down to Ben Luc; they're going to re-supply their second Monitor and two STCAN/FOMs that have been patrolling that area for the past two weeks.

Local intelligence reports had indicated that the VC were out to destroy the Ben Luc Bridge that spans the Vam Co Dong River. It was vital because it linked Highway 4 between Saigon and all points to the south."

"Permission granted and Kay, don't make me regret this decision."

"Aye sir," I replied as I happily exited his office and totally ignored the quizzical look on the Yeoman's face as I passed through.

I went back up to my office to secure my desk and let the guys know that I'd be gone for a few days.

"Where are you headed this time?" asked George as he looked up from the piles of paperwork covering his desk.

"Got the OK to ride RAG 27 down to Ben Luc," I said feeling sorry for poor desk-bound George.

"How did you ever con the old man into letting you go?" asked Ed. "You must be out of the doghouse, eh?"

"Who knows and furthermore, who cares," I replied. "Listen, I'm taking the rest of the day off to get ready and if anyone asks, I'm over at NAVFORV."

"Gotcha covered," said Ed as he went back to eating sunflower seeds that his wife regularly sent to him.

"Some guys have all the luck," murmured George as he continued his labor intensive writing of the Staff's history.

Leaving the office, I practically flew down the stairs because of another small victory attained by my getting back out into the field again. As I made my way along the streets to the BOQ, I shuddered at the thought that I could have been originally assigned to a desk riding Staff position in Vietnam. God only knew what my attitude towards in-country service would have been had it not been for the time spent on Poulo Obi with the Junk Force, brief though it had been. That period of time further kindled my desire to work at something for which I could be proud of and be able to eventually relate to my children.

Entering the McCarthy, I glanced into the bar and noticed Kelleher sitting by himself with a half empty can of Budweiser

in front of him.

"Hey John," I said. "Getting an early start?"

"Not really. Somewhere in this screwed up world, the sun's already over the yardarm. Besides, the cafeteria is closed getting ready for lunch and the maid is still cleaning my room."

"Well, believe it or not, the old man gave me permission to go with you guys. What's the plan?"

"Bring enough gear for a few days along with your rifle and meet me in the lobby tomorrow morning at 0530. The Chief will swing by and pick us up with the Jeep."

"Will do," I replied as I left him at the bar. It was a little too early in the day for me to start drinking, so I headed to my room to get my stuff ready for tomorrow.

As I entered the room, Ba Tu was busily making up the beds.

"Chao *Dai-Uy*, no work today?" she asked looking up at me.

"I have to go on a trip tomorrow," purposely omitting to tell her where because of security restrictions.

"You go long?"

"Oh, just for a few days."

"You be near VC?"

"Ba Tu, no matter where you go in Vietnam, you'll always be near VC."

Nodding her head knowingly, she looked up at me sadly and said, "You be careful, OK *Dai-Uy*?"

"I promise," I replied as she left the room and quietly closed the door behind her.

Once all my gear had been assembled and packed, I decided to answer a couple of overdue letters from my relatives back home. I had been severely lax in that department even though I knew my mother and grandmother would be worried sick every time they watched the grossly misreported news from Vietnam. It wasn't in my heart to tell them that I was enjoying my duty over here and that I couldn't be any happier. Instead, I commented on things like my CHINFO Award and the success of the Newsletter. I had just finished writing a letter to my mother when Captain Park, my Korean roommate entered the room.

"Ah, good to see you again," he said. "They must keep you very busy because our paths hardly cross."

"Yes, I try to get into the field because I hate office work."

Captain Park and I had a very genial relationship partly because of the fact that I had been involved with the Inchon landing. Most Koreans, especially the officers, are slightly aloof and arrogant, but Park was just the opposite. He had told me at length about his wife and little boy back in Korea and his desire to get home as quickly as possible. He was the consummate professional soldier and definitely not a bar hopper.

I went down to the cafeteria to eat a lunch that sadly turned out to be lackluster, then decided to return to my quiet air conditioned room and turn in early. But sleep eluded me until I finished reading two chapters in a book by Wilbur Smith about early Africa. Reading in bed at night had become a habit that helped me clear my mind of the superfluous thoughts that normally kept me awake. Thankfully, it still worked.

PART EIGHT

RAG 27, BEN LUC

The next morning I was up prior to the alarm going off. Having showered the night before, all I had to do was get dressed in the dark so as not to wake up my slumbering roommates and head out. Kelleher was already standing in the lobby puffing away on a cigarette as I came down the stairs.

"All set?" he asked.

"Sure am. I appreciate this chance to get out of the city," I said

"Don't think I could handle being deskbound at Headquarters. There's too much damn traffic, too many civilians and too many chicken-shit restrictions. At least on the river, you're kinda on your own. Know what I mean?"

"Indeed I do, that's why I'm still trying to figure out a way to get back into the field."

"Would you extend a year to get that?"

"Why not? I can't see myself going back to stateside sea duty just yet. I volunteered to come over here as an advisor, not to be a paper pushing office weenie."

"In that case, look around for an advisor whose tour is up about the same time as yours and go after the old man to approve you moving over. You've got nothing to lose and he owes you."

"That's a good idea. Actually, I never considered that approach, thanks."

Just then, the Chief came screeching to a stop out front. I jumped into the back with our gear as Kelleher plopped into the front passenger seat positioning his rifle between his legs.

In order to get to Cat Lai, we had to go over the Long Binh Bridge across the Saigon River and head north on Highway 1. The trip took less than a half hour since there was no other traffic yet on the road. As we entered the little village of Cat Lai, the Chief made a quick left into a US Army compound where we would leave the Jeep. We grabbed our gear and left the base walking towards the pier where RAG 27's Commandament was moored. Since we were a little early, Kelleher decided that we had time for some iced coffee at one of the little shops lining the road.

It was very pleasant sitting around a table under a thatched overhang while we drank our iced coffee. It was sweetened with canned evaporated milk so sugar wasn't necessary.

"Boy, this is the life," I said.

"Yeah, no horseshit regulations to follow around here *Dai-Uy*," said the Chief with a grin.

As we talked, the owner's small son came out to see us. He had on a New York Yankee's baseball cap, no shirt and below his red faded shorts, a prosthetic right leg. That took me by surprise because the boy couldn't have been more that 6 years old.

"This is Vu," said Kelleher picking him up and putting him on his lap. "One of his friends stepped on an old French mine while they were playing in the field outside the base a couple of years ago and Vu caught some shrapnel which resulted in his losing the leg. Cat Lai used to be a French seaplane base and the whole area probably still has mines around the perimeter. Vu was one of the lucky ones because the blast killed two little girls and one boy, who happened to be his next oldest brother."

"God, that's tough. Why doesn't the army clear the area of all that old ordnance?"

"What for?" piped in the Chief. "It helps protect their flank because the local VC also know about the mines."

"So, don't wander into the brush, you're telling me."

"Roger that." said Kelleher tickling Vu and making him squirm with glee.

"He manages really well on that wooden leg. Who outfitted him?" I asked.

"Actually, my predecessor, Lieutenant Stengle was responsible for that. When he heard what had happened, he brought Vu and his mother to the Seventh Day Adventist Hospital in Saigon for treatment. The docs operated on him for three hours, debriding the wound and amputating the leg below the knee. They kept him and his mother there through post-op and therapy until his stump was healed enough for fitting a prosthetic. Then came another two weeks of intensive walking therapy for the little guy; and the best part of all was that it was all done for free."

"That will make a great article for the newsletter. We need more positive stories like that to make it back to the folks at home instead of the garbage being dreamed up and written by the fearless news correspondents on the roof of the Rex."

"Make it happen, Hemingway," drawled Kelleher.

As if on cue, LCDR Rach arrived in his Jeep. His driver pulled up in front of our table as Rach said, "Good morning gentlemen. Are you ready to go aboard?"

"Yes we are, replied Kelleher as he paid our bill to Vu and told him to give it to his father.

We boarded the Commandament as the two diesel engines rumbled gently in the muddy brown river water. Then the order was given to cast off and we were on our way.

The eighty ton craft was a modified LCM-3 that we had initially given to the French. They in turn, replaced the original engines with Mercedes Benz Marines. Eventually, when the US got into the advisory business after the French were thrown out unceremoniously, the Mercedes engines were replaced with American Gray Marines because of materiel support issues.

The Commandament was equipped with one 40mm cannon forward, one 20mm aft, two .30 and two .50 caliber machine guns and an 81mm mortar. Officer's berthing accommodated four below the operating deck and the crew's quarters were below the main deck and slept eight.

Top speed was about 8-9 knots and problems were sometimes encountered when the boat tried to negotiate a river whose current ran 10 knots or more against them.

Sitting atop the Commandament's control deck under a white canvas covering that provided shelter from the hot sun and incessant rains, Kelleher, the Chief, LCDR Rach and I sat on the canvas benches watching our progress and enjoying the scenery as we passed the mouth of the Saigon River to the northwest.

Five miles down the Dong Nai River, we entered the Nha Be River. Passing the huge oil tank farms to starboard, we came to the Nha Be Naval Base, home to several SEAL platoons, PBR units, Swift boats and a VNN Rag unit. We saw ten or eleven PBRs nestled together gently bobbing alongside a barge moored to the pier where their crews were busily preparing for their next mission. This was also the home of Navy Helicopter Squadron 3 Seawolves, or HAL-3 for short. All in all, it was a pretty impressive place.

The majority of the forces stationed at Nha Be operated almost solely in and around the Rung Sat Special Zone, commonly known as the Forest of Assassins. This area consisted of four hundred square miles of mangrove swamp that became eighty-five percent inundated during the wet monsoon season. It was aptly described as the Killer Everglades of Vietnam.

One of the reasons that Saigon placed so much emphasis on the Rung Sat was because it was a natural haven for the Viet Cong guerrillas and units of the North Vietnamese army. Additionally, the Long Tau channel, which was the main shipping route to Saigon from the sea, ran right through the middle of it. The enemy would carry out attacks on shipping in the channel and then melt back into the relative safety of the dense swamp. To try and counter the attacks, PBR Unit 531 was assigned to patrol and protect the shipping on that dangerous stretch of water.

The Rung Sat's eastern boundary was the Thi Vi Go Gia River and almost all of that area had been completely defoliated in an effort to deny the enemy any cover. It was also believed that the elusive VC/NVA had established new base camps in the lush and untouched western side, bounded by the Soi Rap River.

Unheard and unseen B-52 bombers routinely dropped tons of high explosives over the entire western staging area while gunships expended thousands of rounds from their Gatling guns into the thick foliage. Fighter planes from aircraft carriers off the coast scorched the jungle canopy with napalm in a further effort to discourage the enemy from using it as a sanctuary. Despite all this, the enemy prevailed and remained embedded in the area.

Having made good time moving with the current, we arrived earlier than expected at the confluence of the Soi Rap River to port. This river also led to the open sea, but it was shallow and more difficult to navigate.

The Rung Sat loomed ominously on the left side of the Soi Rap where the thick mangroves stretched completely to the river's edge. The area exuded a malevolent and forbidding atmosphere and the total absence of the white long necked cranes that normally soared over the dense forest canopy, gave off an evil aura. In fact, there were no birds or other signs of wildlife whatsoever on that side of the river.

We remained on the Nha Be River for some distance until we finally came to the mouth of the Vam Co Dong River. Entering the river, we encountered an ebbing current that slowed our progress considerably. For the better part of the day, we labored against the tide until we finally reached the Ben Luc Bridge just before dusk.

LCDR Rach maneuvered the Commandament expertly alongside one of the cement pillars supporting the bridge where he had decided to moor for the night. There were two small detachments of ARVN encamped near the approaches on both ends of the bridge, but Rach had made out a night watch bill for the crew of the Commandament to ensure our own security. Two men would be positioned fore and aft on the boat where they would be relieved by two others every four hours until daylight. The man on the bow was responsible for tossing concussion grenades into the river at varied intervals to protect against enemy swimmer sappers.

The sun was about a half hour from setting when a very light breeze softly found its way to us from the north. We sat around talking quietly topside on the Commandament until the sky faded from shades of light purple to black. There was no moon to cast shadows and the darkness was practically complete except for the stars. Their pinpoints of light shone brightly in the night sky until some were blocked out momentarily by passing swarms of bats on their nightly quest for food. There were considerably more mosquitoes than bats, which was the cue for us to turn in under the safety of our netting. Learning to fall asleep with the thump of exploding grenades and the incessant whining of mosquitoes outside my netting was my biggest accomplishment that night.

First light brought about activity aboard the Commandament. Somewhere on the boat, a pot of coffee was being brewed and its tantalizing aroma overpowered the rotting vegetation odor of the river.

As we went topside, we heard excited yells from one of the sailors up forward. He was pointing wildly to the bridge about mid-span where there was a young Vietnamese woman standing on an outer girder facing us. She was dressed in a beautiful pale cream Ao Dai with black pants, her long black hair hung loosely over one shoulder and she held her shoes in one hand. Once she had our attention, she started yelling that she was going to jump into the river. ARVN soldiers started running towards her from both ends of the bridge, but failed to reach her before she launched herself feet first into the river.

Chief Shipp reacted immediately by shedding his flip-flops and dove headfirst into the muddy brown water towards her point of entry. Reaching down, he managed to grab her by the hair and brought her back to the surface. He then encircled her around the waist and made for the boat where our sailors eagerly extended their hands to pull her aboard. Offering little or no resistance whatsoever, she gave us the impression that this is what she had intended all along. A sailor produced a threadbare blanket from below decks that Gunner quickly grabbed and wrapped it tenderly around the young lady as he talked soothingly to her as one would to a wounded bird. The lecher in the old Chief was only outdone by his quick thinking.

When she finally regained her composure, she blurted out a tale of unrequited love. She had been having a torrid affair with a young ARVN officer in charge of the bridge security detachment and ad spent many evenings in his tent making love between silk sheets on his cot. That is until this morning when he said that the affair was over because he couldn't leave his wife and child. Incensed and embarrassed at being so coldheartedly abandoned, she decided that she would fake committing suicide in hopes that he would change his mind. The young smooth-faced Second Lieutenant who was a part of this equation, quickly clambered down from the bridge and joined us. Upon seeing him, she broke down into deep convulsing sobs, body shaking and head held between her hands. Gunner quickly disengaged himself from her as she rushed into the Lieutenant's outstretched arms.

As we sat around watching the tender scene unfold before us, Rach finally stood up and addressed the both of them in his most authoritative voice. He told them to take their sorry fornicating selves off of his boat before he personally threw the two of them back into the river.

They were both embarrassed beyond words in front of the unsympathetic audience that had assembled. She quickly dropped the blanket to the deck as her lover took her by the hand and gently assisted her back onto the bridge.

We all had a good laugh, even despite Gunner's failed plan to hopefully comfort the little lady in his bunk below deck.

Rach said, "There are times and places to bed down a woman, and this definitely was not one of them. In an area such as this, it could prove to be a disaster."

SALVAGE OPS

We couldn't disagree with that logic. Just then, the radio crackled and a hysterical voice broke through the rapidly warming morning air. It was Rach's XO, Lieutenant Dang, who had been aboard the unit's Monitor. His adrenalin charged voice excitedly reported that they had just been hit by a command-detonated mine about seven miles upriver. He said there were no casualties and that he had ordered the two FOMs to try and tow the rapidly sinking craft towards the northern side of the river where it could have a chance at being salvaged.

Rach acknowledged Dang's report and informed him that we'd be there as soon as possible. He then ordered the crew to get us underway. Dang responded with less stress in his voice saying that efforts to beach the vessel seemed to be working.

Kelleher said, "It was Dang's first crack at command and he got nailed. You can tell by his voice that he's scared shitless."

"Hey, how the hell could he foresee a command-detonated mine in the middle of the river. That could have happened to any of us so I can certainly sympathize with him," I said.

"At least nobody got hurt," murmured Gunner.

As we came around a bend in the river, we saw the Monitor to starboard lying on its port side with its bow hard up against the embankment. The forward 40mm gun tub was partially under water and two 3 inch manila lines were lashed around the base of two sturdy palm trees holding the craft in place. The two FOMs flanked the Monitor on either side protectively with both their .30 calibers manned and ready. This undoubtedly was for the CO's benefit as well as for ours. LT Dang was sitting on the bank with his back against a tree looking forlorn and dreading the coming confrontation with Rach. It was written all over his face.

I looked over at Rach and could see the anguish he was feeling too, because no unit commander likes to see any of his vessels damaged and incapacitated. When he spotted Dang, there was no anger in his eyes. In fact, he looked relieved to see that his second in command was unhurt and no casualties were sustained by the crew.

Dang stood up and caught the bow line that was thrown by from the Commandament. He dragged it to the base of the tree that had been his backrest and tied the line around it securely. He then climbed aboard once the bow had settled firmly against the bank several feet from the listing Monitor. He timidly made his way topside to confer with Rach, who was trying to appear nonchalant in order to put his young XO at ease.

While the two officers started discussing the details of the mining, Kelleher and I stood off to one side in order to give the men some privacy. We watched Shipp make a cursory inspection of the craft from the river-bank as he said up to us, "I think it'd be a good idea if we pulled out the 40 mm gun barrel so the VC can't get it. I could do it if someone would give me a hand."

"I'd be glad to help you Chief, as long as you talk me through it," I said.

Rach looked thoughtful for a minute and said, "That is a good idea *Thuong Si*. I'll let Third Coastal Zone Headquarters know and ask them to send a truck to Ben Luc for the gun barrel and any ammunition that we can salvage from her."

Gunner quickly reappeared from below decks wearing a pair of ratty tan colored bathing shorts adorned with small black faded sharks. Apparently the shorts had been white at one time but the brown river waters had discolored them.

Since I hadn't anticipated going swimming on this trip, I didn't bring any bathing trunks with me. So, being an officer and possessing resourcefulness, I stripped down to my underwear and placed my folded clothes on a bench.

"Ready to go Chief," I said as I noticed a small smile of amusement momentarily crossing his face. The others tactfully disregard my near nudity and calmly went about their business.

Gunner pulled a yellow legal pad from his antiquated black government issued briefcase and sketched out exactly what we were going to do once we were inside the semi-submerged turret. For a guy who never went past the seventh grade in school, he had an excellent grasp of the technical side of weaponry. I was really impressed, to say the least. He went over the plan step by step so that I would be familiar with the layout and procedure for removing the gun barrel. He explained that the tools we needed were all clamped on the after bulkhead inside the turret. From the very beginning, the advisors provided tools up the Yazoo to the Vietnamese for maintaining their engines, but the majority of them would ultimately find their way into the tool kits of their personal motorcycles. So I had my doubts as to their existence.

Rach said that he intended to take the Commandament upriver for a few miles to scout out the area, but would leave the FOMs with us for security and in case of any emergency. Since there would be constant radio communications between the FOMs and the Commandament, we were OK with that so we left our weapons aboard one of the FOMs.

Climbing down into the tepid brown river water, we made our way to the Monitor's almost totally submerged turret.

Reaching it first, Gunner looked back at me and said, "This is what pisses me off about these people. The fuckin' XO gets his boat blown out from under him so you'd think he'd be here busting his ass with us; but no! He's an officer and not about to soil his hands as long as the advisors are here to do the dirty work. Aw fuck him! He'd only be in the way anyhow."

I had no reply for that because I knew he had spent more time here in Vietnam than me and I respected his opinion. I knew that he was referring to Vietnamese officers in general, because here I was, alongside him up to our necks virtually in shit creek.

The tide was low and although the turret hatch was above water, the interior was flooded. We climbed inside with Gunner going underwater first in order to get the tools from off the bulkhead. Surprisingly, he came up with two large adjustable wrenches and said that the visibility wasn't too bad since we were close to the riverbank. Further out where the current was running, visibility would be minimal due to the muddy silt bottom being disturbed.

Following Gunner's instructions, I went under and started loosening up the large nuts that secured the barrel. It took several dives of short duration until my lungs became acclimated to staying underwater for longer periods of time. The two of us worked tirelessly until we came to the counter-recoil spring. Gunner hadn't told me that this spring would be under tension, so when I finally managed to release it, it let go with an enormous energy followed by a loud bang. Taken completely by surprise, I involuntarily swallowed a large mouthful of river water. We both came up at the same time. Gunner was trying to suppress his laughter while I was coughing up the highly polluted river water.

"That was the counter-recoil spring *Dai-Uy*. Sorry that I failed to mention that it would probably be under tension."

"That's OK," I replied still spitting up river water. It scared the daylights out of me, but now I know what it's like to drink out of a septic tank. Yuk! Ptui! Aghhh!"

Gunner laughed and said, "We're almost ready to extract the barrel, so let me know when you're set to tackle it again."

"I'm OK, let's do it."

After several more dives we finally succeeded in disengaging the barrel from the housing. The Chief secured a one inch manila line around the barrel behind the flash suppressor so we could haul it out of the turret. Maintaining a solid foothold in the slippery mud proved to be more of a job than we had anticipated.

After a considerable amount of pulling and swearing, we managed to drag the barrel out of the water and laid it on the bank. There were only twelve rounds of live ammunition and four expended brass casings that we could find in the bottom of the turret, so we took them out and piled them alongside the barrel on the riverbank.

Exhausted from our underwater salvage effort, we gratefully sank back onto the grass. Gunner in his tacky shorts and me in my now beige colored skivvies that at one time had been snow white, presented quite a picture. The crew of the FOMs gave us the thumbs up as they broadly grinned from ear to ear. Yes, this beat the hell out of sitting in the office back in Saigon and I was more determined than ever to transfer to a combat unit.

As the Chief and I lay in the shade under a palm tree, a small group of locals from the outskirts of the village had quietly assembled a short distance from the bank. It was probably the first time that they had ever seen an American in his underwear and the other one who looked like an Arab, near their village.

The group was comprised of the usual elderly men who were well past the age of military service, the womenfolk who were left behind by those who were serving and their children. Each woman carried the youngest child on her out-thrust hip while the child maintained a tight grip with their legs around the mother's waist. Now I understood why some children were somewhat bowlegged in this country. The fatter the mother, the more bowlegged the child became, whereas the thinner mother's off-springs grew up with straighter legs.

The longer I stayed in Vietnam, the more I could empathize with these simple village folks. The facts seemed to be that the average farmer and fisherman could really give a good rat's ass as to who was running the government in Saigon. All they cared about was being able to pursue their livelihood without any undue encumbrances from the outside in order to provide for their families. Unfortunately, for most of these people, the politics and realities of war had overtaken them.

A good case in point was that on any given night, the local VC would steal silently into a village and coerce the villagers into planting landmines along the local roads. In addition, they also extracted taxes from them in the form of rice and fish to support their cause. The next day, the government troops would arrive and force them to dig the mines back up again. In some cases, the ARVN would also relieve them of more fish and rice saying that it was in their best interests to support the military. No wonder the indigenous population was confused and angered at being used as pawns for something they felt had little meaning for them. Their everyday lives were being severely disrupted and the land was being overrun by the big, hairy and garrulous rich Americans.

The deep growl of a diesel engine announced the arrival of the truck from Saigon that was dispatched to retrieve the barrel. A short, stocky Vietnamese Chief Petty Officer and his assistant emerged from the truck and approached us with incredulous looks on their faces.

"There's the gun Chief," said Gunner lying on the ground with one hand supporting his head while he pointed with his other towards the water-soaked barrel and ammunition on the bank.

The cherubic Chief looked over at me as I sat with my back against a palm tree in my brown river stained shorts and was trying awfully hard to piece the puzzle together

Finally, he barked some orders to the seaman who quickly took the bitter end of one line from the barrel and secured it around the winch that sat in the forward part of the truck-bed. When the winch was engaged, it effortlessly hauled the barrel over the lowered tailgate where the Chief guided it gently onto wooden chocks on the truck bed. The ammunition rounds were then placed gently into a wooden crate secured to the base of the winch.

The welcomed sight of the Commandament appeared around the bend from upriver. Rach was standing topside with a wide smile to acknowledge my giving him the thumbs up signal while pointing towards the truck.

As soon as the Commandament nosed into the bank, Gunner and I dragged our tired raggedy asses aboard and went topside. Once under the canvas awning, we slumped onto the benches as Kelleher magically produced two cold cans of Falstaff beer from somewhere. Gunner and I decided not to look a gift horse in the mouth and gratefully accepted the cold brew.

"Did you guys have a rough time getting the barrel loose?" asked Kelleher.

"Not really. You were fortunate in having Gunner as your assistant because he's an absolute wizard with weapons."

"It was a piece of cake," said the Chief, "Except for the counter-recoil spring letting go unexpectedly and *Dai-Uy* here swallowed a mouthful of the Vam Co Dong sewage system."

"Ugh! Better you than me shipmate," said Kelleher with a grimace. "There is enough bacteria in that water to contaminate Los Angeles and completely ruin your day."

"Hey *Dai-Uy*," said Gunner looking over at me impishly and laughing, "Think of all the people who took their dumps upriver this morning. Sure hope your immune system is in battery."

"You and me both," I said mournfully as Kelleher and Rach both shook their heads sympathetically.

"What's going to happen to the Monitor," I asked of no one in particular.

"Saigon is sending a salvage team aboard an LCM even as we speak," said Kelleher. "Once they weld some cofferdams inside around the damaged area, they'll pump her out and tow it back to the Eastern Repair Facility in Saigon."

Rach said. "I have ordered the truck to bring the barrel back to Saigon before it gets any later and I also ordered *Dai-Uy* Dang and the two FOMs to stay with the Monitor until the salvagers arrive tomorrow. If we do not leave someone to watch over it, the villagers will assume that it is abandoned and fair game for them to strip it of anything and everything. Then, Dang can return with the Monitor. After all, he's the one who lost it," he said with a wink and a smile.

"Boy, that guy really has his shit together," said Gunner quietly so Rach couldn't hear.

Finally, Rach ordered "*Chung ta di*," or "Let's go," to the Cox'n who began backing out into the slow moving river current.

"We'll head back to the bridge and remain there until the salvage team arrives tomorrow. Besides, this place does not appear to be too inviting after dark," said Rach.

We were slowly making our way back downriver and as we came around the first big bend, all hell broke loose. The quickly darkening night air was filled with green and white tracers coming at us from the tree line on the starboard bank. We all instinctively ducked behind the metal plating and reached for our weapons as Rach ordered the Cox'n to turn into the firing so that our 40mm weapon could bear on to the attackers.

Apparently a small force of Viet Cong had been heading back to the sunken Monitor site as the Commandament suddenly appeared. Momentarily surprised, they immediately took us under fire hoping to sink or damage another river menace.

Gunner and I forgot our fatigue as we quickly grabbed our weapons and joined the fray. Now this is more like it, I thought to myself as the adrenalin kicked in.

We returned fire as the 40mm gun started pumping out rounds towards the ambushers. Only the VC and the NVA used green and white tracers, so we knew this wasn't a case of friendly fire. The night reverberated with the sounds of bullets slamming into our protective steel plating and the steady bang-bang of the 40mm reaching out for the enemy. Our biggest fear as always was having a B-40 rocket fired at us, especially at such close range. They could definitely ruin your day . . . forever.

Suddenly, a fusillade of red tracers started pouring into the attackers from the south. It was an ARVN rapid response team that had been tracking the VC and when the ambush erupted, they immediately engaged them from the rear. "Sure beats the hell out of sitting behind a desk in Saigon, eh *Dai-Uy*?" quipped Gunner as he triggered off round after round into the darkness. When his magazine was empty, he dropped his rifle and magically produced a LAW rocket from beneath the seat. Extending the barrel for firing, he placed it on his shoulder, checked to see that no one was behind him and sent a rocket zooming into the darkness.

A few moments later, an excited voice came over the radio. Rach acknowledged the transmission and turned to Gunner and said that the ARVN leader reported that one of his men had been wounded by an explosion that apparently came from our direction. Since the VC had not thrown any grenades or used rockets, it was assumed that the round came from the river.

"Well Gunner," remarked Kelleher wryly from behind the shield, "it looks like you got one, except he was on our side."

"That's bullshit," retorted the Chief, as he angrily tossed the expended rocket housing over the side.

In any event, we continued to return fire. The green and white tracers diminished in intensity as the enemy suddenly broke off contact and melted back into the blackness of the night.

The ensuing stillness after the short-lived din of battle seemed eerie. Cordite permeated the air around us and the only sounds came from the low rumbling of the diesel engines and the clicking coming from the cooling 40mm gun barrel.

"The VC were most likely heading for the Monitor hoping to finish it off," said Rach. "They did not expect to be caught between us and the ARVN."

Turning towards me, Kelleher said, "Hey Bob; think you can put a story together about this for the Newsletter?"

"Just as long as he doesn't say anything about my nailing a friendly," interjected Gunner glumly.

"No problem. Our taxpayers got something for their money in any event," I replied out of earshot of Rach.

It seemed only a short time before we found ourselves once again nestled firmly bow in, against one of the Ben Luc Bridge pilings. Once the adrenalin rush subsided, it was hard to believe that we had just been involved in a fire-fight. It was about then that I started to feel shitty and my head was beginning to ache.

Noting my obvious discomfort, Rach suggested that I turn in for the night after we have our evening portion of rice. "You have had a tedious day, *Dai-Uy*."

I nodded in agreement but begged off the meal. I just didn't have the energy or the desire to eat anything; I just wanted to close my eyes and go to sleep.

SHOW ME THE WAY TO GO HOME

And crash I did. It was almost 0800 before I surfaced from a deep, dark, dreamless sleep. However, when I tried to open my eyes, the sunlight sent a sharp piercing pain through the top of my head. After attempting several times to reopen them, I found that it was better to keep them closed.

Kelleher had been watching me as he was folding his poncho liner and asked me how I felt.

"I feel like someone was driving a hot marlinspike down into the top of my head every time I try to open my eyes," I said.

"That's weird," he replied. "Do you suppose that Vam Co Dong River mouth rinse you had yesterday has anything to do with it?"

"Don't know, but I'm damn sure heading for the hospital when we get back to Saigon."

"Sounds like a good idea. The salvage team should be here in another two hours and Rach said that's when we would start back. In the meantime, I'd stay in the sack if I were you. I've got some aspirin to ease the pain if you'd like."

"I'd like about a hundred of them," I groaned.

"Right, here're three for starters. Now lie back down and try to get some sleep. I'll wake you if you're needed."

That's the last I remembered until the explosive start of the two big diesel engines awoke me. I got out of my bunk very slowly and made my way to the upper deck. I found Rach, Kelleher and the Chief standing by the forward railing as we headed out into the middle of the river.

"How did you sleep, *Dai-Uy*?" asked Rach as I came up from below.

"Like a dead man, *Thieu-Ta*. I at least can open my eyes a little, but the pain is still there although not as intense."

"You might have gotten a bug in your system from the river water you swallowed. It should pass."

"God, I hope so. Hey John, can I have some more aspirin?"

"Sure," he replied. Take the whole bottle. I've got more back at the 'Q'."

I managed to stay topside until the rice and vegetables were broken out for lunch. Just the aroma from the food made my stomach feel queasy, so I headed below to hit the sack again.

The next time I woke up was when Kelleher was shaking me by the shoulder.

"What's up, John?" I mumbled sleepily as I opened my eyes to the welcomed sight of night blackness.

"We're lost in the middle of the Delta fishnets," he replied. "You're the navigator pal, so come and get us to the Soi Rap."

I once again climbed down gingerly out of the bunk and as soon as my bare feet hit the deck, the fireworks went off in my head again. Man, I could never remember a headache that hurt so much and lasted so long in all my life. "Where are those friggin' aspirins?" I grumbled under my breath as I headed topside.

Rach and Gunner were holding flashlights over a chart of the area and at the sound of my approach, both turned as Gunner said, "Hey *Dai-Uy*, we're screwed up here."

I looked at the chart trying to focus my eyes and asked Rach if he had any idea of our last known position.

"Not since we were in the Nha Be River," replied the CO. "I think the helmsman veered to starboard instead of to port when we entered the Soi Rap. It's too dark to see any landmarks."

I looked around and all I could see were faint lights attached to the many fishing nets that were set in the mouth of the Delta. Before I could offer any recommendations, Gunner was pointing upwards and said, "Hey, there's the North Star and that's the direction we have to go to get to the Soi Rap."

"Good thinking Chief, now all we have to do is maneuver around the outer side of the fishnets heading in that direction until we near the coast. From there, it'll be simple to head east until we find the mouth of the Soi Rap. Even if we miss it, the next one is the Long Tau channel and that'll get us home too," I said.

"Sounds like a plan," chipped in Kelleher. "Let's go for it."

Rach gave orders for the helmsman to steer slightly to the north-east in order to skirt the nets. He also put a sailor on the bow with a battle lantern to help guide us around the nets.

The pounding in my head was still a pain to be reckoned with, so I excused myself and slowly went below to my bunk. Even if we didn't find the Soi Rap, dawn was only a few hours away and then we'd be able to visually get a fix on our position. I ingested three more aspirins washed down with tepid water from my canteen and quickly fell asleep.

The next time I awoke, we were just pulling alongside the pier in Cat Lai. With the shutting down of the engines, Gunner came down to wake me. What he found was a thoroughly sweat-soaked, bewhiskered sorry excuse for an officer. The pain returned, more ferocious than before as I tried weakly to get out of the bunk.

Gunner gave me a hand to stand up saying that "*Dai-Uy* Kelleher wants me to drive you back to the Hospital in Saigon. He's going to stay here for awhile and then come back to town with Rach."

I grabbed my gear and weapon and as I approached Rach, I said, "Thank you for letting me come along with you *Thieu-Ta*. I'm sorry I got sick on you."

"You have nothing to be sorry about," said Rach. "I welcome your company anytime *Dai-Uy*. Now go see a doctor and get well."

With that, I limply shook his hand and followed Gunner off the boat as Kelleher accompanied us to the Jeep. "Hope you feel better Bob. Let me know if there's anything I can do for you," he said as he gently patted my shoulder.

"You're doing enough just letting Gunner bring me to the Croakers."

"OK Chief, take care of our patient. I'll see you tomorrow."

The ride back to Saigon would not be among my more memorable trips because I felt every bump in the road. At every jolt, a sharp needle-like pain exploded behind my eyeballs and my empty stomach began growling like a starving wolf.

When we finally arrived at the hospital, I was quickly admitted. Gunner said he would return shortly to check on me since his house was only a few blocks away. "I'll take your weapon and leave it at my place until you get out," he said. "Is there anything you want me to bring back for you?"

"Nothing, old buddy. I just want to get out of these raunchy clothes and get between some cool clean sheets as soon as I can."

"I'll see you later then, *Dai-Uy*. Try to get some rest and hang in there," said Gunner as he turned and ambled away, one shoulder lower than the other in his inimitable gait.

If Gunner returned to see me, I had no recollection of it. My body was just a lump of clay, immovable in the welcomed peace of dreamless sleep. I spent four days in the hospital trying to do just that, drifting in and out of sleep because the light still caused excruciating pain in my head.

The doctors hadn't prescribed any medication for me after their preliminary diagnosis because they determined that I had a Fever of Undetermined Origin or FUO in medical jargon. Standard procedure was to let the fever run its course rather than inhibit it with any drugs. So, with no nurse coming to dispense medicine, only the daily meals punctuated my day and those I mostly left untouched. Not even so much as an aspirin, can you believe that?

My bed was in an open ward on the third deck of the hospital located about fifteen feet from an antiquated caged elevator just outside the open double doors. Several patients in various stages of recuperation occupied the ward with me but none of them looked any the worse for wear. I didn't see any bloody bandages or other indications of wounds, so I assumed that this was the minimally afflicted floor and I was in the first bed nearest the entrance.

On my second afternoon there, I had just fallen asleep shortly after a meager lunch of tomato soup, crackers and green Jell-O, when I was rudely awakened by a loud squawking rendition of "Rock of Ages." The cacophonous sound was coming from a small portable organ and an electric guitar being played by two gentlemen who closely resembled a shorter version of Ernest Borgnine.

Cracking open my eyes while slowly rising up on one elbow, I saw a pair of twin Caucasian males in front of my bed. They each couldn't have been more than five feet tall, dressed identically in black pants, white Filipino Baranca shirts and light brown, yes light brown wing-tipped shoes.

I glanced around at the other guys in their beds and they all had that same quizzical look on their faces that seemed to say "What the fuck . . ." Then the twin gnomes started singing as they played. I use the word singing only due to the lack of a more descriptive word to aptly identify the complete destruction of a fine old hymn.

A large gold placard depicting cutouts of the two men and two identical sisters with their instruments was attached to the front of the organ. The words "Clarions of Joy" twinkled in blue green and silver glitter above the picture.

Now I couldn't very well attest to the Joy part because up to now, I was experiencing only grief.

I'm sure the two meant well in trying to cheer up the troops, but I wondered whether the USO booking agent back home had ever auditioned these guys. As they finally concluded their discordant offering, the guitar player approached me with a broad friendly smile and asked where I was from back in the States.

Still not thinking clearly, I replied, "Minneapolis."

Upon hearing that, his face beamed even more as he turned and nodded towards his brother saying, "We're from the Twin Cities too."

"Where are the ladies in the picture?" I inquired rather cynically.

"Oh, those are our wives, Abigail and Tabitha."

Ideal names for cats, I thought to myself.

"We met several years ago on the banks of the Mississippi River in Wabasha, Minnesota. We were scheduled for baptism at the same ceremony and it was love at first sight for the four of us. We found Jesus together and ultimately formed our singing group to help spread the word. They're waiting for us in Hawaii at Tripler Army Hospital where we will perform next month after we finish here. Since we still have to journey up to Da Nang and Chu Lai, it was decided that it might not be safe for them there, so we sent them on to Honolulu instead."

Well, I had to agree on one thing, those four were meant for each other. Physically, they were all about the same height and physical appearance, but God forgive me; it was the ugliest quartet of people that I had ever seen together.

It must be true that the Lord performs in strange ways and in this case it was a blessing. Where else could four unattractive people be drawn to each other, find happiness and try to spread their idea of joy to the world?

Then with a serious expression on his face he softly said, "If you don't mind my asking, where did you get wounded?"

"I didn't get wounded; I came down with a nasty dose of Syphillis," I replied matter-of-factly with a straight face.

Well, if you ever experienced a pregnant pause, I did just then. The brothers both gasped and almost choked as their faces reddened with embarrassment. They clumsily took their instruments and beat a hasty retreat to the elevator that fortunately was still open on our floor.

As the gate slammed shut, they descended as fast as the old lift would allow amid cheers and applause from my bedmates. One of the patients towards the rear yelled, "Good going buddy, you handled those guys like a pro."

"Now maybe we can get some peace and quiet around here, after all, it is a hospital," I remarked with a wry smile despite the pain in my head. No sooner had the words left my mouth when the same discordant sounds erupted once again, only this time arising from the elevator shaft. The two "Clarions" had obviously regained their composure and were bound and determined to spread joy in the ward down below regardless of their recent experience. At least now we could have the nurse close the double doors in order to mute the noise and let us get some rest.

BACK IN THE SADDLE

On the morning of the fourth day, the duty doctor signed my release and informed me that I was fit for duty. As I exited the hospital, a Jeep horn beeped twice from curbside. Gunner was sitting slightly hunched over the wheel and said, "How're you feeling *Dai-Uy*? Looks like that rest did you some good, but you seem to be on the slim side of hungry."

"What I need now is some good chow and a cold beer," I said as I climbed into the passenger side. "How about that Chinese place on Ham Nghi where they serve those Imperial Shrimp Rolls?"

"You got it," he said as he swung out into the dusty traffic.

The Canton Restaurant was only a few blocks away from the McCarthy and was always busy, which was a good testament for their food. The one drawback, although it never bothered me, was that you could see into the kitchen from several tables in the dining room. Now that in itself isn't a big thing, but in this kitchen, all the employees were in their shorts and undershirts. Since the owners didn't think that installing air-conditioning in the kitchen was a high priority item, the employees wore as few clothes as possible.

As we waited for our order we could see a bunch of Asians with knobby knees sticking out of their questionably clean shorts preparing the food. It didn't do much for the imagination and we were constantly on alert for curly hairs on our plates. Other than that, the food was good.

The medium sized shrimp were rolled up, dipped in a light batter and gently fried to a golden brown. They were served with a bowl of hot steaming rice that we seasoned with Magi Sauce and bits of fresh red chili peppers. All this was washed down with several frosted 500ml bottles of Tiger Beer. It didn't get much better than that and it sure beat the hell out of "McDog Food."

By the time we were finished, it was almost two thirty in the afternoon and I had no desire to go back to work.

"Hey Gunner, I'm going to take the rest of the day off and start fresh tomorrow," I said finishing off the last of my beer.

"That's exactly what I had in mind. In fact I'm going to head on home so my gal Ann can feel old age creeping up on her."

"Kelleher always told me that you were a lecher and now I believe it. That poor gal of yours probably doesn't get any rest when you're around."

"Ah, she loves it. I always said if it's attention they want, attention they'll get. Besides, a doctor once told me it was good to clear out the tubes regularly as you get older to prevent prostate problems. Did you know the world's highest incidence of prostate cancer is among homosexuals and Catholic priests?"

"No I didn't, but it sounds logical. Seminal fluid shouldn't be stored up for any length of time because the sperm will degrade and probably atrophy."

"Who knows, it could probably lead to Clamidia and Yeast infections. Once I explained it to her she went along with the program. She may not believe it, but she knows it makes me happy."

"Ain't love grand?" I replied. I haven't cut one out of the herd yet to service, but I'm working on it."

"Ann has a good friend that I call 'Fat Betty' and she's available. The only thing is that she's so fat that even when she spreads her legs apart, they're still closed. I don't think you'd want to marine-crawl through her fat just to get laid. Besides, you could never be sure if you were in or just screwing a fold of fat. That thought alone would kill an erection."

"Amen Chief, there are too many good looking women in this country that are slim and trim so one doesn't have to settle for the

'Michelin Woman.' Thanks anyway. By the way, I can make it back to the McCarthy by myself and the walk will do me good."

"OK *Dai-Uy*, don't get lost."

"Never happen, GI."

I walked leisurely along the almost deserted streets back to the BOQ passing several cyclo drivers soundly sleeping in their conveyances. During this time of day, most folks were taking their noontime siestas and it didn't really matter where they snoozed. Stores and kiosks were closed and traffic was almost non-existent except for the occasional military or police Jeeps.

Arriving at the McCarthy, I quickly took the stairs up to my room. Ba Tu had already straightened up and the air conditioning was happily filling the room with cool air. What I needed was a good shower after that ridiculous stay in the hospital. Actually, I felt good but mentally I felt a little drained. Just the mere thought of going back to my office to face another long day of editing articles was depressing.

After a nice long hot shower to loosen up my stiff muscles, I turned on the cold water, which at best was tepid. Leaving the bathroom, I drew the drapes against the minimal light that came through the windows over the narrow entranceway and wearing only my shorts, slipped into bed and was soon fast asleep.

That was the last thing I remembered until I awoke to the sound of the door quietly closing. I looked at my watch and saw that it was 0600, which meant that both my roommates were already gone. If I hurried I thought, I could be dressed and gone before Ba Tu arrived. I didn't feel like having any conversation with her about my recent experiences and a good hot cup of coffee was what my body needed most right now.

Still trying to avoid any idle chatter, I quickly left the BOQ and headed for Headquarters. I could satisfy my coffee craves up in the office and then I'd be ready to relate the tale of my trip to the Delta and its fallout.

Lieutenant Morrow was already in the office and as usual, had a pot of fresh coffee going on the antiquated hot plate.

"Hey welcome back! How was your trip into the badlands?"

"Tell you what, let me get a cup of coffee first and I'll fill you in on all the sordid details. By that time, the rest of the guys should be here and I can tell it only once, OK?"

"Sure thing, but you look a little pale and you've lost some weight."

"You're only noticing that because I'm wearing my work khakis and not my greens this morning," I said smiling.

"Nah, you'd look like a fart-sack no matter what you wore today. Have you seen the Captain yet?"

"Not yet and I'm really not too eager to see his holiness this early in the day."

George brought me a cup of steaming hot coffee as I sat behind my paper-littered desk. "Looks like the guys have been sending me their inputs from the field religiously," I said.

"Why wouldn't they?" he replied, "It keeps the Green Zingers from heading their way." Green Zingers were what we referred to as the 'nasty note' memos that the Senior Naval Advisor sent out to individuals who pissed him off. And he sent out a lot of them.

I wondered if he assigned the XO the job of logging them. It certainly would provide a good basis for his evaluations.

Both Co Mai and Ba Lan stuck their heads in and welcomed me back to the office. I saluted them with my coffee cup and said "Thank You, it's nice to be back." At least this was better than being in that miserable hospital with the wandering minstrels.

A few moments later, the rest of the crew arrived and they all agreed that I looked like shit. What a homecoming! I proceeded to relate my experiences in the Delta; removing the gun barrel, getting lost, the firefight, the nets and the fever that placed me in the hospital. The part where I described the "Clarions of Joy" and my unique way of dealing with them brought laughter to the group.

"So, you're probably not looking forward to any more trips into the field," said Commander Johnson.

"On the contrary Commander, I would really like to get into the RAGS. At least I would feel that I was getting something done in this war," I replied.

Ed just sat there and nodded his head knowingly since he understood where I was coming from. I learned early on that he wasn't as Gung Ho as I was about the war and he accepted his assignment stoically. He, along with the rest of the officers in this office, with the exception of Lieutenant Morrow, was satisfied to serve in a relatively safe billet, get their 'ticket' punched and make it back home in one piece.

I then proceeded to clear my desk of the nonessential paperwork and took care of the more important stuff. This naturally was putting the finishing touches on the next Newsletter. Just as I completed finalizing it, Major Towson stood up and said, "Hey Bob, I'm heading over to NAVFORV and I can drop the Newsletter template over at the print shop if you'd like."

"That'd be great Bill," I replied. That'll let me pump out my trip report and turn it in before my phone starts ringing."

Amazingly, it took about twenty minutes to compose the report that covered what seemed to be an eternity, on my trip.

It was a little before noon when I entered the Senior Naval Advisor's office and found both the XO and the Yeoman absent. The door to the Captain's office was slightly ajar and I could see him behind his desk reading, so I knocked gently and entered.

Captain Bjorkman was comfortably tilted back in the chair behind his desk engrossed in some correspondence. At the sound of my knock, he looked up over his half glasses at me, as I said, "Good morning Captain. I brought you my trip report."

"C'mon in and have a seat. I hear you had quite an experience. Do you still feel like you want to get back out in the field?" He asked with a smirk.

"More than ever sir; Here's my report," I said as I handed him the sheaf of papers.

He leaned forward in his chair as he started to read it. After digesting it, took his glasses off and looked me straight in the eyes. "I must commend you and Chief Shipp on removing the gun barrel, although I'm not sure as to exactly what the VC would have done had they gotten their hands on it. As for the rescue of the despondent Vietnamese woman who jumped off the bridge, that falls into the 'humanitarian' phase of our presence here. Your hospitalization however, was unfortunate and I hope that your swallowing that foul river water doesn't present any long term health problems for you. How do you feel now?"

"Actually I feel pretty good. After all I've had four days of nothing but bed rest in the hospital, so things are pretty much back to normal," I replied.

"Well, in that case if you feel up to it, I have another short assignment for you. The Public Affairs folks over at NAVFORV informed me that they've cleared an NBC Journalist to accompany the HQ-400 Medical ship and the HQ-401 PSYWAR ship on a trip down into Hoa Hao country and I want you to go along and babysit him so to speak. Just make sure he doesn't get involved in anything that would cast aspersion on our advisory efforts, if you get what I mean. The trip should last about a week and incidentally, try to avoid swallowing any more river water. Oh yes one more thing, is there anything that needs doing for the next edition of the Newsletter?"

"No sir, the paperwork is over at the print shop now and will be distributed on time."

"Good, good," he replied as he settled back in his chair. "The ships will be at the pier in front of VNN Headquarters tomorrow morning and my understanding is that you will ride the HQ-400."

"That's good because Captain Tai and I are friends," I said.

"They're scheduled to depart at 0815, but you know how that goes. Just make sure you're both aboard before then."

"Will do Captain," I answered as I rose and left his office. That wasn't too bad, I thought to myself as I climbed the stairs back to my office. He is one tough guy to figure out.

The laughter started the minute that my office mates heard that the old man was sending me down to the Delta again. Ed remarked in his easy going manner, "Do you suppose he found out that his life is so much more relaxing without you around to muck things up?"

"Could be," I retorted, "But then again, who cares?" "Beers are on me on top of the Brinks, if you'd care to kill an hour or so after work," I announced. The Brinks was also a BOQ, located just four blocks up from Headquarters on Hai Ba Trung Street. It too boasted a rooftop eatery and bar for officers and similarly ranked civilians like the Rex two blocks over. The Brinks quality-wise however, was a cut below the Rex, but as we were fond to say in the Navy, "Any old port in a storm."

The five story building was constructed atop an open parking area surrounded by a high brick perimeter wall with a wide gated entrance on Hai Ba Trung. The residents and patrons normally parked their vehicles in the vast street level parking area under the building which was much safer than parking outside on the street.

On the 22nd of December 1964 when security was lax, VC Sappers entered the area in a canvas covered truck and managed to park it amongst the other vehicles. The explosives laden truck went unnoticed for two days and on Christmas Eve, just as the Holiday festivities got underway, the explosives were remotely detonated. Fortunately the building remained standing, but the horrendous blast resulted in some 100 plus US, Australian and Vietnamese personnel injured and two US killed. Now in 1967, the episode had faded with the constant changing of the guard and a false sense of normalcy had returned.

Before leaving the office, I made a call to the Personal Response Office over at NAVSUPPACT and got one of the Yeomen. "This is Lieutenant Kay down at VNN Headquarters and I was wondering if you had any pamphlets about the Hoa Hao available."

"Sure do Lieutenant. When do you need it?"

"By tonight if possible; could you drop it off at the McCarthy BOQ desk and tell them it's for me if it's not too much trouble?"

"No problem. I live at the Plaza so it's on the way."

With that done, I joined George in Ed's Jeep and headed for the Brinks. Commander Johnson and Lieutenant Commander Klamath had already departed. We left word with Ba Lan for Major Towson to join us if he returned before the girls left for the day.

The rooftop bar area was not crowded since many of the patrons preferred to imbibe much later in the evening after the sun went down. We naturally had no such compunctions, drinking whenever the opportunity presented itself and this was one of those times. We sat at a table on the patio in order to get some of the rare breeze that was occasionally blowing across the roof-tops. The patio's overhead was constructed of green corrugated plastic sheets that did a good job of keeping the midday sun at bay. When the petite waitress arrived, I ordered beers all around except for George, who stuck to his Coke. I can only imagine what it was like for him growing up in an Orphanage. He had missed so much in life and I sincerely hoped that he'd get married and make up for it when he returned home, although there was never any mention of a girl in his life.

The ice cold beers and Coke were served along with a huge bowl of fresh pop corn. As we took turns dipping into the bowl, the conversation drifted to my Hoa Hao trip in the morning. Commander Johnson said that his counterpart related a story to him about the Hoa Hao. It seemed that a few years ago the local VC had paid a visit to the Hoa Hao village in an effort to intimidate their elders. The Hoa Hao, who had a lifetime of being oppressed by the French, Japanese and the Diem regime in Saigon, calmly subdued the two VC emissaries and hung them from the branch of a huge banyan tree just outside the entrance to the village. Needless to say, they were never approached nor bothered again.

"Hope you people don't get that kind of welcome," remarked Klamath as he puffed away happily on his ever-present briar pipe.

"I don't think that'll happen. After all, we're going down there offering free medical care, medicines and a Vietnamese version of a USO show," said Commander Johnson.

"What's your roll in all this?" asked Ed.

"Believe it or not, I'm babysitting some NBC correspondent who finagled this trip out of NAVFORV's Public Affairs Office. The good Captain wants me to make sure he sees how well the Viet Navy interacts with the Hoa Hao and he'll be able to observe firsthand the compassion that they have for their countrymen."

"Boy that sounds like a hard row to hoe," murmured Klamath. "But then again, the crews of the HQ 400 and 401 are specialists in their trade and not the normal run of the mill 'My daddy's pull got me into the Navy' sailor."

George, who had been taking it all in said, "That's the kind of assignment I'd like. Being aboard as a ship's advisor instead of laboring away with the darn history log that will most likely wind up unread in the basement of the Navy Department."

"Ah George, you'll get your chance," I remarked feebly.

"Yeah, only if you extend your tour for six or twelve more months," said Klamath gently sucking on his pipe.

"Maybe I'll just do that," answered George seriously. "I can't see going through that entire Counter-Insurgency crap just to sit in an office like Ben Cratchett used to do for Scrooge."

That brought laughter into the conversation as I ordered another round for the table.

"Are you calling our good Captain, Ebeneezer Scrooge?" asked Ed raising his eyebrows in amazement. We were all taken by surprise at the strident tone taken by the normally mild mannered Staff Historian.

"Seems appropriate to me," said George defensively. "But I'm like you Bob; I want to put some time in the field too, so that if and when I ever have children, I can tell them I was an advisor to the Vietnamese Navy, not holding down a standard gray navy chair made by a low bidder in Brooklyn. Know what I mean?"

I think all of us around the table understood George's frustration and got a better read on the quiet, likable lad from New York City.

With that, we were ready to go our separate ways. Ed asked me if I wanted a ride to the McCarthy, but I said, "Thanks, but I can hoof it from here."

George decided to stay and have his usual two cheeseburgers and fries, served with lettuce, tomato and another Coke.

After a slow, descent in the sluggish elevator, I exited the building and turned right at the corner heading towards Tu Do Street. I crossed the bar-filled street and continued walking straight past the side of the white National Assembly Building on the left which brought me to the Continental Hotel on the right. A small park occupied the center of the street between the Continental Hotel with its famous outdoor veranda and the newer Caravelle Hotel across the street. Next to the Caravelle was the PTT building where all the Journalists in-country transmitted their latest stories back to their parent newspapers.

A huge bronze statue that depicted two Vietnamese soldiers with rifles crouched forward as if in combat, occupied the park. It was meant to be inspiring, but the story that had been going around was that the soldier in the back was an American who was pushing the reluctant ARVN into battle.

The intersection of Le Loi and Nguyen Hue, known as Lam Son Square, was generally considered the center of downtown Saigon. In the square there was a circle that contained a water fountain that sometimes functioned. When it was working, water would cascade down into the pool at its base. As I crossed diagonally across the intersection dodging the ever-present traffic, I arrived at the McCarthy BOQ, picked up my promised pamphlet on the Hoa Hao and headed for my bed. My reading light must have been 15 watts, but it allowed me to read the thin pamphlet without bothering my sleeping roommates.

OFF TO HOA HAO

Once again both of them had already departed before I woke up, and that was OK with me because it meant that the shower was all mine again; so I quickly took advantage of it. I had already packed a small bag the night before with the essentials that I needed for the trip. All that was left was to fill my canteen with some good potable water since I wasn't too sure about the quality of the ship's water supply. Looking around the room I saw a Smirnoff Vodka bottle sitting by Captain Tolliver's bed stand, so I proceeded to fill my canteen from it since mine was empty. As I may or may not have stated before, one of our maid's duties was to fill the recycled liquor bottles with potable water daily. Ba Tu was very reliable at replenishing our supply, so we knew the water was fresh every day. I then headed down to get some breakfast figuring that it was better to start out on a full stomach. Finding any empty table at Dawn's station, I ordered a double order of scrambled eggs, crisp bacon, home fried potatoes and whole wheat toast. Two cups of strong hot coffee helped wash the food down and I was off and running down to the pier.

Standing at the head of the jetty that led to the pier, there was a lone bored looking civilian smoking a cigarette. My first impression of him as I approached was that he had an uncanny resemblance to the actor William Holden, with the exception of a mediocre attempt at a mustache a la Errol Flynn. He was wearing the traditional short sleeved light tan "Bush Jacket" that was the uniform of the day for the media people in-country. Lightly creased khaki pants coordinated fairly well with the jacket and the cuffs were hemmed up about three inches showing off his rugged high top Red Wing boots. Assuming he was the Journalist that I was supposed to meet, I went up and introduced myself. "Hi, I'm Lieutenant Bob Kay from the Naval Advisory Group."

"Pleased to meet you Lieutenant, I'm Wilson Hall from NBC," he said with a soft gravelly voice as he reached out to shake my hand. His handshake however, was disappointingly feminine-like. I was slightly put off by the encounter because I come from the school of firm handshakes between men. Not the bone-crushing macho grip that some guys like to intimidate you with, but a genuine, even-pressured hand clasp. To me that indicates strength of character. But then again, that was just one of my many quirks and it's not a foolproof indicator of manhood by any means.

"There are three others that are also coming along; my camera operator and two USIS military reps. They should be here at any time," said the journalist.

Just then a green painted Scout skidded to an abrupt stop by the curb at the foot of the jetty and three passengers got out. One was a young US Army 2nd Lieutenant, a middle-aged Major and a wiry looking Vietnamese civilian. They unloaded a fairly large black shoulder video camera and three small duffle bags that must have been their personal gear from the rear of the Scout.

"That's them now," he said as the three approached us. The Lieutenant did not seem to be in any hurry while the Major and the Viet hustled up the jetty.

"This is Major Grant Reese, Lieutenant Tom Tully from USIS and my cameraman Mr. Phan," he said introducing the trio. The Major was a little long in the tooth for his pay grade, so I assumed that he was prior enlisted. He was about my size, with huge farmer-like hands, although his frame was on the medium side. His thinning hair was corn-silk yellow and tufts of it stuck up from the top of his tee shirt under his greens. The eyes were a washed-out brown and wrinkles had been making steady inroads on his face. The voice had a soft Texas twang, although not too pronounced. Tully, on the other hand, resembled a wise-ass from the streets of New York. His countenance seemed greasy and his thick black eyebrows hovered over black eyes that were constantly in motion as if expecting a VC to suddenly jump out and attack him. An aquiline nose that turned down sharply at the end sort of reminded me of the Wicked Witch in the Wizard of Oz. He was most definitely not recruitment poster material by any means. Phan, the cameraman appeared to be a happy-go-lucky individual in his late twenties and struck from the same mold as other Viets his age. He carried a huge video camera on his shoulder and had a large case of audio equipment at his feet. Almost immediately I wondered why he wasn't in the Armed Forces of Vietnam. It had become second nature for me to wonder about things like that.

This is Lieutenant Bob Kay from the Advisory Group who will be chaperoning us on the trip," said Hall to the trio.

Tully quickly replied, "If the Lieutenant is coming along, there's no reason that I'm needed. Two military types should be enough to show the flag, so I'll just mosey on back to the office and tell them you're in good hands," he said looking at Reese. "Besides, I'm not a very good sailor and it'll save manpower."

The Major took this in stride and apparently could have cared less about Tully's intention of bailing out of the trip. Strange folks these Army guys I thought, but replied, "That's OK by me if it's OK with you folks. Besides, the current in the rivers along with the wave action once we clear the Delta can cause '*mal de mer*,'' I said facetiously.

Catching my sarcasm, Major Reese finally said that it would be fine if the Lieutenant stayed behind. No sooner were the words out of his mouth when Tully grabbed his mini-duffle and beat feet off the jetty heading for Tu Do Street.

"Must have something important to tend to in town," I mused aloud as Hall nodded his head in agreement. The Major, on the other hand said snidely, "I'll miss him like bleeding hemorrhoids because he's a worthless piece of shit. His old man is a chicken colonel with the Rangers up in Hue and there's no doubt in my mind that Daddy played a big part in having his son assigned to a desk in USIS/Saigon. They tried to make a Public Affairs Officer out of him, but it was obvious he was short on talent and long on political pull. Believe me; we're better off without him. He'll most likely go back and say that we didn't want him along."

Slightly taken aback by the whole scene, I said, "If you need me to back you up when we return I'll be there. Well then, are you folks ready for a boat ride into the unknown?"

It's a damn sight better than hanging around Saigon drinking myself to death," said Wilson.

"I hear you. I'm presently attached to Staff here and it's driving me crazy. Before being shanghaied back to Saigon, I was attached to a Junk Group on a little island south of Camau."

"Sounds like there's more to that story," he said raising his right eyebrow slightly.

"There is and I'll be glad to tell you about it on the way down to Hoa Hao. C'mon, we might as well get aboard."

The RVN Hat Giang HQ-400, with a distinctive large Red Cross painted on her hull amidships, was tied up at the pier at the end of the jetty. Having researched her pedigree, I learned that she was the ex-USS LSM-335 and was transferred to the Vietnamese Navy in 1955. She was 203 feet long with a beam of 34.5 feet and just right for maneuvering on the rivers and along the coastal waters. She was modified into a Medical Assist ship with a full complement of medical personnel and equipment aboard.

The ship's Captain, Lieutenant Commander Tai, in his faded blue working uniform, met us at the quarterdeck as soon as we stepped aboard. He was approximately five feet seven inches tall with a soft body that apparently had not been exposed to too much rigorous physical activity. That would imply that his mental ability was his long suit. He wore a perpetual grin that exposed his overly large upper teeth which some people found to be a disconcerting physical trait in some of the Vietnamese.

I had met him several times before at VNN Headquarters and he had the reputation of being one of the better officers. He had been to the States for training and his liking for all things American was well known. I knew he would go out of his way to make this a pleasurable trip, especially when the opportunity to get some good press was presenting itself.

I introduced Major Reese, the Journalist and the cameraman to the Captain and Tai said, "I was under the impression that there was another officer coming aboard."

"He had a sudden emergency back at the office, but we can handle the situation easily," said Reese.

"I had billeted you with Lieutenant Kay and the Lieutenant with Mr. Hall, but under the circumstances Major, you can occupy my At-Sea cabin and Mr. Hall can share his with Lieutenant Kay. Please follow my Chief Master at Arms," indicating an intense muscular individual who had quietly approached us. "He will show you to your quarters. We will be getting underway on schedule and if you'd like, please feel free to join me on the bridge once you're settled in."

We all thanked him just as the stern-faced CMAA asked Major Reese to follow him up to the Captain's sea cabin. Turning to us, he said that he would be right back to take us to our quarters. Now this guy impressed me because he reminded me of an Oriental Wyatt Earp. There was no doubt that he carried out his duties as the ship's Head Sheriff with absolute confidence. He surprised me later however, after showing us to our stateroom; he smiled broadly and said, "Lunch will be served in the wardroom at 1145. I'm sure you can find it *Dai-Uy*. I will bunk Mr. Phan in the Chief's quarters where I'm sure he will be most comfortable."

"Yes, thank you Chief," I replied.

The stateroom was typical of junior officer's accommodations aboard naval vessels measuring eight feet by six feet. It contained a double bunk against the outer bulkhead, two fold-up desks with two chairs that had seen better days and a stainless steel sink with a medicine cabinet above it. "All the comforts of home, I said glibly. Would you prefer the upper or the lower?"

"I'll take the lower bunk, since I'm not as young as you are," Hall said as he flopped onto the bunk. He made the right choice as far as I was concerned because the upper bunk had a porthole in the bulkhead that was level with my head when I lay down. The air conditioning systems on these old ships were old and were known to break down, having seen better days before we turned them over to the Vietnamese. The porthole had a screen insert and an outer air scoop that normally directed a flow of air into the compartment while underway. That would definitely benefit me. Besides, since I was the tour guide it stood to reason that I should have some perks.

The sound of scrambling feet above and the slight rumble from below decks announced that we were getting ready to get underway.

Wilson asked me to bring him up to speed about the Hoa Hao since he didn't have a clue about them. Apparently, someone in his home office decided to lay this assignment on him probably to get him away from the Saigon bars for awhile. Acute alcoholism doesn't go unnoticed for very long in the correspondent's community and in that cutthroat profession, word is bound to trickle back to the home office. It's inevitable and for that, I started to have some sympathy for the man.

I sat down in one of the chairs and proceeded to explain what I had learned about the Hoa Hao from information provided to me by the Personal Response folks at NAVSUPPACT. That office had been created to familiarize newly arrived navy personnel with the customs, history and religions that they were apt to encounter during their Vietnam tour. It went into considerably more depth than the information that was being presented at Coronado and I had frankly found it fascinating.

The Hoa Hao religion was formed as a militant sect and a secret society of the Buddhist religion in 1939 by a twenty year old Buddhist Reformer named Huynh Phu So. He was born in 1919 in the village of Hoa Hao, District of Tan Chau located in Chau Doc Province. The religion is a combination of Animism, Buddhism, Confucianism and Taoism and is very nationalistic and extremely xenophobic. It primarily emphasizes the importance of home worship instead of erecting and attending pagodas and temples. It rejects the use of statues, gongs, bells or burnt offerings and uses their financial resources to assist the needy among their people. Under a Buddhist monk named Thay Xom, Huynh Phu So studied the art of acupuncture, hypnotism, Buddhist philosophy and a smattering of sorcery. To help in identifying his teachings, he named the new religion after his village of Hoa Hao and it remains the same to this day.

His apparent "gift of prophecy" foretold the defeat of the French in World War II, the coming of the Japanese invaders and the ultimate arrival of the Americans. This, along with his skills of healing by acupuncture and herbs, made him extremely popular among the people. Additionally, his hypnotic stare earned him the nickname of the "Mad Bonze."

The neophyte religion joined forces with the Cao Dai in their armed resistance against the French and later in 1942 against the Japanese colonialists. Eventually the French considered his preaching to be extremely anti-French and strongly political. His growing popularity made them uneasy and they viewed him as a real political threat so they exiled him away from Saigon to the city of My Tho where he succeeded in gaining many more converts. Fully exasperated by now with his preaching, the French placed him under house arrest under trumped-up charges and later detained him in a Psychiatric facility in Cholon. He managed to convert the Director/Psychiatrist, who declared him sane and released him. Immediately, the French exiled him to Vinh Long in Bac Lieu Province where he continued to convert the populace into the Hoa Hao. The frustrated French once again exiled him to Laos only to have the Japanese insist that he return to Saigon to use as their protégé in October 1942.

After the surrender of the Japanese, Huynh Phu So aligned the Hoa Hao with the National United Front which was a Viet Minh organization. This was short lived because neither the Hoa Hao nor the Cao Dai adherents could accept the Viet Minh leadership. This soon caused the downfall and dissolution of the United Front. Huynh Phu So then became an avid anti-Communist and anti-French politician and despite this, the Viet Minh appointed him to the nine-member Executive Committee for South Vietnam hoping to placate him and his followers. However, since six of the committee members were Communists, disharmony broke out between them and Huynh Phu So finally fled for his life in 1946.

In April of 1947, in response to conciliatory overtures by the Viet Minh to meet with them in Long Xuyen, he was captured, tried and executed by the Communists. The Hoa Hao party however remained intact and turned their full wrath against the Viet Minh. The followers were never told of his death rather that he had temporarily withdrawn and would eventually return. The Hoa Hao still refuse to comment on the subject and is the basis for their extreme hatred for everything the Communists stand for and continue to destroy all of them who enter their domain.

Upon the defeat and expulsion of the French, President No Dinh Diem commenced his oppression of the Buddhists and the Hoa Hao in the south. Diem was cautioned by the President Kennedy to stop antagonizing these people but he stubbornly refused. Ultimately, he was assassinated along with his brother who had the misfortune to be with him at the time. There are many who still believe that the CIA was responsible but nothing ever came of it. The Hoa Hao then centralized themselves back home in the Delta where their movement had originated and continues to this day oblivious to all the politics going on around them. They sought seclusion, isolation and declared all government factions and Vietcong as persona non grata.

"And that's the story of the Hoa Hao in a nutshell. I hope it'll help you out during the next day or so and in fact, I'll give you the literature that I have," I said.

"Hey, that's exactly the background info that I'll need to complete this assignment properly. Thanks a million."

"This two ship effort on the part of the government is an attempt to soften the animosity that exists between the Hoa Hao and Saigon," I said. "All previous diplomatic efforts had failed to rally the group's support in the war against the north."

Wilson, lying on his side in the bunk with his head propped up on his arm, said, "Do you think we're doing any good here?"

"Well, I haven't met anyone in Vietnam's outback that would refuse free medical treatment, no matter how minimal and where it comes from. Also, the chance to see some live entertainment is appealing to these folks. I don't think you'll find any TV sets in Hoa Hao and the main source of enjoyment for the adults down here is copulation."

"Should be interesting, to say the least," Wilson replied. "Hopefully, I can put together something that should satisfy the fat cats back at NBC."

As stated by Captain Tai when we boarded, the ship did indeed get underway exactly at 0830. Wilson and I had been talking for about two hours and he said as he swung his feet out of the bunk, "It's almost time for lunch. How about we take a turn around the deck and take in the scenery?"

I'd almost forgotten that these landlocked Journalists rarely got the opportunity to sail on any of the waterways that provide sustenance to the people of Vietnam, so I agreed.

We were traveling at about 8 knots and were somewhere on the Soi Rap River on the way down to the open sea. The sky was a cloudless cerulean blue with a slight brownish haze hovering over the riverbanks. "The odor of rotting vegetation and the smell of burning charcoal fires is commonplace along the rivers of the Delta," I said to Wilson.

"Strange that you don't see many birds flying around," he mused after looking around the horizon.

"Probably because they've all been killed and eaten and their proliferation has been set back quite a bit." I said.

We made our way into the ward room and found Major Reese sitting at the smaller of the two tables having a quiet relaxed conversation with the Captain.

"Good afternoon gentlemen, please join us," said Captain Tai as some of the other ship's officers filed into the Wardroom. "I hope you found your accommodations satisfactory."

"Yes sir, they are indeed adequate. We seem to be making good time," I said.

"Actually, we're a little ahead of schedule. I received word earlier that the HQ-401 is already at Hoa Hao and is already making preparations with the villagers for our arrival."

"When do you anticipate reaching there, Captain?"

"I plan to steam through the night and arrive around eight in the morning. Since there's a bright full moon tonight navigating will not be a problem. I don't foresee anything in the way of hostilities because the word has been spread well in advance of our arrival. The VC would rather take advantage of the medical care we provide than to attack the gift-givers. Returning is another matter, but one which we will address when the time comes. In the meantime, I hope you will join us for a simple lunch."

I noticed a savory aroma coming from the galley and immediately recognized it as *Pho*. My senses kicked in and I quickly remembered the excellent beef soup that the Vietnamese enjoy so well. "A simple lunch" was an understatement.

It might have been a simple fare for the Vietnamese but it was an offering fit for a king as far as we gringos were concerned.

Major Reese and Wilson appeared to actually relish the soup as evidenced by the way they dispatched their portions. After the Mess Attendant cleared away all the bowls, cups of green tea were served all around and it was a perfect finish to a very hearty and satisfying meal.

Captain Tai extended his invitation for us to join him up on the bridge and we assured him we would take him up on his offer. Wilson, the Major and I headed back to the fantail after leaving the somewhat cooler but stuffier air in the Wardroom. The breeze off the water felt refreshing and Wilson immediately lit up a cigarette and offered them around. The Major said he had given them up years ago and I said that I had never started, although I had indulged a pipe for years without inhaling. It had been a security blanket in that it helped me concentrate on whatever work I was doing. The biggest assist I had however, in giving it up, was that it required too much junk to lug around. There was the pipe, tobacco pouch, butane lighter, a combination tamper and bowl scraper and pipe cleaners. There were just too many items and too few pockets, so I reluctantly, albeit fortunately, became a non-smoker.

There were a few small fishing boats plying their way around the myriad of fishnets that were situated all over the Delta. The local fishermen found that the confluence of so many rivers emptying into the South China Sea was an excellent place for snaring fish, coming or going. They hastily avoided our larger vessel as soon as they spotted us coming because they disliked having their boats boarded and searched continuously by the various patrols that criss-crossed the Delta.

As we approached the mouth of the mighty Mekong River, two US Navy PBRs appeared from out of nowhere apparently to escort us. One boat positioned itself ahead of us and the other trailed about fifty yards astern.

Once we entered the Mekong River, the cool breeze we had enjoyed before turned tepid and the humidity had noticeably increased. The thick vegetation bordering both sides of the river seemed to exude its dank sultry breath over the entire area. It was the typical environment of the rain forests in the Amazon and Orinoco Rivers in South America. It wasn't as stifling because of our movement over the water. We would follow the Mekong until it intersected the Song Tien Giang River which would take us to Hoa Hao. Reese broke the comfortable silence as he remarked that this river was reputed to contain over two hundred species of fish and over a hundred species of fresh water snails.

"Wow," I said, "that's a lot of marine life for this old waterway. But then again, it's the 10th or 11th longest river in the world, stretching all the way from South Vietnam to China's border with Tibet."

Wilson sighed as he flipped the remnant of his cigarette arcing out into our wake and said, "I'm sure glad you walking travel folders accompanied me because I can use all the filler material I can get for my report."

"Glad we could be of service," quipped Reese. "There's so much history to this country and to think that just a few years ago, few Americans knew where Vietnam was geographically."

"Well, I'm about ready to measure my rack until supper," said Wilson. "This is all brand new to me, but I'd like to come back out on deck after supper and enjoy the ride for awhile."

"Sounds like a plan," said Reese.

"Me, I'm going topside and join the Captain on the bridge. It's been awhile since I stood on a bridge deck underway and I kinda miss it," I remarked with a smile.

The atmosphere on the bridge was like any other military ship in the world. The helmsman seemed relaxed but was alert for any sudden change in course directed by the Officer-of-the-Deck because he was navigating by the Mark 1, Mod 1 eye-ball rather than from the Navigator's chart. Tonight, this was totally acceptable because the full moon's brightness illuminated the entire river and the sky was cloudless. Lookouts were posted on each wing of the bridge to scan the river ahead for any potential problem. The warm breeze against your face had a tendency to lull one to sleep and having been with Vietnamese sailors for awhile, wondered if they occasionally closed their eyes as they peered through their binoculars while leaning against the bridge's splinter-shield. The only sounds to be heard were the swish from the ship's bow cutting through the brown water and the deep rumble of the accompanying PBR's Jacuzzi engines.

Inside the pilothouse however, everyone was intently absorbed in their assigned duties, more than likely because Captain Tai was sitting in the bridge chair. He was relaxed and calmly taking in everything that was going on around him. Lieutenant Mai's voice, the XO of the HQ-401, was coming from the comm speaker passing on information about the preparations at Hoa Hao since they had arrived earlier in the day. The transmission was rogered for by the young OOD once Captain Tai acknowledged it with a nod of his head. That's when he saw me enter the bridge from the inside passageway ladder. "Come in *Dai-Uy*," he said as he ordered the Quartermaster to give me his stool and had it placed near his chair. "Well how do you like having a steel deck under your feet again instead of bouncing around in those Junks?"

"It feels great, but it's a lot different being out here than back home with the fleet. All the training and repetitive drills I've endured in our Navy seem so far away since having being under actual combat conditions. I know that I'll have a problem responding to those drills with any kind of enthusiasm if I ever decide to return to stateside sea duty."

"Yes, I can understand that," said Tai. "Here in Vietnam, we have been doing this for so long that most of us do not know any other way. Hopefully, someday peace will come to my country and we will be able to enjoy our old age quietly and do the things that make us happy with our families. Although I am a military man, I do not enjoy the killing of warfare. It's so senseless to lose the potential of our country's youth simply for ideological and religious differences. Don't you agree?"

"I do. After all, even though America has been through a few of those conflicts, they were fortunately not fought on our home soil for over one hundred years. Fighting in your own backyard keeps you on the defensive and saps the energetic effort that should be directed towards improving life. There's no future in dying in battle."

"I must agree with you there. Some people think that war is exciting and romantic, as shown in the movies. But there is nothing exciting or romantic about seeing someone get horribly maimed for the rest of their life or killed outright," said Tai as he scratched the side of his head.

"So far, I have enjoyed my stay in Vietnam because it has given me the opportunity to observe another culture and become part of it. Being an advisor has provided a good insight into the Vietnamese people that cannot be fully understood by American troops isolated in their units or our sailors manning the ships at sea. Sure, they can later say that they were in Vietnam, but what knowledge did they bring back with them about the country and its people?"

"You are right *Dai-Uy*. Even though I spent some time in your country, I never really had the time to fully appreciate your culture. First of all, it was too overwhelming and secondly, I had been subjected to the narrow-minded thinking of our former French occupiers of my country. Perhaps someday, I and my family would be afforded the chance to spend some time in the United States and experience all the wonderful things that exist there."

We both became silent, each lost in his own thoughts. My butt was starting to hurt because the stool was not adequately padded and one of the legs was shorter than the rest. The movement of the ship caused me to rock ever so slightly and after awhile it began to annoy me. I finally stood up and said to the Captain that I had enjoyed talking with him and that I was heading below.

"Goodnight *Dai-Uy*. I hope you have a pleasant sleep."

"Thank you Captain; see you in the morning," I replied as I turned and headed back down the ladder to my stateroom. Before I even opened the door to my room, I could hear Wilson's sonorous snores coming from within. He must have really been tired and the fresh air didn't hurt any either. It was quite different from the cigarette-laden air of the Rex rooftop or the streets of Saigon. Whatever the cause, he should wake up in the morning more refreshed and I could only hope the same for me. I peeled off my clothes and climbed into the top bunk clad only in my shorts. I didn't need to open the porthole because the ship's ventilation system was working perfectly and laying my head on the pillow was the last thing I remembered until the next morning.

Wilson was already awake and shaved when I finally opened my eyes. "Man, was that a great sleep or what," I asked.

"That's an understatement," he replied. "I sure hope we don't have tea and soup for breakfast because I'm hungry.

"Well, just let me shave and get dressed and we'll make it to the Wardroom and see. I'm sure Tai will have coffee and French bread for us."

Entering the Wardroom, we found Reese sitting alone. The mess attendant was just bringing out Reese's breakfast and lo and behold it was two fried eggs, two strips of crisp bacon, a cup of coffee and a basket full of French bread. "It seems that Captain Tai has a flare for the dramatic," Wilson said.

"I guess his tour in the States had something to do with that." The aroma coming from Reese's food made me realize how hungry I really was. The mess attendant politely asked us what we would like for breakfast and Wilson and I said that we'd like the same. The young man nodded, smiling slightly and said that the food would be along momentarily. He reappeared almost immediately and filled our cups with freshly brewed French roasted coffee.

The food had arrived and we were just finishing up with a second cup of coffee, when Captain Tai entered the Ward Room. As the three of us started to rise in deference to the CO, he motioned us to remain seated. He pulled up a chair to join us and asked the Mess Attendant for a cup of coffee also. "The breakfast was wonderfully delicious," said Wilson, to which Tai nodded his appreciation, exhibiting his radiant smile.

"I am happy that it met with your satisfaction. From my short time in your country I learned that bacon and eggs is much more preferred for breakfast than a bowl of *Pho* or plain French bread and coffee."

I answered by saying that I have thoroughly enjoyed eating fresh warm French bread, liberally buttered, some hard cheese and a good cup of coffee.

"Me, I've learned to start my day with a strong cup of coffee so that the caffeine kicks in and gets me on my way. I was never much one for bulky breakfasts being in the news reporting business. Lunch and dinner were more important because business can readily be conducted at a leisurely pace whereas breakfast is not a good venue for serious conversation. Besides, who feels like talking when you're trying your damndest to wake up or shake off a hangover?" remarked Wilson.

Reese was noncommittal by saying that since he had spent a considerable amount of his career on an army base, meal time, no matter which one it was, was an exercise in information gathering and dispensing. I had to agree with that completely.

"When you gentlemen finish your breakfast, we should just about be making our approach to Hoa Hao. The HQ-401 is already bow-in on the beach and there's room for us to pull in alongside. This way, we can put our bow ramp down which is better than using the accommodation ladder and being ferried to the beach by small boat," announced Tai as he departed the Wardroom.

Reese, Wilson and I upon finishing our coffees, immediately went to the nearest head to complete our morning constitutionals. Once finished with the essentials, we went back up to the flying bridge so we could observe our approach to Hoa Hao.

HOA HAO

Once in sight of Hoa Hao, our two escorting PBRs quickly executed one hundred and eighty degree turns and with a squeal from the lead boats siren, headed back to their base. The maneuver of reversing direction on a dime is one of the boats' greatest attributes. A great bunch of guys!

As stated before, the RVNS Hau Giang HQ-401, (ex-USS LSM-110), had departed Saigon earlier and was now bow-in to the beach at Hoa Hao with her ramp down. The ship had been transferred to the French in 1954 and later to the Viet navy in 1955. Although she too had a large Red Cross painted on her hull, her main function was as a Psychological Warfare platform. There were about 400 smiling villagers standing around the perimeter that had been marked off by the 401's crew to keep them at a distance while our ship made its approach to the beach.

"Where did all these folks come from?" asked Wilson. "They can't all be residents of Hoa Hao, right?"

"No," I replied. "Remember Tai told us that the word had been put out announcing our intended visit and they have come from all over the immediate area to join in the festivities and get free medical and dental treatment. You can be sure that there are many VC among them but they won't pose any immediate threat. Why bite the hand that feeds you?"

A crewmember of the HQ-401 was speaking over a hand-held loudspeaker to the crowd. He was telling them to stay behind the perimeter for their own safety while our ship was making its landing. He continued to say that once the ship was beached that medical and dental screenings would commence only for adults over the age of 17. The younger children should proceed to the center of the village where entertainment would be presented by the crew of the HQ-401. After lunch, all the younger children will get the opportunity to be examined by the medical teams. Then after supper, a musical play will be presented for all back in the village's center. A slight ripple of applause trickled from the crowd as they muttered their approval.

Tai had translated the announcements for us and said, "Well gentlemen that will be our schedule for this visit. I hope you find it both interesting and informative."

"Sounds good to me," said Wilson. "But how can you expect to give medical treatment to all these people in such a short time?"

Tai replied, "For most of these villagers, it will be the first time that they have come in contact with anyone who has had medical training. However, if anything serious is discovered, the individuals will be informed how they can seek further medical attention and the consequences for ignoring the advice

"And it puts a positive spin on the Saigon government," added Reese softly to me. "It's the whole idea behind this endeavor, you know 'Win the minds and hearts of the people' and all that."

"I know, you can lead a horse to water but you can't make him drink,' said Wilson.

With the ship securely beached and its bow ramp down, medical personnel had already set up examining stations in the well deck. The first two stations were for initial screening manned by senior chief medical petty officers. Here, each individual would state his or her complaint and then be directed to a particular station marked by numbers. The crewman with the bull horn then directed those who wished to be examined to form two single lines leading aboard to the screeners, while the children were herded by female Navy personnel to the center of the village.

One of the seamen came up to the signal bridge and said that the Captain requested our presence on the bridge. As we entered the pilot house, our cameraman Anh was just coming up the outside ladder. "What's up?" he asked Wilson.

"Don't know, but we're about to find out."

The Captain was still sitting in his bridge chair and turned to us as we approached. "You have been invited to visit the Hamlet Chief in his house along with me and Captain Thanh from the HQ-401. It is protocol and a good opportunity to introduce you to this elderly but very influential leader of the Hoa Hao. So, if you feel up to it, I suggest we go."

With that, we all filed down the ladder into the well-deck and out onto the beach. Captain Thanh was standing at the edge of the village giving last minute instructions to some members of his crew involved with the presentations. We joined him as Tai made the introductions and hands were shook all around.

"Time to pay our respects," said Thanh as he started to lead us to the house of the Hamlet Chief. "The village leader here in Hoa Hao is in his early nineties and has led these people since the Japanese occupation. Also, don't be shocked at his uncanny resemblance to Ho Chi Minh. It is purely unintentional because there is no love lost between the two gentlemen. Further, do not be taken in by his frail appearance for he was and still is a ferocious jungle fighter."

Wow, I thought to myself, it's almost like meeting a living legend and we are probably among the minority of privileged Americans who will ever get to meet this man.

As we came to the clearing in the center of the village, the PsyOps crew from the 401 had about a hundred children hunkered down on the ground in a semi-circle. One of the petty officers was leading them in a group songfest as the high-pitched voices of the children rang out over the surrounding jungle with pride as only they can exhibit when they get a chance to join in with the grown-ups. Off to one side, a male petty officer was setting up a chalkboard where he would present the "Saigon" message in terms that were aimed at the younger generation.

Behind the song director, a Punch and Judy stage was quickly being constructed by the PsyOps crew. Once the singing and light indoctrination portions were finished, the children would be treated to several puppet shows. This was the high point for the kids; a chance to laugh and be carried away to a mystical place free from their humdrum lives and away from the war that was going on all around them.

The Hamlet Chief's house was set back in a small shaded bamboo grove not too far from the center of the village. An unpainted wooden makeshift fence encircled the right side of the yard and contained a few clucking chickens pecking happily at the dirt. Several various sized clay pots containing colorful flowers that I did not recognize, were set on the three wooden steps that led to the porch. The house itself was easily the largest one in the village and its tall canted roof indicated that it had high interior ceilings. It was well constructed and built out of a very dark wood, probably monkey pod that most likely was local to the area. Long faded plastic strips were hanging in the doorway that allowed the occasional breeze to waft into the house while keeping any flying insects outside.

Thanh knocked on the doorjamb and courteously called politely to announce that we had arrived.

A voice came from within beckoning us to enter. We removed our boots, (which is the custom when entering someone's house in Vietnam), and set them outside the entryway. The six of us in stocking feet filed through the darkened entrance. The interior of the house was remarkably cool and in shadows with no sunlight filtering in so it took a few seconds for us to adapt to the dim surroundings. The Hamlet Chief came slowly forward to greet us with enthusiasm that belied his advanced age. He was a shade over five and a half feet in height, slightly stooped, extremely slight of build and possessed the most penetrating pair of eyes that I had ever seen in an older person before. The eyes were accentuated by thick gray eyebrows that matched the color of his thinning hair that barely managed to cover his head. The wispy long goatee and drooping mustache did indeed make him a Ho Chi Minh look-alike.

As he shook hands with each of us bowing in turn, I noticed the skin of his hands was almost translucent. The gray-blue veins that carried his life's blood through his body were in stark contrast to the pale skin. But his hands were rock steady and firm as he greeted us. Meanwhile, a young teenage boy dressed in a white long-sleeved shirt and long black pants, started lighting oil lamps around the room. The Hamlet Chief proudly introduced him as his grandson Khoi.

"Although he is only sixteen, he takes very good care of me since my wife passed away last year. His parents were killed accidentally by the ARVN several months ago along with his younger sister. He was the sole survivor of that terrible event but unfortunately did not escape unscathed, as you can see."

The once smooth-skinned handsome face had been badly burned on the left side and he was very conscious of the ugly purple scar that marred his appearance. For that reason he tended to keep that side of his face turned away from any conversation directed towards him. "He's had a difficult time accepting his fate because of the way the children stare at him. I had hoped that having him here with me would ease his pain somewhat, but alas, progress has been rather slow."

Taking in the surroundings, I noticed the intricate scrolled woodwork that adorned the large room. Several old heavily framed pictures were hung on the walls that were obviously of his family and ancestors. He bade us to be seated in the various heavy dark-wooded uncushioned chairs around a small low round table set in the center of the room. Glancing upwards towards the ceiling, I could see that it was open up to the rafters. This feature is common to the tropics since hot air rises and the cooler, denser air remains below. One thing came to my attention and that was that there were no ceiling fans or electric lights anywhere. It was unbelievable that this village existed without electricity. Fortunately, the HQ 401's crew had rigged lights in the center of the village fed by huge cables that snaked over from the ship to provide the necessary lighting for the show.

While the old man was speaking to us, the boy left the room and returned a few minutes later carrying a black lacquered tray inlaid with mother of pearl figures. On it was a beautiful porcelain teapot and several small delicate matching teacups without handles. Khoi then proceeded to pour each of us a cup of the steaming liquid.

Apparently the Chief was also conversant in French as he freely interjected words such as '*maintainment*,' '*ecoutez-moi mes amis*', '*mais ouis*' and '*d'accord'* into his Vietnamese dialogue with Thanh and Tai. From what I could make of the conversation, the elder was asking how the war with the north was progressing. Naturally, both officers replied with the politically correct responses glorifying the Saigon government. Wilson, Reese, Pham and I sat back politely on the hard chairs sipping the hot but delightfully fragrant tea. We grinned a lot whenever the Chief looked our way which also brought a small smile to his wizened face.

Shortly, Tai leaned over and said softly that when he asked the old man if the local VC gave him any trouble, the answer was short and succinct. He said they used to come by the village every so often trying to recruit followers by first being polite. When that hadn't worked, they tried to intimidate the villagers, but to no avail. They continually sought food and clothes, until finally his patience ran out and he ordered the last two Viet Cong representatives hung from the large banyan tree by the entrance to the village. From that day on, the VC never bothered them again.

"Boy, the old gent has balls and that's what you need in a strong leader. Remind me to stay on the good side of him," said Reese whispering to me out of the side of his mouth, while still maintaining a smile.

When our fifteen minute visit of respect was over, we all stood and bowed as we shook hands in turn with the old warrior. He smiled broadly as he patted each of us on the back on our way out. After putting on our shoes, it felt good to be back out in the sunlight as we headed towards the children and the community songfest. "There's one thing that bothers me about the hangings," said Wilson. "How come there was no retribution from the VC when they learned that their brothers had been hung?"

I replied, "That's simple. You have to understand that the VC are dedicated to their ideology and in following the precepts set forth by Ho Chi Minh. They respect force and resistance because that's what they have been taught all these years. Why else would they hide and live underneath the ground in tunnels for months on end enduring that kind of lifestyle? And think about the many thousands in their ranks that trudge down the Ho Chi Minh trail from the north bearing unbelievable burdens while being attacked constantly from the air. That takes initiative and absolute stubborn adherence to their cause. From what I've seen so far the South Vietnamese do not possess that type of fervor. So, once the Hoa Hao took their stand, the VC backed off and left them alone."

"That makes sense," replied Reese. "But it still took guts for them to stand up to the VC. You have to respect them for that."

"And the VC did just that," I added.

"Say Captain Thanh, just how much dental and medical care can be administered to so many people?" asked Wilson.

Thanh replied "Most of the complaints are the usual maladies of youth and advanced age. Cataracts and glaucoma are normally treated with a month's supply of eye drops. The doctors lance boils and Tuberculosis, which is prevalent in Vietnam, is treated with placebos. The people seem to be satisfied with that. "The dentists do basically prophylaxis work, extracting bad teeth, treat gum diseases and generally try to stress good hygiene. If anything serious is detected, the individuals are advised to go to Chau Doc where there are some medical and dental facilities. Alas, many of them do not take the advice and choose to suffer rather than seek further professional help."

As we approached the mass of smiling, happy children with their shiny black heads of hair, crude wooden chairs were being set up for us off to the side where we could see the show. "I wonder what Lieutenant Tully is doing back in Saigon?" I said.

"Who gives a rat's ass," growled Reese as Wilson and Cameraman Pham nodded in agreement. It was plain to see that young Tully was pretty high up on everyone's shitlist.

The singing session was coming to an end and it was pleasant to hear the young high pitched voices resounding through the surrounding trees. As the grownups returned from their various medical and dental exams, they eagerly squatted down behind the cordon of children to enjoy the next part of the show which was the puppets.

"OH, I FORGOT TO TELL YOU - THEY DON'T WEAR DIAPERS"

Everyone eagerly turned their eyes towards the small stage in rapt attention. There were two puppets having a dialogue with each other amidst numerous punches and kicks being thrown that were accentuated by a sailor behind the stage banging medium sized cymbals and a small bass drum that provided emphasis to the action.

If you've ever seen a Punch and Judy puppet show, its theme is the same throughout the world: Rapid dialogue punctuated by jumps and punches that keep the audience deeply immersed in the byplay. This one was no different. Everyone clapped and cheered whenever Punch got pummeled by Judy and browbeaten by her caustic and seemingly unceasing harangue.

The show lasted about forty five minutes and then the curtain fell, much to the dismay of the children. It was time for the noon meal so the children quickly dispersed, each heading for their homes. A long table was quickly being set up for us guests and the elders. We were invited to bring our chairs around the table that was conveniently located in the shade of an enormous banyan tree. We were served by several of the wives with steaming bowls of steamed rice and generous amounts of white meat fish that probably had been netted in the river. Small ears of corn were also served that had been cooked in their husks over a charcoal fire and individual glasses of coconut milk were passed all around to quench our thirst. Hardly any conversation went on during the meal and it was fine by me as I realized that I was actually hungry. I found the fish tender and sweet, while dipping each morsel into the little dish of *Nuoc Mam* set before each person. The pungent chili peppers really spiced up the sauce and the tepid coconut juice gently soothed the pallet.

Finally, the Hamlet Chief quietly addressed all at the table, as Captain Tai quickly translated for our benefit. “He thanks all of us for our efforts here today on behalf of the people of Hoa Hao and wishes us many blessings in our future endeavors. We are most welcomed to return anytime and will always be considered friends of his people.”

“Tell him we wholeheartedly appreciate the opportunity to visit his village and partake of their hospitality,” said Major Reese. Tai once again relayed the remarks to the Chief and the elders who nodded their heads in acknowledgement.

After the meal was concluded, we were invited to take our chairs back for the rest of the show. We were informed by Tai that we would now be treated to a traditional classic Vietnamese opera known as *Hat Cheo*, the highlight of the entertainment.

The opera has been around since the 11th century and some believe that this classical Vietnamese music was strongly influenced by Chinese, Mongolian and Japanese opera. The stories depicted often rely on historical themes, tragedies, folklore and are presented with the actors dressed in elaborate costumes and stylized makeup. The men are bearded, wear long silk gowns and wear pillbox-type hats. The women are attired beautifully in long gowns and if not wearing tiara-type headdress, wear their hair up, coiled and coiffed. In every play, there is a buffoon who wears a short jacket and is identified by an accompanying deep bass drum accenting his lines. The musical background is composed of crashing cymbals, a three stringed lute, a bass drum, a one string Chordaphone and a beautiful sounding 16-String Zither.

A pleasant addition to the show was the inclusion of one of the young men from the village playing the part of the princess' true love. The HQ-401 director of the opera, at the bequest of several villagers, allowed the 16 year old to replace the regular player in order to showcase his talent. And talented he was.

It is relatively easy for non-speaking Vietnamese Westerners to follow the plot of these operas just by watching the dramatics being displayed by the actors and the vibrant music emphasizing critical points in the play.

All in all, it was an enjoyable experience because the entertainment made the war seem light years away. Now I can understand why the PsyOps people run these events throughout the country. It not only takes everyone's mind off the conflicts but it also shows that their government is interested in their well-being. At least that's the end result that is strived for.

When the show was finally over, the villagers were in no hurry to return to their homes. Rather, they stood around chattering happily while discussing the various aspects of the opera. We, on the other hand, deciding to escape the inevitable mosquitoes that come out at dusk, respectfully bade our congenial hosts goodbye with the usual promises that we would once again return to Hoa Hao. On the way back to the ship, I asked Mr. Pham if he had recorded sufficient amounts of the day's activities to satisfy the powers that be in Saigon.

"Sure thing *Dai-Uy*," he replied. "I've got more than enough footage to substantiate this trip."

"Great. I'd sure like to see the finished version if I can."

"No problem. I know where to reach you at and I'll give you a ring, probably in a week or so."

RETURN TO SAIGON

As we boarded the ship through the open bow ramp, I could hear the sounds of the sailors preparing to get underway. Captain Tai informed us that we would head for Saigon immediately and steam in company with the HQ-401. He said that by the time we awoke the next morning, we should already be tied up to the pier at Bach Dang. I'm sure the rest of our party felt as tired as I did and the thought of a good night's sleep was uppermost in my mind.

Bidding the Captain "goodnight," we headed for our staterooms. Once inside ours, Wilson asked, "Do you still have any potable water in your canteen? That coconut juice didn't really slake my thirst any."

"Sure," I said as I handed him my canteen that I had left on my bunk this morning.

Slowly unscrewing the black plastic cap, he lay back on his bunk and took a deep draught. He immediately jumped up, red faced and coughing while spewing liquid all over the deck.

"What's wrong?" I asked worriedly.

"Holy Christ, that's not water, it's pure friggin' vodka." He exclaimed hoarsely. Don't you navy-types believe in drinking plain everyday water?"

That's when it dawned on me that I had filled my canteen from Tolliver's bottle thinking it was water when it was actually his personal vodka. I was embarrassed and felt like a rookie in front of this civilian. I'd have to tell Tolliver about my mistake and get him another bottle of vodka. Otherwise, he might think one of his roommates or Ba Tu was nipping from his supply. Meanwhile, I tried weakly explaining the honest mistake on my part to Wilson who was finally settling down. As I apologized and begged his forgiveness, he looked at me and said, "Well, since we've got a canteen full of good vodka, there's no sense in letting it go to waste. Care to have a nightcap with me?"

"I'll pass and again, I'm really sorry."

He smiled as he tipped the canteen up one more time, mumbled "Goodnight" and then handed it back to me.

Snapping off the compartment's light, I climbed wearily into my upper bunk and that was the last thing I remembered until the next morning when the sound of Saigon's traffic awoke me.

I quickly jumped down from the bunk and in doing so, woke up Wilson who had been deep in sleep, thanks to the vodka nightcap. "Are we here already," he asked in a hoarse voice as he rubbed his sleep-filled eyes."

"That we are. Would you like to come with me to the McCarthy and get some breakfast?"

"No. But thanks for the invitation. I think I'll meander on home and hit the sack again. No sense in going back to work right away. Besides, we always get a day of rest after returning from an assignment."

"In that case, I'll head over to the Meyerkord PX and pick up a bottle of Vodka to replace the one I emptied into my canteen by mistake. I can only imagine what ran through Tolliver's mind when he discovered that his vodka level had considerably diminished."

We both assembled our gear and made our way to the Quarterdeck where we found Captain Tai talking to Major Reese and the cameraman Mr. Pham. Upon seeing us, Tai smiled and asked if we would like some coffee in the Ward Room before we disembarked.

Wilson answered for both of us and said, "Appreciate the offer Captain, but we all have things that must be attended to. By the way, I'll see that both you and Captain Thanh each receive a copy of the documentary when it's finished."

"I look forward to seeing it."

As we shook hands with Tai I said, "It was an honor to be aboard for the trip and I hope to see you again soon."

"It was also a pleasure to have you gentlemen along with us to Hoa Hao, and hope to see you again in the very near future."

With that, the four of us crossed over the gangway and made our way down the quay wall to the street.

The early morning air was already beginning to thicken with the smog that seemed to blanket the city. The first trickle of perspiration was starting to run down my spine and that's when I decided to go across the street to my office and get out of the sun. Major Reese, Wilson and Mr. Pham headed off to Nguyen Hue after we said our goodbyes, each eager to be on his way. I climbed the stairs up to my office where I found only Co Mai sitting at her desk diligently working on a broken fingernail.

"Good morning *Dai-Uy*," she said as she glanced up smiling. "Did you enjoy your trip to Hoa Hao?"

"Good morning Co Mai, you're looking particularly lovely this morning," I said cheerfully knowing that the compliment would make her day. "No Mrs. Lan today?"

"She's been out since yesterday with a bad cold, but I think she will be back on Monday."

"I was really impressed with the Hoa Hao, but I feel much better now that I'm back in Saigon. Maybe later I can tell you all about the trip, but right now all I need is a good, long hot shower and some food."

"OK," she said coquettishly. Even though she always wore a sexy mini-skirt to work none of the guys in the office to my knowledge had ever made a run on her. Maybe she had better luck on the outside; at least I sincerely hoped so for her sake.

Entering the rear office, I found Ed sitting at his desk reading a Stars and Stripes while George was hunched over a bunch of paperwork. I felt really sorry for him because he craved a combat assignment and here he was, stuck in the mud. I sure hoped for his benefit that somewhere, somebody would actually get to read the product of his efforts.

Ed looked up and said, "Hail the wandering Greek. How was the trip this time?"

"Pretty good; I'll fill you in later. Right now I've got to get over to the PX and replace a bottle of vodka that I used inadvertently that belonged to one of my roommates."

"I need a few things myself, so I'll give you a lift if you'd like."

"That would be great and from there I'm heading to the BOQ to wash the Delta bacteria off of me and then get something to eat."

Ed rose from his chair, threw his Stars & Stripes in the trash basket, grabbed his hat said to no one in particular, "We're outta here."

Making our way to his Jeep in the courtyard, I was conscious of the shipboard diesel oil smell that permeated my greens. Now I knew what the guys on the old diesel submarines used to complain about. I really looked forward to the shower, but the trip to the PX had to come first. I wanted to have that replacement bottle of vodka in case Captain Tolliver was still in our room. The more I thought about it, the more certain I was that he'd be pissed about his missing vodka. I know I would be if it had happened to me. It's bad enough to be thrown into a BOQ room with two strangers and find out one of them was messing around with my stuff. This made it more imperative than ever to replace the booze as quickly as possible in order to maintain the peace and harmony in our room.

Pulling out of Headquarters, we hung a right and headed for Ham Nghi. We followed that until we hit the Le Loi—Trung Hung Dao circle, went across it and took another right to get us behind the large Cholon marketplace. From there, the Meyerkord was only two blocks back on Nguyen Du. The Meyerkord BOQ was originally an apartment house that was converted to billet military officers and visiting entertainers. It not only sported a fairly well stocked PX and liquor store, but had a pretty good snack bar area where the food was good. The facility was named after Navy Lieutenant Harold "Dale" Meyerkord, the Senior Advisor killed with RAG 23.

Fortunately, the PX wasn't crowded and we finished our business quickly. With the replacement quart of Vodka tucked safely under my arm at the exorbitant price of $2.80 MPC, we got back into the Jeep and headed to the McCarthy to drop me off. Along the way, Ed asked if I was interested in going to the Dragon later on in the evening. I replied that I was pooped after the long river trip and wanted to get a shower and hit the sack early. Actually, I wasn't in the mood to visit Lan and Tuyet and go the "Saigon Tea" route. In all honesty, I was trying to avoid the pitfall that so many lonesome GIs fall into while overseas. For most of them, it was probably the first time that they found themselves away from home with temptation all around them. One didn't have to look hard to find one pretty girl after another in this place. Unfortunately, these young warriors fell in love at the drop of a pair of panties. The girls themselves aspired to catch a good looking American and have him take them back to the USA with them. The problems usually start there because a fairly prosperous "bar girl" usually has a maid or relative that cooks and cleans for her at home. Once the GI gets his new bride back to some rural place in Georgia, she finds herself alone at home while he goes off every day to make a living. Oh sure, he has provided all the comforts at home such as a washer/dryer, vacuum cleaner, microwave oven, etc., but then she faces the reality that she has to run all these appliances herself. It's easy to see how so many of those girls become disillusioned and unhappy. I for one didn't want to go that route-at least not yet. I really believed that Ed was using me as a co-conspirator to get into Lan's pants, because he wasn't making any headway on his own.

As he pulled up in front of the McCarthy to let me off, his disappointment was obvious and I told him I'd love to have a rain-check on the Dragon Bar. He nodded but his abrupt takeoff into traffic indicated his true feelings. I just didn't feel like socializing in an area that was getting predictable, if you know what I mean.

As I entered our room, I heard someone in the shower and hoped it was Captain Tolliver. I sat on the edge of my bed and took my boots off to give my tired feet some air and just then Tolliver came out with a towel wrapped around his ample body.

"Hey buddy, glad to see you back. Where'd you go this time?"

"I was down in the Delta at a place called Hoa Hao. Like they say, 'Nice place to visit but I wouldn't want to live there' By the way, I'm returning the Vodka that I took for my canteen by mistake thinking that it was potable water."

"Damn, I was beginning to think that I had drunk the stuff and didn't remember or that maybe Ba Tu was sneaking nips on me."

I then related the story about Wilson drinking the vodka and expecting water. That cracked Tolliver up and he laughingly said, "Only in this shithole could a mistake like that happen."

"Amen to that. If you're finished with the head, I'd like to wash the Delta crud off my body."

"It's all yours and thanks for replenishing my supply of liquid courage and relaxer *extraordinaire*."

I can't recall how long I remained under the wonderful hot soothing shower, but once I finished, my mood was definitely upbeat. I decided to take a short nap, since it was still early in the day and I didn't feel like battling Saigon's humidity and heat. I set my alarm for 1730 (that's 5:30 PM for you civilians), hopped onto my bed and covered myself with the ever popular camo poncho liner.

It seemed as if it was only a few minutes since I had laid down when my alarm clock rudely brought me back to the land of the living. I must have been tired because I couldn't recollect any dreams whatsoever. I put on a set of my wash khakis and planned to mosey on down the street to get something to eat. One of the prime rules is to get something solid in your stomach before starting to drink. And, I was planning to down a few beers as sort of a celebration for returning unscathed back to Saigon.

I was in the mood for a good old American styled hamburger, with a thick slice of onion and surrounded by crisp French fries. The nearest place to get that was at the USO which was just down the street. The cafeteria at the McCarthy also served hamburgers, but they couldn't compare to the ones at the USO. I preferred my burgers crisp on the outside but not well done on the inside. Additionally, the fries at the USO were fresh and crisp whereas the cooks at the BOQ served preheated potatoes that arrived warm and limp. So, the choice was easy. A further reason for my choice was that I wasn't in the mood to socialize with anyone I knew and the USO was a safe bet for that.

After having successfully consumed the hamburger, onion and fries washed down with a fresh hot cup of coffee, I was ready for the next step in my night out. The meal definitely lived up to my expectations and fortunately tonight, the USO was not overcrowded affording me a quiet table off to the side. Moments such as these can be prized when one considers the huge amount of people that inhabit Saigon at any one time.

I decided to head down towards the river by Bach Dang, which was only a couple of short blocks and found myself in front of the Majestic Hotel. It was another example of early French colonial architecture. Previously built in 1925, consisting of 4 stories, it was expanded in 1965. Two more floors were added and the rooms were updated. The entrance sat on the corner of the building at the confluence of Nguyen Hue and Bach Dang and was covered with an opulent overhanging rococo canopy.

Upon entering the immense lobby, the concierge's desk was on the left as I headed to the rear for the elevators. Taking one that was already open, I headed for the roof garden. Strains of music wafted down the elevator shaft as the ancient lift shook its way slowly to the top floor.

The roof garden was semi-enclosed and tropical palm potted plants were in abundance. Performing on the stage were five young and highly animated Vietnamese. The band consisted of a drummer, a bass guitar player, two more guitars and a young attractive girl at the microphone. They appeared to be in their late teens and the boys wore black pants with white, open-necked shirts. The singer wore a tight mid-riff top with matching short shorts and white knee high boots. With her page boy haircut she reminded me of a young Keely Smith who sang with bandleader Louis Prima whom she eventually married. They were doing an excellent rendition of Lulu's "To Sir, With Love."

I found a vacant table away from the band and close to the outer railing where I could gaze out upon the river and the busy nighttime traffic below. The waiter appeared miraculously in his crisp white jacket and black creased trousers and asked softly, "What would *Monsieur* like to drink this evening?"

Having been thinking about our village in Greece and my relatives a lot lately, I decided to have a Ricard, which was as close as I could get to Ouzo. The waiter appeared shortly with my drink and also placed a small plate of plain pistachio nuts on the table. That was something I had never seen before in-country, complimentary pistachios and they were good and fresh. Finally, as the combination of the alcohol, pistachios and the fairly decent music invaded my senses, I was beginning to relax.

After my second drink arrived, a man approached my table and asked "Do you mind if I join you?"

I surreptitiously leaned over and glanced down at his feet to check out his socks. Fortunately, they were khaki colored and just visible above a pair of dusty chukka boots. It was rumored that in Vietnam, homosexuals wore white socks for identification of the species and I definitely wasn't interested in that form of interaction. That's me, pussy and beer and in any order because I am not a big fan of bumping snakes with another male.

"Be my guest," I replied.

"I just didn't feel like drinking alone," he said, "and you looked like the only sober and intelligent guy in the place. My name is Vince Slavin," reaching his hand across the table.

"I'm Bob Kay," I replied taking his hand a little cautiously.

"Well, I can see you're a little skeptical about whom you talk to and I can certainly appreciate that. I'm a correspondent with the Newark Star Ledger in New Jersey and I find that drinking with my fellow journalists usually turns into a boozing marathon, so I try to avoid them"

"I'm familiar with the Star Ledger," I replied. "I was born in Newark, but raised mostly in Jersey City."

"Hey, how about that?" he said earnestly. "Do you have family back in Jersey?"

"Yes, my mother lives in Irvington."

The waiter appeared quietly and Vince ordered a "33" Beer. "Bob, would you mind very much if I did a short interview with you for the hometown paper? It'll be just a short synopsis of your tour here, nothing fancy. The folks back home need to hear the human side of this war and not just the canned drivel that is shoveled at them every day.

"Sounds OK to me," I replied.

With that he took out a small camera and took a head shot of me. Then he proceeded to ask questions as to how long I've been in-country, where I worked, and so on.

I answered his questions with fairly short answers, but as the evening progressed, I felt a little more comfortable with him. I went into the Poulo Obi experience with the Junk Force, the theft of the VC shrimp in the Bo De River and my ultimate transfer to Advisory Staff Headquarters in Saigon.

He wrote rapidly in his small notebook and after a few more polite queries asked, "What was with the checking of my shoes when I arrived?"

"I was looking at the color of your socks," I replied and went on to explain about the homosexual connotation of white socks.

Upon hearing my explanation, he leaned back in his chair and laughed. "I can see why you were suspicious of my motives in joining you," he said.

"With all the good looking women in this country, playing footsy with another guy is just not a viable option with me."

"Me either," he replied. "You know, finding you this evening has been a life-saver, so to speak because I hadn't filed anything back to the home office in a few days and I'm sure they are getting fidgety about now."

I nodded knowingly and said, "And a little personal interest story doesn't hurt once in awhile."

"You got it," he said. "The interview should be in the paper in about two to three weeks, so tell your folks to be on the lookout for it. By the way, do you mind if I ask you another question that has been bothering me for awhile?"

"No, go right ahead, as long as it's not classified," I said.

"What's with this taking of ears shit that has been going around? Are our guys really turning ghoulish with nothing better to do than desecrate the dead?"

I took a deep breath and took my time answering his question because I wanted to make sure he got it right. "Before we started cutting off ears, there was no true method of getting a true body count. The Viet Cong and the North Vietnamese soldiers always remove their dead in order to keep their fatalities from us, especially since they know of the big push from MACV for enemy body count for the hometown papers. Let's say for example a US patrol was sweeping a particular area and killed five VC. They would make note of them in their after-action report and the five were reported to MACV. Later, a small group of Vietnamese Rangers crossed the same area from another direction and came upon the bodies. Bang, another five enemy dead were reported. Now multiply this by a few more friendlies coming upon these same bodies and you can see how the original five has now grown exponentially and distorted the actual body count. Finally someone got the bright idea to hack off the right ear from any dead, regardless of who killed them so that anyone else coming across the remains would know that these bodies had already been tallied."

"Wow, that makes sense," said Vince. "I'll make sure the word gets around to my erstwhile colleagues who have been reporting under less than factual conditions. Thanks a million buddy; it helps to renew my faith in you guys in the field."

"Hey, remember that's what the real purpose behind the ear cutting was about, but there are still some whackos in khaki and coke-heads taking them for souvenirs or using them for ash trays or making them into necklaces to impress the rear echelon troops who never get to see combat."

I left Vince sitting at the table happily scribbling away and we both promised to keep in touch once we were both "back in the world." I made it to my bed in the BOQ none the worse for wear and again, I didn't disturb my roommates.

I never did tell my mother about the article but she later received a phone call from a friend of hers telling her one day to look at last night's Star Ledger. From there, the Jersey Journal in Jersey City picked up on it and ran the story too. Later, my mother told me that she had received a nice letter from a New Jersey Congressman congratulating her and extolling the State's extreme pride in having one of their finest serving in Vietnam. To think all this started during a quiet night out on the town in Saigon!

The next morning began like any other duty day with the exception that I skipped having breakfast down in the cafeteria. Instead, I stopped at a small kiosk at the lower end of Nguyen Hue and ordered their specialty, a scrambled egg sandwich on warm fresh French bread. I added that I wanted it "to go" so the mama-san neatly wrapped it up in a sheet of newspaper. I would keep it until I reached my office where hopefully a pot of newly perked coffee would be available. It was Saturday and work at Headquarters went on as usual. The "Newsletter" was already being distributed for this month so I only had my trip report to knock out for the Captain.

Since I was the first one in the office, I was obliged to make the coffee. I sat at my desk reading through the material in my in-basket and there was nothing of importance except for a letter from one of my Greek friends in San Diego. By the time I finished reading about the social scene in California, the coffee was ready and I could finally get to my cold sandwich. No matter, it tasted out of this world.

As if on cue, the rest of the crew noisily arrived and headed for the coffee pot with their cups. It took me about an hour to type up my trip report for the boss and as per usual, I passed the carbon copy around for each of my officemates to read. This served several purposes in that it precluded me from having to repeat the narration without an interruption, provided five excellent proof-readers and gave them something different to read while they had their morning coffee.

"Good report," said Commander Johnson. "Looks like you had a nice cruise in the Delta without any Purple Heart opportunities.

"Oh, the bad guys were there alright, but they were lined up for the Med-Cap and the entertainment. One thing for sure, I wouldn't like to piss off the Hoa Hao anytime soon. No sir!"

"This place is amazing," said George. Too many indigenous people in this country are killing each other, and for what?"

"What about that militant French priest with his rag-tag army that takes on the VC down around Rach Gia? Even the government troops try to avoid confronting this group because they don't want to get their butts kicked. The Padre's quasi-militia lives off the land and moves around at will, more than likely with the blessing of the Province Chief. The locals protect them by providing food, shelter and most of all, with their absolute silence."

Once everyone in the office had finished reading my report without any recommended changes, I signed the smooth copy and headed down below to see the Captain.

It seems that every time I entered the Captain's outer office, the occupants appeared frozen in time. The XO was still reading a copy of Stars and Stripes while simultaneously snacking on cold Pop Tarts and the Captain's Yeoman was busily typing the endless amount of verbiage generated by the Boss. I guess the Captain figured that a massive quantity of paperwork issued from his office would be an indicator as to how well he had a grasp on the Advisory effort. Oh well, who was I to argue?

The XO looked up and said, "Howzit going, lad?"

"Pretty good, sir," I replied as I headed over to the Yeoman's desk. "Is the Captain in?" I asked the typewriter twat.

Without taking his eyes off his machine, Norman replied rather aloofly, "He's over at NAVFORV."

"OK, see that he gets my trip report when he returns," I said as I placed the papers in the Captain's "In Box."

As I was leaving, Commander Selfridge stopped munching long enough to ask me if I had enjoyed my trip.

"It was pretty eye-opening to say the least. You should see the documentary on the trip that USIS will air on AFVN television soon. I'll try and find out when and let you know Commander."

The XO nodded once and returned to reading his paper. With that, I exited and headed back up to my office. Ba Lan and Co Mai were already sitting at their desks by the time I had returned

Ba Lan asked in her usual soft voice, "Did you enjoy your trip?"

"It was nice, but I am glad to be back in Saigon where I can see you two lovely ladies every day," I said.

With that, they both blushed shyly.

PART NINE

THE SILENT VIPERS

The reedy, sing-song music, accentuated by the monotonous crashing of tin cymbals, emanated from a small portable Japanese radio. Since it was a month into the Southwest monsoon season of 1967, static was a constant annoyance. This was due to severe thunderstorm activity somewhere in the area.

Khoi, a young boy no more than 17 years of age and slight of build, was sitting with his back against a large banyan tree deep in the heart of the Parrot's Beak. This area consisted of mainly dense jungle in southeast Cambodia that protruded into South Vietnam and was located about 45 miles west of Saigon. It was known for its excellent concealment and used by enemy forces that traveled unhindered between Vietnam and Cambodia.

The tree was located inside a small VC base camp situated under a jungle canopy that prevented prying eyes in the sky from detecting their presence. The thick overhead foliage also kept smoke from their camp fires go undetected and the group moved around freely. The boy's most noticeable feature was a horrible purple burn scar on the left side of his face. The injury was the result of South Vietnamese troops raiding his village and his miraculous escape from their burning hut. Unfortunately, his mother, father and younger sister weren't so lucky because they were killed during the attack. With no other relatives in the village to care for him, Khoi was forced to go and live with his paternal grandfather who was the Hoa Hao leader and Hamlet Chief of the village further down in the Delta. But he was not happy there because of his physical appearance and the other children made him feel uncomfortable. Despite the love from his aging grandfather, it was painfully obvious to Khoi that the older people pretended not to notice his disfigurement in deference to his grandfather. He was there less than five months when his grandfather suffered a massive fatal heart attack during a heated confrontation with some local VC who were trying to conscript recruits and coerce assistance from the villagers. They failed in both cases. Chu Bay the VC leader happened to be the estranged son of the Hamlet Chief and the younger brother of Khoi's father. Since the boy had no other place to go, he left with Chu Bay.

From that moment on, Khoi rallied heart and soul to the cause of the Viet Cong and soon found absolute peace among his new found comrades. He studied Ho Chi Minh's writings religiously and was eager to learn the many subtleties of terrorist warfare. This fact did not go unnoticed by the rest of the men as well as his uncle and mentor.

Today, he appeared oblivious to the raucous sounds coming from the radio because he was deeply engrossed in cleaning his AK-47 Chinese communist rifle. It was his own personal weapon and had been given to him a week ago by his uncle and leader of the small band of Viet Cong. The gift was a symbolic gesture as a reward for getting his very first kill during a well planned and executed ambush the week before.

Khoi's old rifle had malfunctioned and the boy had been crouching with racing heart in the underbrush. A severely wounded Regional Popular Force trooper, who had been shot by someone else in the ambush party, had fallen a few feet from where Khoi had been hiding. He stared wide-eyed at the man while subconsciously holding his breath. The wounded man's eyes opened lethargically and settled accusingly on Khoi.

A tremor of fear caused a little leakage of warm urine down Khoi's leg, but he quickly regained control although somewhat embarrassed. It was then that he remembered the long slim knife at his side. Slowly unsheathing it, he held it out in front of him as he started to inch forward. Hugging the ground as much as possible, he extended the knife until it pressed up against the quivering throat muscles of the fallen man. At its touch, the trooper's eyes widened with fear realizing that his pain was yet to be over. With a quick thrust, the slim blade entered piercing the man's carotid artery causing bright red blood to spurt forth instantly wetting Khoi's hand as he pulled the blade from the soldier's neck. Within a few seconds the trooper died with his hands curled as if in supplication to a God who obviously had not watched over him.

Comrade Trinh, the oldest of the group and who had also fought against the French at Dien Bien Phu, witnessed the boy's first kill. He later related what he had seen, with some flowery embellishment, to Chu Bay after they returned to their camp. This made the uncle enormously proud of his nephew.

Later that evening as the men sat around the soft glow of their campfire, Chu Bay presented Khoi with a brand new AK-47. It had been part of a resupply shipment that had been carried for more than two months down the Ho Chi Minh Trail from the North.

The semiautomatic was the favorite weapon of the Viet Cong and were delivered in large numbers down the trail by way of Haiphong from a communist arms factory in Czechoslovakia. Little by little however, Chu Bay's group was acquiring newer and better weapons and it was a quantum leap from the old French rifles that they had first carried into battle.

Chu Bay had been the local Hamlet Chief of a small village just west of Can Tho; that is until he was pressed into leading the small band north into the jungles of the Parrot's Beak.

Over time, the group quickly earned the name of "The Silent Vipers." It was bestowed upon them for their highly successful assaults on the local South Vietnamese forces in and around the area. This had been going on for three months now and the band was becoming increasingly raggedy. The only thing that kept the hardened jungle fighters together was their enormous success and the apparent charmed life that they were enjoying.

Bright flashes of sunlight filtered through the overhead canopy of trees that made up the Parrot's Beak. They reflected off the droplets of rain that moments before had just fallen in a deluge onto the leaves.

Visitors noticed very quickly upon coming to this part of the country, the speed with which the torrential downpours come and go during Monsoon season. Perspiration was always an irritating and constant companion caused by the humidity that lingered in the upper 90% range. Dehydration soon becomes an enemy that has to be dealt with along with the incessant insects and bugs that infest the waterlogged undergrowth.

Leaches are another of the disgusting forms of life that drop silently from the overhanging branches onto the unsuspecting traveler. They also infest stagnant water and will find their way to a person's skin if left unprotected. You haven't lived until you have had one or more of these creatures attached to your body as they gorge themselves on your blood. To remove them effectively, it is necessary to touch a lit cigarette to their tails which forces them to disengage their heads from beneath the skin. Pulling them usually results in separating the body from the head that remains embedded under the skin, and which ultimately causes infection.

So much for the tropical paradise: Living among the small band of men, were about nine females between the ages of thirty five down to a girl of seventeen. A few had already attached themselves to some of the men, while others remained aloof but nevertheless professional. The seventeen year old was named Ngoc and she was slight of build, with short cut black hair and a constant unsmiling countenance; and that is until she was in the presence of Khoi, her new "Hero."

Ngoc had been born in a little village near Long Xuyen and had lost her father when she was just thirteen and a budding young girl. Her father had been killed by an attacking aircraft as he worked in his rice paddy late one afternoon. She never knew whether it was an American plane that took her father away or one of the cocky South Vietnamese pilots that filled the skies. Since Ngoc was the seventh and youngest child in the family, the sudden loss of her father made it almost impossible for her mother to make ends meet. In order to stabilize the household, three of the oldest siblings were sent to relatives to work off their keep, while the mother and the three oldest children, along with young Ngoc, headed for Saigon to join a semi-wealthy uncle.

This arrangement soon ended in disaster when the uncle tried to force his attention on the innocent Ngoc one evening when her mother went to the market. Ngoc managed to evade his advances, but the air hung heavy in the household for the next few days.

Finally the uncle arranged for Ngoc to be sent to live with a Chinese family in Cho Lon under the pretense that Ngoc would be a baby-sitter. In reality she became another participant in a group of young girls that made up Madam Ha's infamous prostitutes. Her notoriety centered on having an endless supply of virgins for the ever-growing demand by wealthy Chinese business men who craved the feel of the uninitiated. Great sums of money changed hands in these arrangements. But what the dirty old men who beat a path to Madam Ha's door didn't know, was that after each deflowering, the girl would be rushed to a local Chinese physician who, in turn, re-sutchered the hymen to its original state. The girls would then be sent to another province where Madam Ha had a similar establishment where the product could again be marketed without fear of being discovered.

During Ngoc's first repulsive encounter with a seventy year old Chinaman who had a problem getting an erection, she managed to escape any serious damage. He pawed her mercilessly, licking her budding breasts and her face with his odorous tongue that reminded her of a dog. He groped at her vagina with his arthritic fingers but was unable to part the lips, so he finally flipped her over and laid his pasty-white cadaverous body on her back while grinding his flaccid penis between her buttocks. In this way, however miraculous, he reached a climax. Lying atop her for several minutes savoring his orgasm, he whispered harshly into her ear that she was not to speak of his failure to anyone. She agreed, immediately relieved that she had been fortunate to escape with only a sticky mess around her ass that a shower in hot water would remedy. For some reason she had expected the vile impotent old man to climax with a puff of dust.

Madam Ha appeared satisfied that Ngoc's first go at the job went so flawlessly. She told her to "rest up" and tomorrow she would make a trip to the Doctor who supposedly would examine the vagina for any damage. At least that's what Ha had told her. But Ngoc had a better idea; she would get herself away from this charnel house and make it on her own back into the safety of the Delta.

After leaving Madam Ha's presence, she managed to slip out the back door and make her way through the alley to the street. She mingled in easily with the teeming flow of humanity that made up the Chinese section of Saigon called Cho Lon. She had some money tucked away that enabled her to hail a pedicab with an aging driver who agreed to take her to the bus terminal on the southern outskirts of the city.

Arriving at the destination, she found herself in an open area amidst several crowded busses that belched noxious diesel fumes into the already smog-ladened air. She made her way to a small kiosk where an overweight, baldheaded Chinese sold tickets and discovered that she had enough money to get on the bus for Chau Doc, which was about to leave momentarily. The top was completely covered by baskets and cardboard boxes filled with purchases destined for the countryside. The interior of the bus yielded one lone seat in the middle of the back row. It was occupied on either side by two women carrying baskets with live chickens whose heads were protruding from the covers. This, to Ngoc, was considerably better than being pawed by that disgusting old man at Madam Ha's.

Several hours of bone-rattling jarring in the back of the bus, finally ended in the bustling Delta city of Chau Doc. By now, Ngoc was famished and driven almost to the point of nausea by being subjected to the odorous smells of the restless poultry around her. Stepping down off the aging conveyance, she made her way to a small group of tables in front of a shop selling *Pho Bo*, or Beef Soup. The lone customer seated at her table of choice was a young lad whose good looks unfortunately were marred by a large puckered purple scar on the left side of his face. Looking up at her, he turned his face slightly in an unconscious effort to hide the scar. At the same time, he blushed with embarrassment as he nodded to the pretty girl standing in front of him

"Is the soup good?" she asked lightheartedly as she sat down.

"Good is relative," he replied in a voice belying his shyness. "Actually, it is very tasty and has some nice lean pieces of meat in it."

"I'm starved," she said as she motioned to a young girl who was waiting on the customers. "I'll have what he's having along with a glass of coconut milk, please.

The boy looked up from under the black hair that almost covered his eyes and said, "I saw you get off the bus. Are you visiting family here?"

"No," she replied. "Actually, I'm running away from a bad situation." She then proceeded to tell him of her bad luck and equally bad experience in the big city.

He took it in very quietly and for some reason felt a connection with this slim young girl that he had never felt before. He related his own history, leaving out the part where his peers humiliated him in the village. And then very softly, he told her of his decision to join his uncle in the fight for freedom. Surprisingly, she agreed on his choice and boldly asked if it were possible for her to go with him in order to settle her own score with the government.

Khoi was dumbfounded, but he regained his composure enough to quickly reply, "I don't see why not," as he picked up the check for her meal. The world suddenly didn't seem like such a bad place after all, he thought. "My uncle and a few of the others came to Chau Doc to get some supplies so I decided to get some good soup. I will introduce you when we meet him by our old truck and don't worry, you'll be accepted, honest."

Arriving at the appointed place where the truck was parked off the beaten path, Khoi and Ngoc approached the dusty, old nondescript vehicle carefully. Just then, his uncle's voice came out of the cab saying, "It's about time you returned nephew. Did you enjoy your soup and who is this that with you?"

Khoi straightened up imperceptibly as he introduced Ngoc to his uncle, while holding her hand tightly in his. This did not go unnoticed by Chu Bay as he listened to the boy explain the girl's predicament and her desire to join the group. The young couple stood looking up at Chu Bay in the cab of the truck for what seemed an eternity, until the older man nodded his head.

"Yes, she can join us as long as she pulls her share of the load," he said solemnly. "But, her history is not really anyone's business so it should remain among the three of us, understood."

Nodding their heads in unison, both Ngoc and Khoi let out audible sighs of relief after thanking the uncle profusely. Chu Bay slowly inhaled his Ruby Queen cigarette as he thought back to when he was in love as a young man. Unfortunately, the girl of his dreams at the time did not share his ambition to side with the Viet Cong and unceremoniously broke off their relationship. Oh, how he envied his nephew. But then again, these were strange times and things were just not conducive for such adventures of the heart. Instead, he grabbed what intimacy availed itself whenever one of the obliging female camp-followers in the group crawled under his blanket in the dark of night. But aside from that, he still had his cigarettes that he enjoyed whenever he went on a supply run. He specifically forbade any of his group to smoke while they were in the jungle because he knew that smoke from a cigarette was detectable at a great distance. He harped constantly to his people to dispose of any litter around the campsites that could give away their position. They were pushed to religiously sanitize the area prior to departing so as not to leave any sign of the group's passing.

Of late, there had been subtle hints from the upper echelon that a new massive offensive was in the works and he did not want any problems to get in the way. He couldn't help but wonder what their part in it would be, and as always, time would tell.

PRE-TET SAIGON

The next few days were totally uneventful as far as work was concerned, but in the city of Saigon, a surge of electricity was in the air. Not only could one feel the energy, it was evident in the way people went about their daily routines. They were more animated because of the planning and anticipation of being with their families during TET, relaxing and celebrating life's renewal. It gave pause from the death and destruction that the war had brought, if only for a short time.

It was agreed to by both sides to observe a cease-fire truce during the observance of TET. This was a good sound strategy on the part of the North who understood that since everyone wanted to go home during for holiday, disrupting that would alienate the people of the South and would greatly hinder any efforts for uniting the country under one rule.

I was sitting at my desk all alone on Sunday morning as it appeared the rest of my office-mates were probably sleeping-in. I started reading an article that I had previously written for last month's Newsletter concerning the TET Holiday. I felt that some background description of the customs surrounding the New Year would be beneficial to the Advisors in the field. This subject had been covered in Counter-Insurgency School, but at the time, few students appreciated its importance.

Tet Nguyen Dan or Feast of the First Morning is commonly referred to as simply TET. It marks the beginning of a new year on the lunar calendar and also marks the start of spring. Although the celebration traditionally lasts for seven days most businesses usually allow only the first three days off and preparations are begun weeks in advance. Homes are cleaned throughout in order to get rid of any bad fortune experienced during the past year and are decorated with bright yellow flowers called *Hoa Mai* which represents Spring. Homes are repainted in some instances to bring forth a new look in hope of avoiding any impending bad luck. Everyone gets new outfits and shoes, old debts are paid and existing differences are settled between families and friends. A

New Year's tree called *Cay Neu* is planted in front of each home and is traditionally a bamboo pole with its leaves removed. The pole is then decorated and wrapped with lucky red paper since it is believed that the color red wards off any approaching evil spirits. The tree is taken down on the seventh and last day of TET. It should be noted however, that household cleaning is not done once the TET observance is underway for fear of sweeping out any good luck that may be present.

A special ceremony called *Le Tru Thich* is celebrated commencing at the stroke of twelve on New Year's Eve. This ceremony includes gongs, firecrackers and other loud noises in order to frighten off evil spirits. It also helps to usher out the old year and welcome in the new. This is similar to the way we celebrate our New Year with noisemakers and fireworks.

The events on New Year's Day will determine an individual's fortune for the rest of the year. Children are forbidden to cry or fight at any time during TET and only good relationships are encouraged. Visiting friends or relatives who are in mourning during this period is frowned upon because it is associated with death and suffering. Family members exchange gifts with each other and adults give lucky money known as *Li Xi* in small red and gold envelopes to the children.

One of the oddities that I noticed in Vietnam was that our civilian Vietnamese workers got to take off not only for all their religious and civil holidays but for all the standard American holidays as well. We, the gringos on the other hand, were tasked with putting in ten hours a day, seven days a week. We did get off for the first day of TET because absolutely nothing would get done without counterpart interactions.

This is where the Viet Cong pulled a fast one on us. As we learned later on, the Viet Cong for weeks had been secretly infiltrating the main cities of the south. Approximately five battalions of VC/NVA arrived in elaborate funeral processions with their weapons concealed inside the coffins. Others smuggled grenade launchers, rockets and hand guns underneath baskets of flowers and vegetables in trucks and carts supposedly bound for the central markets. Additional AK-47s and ammunition were wrapped and dropped into the nearby rivers. Due to the exceptional design of this weapon, dirt, water and grime had no affect whatsoever on its performance, unlike our M-16s that failed to fire when even slightly fouled. So when it was time for these weapons to be retrieved, they were ready to be used.

The guys drifted in slowly during the next couple of hours and each proceeded to delve into his in-basket as required by the front office. It was the same hum-drum monotony broken only by Ed telling me that Tuyet had been asking for me when he had gone to the Dragon the night before. He also said that most of the girls there would be going home to their families for TET, but Lan and Tuyet would be returning on Sunday, the fourth of February. So that bit of information helped me decide what I would do for entertainment for the next week. Since Ed didn't make any suggestions, the subject was dropped after I thanked him for the heads-up.

SILENT VIPERS ON THE MOVE

As the battered truck slowly labored up the slight grade to the village where the vehicle was to be left, Khoi gently nudged Ngoc awake. She had been sitting between Chu Bay and him in the cab and had fallen asleep with her head on Khoi's shoulder. Waking with a start, she soon realized where she was and gave Khoi a small embarrassed grin.

"We have to walk in from here because the road doesn't go to our base-camp," said Chu Bay. "When we get there, I'll introduce you to the other women so they can get you settled and you can meet the rest of the men later."

Khoi started to say that he was told that he would do the introductions, but a stern glance from Chu Bay left the words unsaid in his mouth.

The truck was quickly unloaded and the supplies were divided equally amongst the small party. After a twenty minute's march, they reached the edge of the mangrove swamp and their campsite. A shrill bird-like whistle shattered the silence, but it was only a warning to the camp from a perimeter guard that someone was approaching.

Chu Bay was greeted by a visitor who had come a long way and had been patiently awaiting his return. The two men shook hands warmly and sat down around the fire.

"I bring important orders for your group," said the gaunt visitor quietly. "Our superiors in the north, having recognized the excellent work your men have accomplished, wish to reward you. You are to make your way immediately to the Cholon section of Saigon and rendezvous at the Quang Buddhist Pagoda where you will link up with a group from Tay Ninh. There you will receive further orders. Since the Pagoda is the home of militant Monks, the threat of detection will be practically nonexistent."

With that, the visitor stood up and bade Chu Bay good fortune and slipped back into the jungle with his traveling companions.

This is what we have been long awaiting, thought Chu Bay excitedly as he gathered his leaders to pass the word. "We leave at first light to fulfill our destiny and reclaim our country," he exclaimed proudly.

It was a foregone conclusion that Ngoc would share Khoi's sleeping mat, so that, along with the knowledge that tomorrow the group would be on the move, made her slightly apprehensive. This was the beginning of a great adventure for her and one that she had never believed possible only a short time ago. Yes, fate did indeed move in strange ways, she thought.

Although it was late, the electricity that emanated from the group was almost tangible as they made their final preparations for the journey that lay ahead. It was a certainty that sleep would be hard to come for most in the few short hours that remained before daybreak. Ngoc and Khoi were almost guaranteed a good night's sleep after their initial love-making.

The small campfire that had been used to prepare the morning tea was quickly extinguished and covered over leaving no trace of it having ever existed. The campsite was thoroughly cleaned and meticulously examined for any tell-tale traces of the group and only then did each person shoulder their own meager personal belongings. The men however, would also carry the new supplies divided up equally among them.

The group was broken up into smaller units of twos and threes in order for them to remain inconspicuous on their journey. Ngoc and Khoi were to accompany Chu Bay. However, all their weapons were wrapped up and transported to a place where they could be retrieved later. Khoi was heartsick that he had to give up his prized AK-47 that had yet to be fired in anger, but was assured that the weapons would be available at their destination.

Chu Bay gave them each a specific route to follow as they departed at staggered intervals in order to blend in with other travelers heading to Saigon for TET. As he bid each group a safe and uneventful journey, he reminded them to avoid confrontation at all costs and added, "To appear innocuous guarantees safety among the masses." This was in keeping with the teachings of the revered Communist leader Mao Tse Tung who said, "To be successful, guerrillas must learn how to swim among the people like fish in the water."

After the last group departed, Chu Bay told Ngoc and Khoi quietly that they would head back to the village to get the truck. "There's no reason for us to have to walk. Besides, our papers are in order so we'll be able to get to the pagoda before any of the others. I think that this is the operation that we all have been waiting for and it's best if we get there early in order to be well prepared.

As they made their way back to the truck, Khoi respectfully asked his uncle, "Won't the others be angry when they find out that we came up in the truck and they had to walk burdened with their belongings?"

"Trust me nephew; they will walk only until they can find some kind of transportation. Those that have proper papers will look for a conveyance of some sort, perhaps a motorcycle, bus, sampam or ox-cart. I do not worry about them because they are clever in the ways of survival. The remainder will either make the journey on foot as ordered or they will simply melt away into the countryside and disappear. The life we have led in fighting for what we believe is not something that everyone can easily adapt to. The weak always fall by the way-side leaving only the most determined and courageous to stand with us."

They walked silently in a single file with Chu Bay in the lead, Ngoc in the middle and Khoi bringing up the rear. As they entered the village, no one paid them the least bit of attention as they made their way to the truck that was parked behind the village chief's hut. This was indeed unusual for the average Vietnamese who are basically overly inquisitive, to ignore the newcomers. They knew exactly who Chu Bay was and were prepared to remain totally oblivious rather than initiate some sort of a confrontation with him.

Once inside the cab, Chu Bay lifted up the floor mat and retrieved the ignition key he had left there. Despite the truck's antiquated appearance, the engine fired up on the first try. Chu

Bay smiled in satisfaction as he maneuvered the truck back onto the dirt road that led away from the village.

After a few kilometers of dusty travel, the road intersected the two lane highway that would lead them to Long Xuyen. The journey took them southeast rather than north because of the many rivers that lay between them and Saigon. Besides, following the main road out of Long Xuyen, they would eventually reach Highway 4 that would lead them directly to Saigon.

They stopped innumerable times to rest, eat and to attend to nature's calls as required, and their spirits remained high. Ngoc even exhibited a fairly good singing voice as she went through some of the songs that she knew. This pleased Chu Bay immensely and he was glad that he had allowed her to accompany them. When it came time for them to sleep, they'd pull off the road under a stand of trees, eat the food purchased from the innumerable roadside vendors and turn in exhausted from the journey. Chu Bay curled up across the front seat while Ngoc and Khoi were relegated to the rear of the truck. With the back canvas flap tied securely in place, the youngsters entwined themselves together as they lay atop old rice sacks. Chu Bay's soft voice came back at them from the front saying, "Try not to make the truck shake too much so we don't attract any unwanted attention." The youngsters giggled self consciously as they tried to muffle the sound into each other's shoulder.

"Good night Uncle and sleep well," croaked Khoi."

After two days on the road they passed the cities of Can Tho and My Tho, encountering no problems at the various checkpoints that had become lax due to the upcoming TET Holiday. When they finally arrived at their destination it was dusk as Chu Bay pulled up to the side of the Pagoda in Cholon. As the trio entered the Pagoda through a side door, they were met by a very stern-faced middle-aged monk who motioned them to follow him. Once inside the spacious Pagoda, soft cymbals clanged and small bells tinkled along with the ever familiar odor of burning joss sticks. The monk did not identify himself but instead asked for the keys to the truck. Before Chu Bay could utter a protest, the monk produced two sets of keys and said, "Two motorcycles for your use are beside your truck which will get you safely to your next destination. The truck will draw too much attention the further you go into Saigon and we have other uses for it. You are to go to *Pho Binh*, or as the Americans call it, Binh's Soup Shop near the US Embassy. Sit down and order a meal. The owner will join you at the table and from there, you are in his hands. Here are directions to the shop; goodbye and good luck."

True to his word, there were two motorcycles parked alongside the building. A cream and blue colored 50cc Honda and an older black Suzuki recognized by the tinny ring-a-ding-ding sound of its engine.

They were led once again to the side door where they exited the quiet serenity of the Pagoda. The air seemed much muggier than before as Chu Bay straddled the Suzuki, leaving Khoi and Ngoc to ride the Honda. Both machines fired up at the first try and they were off to their next destination. It was apparent that Chu Bay was familiar with the streets of Saigon because he never once checked his written directions. The two cycles blended in easily with the normal street traffic and once again, they encountered no difficulties enroute.

The famous soup shop was crowded with noisy patrons, both civilian and military, Vietnamese and Caucasians, all happily enjoying the pre-holiday festivities. Chu bay led them to an empty table towards the rear near the kitchen where they seated themselves. In a few moments, an older man approached holding three menus and as he placed them on the table, introduced himself as the owner, Ngo Toai.

"We have been waiting for you. Did you encounter any problems on the way here from the Pagoda?" he asked in a casual voice.

"None whatsoever," replied Chu Bay.

"Good, then you should be ready to enjoy the best *Pho Bo* in Saigon," he said as he turned and disappeared into the kitchen.

A young girl came out bearing three steaming bowls of soup on a tin tray, along with three cans of American orange soda.

"Enjoy your soup," said the girl as she gave them spoons and napkins. "The meal is on the house and when you're finished, make your way up the stairs through the doorway marked 'Private' next to the toilets. Someone will show you where to sleep and your motorcycles will be locked up in the shop once we close."

The meal was indeed good and gratifying as Khoi sheepishly said that he could go another helping. That is until Chu Bay gave him that look that said "one is enough."

They made their way up the stairs and entered the second floor apartment as directed and were met by a younger man who introduced himself as Choi. "Greetings comrades, please make yourselves at home and pick any of the empty cots that you find. You will be safe here as everyone in the shop and many of the patrons are sympathetic to our cause. This room has been our central meeting place where the upcoming events have been meticulously planned for several months now. You three have been assigned to Group 3 that will concentrate on attacking the Radio Station once the grand push is started."

"Do you mean that we are attacking Saigon during the Cease Fire truce?" asked Khoi.

"Yes, not only in Saigon, but throughout the country. Once the populace becomes aware that we have taken this action, they will join us in droves to help defeat the puppets in power and restore Vietnam to the people. Now try and get some sleep for tomorrow someone will come and lead you to Group 3 in Gia Dinh. They will give you your weapons and brief you on your target."

As Choi departed, the trio each picked a cot and hoped they'd be able to sleep now that the impending action had been revealed to them. The ample servings of hot soup however, helped to bring sleep quickly to the three weary travelers, each lost in their own thoughts.

VIETNAMESE NAVAL HEADQUARTERS

The next two days were pretty much a carbon copy of Sunday, with the exception that an "All Hands" memo had been issued from the Captain. It warned us to be alert and basically watch our respective backsides during the upcoming TET holiday.

On Tuesday evening on my way to the BOQ after work, I noticed something out of the norm: Large French flags were prominently displayed from the Majestic, Continental, and Caravelle Hotels, while smaller flags adorned several of the lesser businesses in and around the downtown area. This puzzled me because the average citizen did not regard the previous occupiers of their country with any great amount of respect. Nor did it connect in any way with the celebration of the Vietnamese New Year.

Shrugging it off, I decided to have a quick supper in the dining room and then perhaps a beer or two afterwards. The meal was uneventful and when it was over, I was glad to leave the low buzz of conversation mixed with the clattering of dishes from the kitchen. I got up and made my way into the bar that was doing a brisk business. Since most of the bar girls in Saigon headed home to their families for TET, the hard core girls who stayed behind to work held little interest for the average bar-hopping GI. Hence the BOQ bar flourished, because requests for "Saigon Tea" were nonexistent.

Anna, the long-haired bartender, greeted me immediately as I took a seat towards the rear.

"Long time-no-see, *Dai-Uy*," she said as she placed a coaster in front of me.

"I was down in Hoa Hao and then I had to catch up on all my work once I got back," I replied. "I'll have a beer, please. How have you been?"

She leaned towards me over the bar and softly whispered, "Do you remember that restaurant you told me about out in Thu Duc?"

"Yes, *Le Biche Du Abois,* the restaurant a few miles north of Saigon." Loosely translated it meant "The Deer in the Woods." It is located in a peaceful countryside setting and the food is European style and outstanding. Eating there always made one forget about the chaos of the world around you. I was originally introduced to it by a Vietnamese Naval officer who brought me along to help celebrate his promotion to Captain just after I came up from Poulo Obi.

Anna continued, keeping her voice low. "I was out there yesterday with a friend of mine and towards the end of our meal, the owner came to our table very nervous. He told us that we had to leave immediately and to forget about the check. This was repeated by the waiters to the other patrons and it was clear that something was wrong. The owner had come to us because he knew the American who had brought me and that he worked in the US Embassy. As we all quickly filed out of the restaurant, I looked back towards the kitchen area and saw several men with guns through a little window in the door. I became frightened, which was obvious to my friend and as he started his car, told me to look straight ahead and relax. What do you think?"

"Did you get see what type of weapons they were carrying?"

"No, I was too afraid to look," she said softly as her eyes cast downwards.

I knew that if she had gotten a good look at them she would certainly have recognized the standard AK-47.

"Strange, really strange," I said. "There hasn't been any VC activity reported in the Thu Duc area that I know of and why, if they were VC, didn't they just kill you and your friend? After all, you know how they abhor Vietnamese women who fraternize with Americans."

"That bothered me too," she said shaking her head, still obviously shaken.

She drifted to the front of the bar while I drank my beer and pondered what all that had been about. Maybe it was just a couple of angry locals venting their frustrations towards the owner who allowed such permissiveness between their women and us foreigners. But if so, why didn't they come out and rough up the non-Asian men to make a point? What I didn't realize then and was about to find out in the very near future was that this was the beginning of the 1968 TET offensive.

I had another beer from the other bartender whose name I didn't know and after downing it, decided to call it a night. I guess I just wasn't in the mood to party since some of the bar patrons that I recognized didn't interest me for conversation. I waved to Anna on my way out and she waved back, still with that worried look. She had really been rattled by that experience.

Quietly entering my darkened room so as not to waken anyone, I discovered that I had the room to myself. Neither one of my roommates were there, probably at a pre-TET party somewhere.

The next morning I awoke, shaved, showered and headed down to the dining hall. I noticed a definite air to the place that was also not normal. The chatter of the diners seemed a little more subdued and there appeared to be more people there than usual. I sat down at a table with a Navy Lieutenant whom I recognized from NAVFORV and asked him what the excitement was about.

"Where have you been? The VC attacked not only Saigon but every major city in South Vietnam. In fact, there are MPs outside that have kept us cooped up inside. Word is that we are all confined to our billets until further notice."

That explained what Anna had been telling me about her Thu Duc restaurant experience. Those guys in the kitchen were most likely part of the attackers working their way into position and waiting for the green light from Hanoi. A million thoughts raced through my mind and uppermost was to go to my room and strap my snub-nosed .38 pistol under my greens.

When I returned to the main floor, I noticed a memo from the SOP (Senior Officer Present) posted on the bulletin board. It announced that there would be a meeting in the Dining Hall at 1000 hours. Since it was only 0930, I decided to go in, find a seat and have another cup of coffee. There were already several people sitting around the tables and talking among themselves. I joined two other naval types and they were as much in the dark as I was with regards to what was happening outside. Finally at 1000 on the dot, Army Lieutenant Colonel Fletcher, who was the SOP at the McCarthy, asked for our undivided attention.

"As you may or may not know, the Viet Cong along with units of the North Vietnamese army have simultaneously attacked the major cities throughout South Vietnam. It's unclear at the moment what the exact situation is, but we here are going to 'Battle Stations' until further advised. I have posted a watch bill outside my office next to the main desk and would ask each of you to read it and make the necessary preparations. These are four hour watches and I do not foresee any problems arising from that since we have no indication as to when our restriction to quarters will be lifted. I have assigned three men to the front perimeter outside the building, two inside the front doors, two at the rear door leading out from the kitchen and one man on the roof. These watches will commence at 2000 hours this evening and continue until further notified by me. Weapons will be carried by those on watch and safeties will be on unless the situation requires the firing of said weapons. For those of you posted outside of the building, your rules of engagement are hereby modified: Shoot anyone you deem to present an immediate danger to you rather than wait for them to take the first shot. Any questions so far? The MPs who are presently posted outside the front entrance will be relieved by the three men assigned by me at 2000 hours. As you can see, many of the Vietnamese personnel employed at the McCarthy are still here and will remain inside. Meals will be served as usual. I'm not certain how many room maids are still here but we'll have to make do until travel restrictions are lifted. None of the female military personnel have been given any duties as there are enough male occupants to have a seven section rotating watch bill. Somehow I don't think that this will last more than a couple of days. Feel free to see me if there are any problems and I'll try to keep you posted as information comes in. So now, if you will please check out the watch bill and initial your names, I'll have a better idea as to who is aboard and make any changes required."

As the Colonel left the dining room, the murmur of voices erupted, mostly in discussions of what was just presented to us. Who could have figured that the annual TET cease-fire would be broken? It only made each of us acutely aware as to what kind of enemy we were facing, and it didn't make us feel any better.

I sat around for awhile waiting until the majority of the people went to check the watch bill. Most of them eventually drifted into the bar or up to their rooms still chattering among themselves. When I finally made it to the watch bill, I was surprised to see that my name was posted to the first watch out front part of a group of three. I quickly glanced at the other two names beside mine and they belonged to a Marine Captain and an Airborne 1st Lieutenant. With nothing else to do until that evening, I decided to go back to my room, check my rifle, ammo and get some more sack time.

The significance of the French flags flying throughout the city meant that the local French must have somehow learned about the impending attacks. It was now clear that by displaying the flags, it identified the property as that belonging to a loyal sympathizer. Ah, you had to admire these two-faced weasels.

After getting a few hours of quality sleep, I awoke to find that neither of my roommates had returned. It was close to 5 o'clock, so I dressed in my greens and donned my combat boots figuring that they would keep me warmer during the night and offer better protection from mosquitoes that might be around. I made my way into the dining hall that was only partially full and had a mediocre supper of chicken fried rice, stale apple pie and coffee. After that, I went back up to my room to make a "head call" and assemble my gear for my coming watch. The only sound that I could hear distinctly was the constant thumping of the big diesel generator below. I could not imagine what lay ahead since I had never been in a city that was under attack and where the enemy could not be differentiated from the good guys. Well, self preservation dictated that "When in doubt, shoot and ask questions later."

THE CIRCLE, DOWNTOWN SAIGON

I came down around 7:30, which was 15 minutes earlier than I would actually have had to assume the watch. My two watch-mates arrived almost simultaneously and the three of us somehow knew that we were to stand the first watch together, so we introduced ourselves to each other.

"I'm Bob Kay" I said shaking each man's hand.

The Marine Captain was dressed in typical VN Marine black and green Tiger Stripes, standing about an inch over six feet tall with closely cropped blonde hair and grey eyes. He carried his

200 pounds well distributed over his muscular body and said in a no-nonsense voice, "Mark Williamson," with a grip to match.

The third and junior member of our group was a medium height, tanned, stocky, but well-built Airborne First Lieutenant with short jet black hair and eyes to match. Because he was slightly older than the standard First Lieutenant, I assumed that he had previously been a sharp non-com enlisted who got commissioned.

"I'm Pete Thatcher," he drawled. "Did we make somebody's shit-list or was this just the luck of the draw?"

"Nah, we're just lucky," said Williamson as he adjusted his M-16 bandoliers over his shoulder. Looking at me he said, "I see you're still lugging the M-14 around with you. Hope the Navy taught you how to handle it."

"Well I survived Underwater Demolition Training and made it to the teams as an enlisted man which allowed me to swim off the coast of Inchon, Korea just before the invasion. When I returned to active duty with a commission, I turned down the offer to go into the SEALs because at 31 years of age, I didn't feel as if I could keep up with the new breed of 19 year olds. And, before I wound up here in sunny Saigon, I was in the Junk groups playing tag with Charlie off the coast of the Camau peninsula. I would think that qualifies me to handle a weapon, don't you Captain?"

"Yes, it does and don't take it personal," he said genuinely. "I just like to know who I'm going to the dance with."

Thatcher began chuckling to himself as he hefted a short barreled 12 gauge Ithaca Pump shotgun and a Mark 30 grenade launcher with two bandoliers of shells. "Let's get this ballgame going since we've covered our bonafides. If 'Charlie' comes nosing around, he'll find out he just won the Tri-Fecta."

As the three of us headed out of the entranceway, Williamson said "We'd probably be better off if we positioned ourselves in the Lam Son circle. That way, we can see all around us."

"Sounds good to me," I replied.

Thatcher chimed in suggesting that we check out the kiosks lining both sides of Nguyen Hue first, just in case.

"Good thinking, Pete,' said Williamson. "You take the ones on the far side of the street and Bob can check this side. I'll come down the middle and back you guys up. Just go down as far as the USO. That should be enough, OK?"

"Let's do it," I said. All the kiosks were darkened except the second one on my side of the street. Apparently the owners sometimes slept in there, a fact which I hadn't even considered before. I silently approached the near side of the kiosk where I could see a faint light leaking through the wood framing along with muted conversation. Glancing upward, I spotted the tell-tale gypsy-wire running from the roof of the kiosk to the nearby light pole where the occupants were pirating electricity from the city. Almost everyone that could bribe a Utilities inspector did it, so there was no surprise here. I banged lightly on the wood siding and hissed "*Tac dien di*," which meant "extinguish the light" in Vietnamese. The light immediately went out and silence closed in around the kiosk.

"Everything OK?" asked Mark softly to which I responded silently by giving him a thumbs up. We continued down the street until we reached the USO and then retraced our steps slowly and headed back towards the circle. The streets were eerily quiet for this time of night and it exuded a ghostly quality to the entire area.

CIRCLE AT NGUYEN HUE & LE LOI - DOWNTOWN SAIGON

The circle was approximately thirty feet across and at one time held a working fountain. It was constructed of cement and the outer edge was about eight inches high. The top of the edge was six inches wide and the inner surface gently flowed towards the center at a thirty degree angle until it reached a smaller cement circle four feet in diameter that contained some capped-off pipes. The sloping area between the inner and outer circle was covered with sparse grass that was struggling to survive and only the rain provided it with any sustenance.

The three of us approached the circle at a slow pace keeping a wary eye out for anything suspicious. Just as we were crossing the street, a faint voice called to us from one of the entrances just off the corner of Nguyen Hue on Le Loi. Pete, being the closest turned and carefully approached the small gated entrance to one of the civilian hotels. There were two male civilians on the inside of the high closed accordion style gate. Before Pete even reached them, they both started whispering excitedly at the same time. "We're Americans and are attached to USAID. This is our billet, but we have no protection, no instructions or any information about what the hell is going on."

Pete replied softly, "Just take it easy and relax. We've stationed security in the circle and it will be maintained until word reaches us to the contrary. The Senior Officer in the McCarthy is in communications both with MACV and the Embassy. The VC and the North Vietnamese army violated the cease fire treaty by staging coordinated attacks all over the south. We've been ordered to stand fast and remain in our quarters until further notice, so pass the word and go hit the sack. Your tax dollars are hard at work here tonight, so relax.

Having calmed the men down somewhat, Pete returned to the circle where Mark and I had already hunkered down. He related his encounter with the two civilians finishing sardonically with, "Just like those friggin civilians; they look down on us service-types until their lily-white butts are in a jam and then they come looking for us, big time."

"Sounds awfully familiar but fortunately, those folks are in the minority," said Mark setting his bandolier down beside him.

Once we were comfortably situated within the circle, each covering a third of the quadrant, we settled in as best we could for our assigned vigil. We were not given any specific marching orders with regards to our duties out here, but we understood that we would be the outer listening post and initial contact point for the BOQ. There was an earthy musty smell coming from the ground and odds were that the circle initially contained a working water fountain when the French constructed it. But as city officialdom changed, so did the local street scene. Someone must have decided that the city should not have to pay to have a fountain pumping water continuously for simply esthetic reasons, so "poof," out it came.

About forty-five minutes had passed since we had assumed our positions, when the sound of an approaching automobile engine broke the silence of the night. The sound was coming from the direction of the Opera House and Hai Ba Trung Street. Almost immediately, two headlights appeared heading our way rather quickly. Williamson immediately jumped up and waved at the vehicle to stop while Pete and I covered him with our weapons. The car was an old, white Volkswagen beetle with a crudely printed sign on the side reading "*Bao Chi*" or Press. As the vehicle pulled up, four Caucasian faces cautiously peered out.

"Don't you guys know that a military curfew has been imposed on the city and no one is supposed to be out on the streets?" said Mark in an imposing voice.

The driver stuck his face partly out of the vehicle's window and replied rather officiously, "We know about the curfew, but we represent the Press and it's our job to get the latest news for the folks back home."

"I've got news for you mister; the whole country is under attack by the Viet Cong and the North Vietnamese army. Nobody, except on official business, is authorized to be cruising around the streets. It's not safe or smart. So please turn around and go back to where you came from before someone gets hurt. The entire city is under lockdown and the ARVN have set up numerous roadblocks all over. You don't want to be mistaken for one of the bad guys, do you?"

"We hear you Captain," a voice from the rear of the car said, "and we'll take your warning under advisement."

The passenger in the front leaned over and added his two cents worth by saying, "We're just doing our job same as you, and though we appreciate your advice with all due respect, we're going to continue on our way. With that, the vehicle started up and roared down Le Loi in the direction of the Cholon Market.

Before Mark even got back to his place in the circle, a flurry of gunshots followed by a dull thud reverberated from the direction the vehicle had taken. We learned later that the ARVN, who had been set up around the circle by the Cholon Market, had opened fire upon seeing the speeding vehicle approaching them. One can understand their apprehension at actually being attacked in their capital city during a Holiday, but sound leadership and common sense were not present in this case. They had enough firepower to halt the vehicle to check it out just as we did, but chose to shoot first. All four journalists in the car were killed and I was sure that repercussions and finger-pointing would follow when and if things settled down.

When we heard the shooting, Pete remarked dryly, "I'll be willing to bet that those four guys just bought the farm."

"Damn, when are these correspondents going to learn that '*Bao Chi*' doesn't make them bulletproof?" Mark said stoically.

"Yeah, look at Ernie Pyle during the second world war and 'Dicky' Chappelle in 1965 with the Marines up north. They voluntarily imbedded themselves with the grunts and understood the dangers of combat before they got killed. These other clowns just sit around the bars in their safari jackets and write their bylines while knocking back the cheap booze every night. That's some journalistic integrity and the folks back home believe all the shit that they put out," I remarked emphatically.

"Boy, that's profound," said Pete.

"Yeah, but all too true," agreed Mark.

Just then, more firing erupted and we could see white, green and red tracers arcing into the sky from the direction of the US Embassy and the waterfront by VNN Headquarters. "Looks like someone has their hands full," remarked Pete as he took a much tighter grip on his shotgun. The firing continued unabated in the distance for approximately ten minutes, then subsided into sporadic gunshots.

The three of us settled back in silence, ever vigilant and each with our own thoughts. Pete raised his head and whispered as he pointed towards the Caravelle Hotel, "Look at the size of that rat that just climbed out of the sewer opening on the corner." It was huge and the biggest rat that I had ever seen even compared to the brutes that inhabited Poulo Obi.

Mark said, "Man, it's bigger than a friggin' possum."

As we watched the enormous rodent calmly sniffing around the curb, a mangy white cat was slowly making its way towards the corner from Nguyen Hue. Upon spying the rat, the wary cat came to an abrupt stop, stared at the rodent for several seconds and quickly disappeared under a parked car across the street. "That's a good lesson in Survival of the Fittest," said Pete.

"Well, he'll live to flee another day," I quipped. "Who said animals are dumb?"

Time dragged by slowly with nothing but intermittent shooting off in the distance to break the otherwise stifling silence. It is really tough to be involved in a situation like this without knowing what side is winning. Oh sure, we were confident that the guys in the white hats would prevail in the long run, but it was the interim period that concerned us the most. And still, we maintained our vigil in the heart of downtown Saigon.

Glancing at my watch for the umpteenth time in the last hour, I was relieved to see that it was 2230. We should be getting relieved by the next trio of watchstanders within the next 15 minutes, although I must admit that I was not really tired. The long nap I had taken earlier, plus the adrenalin rush of possible enemy contact, helped to keep me wide awake. Just then some movement occurred by the entranceway to the McCarthy. From out of the shadows, a man bedecked with a helmet strapped on his head and a water canteen bobbing on his ample hip made his way crouching low and zigzagging towards us. Huffing and puffing from the exertion expended in the sinuous path he took to reach us, he reached the inner confines of our circle. Mark, Pete and I just stared at the newcomer who turned out to be an army Captain with a Finance insignia on his collar.

"Hi guys, I'm Al Pinto and I'm one of your reliefs," he said obviously short of breath. "The others are coming shortly."

"Where's your weapon?" asked Mark curiously as his eyes continued to roam over the portly and out of shape Captain.

"Uh, I left my .45 in my desk at MACV and was never issued a rifle. I figured that I could use one of yours," he said a little uncertain.

Pete stood up and offered Pinto his shotgun. The Captain in turn, seemed completely at a loss as he hefted the weapon and examined it closely.

"Have you ever fired one of these babies before?" asked Pete.

"No, not really," replied the Captain a little sheepishly and by now, clearly embarrassed.

"In that case, I'm going to make a suggestion that you head back to the BOQ and tell those other two that we've got the situation under control and that we intend to stay here until 4 AM. Your job, along with the other two guys, is to keep us supplied with hot coffee and maybe a sandwich or two, OK? You can lose the helmet and canteen on your next trip out," said Mark. "And by the way, never strap your helmet under your chin because if there is a concussion close by, the force will tear your head off. If it's loose, only the helmet will come off."

Without showing any visible emotion after being summarily rejected for duty, Pinto nodded and almost tripping over the lip of the circle, quickly resumed his zigzag run back to safety.

"Boy, was he a trip, or what?" I asked.

"I hope you guys didn't mind my volunteering us for an extended watch. I figured if you're like me, I wouldn't be able to close my eyes knowing he was out here protecting our asses," said the Marine.

"No problem, Cap," replied Pete, to which I nodded in approval.

"Didn't they teach weapon handling at Army OCS?" I asked.

Pete replied slowly, "Sure they did, but some of those primadonnas act like the stuck-up British aristocratic broad that put on her white lacy gloves on the night of her honeymoon so she wouldn't have to handle the ghastly thing."

With that, Mark and I both cracked up laughing. "Well, it takes all kinds to run an army and I hope he is better at doing the payroll," said Mark.

A half an hour had passed since Mark had sent our "relief" packing, and we were pleasantly surprised to see him casually strolling back towards us. Another officer was with him who was carrying a cardboard box, while he proudly carried a .30 caliber carbine. This time, neither one of them wore helmets. The box was packed with three large containers of coffee, six ham and cheese sandwiches and 3 packs of oatmeal cookies. "Here's your care package as requested. This gent here is Lieutenant Gormes from NAVFORV and he was part of my watch team," announced Captain Pinto somewhat officiously.

We greeted them with nods and eagerly dug into the chow since none of us had realized that we were as hungry as we were.

"Will there be anything else you men need?" asked Pinto as he handed the empty carton back to Gormes.

"No, we'll be just fine until we get relieved," said Mark. "Many thanks to you and the kitchen crew for the Mid-Rats. It's much appreciated."

The Captain crinkled his eyebrows up at the term Mid-Rats, probably never having heard that term before. I explained that this is what we in the Navy call Midnight Rations for the folks that stand the Midnight to four AM watches. Understanding then smoothed out the Captain's features and he smiled knowingly.

"It figures that you Navy types have to have a language all your own," he said as the two men started back to the BOQ.

The next few hours passed without incidence. Not so much as a breeze was discernible as the fetid air seemed to just weigh down on us. This was supposed to be the dry season which would normally have cooler temperatures, but it didn't really seem so this night. It was strange indeed; there were no birds chirping quietly in the trees and few, if any, bats out hunting night flying insects. Nothing seemed to exist except our individual heartbeats.

Sometime close to 0230, another vehicle motor broke the evening silence. It was coming from Le Loi and it turned out to be an MP Jeep, equipped with a .50 caliber machine gun with its gunner standing upright on the rear seat. Next to the driver sat an

MP Sergeant with the butt of an M-16 resting on his knee. They approached the circle warily until they recognized that we were US military. The sergeant threw us a casual salute upon seeing that we were officers but only Mark returned it.

"How's it going Captain?" asked the sergeant.

"It's been pretty quiet since the ARVN shot up a VW beetle filled with four press-types. We tried to warn them to keep off the streets, but you know how they are," answered Mark.

"You can imagine how we feel tooling around these streets, especially with the trigger-happy ARVNs manning roadblocks all over the place. Our Major sent two units out to poke around and try to get a feel of the situation. We lucked out with this milk run around downtown, but the other guys were heading out into Cholon. My money says that the bad guys are holed up in those Chinese rabbit warrens."

"Well, if they're not there now, I'll bet they used Cholon as a staging area for all this bullshit," surmised Pete.

"As long as you guys are OK, we'll move on." With that, the Jeep roared off heading east towards the river and Khanh Hoi.

The growling of the vehicle's engine followed it down Nguyen Hue and the deathly silence once again returned only to be broken by the occasional sound of helicopters circling the city. A continual ring of flares were being dropped all around the outskirts of the city, but for the most part it was quiet.

As the hands of my watch neared 0430, we heard a whistle from across the square by the entrance to the McCarthy. The Finance Officer was standing there waving his arms and trying to get our attention. Mark stood up and shrugged his arms to the side and up in the universal gesture meaning "What's up?"

Captain Pinto continued to wave, only this time he was beckoning us to return to the BOQ.

"What the hell is that all about?" asked Pete.

"Dunno, but it looks like they want to pull us in," said Mark and with that the three of us gathered our gear and headed back slowly to the McCarthy.

Upon reaching the lobby, we were met by the over-exuberant Captain Pinto who rushed towards us breathlessly announcing that we were ordered to stand down and no further outer watches would be required. The only ones that were to be maintained were the two men assigned inside the front lobby, two by the rear door in the galley and one on the roof. "The Colonel is in the mess in case you want to see him," he added.

When he finished his oration, he stood there fixedly staring at Mark as if he were waiting for a friendly pat on the head for his report. That's when I thought to myself that he would have made a good Supply officer in the Navy, well perhaps.

BACK TO THE BOQ

The three of us slowly wandered into the dining hall to get ourselves some fresh coffee. The Colonel was sitting at one of the tables and waved us over.

"Grab a seat and fill me in about what happened out there last night." He said.

We sat down as coffee was brought to us by one of the VN waitresses. Then Mark proceeded to relate what occurred with the four press people in the VW and the reason we opted to extend our watch after getting a load of Captain Pinto.

The Colonel chuckled over the last part, nodding his head knowingly. "I'd have done the same thing had I been in your shoes," he replied considering the Captain's unmilitary-like bearing. "However, those four jerks in the VW never made it because they tried to push their luck with the ARVN. The bodies are still in the car outside the barricade and will probably stay there because the VNs are trying to send a message. This is their country and no one is going to bully their way through them, regardless of how important they think they are."

"Can't say I blame them," I remarked. "The US press has never had anything good to say about the ARVN anyway so I can readily understand their resentment."

"Yes, it's too bad we all can't be on the same page about this conflict. It certainly doesn't help the people back home to fully understand what's actually at stake here with the biased slant the media generate in their reports. There are only a handful of correspondents who tell it like it is, but they are over-shadowed by the elite press majority."

"How come we're cutting back on our watches?" asked Pete.

"Word is that the initial coordinated attacks have been beaten back in our area. The bad guys hit the Embassy, Vietnamese Naval Headquarters, the Presidential Palace, Long Binh, Bien Hoa airbase and Tan Son Nhut. There are still pockets of resistance, especially in Cho Lon, Gia Dinh and the Phuto Racetrack. "I'm not up to speed on what's happening throughout the rest of the country, but if it's anything like Saigon, our guys have pretty much got a handle on things. The next few days should tell the story. If you've nothing better to do, you guys ought to head up to the rooftop. There's a crowd up there having a party and watching the fireworks going on around the city." Mark said, "I think I'll just get some sack time before the sun comes up. Besides, who knows what tomorrow may bring, to quote an old axiom."

"I'm game for hitting the roof," said Pete looking at me.

"Yeah, I guess it's worth an elevator ride to join the party," I replied as I stood up and stretched the old back muscles.

The elevator came to a shuddering stop as it reached the top floor and instead of loud music being pumped out of a boom-box, only the low murmur of soft conversation was heard. We stepped out into the hallway and made our way to the rooftop patio. To our surprise there were only about twenty people standing around the perimeter of the roof. They were watching the flares being continuously dropped around the city to light up the ground for patrolling gunships. Some of the onlookers were decked out in shorts and flip-flops holding cans of beer while others were in their wash khaki pants with glasses of some kind of refreshment.

Standing by the doorway with his usual glass of Wild Turkey making repeated trips to his lips, stood Lieutenant Commander Link Richards. He stood about 5 feet 9 inches tall, very well tanned and had a wiry frame. His head was completely bald and he stood with a slight hunch to his shoulders. The huge anchor tattooed on his right forearm indicated that he had come up through the ranks and was now the Senior Advisor attached to the Vietnamese Third Riverine Commander. Our paths had crossed several times since I had been assigned to Saigon and he seemed a likable individual in the ever rotating mass of personnel passing through Vietnam.

Spotting me, he asked, "How's your Newsletter coming along?"

"Just fine," I replied, "But I'm still waiting for a good job in the field to open up so I can get back to doing what I came here to do."

"Would you be interested in a spot with the RAGs? Lieutenant Sanderson is slated to leave in March. He's with RAG 24 based in Tan An and he'd like nothing better than to know who his relief is, the sooner the better."

"Thanks for the tip; I'll talk to the old man first chance I get."

"Let me know because I can appreciate you wanting to get out from behind that desk and from under the old man's thumb."

"Amen to that and thanks."

Pete had managed somehow to get his hands on two cans of ice cold Schlitz beer and handed me one.

"This beats breakfast any day and it'll sure help me unwind when I hit the sack later," he said.

"Uh huh," I mumbled as I let the cool liquid pass over my lips just as a small hand touched me on the shoulder. I turned and recognized Quyen the waitress from the cafeteria and she was still in her work clothes.

"Looks like you were stuck here instead of being home with your family," I remarked.

"No problem." She said. "My family live near Nha Trang and this year I decided to stay here and work over the holiday to make some extra money."

"Well, you're probably better off here than up north. At least you have enough protection around you, more so than if you had gone home."

When the conversation between Quyen and I commenced, Pete casually sauntered to another part of the roof patio thinking that he was giving me a clear shot at the young lady. But, this was not my intention, although I appreciated his consideration. That's what real buddies do for each other even though we hadn't met prior to standing watch together in the center of town.

As Quyen and I continued our dialogue, I noticed that she had moved close enough to me so that our bodies were touching. In a tremulous voice just barely loud enough for me to hear, she asked, "Do you want me to come with you to your room?"

I was taken by surprise by the demure offer and most likely had it happened at any other time, I might have read the signals earlier. But, being the gentleman that I was, even with the lack of sleep, I regained my composure. I held her gently by the arms, looked into her eyes and said, "Quyen, I would like nothing better than to bring you to my room, but I have two other officers as roommates and they are in there sleeping." Although that was not a true statement, it was the best excuse that I could come up with at the time.

She let her eyes drop down and seemed to be genuinely embarrassed by my refusal. Her soft voice then said, "Maybe some other time *Dai-Uy*, whenever you want."

She gently touched my arm briefly as she left to join two of the other waitresses sitting around a small table. Moments after she sat down, the eyes of the other waitresses fell on me almost accusingly. Well, I guess I just qualified as the "a-hole of the day" in the eyes of the McCarthy's serving staff. You can bet that the infamous "bamboo grapevine" will circulate this boorish behavior by noon tomorrow. Pete looked at me from across the patio and shrugged his shoulders as his eye-brows arched upwards in the universal gesture meaning "What's up, over?" In response I too could only shrug. The only thought that came to my tired mind at this point was that in no time at all, I could have had that girl eating out of my wallet.

I decided to head down to my room and see if I could stretch out for at least an hour. As I entered the corridor, Link's room was just to the right with the door open and he was breaking the seal on another bottle of Wild Turkey. Whew! I don't know how some of these guys do it with the booze consumption. Perhaps it's in their genes or they might have accidently stumbled on a new deterrent for abstract boredom.

Since the elevator was in use, I decided to take the stairs to my floor. What the heck, it was downhill all the way, right? The room was still empty, regardless of what I had told Quyen and I wondered where my two roommates had spent their evening. Flopping onto my bed fully clothed, I set the alarm for two hours. That's all I remember till the incessant beeping brought me back to consciousness.

I got up from my bed feeling sluggish as if I had been swimming in a sea of oatmeal and was trying desperately to reach the surface for some fresh air. The water that came out of the bathroom sink tap was tepid at best, but it would have to do. I splashed it vigorously on my face hoping that it would wash away the malaise and afford me some hidden reserves of energy to let me make it to my office. I had no idea what I would find there, but it was better than moping around the BOQ where too little information was available as to the current situation.

I made it down the stairs to the foyer, encountering only an Army First Lieutenant who was sitting on a folding chair and obviously one of the guards assigned to watch the entrance. He merely glanced up at me as I exited the building, which was good for me since I was in no mood for any conversation. Once out on the street, the sun hit me like a hammer which forced me to put on my sunglasses.

I was dressed in my greens with my .38 pistol in its shoulder holster under my left arm because I didn't think it was wise to venture forth unarmed. I headed straight down Nguyen Hue hugging the buildings on the right hand side. As for anyone else in the street, there wasn't a soul in sight, which made it eerie for this time of day. Once I reached Ben Bach Dang, I jogged quickly across the street and headed for the Tran Hung Dao statue. As I approached Don Dat Street, I saw a roadblock being set up by several Vietnamese sailors blocking off Ben Bach Dang and the entrance to Vietnamese Naval Headquarters. It seemed strange because I would have assumed that the roadblock would have been setup yesterday immediately upon hearing of the attacks around the country. But then again, who was I to presuppose the workings of the Asian mind?

The sailors paid me no mind as I crossed over the sidewalk and headed for the entrance. That's when I saw an old battered white Simca automobile in the street with its four doors wide open. The guard post, which was a cylindrical concrete structure attached to the left side of the compound wall was blackened and a huge hole had been blown in the wall next to it. The gates were ajar just enough for me to pass through into the compound. I saw six blood-soaked bodies arranged in a row lying on the ground. They were dressed identically with dark pants and white shirts, each with a white rag tied around their upper left arms. I learned later that this was common with the VC so that when they were wounded, it was easier for their comrades to grab them by the rag and drag them off.

As I looked up at the face of the building I could see bullet pockmarks all over its surface. On the second deck, there were two manned .30 caliber machine guns positioned facing the main entrance. One of the gunners was a Vietnamese Lieutenant and the other was an American Advisor, LTJG Summers who was assigned to the Comm center at headquarters. He waved to me and yelled down for me to come up.

Taking the steps two at a time, I made it to the second deck and headed for the front portico. Summers looked a bit haggard as he leaned out over the four foot wall gazing down on the bodies lying on the hot cement. "Looks like you folks had some excitement," I said approaching him.

"You could say that. We got a tip last night that something like this was going to happen, so we went to General Quarters. Since Dai Uy Mang and I were the only officers on duty in the Comm Center. We got to man the .30s. When the Simca turned into the street and stopped, it looked just like those comic cars in the circus where all the clowns come pouring out. The exception being that these clowns had guns. One had a shoulder fired B-40 rocket launcher that blew a hole in the wall and another guy had a grenade launcher that hit the guard's post killing a young sailor. Our Vietnamese were shooting at them from every window while Mang and I riddled them with the .30s. We got them all before they could breach the compound and managed to take one of them alive but wounded. He's being interrogated as we speak by the

Vietnamese Intel guys on the next deck up in the building on the right. I wouldn't want to be in his shoes right now."

Just as we were talking, the shutters from the third deck window of the Intel Office flew open and a white shirted body came hurtling out over the sill. His hands were bound behind him and blood was streaming from a cut on his head as he plummeted down screaming towards the cement in the courtyard below. I could have sworn I saw two sets of hands from inside propelling him out the window, but I would never admit to it if I were ever asked. "I guess he wasn't too cooperative up there," I thought.

"Well, that's seven for seven, but it's a pity we lost that young sentry," said Summers.

"What do you expect when they still follow French basic designs? By rights, that sentry booth should be entered from inside the compound not from the outside. Once he was out there, he didn't have a chance in hell of surviving," I said angrily.

"Where are you headed now," he asked.

"I figured to come down here to see if anyone else showed up, but I guess not."

"The Old Man arrived a few minutes ago so he's probably in his office."

"Well, in that case, I'd better head down there to see if he's got anything for me to do," I said as I patted him on the shoulder and headed back down below.

Entering the Senior Advisor's office, I saw that it was empty but the Captain's door was slightly open. I knocked softly and immediately heard the CO answering, "Come."

I entered the office and found the Captain sitting behind his desk as usual wearing his well starched greens. "What brings you down here Lieutenant?"

"I thought there might be something for me to do here rather than just sitting around the BOQ."

"Where did you spend last night?" he inquired.

"I was with two other BOQ mates positioned inside the circle at Nguyen Hue and Le Loi for eight hours."

"Why the heck did you stand an eight hour watch with so many other officers in the BOQ?"

"We didn't intend to Captain, until we got a look at the guys who came out to relieve us. The three of us unanimously decided right then and there that we'd rather stay on than entrust our safety to those greenhorns."

"Why in blazes were you guys out in the open like that in the first place?" he growled.

"We were just following orders from the Senior Officer of the BOQ, Captain."

"Hmmph," he said shaking his head in disbelief. "Well, there is nothing for you to do here at the moment, so I'd suggest that you return to the BOQ and stay there until otherwise ordered."

"Actually, I was thinking that I'd go over to JUSPAO and see if the 5 o'clock Follies were going to be held. If so, I'd be able to get a better handle on what has transpired around the country; that is if it's all right with you."

"Good thinking lad. You may have the makings of a first class journalist yet. Hop to it and keep me advised."

"Will do sir," I said as I turned and left the office somewhat relieved by his amiability.

Since it was still too early to go to JUSPAO, I traced my steps back to the McCarthy, only this time on the opposite side of the street from before. Entering the BOQ, I managed once again to avoid anyone that I knew except the same First Lieutenant still perched on his chair in the same position as I had seen him earlier. That sure didn't give me that warm and fuzzy feeling of security that I so sorely needed about now. But on the other hand, it was better than nothing and better him than me on that uncomfortable chair, right?

I went into the nearly deserted bar and mounted a stool in front of Ping, one of the other bartenders. She was a pert young lady in her early twenties, SOS, (standard Oriental size), with small breasts, short cut black hair and one of the nicest backsides that I had seen up to now. Ping had completed almost two years of university studies preparing for a career in medicine. But, like so many cases, the war had caused a delay in her plans; ones that she fully intended to resume once things returned to normal—if ever.

"What would you like *Dai Uy?*" she asked in her soft, almost bashful voice.

"I'd like a one week R & R trip to Singapore with you as my companion," I said smilingly. "But I'll settle for a cup of coffee with milk and sugar since I don't think my offer is appropriate or appealing."

"Why do you say that? All you have to do is ask and who knows what my answer would be?" she said coquettishly. "Besides, I have an aunt and uncle who live in Singapore and it would be nice to visit them."

I was immediately taken aback by her straightforward answer. What was I getting myself into, I thought while a kaleidoscope of pictures of the two of us naked in a Singaporean hotel ran through my mind at lightning speed? "Uh, I'll have to check back with you once things quiet down here," I stammered trying hard to sound upbeat. In reality, I was surprised and scared at the same time.

"OK," she said softly. "The door is open for you when you're ready and please enjoy your coffee."

I sat there dumbfound as she went to serve a customer at the other end of the bar. Actually, I think that this is precisely the reason I was so content to be over here. Everyday brought a new adventure of sorts and the place was crawling with good looking women. Too bad the recruiters back home couldn't use that as a benefit for inducing young men to enlist and volunteer for duty over here. I'd be willing to bet that there would be more than a few takers.

I finished my coffee, even though I hardly tasted it and headed over to JUSPAO. Once again I passed the young Army Lieutenant holding down the chair in the foyer and I wondered if he was asleep with his eyes open. For sure he was definitely one of the guys that folks referred to as a "REMF."

FIVE O'CLOCK FOLLIES

As I crossed Le Loi and passed the circle that only a short time ago had been my battle station, I could now see why Captain Bjorkman's assessment was that it was a poor choice for a perimeter defense. One bad guy with a grenade could have nailed the three of us easily. Oh well, we got away with one, but you can bet that I'll be a little more selective next time.

The uniformed short-statured wizened Nung guard that was just inside the JUSPAO entrance gave me an indifferent once-over as I came through the door and immediately resumed his stare off into infinity. It must be great to have a secret place to mentally retreat to when boredom is your chief commodity. I entered the rear of the large auditorium to find it was jam-packed full of correspondents, photographers, freelance journalists and a small group of military personnel. The many conversations among the attendees sounded like the buzz caused by a swarm of angry wasps just prior to making an attack on some unsuspecting human. As I looked around for familiar faces, I recognized several down in front of the large stage. Ed Bradley from CBS stood out clearly as he waited for the briefing to begin. Other correspondents I recognized were Wilson Hall from NBC, Peter Arnett from AP (Associated Press), and my recent friend Vince Slavin from the Newark Star Ledger.

Well, I surmised that this briefing should probably be one of the most significant ones to date because it would shock the folks back home to learn about the great TET Offensive. I took a seat in the back row trying to remain as inconspicuous as possible amid all the noted luminaries of the press corps. In short order, Captain Meehan of JUSPAO came out on the stage to the podium very stoic and purposeful. He held a sheath of papers in his hand that he spread out while adjusting the microphone and began to speak in a clear, well modulated voice . . .

"In the very early hours of Wednesday, the 31st of January 1968, more than one hundred targets throughout South Vietnam were simultaneously attacked by Viet Cong and North Vietnamese army units thereby breaking the TET truce. In our local area, the targets consisted of The American Embassy, The Vietnamese Joint General Staff Headquarters at Tan Son Nhut Airport, the Independence Palace, Vietnamese Naval Headquarters, the National Broadcasting Station and the Philippine Embassy."

During the briefing, as a detailed report on the Embassy attack and the number of enemy dead was concluding, a correspondent from Reuters stood up and asked the briefer if the Viet Cong sappers at any time were given the opportunity to "*Chieu Hoi*?" This was met immediately with "boos" and "cat-calls" from the entire group. Reuters was notoriously biased against the U.S. effort in Vietnam and always printed negative reports that were widely circulated and read throughout Europe.

"ER, COULD I INTEREST YOU IN THE CHIEU-HOI PROGRAM?"

The *Chieu Hoi* Program was a Psychological Warfare tool adopted in 1963 whereby an enemy soldier was invited to give up his arms, return to the south with immunity and get re-educated in order to become a viable citizen. I have heard of cases where a pitched firefight was just about over and the enemy, realizing his days were numbered, would throw down his arms and say "*Chieu Hoi.*" Unfortunately, many American GIs understood this ploy and either took them prisoner or shot them figuring that a true rallier would have made the choice before the encounter. Perhaps a bit cynical, but it makes sense. If one intended to come over, then he wouldn't have pulled the trigger in the first place.

Quite unexpectedly, General Westmoreland came onto the stage and took over the microphone. He basically reiterated what had already been reported and continued by giving body counts and instances of US and Vietnamese Forces' successes in throwing back the insurgents throughout the country. At this point, the correspondents began taking this oratory with a grain of salt since reports of inflated body counts had been highly suspect during the last few months in order to deflate the opposition to the war at home. Sensing the mood in the auditorium, the General quickly concluded his remarks and turned the mike back to Captain Meehan who resumed his briefing.

One other notable bit of information added on at the conclusion of the briefing was that when the fight at the embassy subsided, it was discovered that Ambassador Bunker's driver, Nguyen Van De, had been seen shooting at the MPs. He was among those who were subsequently shot and killed: So much for background checks and vetting of employees.

The questions that followed at the end of the briefing from the audience were as nonsensical and redundant as always. It appeared that many of the correspondents did not listen to the previous questions because they were too tied up in their own little world and repetition occurred, much to the exasperation of the briefer. So, being out of patience with this crowd, I got up and made my out of the building. I knew that I couldn't bear to hear one more asinine question thrown out at my poor friend.

On the way back to the BOQ, I decided to see if the corner coffee shop on Tu Do Street was open for business. It was, and I had no difficulty in finding an empty table since I was the only customer. The staff consisted of the owner and his wife who had been sitting pensively at a back table. Both their faces split open with wide smiles as I entered and this was the sort of greeting that I enjoyed. The mama-san fussed over me with the silverware and an English version of the menu, while the husband went expectantly into the kitchen. I ordered coffee, a croissant with orange marmalade and a half a grapefruit. It wasn't the usual large order normally consumed by the average American but any business was better than none at all. The meal was good although I felt awfully conspicuous being the lone patron. Finishing up, I thanked the owners politely and made my way back onto the nearly deserted street.

With my stomach quieted and nothing else to do, I headed back to the BOQ where I hoped to find solitude as I lay in my bed and read the latest Louis Lamour novel. He was one of America's greatest western writers and although I wasn't a big fan of cowboy literature, a friend once told me that his cardiologist recommended that he read Lamour mainly for the gentle flow of his writing. It worked for him so I hoped it would work for me.

The fighting in Saigon had pretty much abated by the first week of February, although pockets of resistance remained in Cholon and Gia Dinh until the end of the month. The main area of contention was the Phu Tho Racetrack which sat at the hub of several of the main streets in Cholon. The insurgents had overrun it early on in the attacks in order to deny its use as a landing zone. This racetrack was the home of some of the most crooked horse races in history.

I'd heard remarks from those who attended that some of the horses were so doped up prior to the races that they had trouble even finishing. So it was obvious that looking for an edge wasn't solely an Occidental cultural trait after all.

Although American troops from the 7th Infantry Division succeeded in retaking the racetrack with the aid of U.S. helicopter gunships, many of the VC disappeared into the back alleys in and around Cholon.

The fighting to the northwest of Saigon in Gia Dinh took a little longer than the operation to the south in Cholon. There were many factories and warehouses located throughout Gia Dinh in which the attackers had sought refuge. Knowing that the government forces would come in with helicopter gunships and mortar fire to root out the insurgents, the wealthy Chinese who owned these properties were rumored to have made a substantial payoff to the Vietnamese Airborne Commander to use only ground troops in order to spare their destruction. Yes, the cleanup in Gia Dinh would have happened much sooner except for that fact.

It was apparent that the failure of the TET Offensive rested primarily on the north's misguided belief that the attacks would spur a massive uprising of the population against the Thieu government. But it never came to fruition and they were left with their pants down in total failure.

Meanwhile, work continued on at VN Naval Headquarters as reports from the northern part of the country came in describing the final mop-up of the enemy attackers in Hue. Saigon itself rebounded as if nothing had happened and the traffic was as congested as usual.

The monthly blurbs from the field came in sporadically, but with enough of them so I could edit the inputs and fill the newsletter in order to keep the good Captain mollified. One story in particular came from up-country in Two Corps where one of the Assistant

Advisors of a Junk Group described a harrowing experience. It happened late on a Friday night while an eight man unit was deployed in ambush alongside the confluence of two canals that were suspected of being VC transit routes. This young officer along with the group's Executive Officer and six of their crew had been hidden among the saw grass and mangrove trees that covered both sides of the canals for more than three hours. Quietly enduring the night noises and the incessant buzzing of mosquitoes, the group lay in silence hoping to hear the soft slapping sound of approaching sampams. About the time that they were deciding to call it a night, a slight rustle of grass behind the Advisor got his attention. As he turned slowly and carefully parted the saw grass, he found the huge face of a tiger staring back at him with fierce yellow-green eyes. In an instant, the officer let out a yell and in the famous quip by comedian Bill Cosby who said "First I said it, then I did it," the officer shit his pants. Simultaneously, the huge cat let out a horrendous growl and disappeared back into the tall grass. It was only then that the acrid stench of the animal remained to verify what all had heard. With the ambush now a foregone conclusion, everyone started chattering nervously as the XO ordered them back to their Junk. Once safely aboard, the talking continued as they made their way down the canal towards their base. The young officer however, was relegated to sit downwind at the stern of the boat until he could clean himself up. One of the sailors jokingly yelled out,

"Hey *Trung-Uy*, you lucky tiger no want eat you because you smell so bad." That brought laughter from everyone.

Upon returning to the base where their story was told to the Commanding Officer and the senior Advisor, more laughter ensued. It naturally spread through the base at lightning speed and the officer became an instant celebrity, of sorts.

THE UNREFUSABLE OFFER

The next few weeks passed by with not much happening except for the normal business of the day. The city had quieted down and we were once again in a pre-TET disposition. Then late one afternoon, I received a phone call from LCDR Richards, the Third Riverine Advisor.

"Are you still interested in being a RAG Advisor?" he asked.

"You bet I am Commander."

"The Advisor of RAG 24 is due to rotate soon and if you're still serious about relieving him, I'll talk to the Captain and put in a plug for you as my choice."

"That would be great. I never believed it could happen."

"Well, don't count your chickens too fast young fella because you can never anticipate Bjorkman's reaction."

"I hear you, but I'll keep my fingers crossed just the same, and thanks Commander."

The next morning, Norman the Captain's Yeoman called me on the phone and said that the boss wanted to see me in his office. I assumed that it must have something to do with my conversation with LCDR Richards yesterday and hoped that it was. I almost went ass-over-teakettle as I ran down the stairs and ended up caroming into the wall because the tile deck was still wet from having been freshly mopped. Quickly regaining my balance and composure, I crossed the courtyard and entered the Senior Advisor's office. The tit-less Yeoman Norman looked up and nodded his head towards the CO's office. Oddly enough, he was the only one in the front office which could only mean that the XO was probably on a Pop-Tart run.

I knocked on the closed door and was immediately summoned to enter. The Captain was sitting behind his desk with his glasses low on the end of his nose. As I approached, he casually leaned back in his chair, crossed his legs and invited me to sit down.

"I had a call this morning from the Third Riverine Senior Advisor and he requested that you be transferred over to him to relieve LT Sanderson in RAG-24. I seem to remember when you first reported in that you were unhappy about being pulled out of the field, so this didn't come as any big surprise.

"Yes sir, I never gave up hope of getting back to do the job that I was trained for; although truthfully, I learned a lot since I've been on your staff." (Kiss, kiss, kiss)

"But since we're being honest, your current tour is almost over and career-wise you should be heading to Destroyer School."

"I appreciate that Captain, but I should also remind you that I am still a reservist and haven't augmented to the regular navy yet. I wanted another opportunity to serve in the field as an advisor and then make up my mind as to whether or not to pursue a career in the navy."

He knitted his brows as he started slowly rubbing his chin. Finally he said, "OK young man, although you were brittle in the beginning, you performed professionally and I commend you for hanging in there this long. I'll inform LCDR Richards that you will belong to him starting next week and I'll get Personnel at NAVFORV to send me a replacement for you."

With that, he stood up and extended me his hand over the desk and said, "Best of luck on your next tour Lieutenant, and again, thanks for a job well done."

"Thank you Captain, for everything," as I quickly turned and exited his office with my heart pounding. The tough old bastard wasn't so bad after all, I thought as I headed back to my office to spread the good news.

As I would have expected, the guys in my office took the news of my extension with varied casual congratulations, although Ed and George understood that this was what I really wanted. For the most part, the others probably thought that I was crazy for staying on for another combat tour because each of them was content to do their year sitting in a reasonably safe Staff billet and getting their ticket punched for their next promotion. Ed never said much about it but I knew he was looking forward to getting home again, whereas George envied me and was determined to extend his tour for a combat billet too.

The rest of the work day was devoted to making a "Who's Who" list that I would pass on to my relief and any other pertinent information that he would need. I did this religiously because I knew the newby wouldn't be able to digest all the information that needed to be passed on before he officially relieved me. By the time I finished, everyone else had already left and in a way it was good to be alone. I locked up my desk and decided to saunter down to the USO for a hamburger and then perhaps to the Golden Dragon and see if Tuyet had returned.

As I was walking along a side street towards Nguyen Hue, I spotted an older man wearing striped pajamas, white socks, open-toed sandals and a Panama hat walking towards me in the opposite direction. The reason I noticed him was because as a rule, the majority of Vietnamese are generally shy when meeting a foreigner and invariably lower their eyes. This particular man had focused his eyes directly at me and immediately set off alarm signals. As he approached to within arm's length, he quickly took off his hat and held it up in front of my face. At the same time, I felt a tug at my shirt pocket and I immediately grabbed his wrist and twisted it backwards. He let out an unholy howl as I heard his brittle wrist bone snap and he fell to the ground dropping my Cross pen that he had tried to steal.

A crowd materialized out of nowhere and surrounded us just as a National Policeman roughly pushed his way towards us.

Fortunately for me, he spoke reasonably good English and several of the onlookers explained spontaneously that the old man tried to steal my pen. My left shirt pocket flap was ripped along the seam in testament to the theft and with that, the police officer handcuffed the still screaming thief and pulled him to his feet.

He looked at me and said "OK, OK! You go now," as he motioned me on my way, which I was only too glad to do. After that little encounter, I decided to forego the hamburger and head directly to the safety of the Dragon and a bottle of ice cold "33" beer.

As I entered the cozily lit interior, I looked around and spotted Lan, Ed's paramour, sitting at a back table with a couple of the other hostesses. Upon seeing me, she stood up and came over to greet me with a smile on her face.

As we sat down, Marie also came over and stood with her hand lightly on my shoulder.

"What happened to your pocket?" she asked when she saw the tattered flap on my shirt.

I related the story of the old guy in pajamas and both their brows knitted tightly in concern. "I'm OK, nothing to worry about," I said trying to sound casual.

"You have to be careful," said Marie. "Many VC still in Saigon and can hurt you easy."

I shrugged it off and said that I was always careful and that I could really use a cold beer about now. Marie went to place the order and Lan leaned towards me and said softly, "Tuyet has returned to work now that she has a new baby boy. Would you like to meet her?"

"I'd like that very much," I replied as she turned and beckoned to one of the girls who had been sitting with her.

Actually, I didn't know what to expect because I had heard so much about her from Ed that I was taken a little by surprise. Tuyet was about one inch over five feet tall, wearing an apple green Ao

Dai with white pants that showed off her petite figure to perfection. She had semi-long black lustrous hair that she wore over one shoulder and framed an oval face with a cupids-bow mouth. My first impression was that she had some faint Chinese features which I learned later came from her mother's side.

Lan made the introductions as I stood up and took Tuyet's delicate hand in mine. Her voice, when she said "Pleased to meet you, *Dai Uy*," sounded like crystal bells tinkling while her face crinkled up in a smile that showed her small even white teeth.

"Please sit down," I said as I pulled a chair out for her.

"I will leave you two alone to get to know each other," Lan said as she got up and returned to the other hostesses.

Marie brought my beer to me personally as Tuyet and I were making small talk. I ordered a "Saigon Tea" for her and I could see that Marie was satisfied that another loyal patron had just been added to her clientele.

I managed to consume half of my cold beer after waiting until Tuyet's "Tea" arrived and it had been well worth the wait.

I proceeded to tell Tuyet of my new assignment to the River Assault Group and that I would be going home for a month's leave and return for another year. She reacted exactly as I hoped she would; her face lit up like a Christmas tree and genuine joy was written all over it.

"When you go?" she asked quietly.

"Probably by the end of the week at the earliest; I'll have to take my relief around and introduce him to everyone before I go.

After another round and more small talk, it was time for me to return to the BOQ and get ready for the next day. Tuyet walked me to the door and said "Please be careful and come see me when you come back, OK?"

I assured her I would and headed back to the McCarthy feeling much better about life in general.

The next morning in the office, I recounted my earlier evening's experience to Ed and I could see that he was pleased that I had finally gotten to meet Tuyet and that we had hit it off. He now knew that he had a willing partner in the Dragon run.

As I was deep into working on yesterday's Stars and Stripes crossword puzzle, Co Mai came over to my desk with a young officer in tow. Pointing to me she said, "This is Lieutenant Kay" and quickly returned to her desk in the outer office.

I stood up and extended my hand to the newcomer and said "I'm Bob Kay, can I help you?"

The young LTJG, dressed in starched wash khakis with wavy dark brown hair worn just short of being non-reg with sleepy eyes nodded and replied, "I'm Tod Beasley, your relief."

Smiling broadly, I indicated for him to sit down in the chair alongside my desk as I asked him where his last duty station was. "I was attending Fleet Sonar School at Key West, but I came down with Mononucleosis and they set me back a class. I got mad and registered a bitch which resulted in my being sent here," he said glumly.

"Yeah, I guess you really pissed someone off; it happens. By the way, do you have any journalism experience?"

"No," he answered, but I was the recording secretary for the Student Council at UCLA where I majored in Sociology."

A fat lot of good that was going to do him, I thought to myself. "Well, that's not a problem because I didn't have a background in it either and I made out just fine. Everything pretty much runs on automatic, except the editing part which you will have to do and it's not a big deal."

I quickly filled him in on how I wound up in this job and stressed the Captain's paternal interest in the "Newsletter." He sat there taking it all in but I got the impression that his interest was slightly below sea level. Although I could really sympathize with him looking back on my initial exposure to the job, he was my ticket out of here and I didn't intend to blow it. With that out of the way, I introduced him to the other guys in the office and then said that I would take him around to meet the rest of the players involved with the job. Now I'm not much on reading body language, but Beasley appeared to be wishing that he was back surfboarding in sunny California and sucking on limes.

"Cheer up," I said with a smile. You'll do just fine."

Ed, with a slight smile on his face said, "You can use my Jeep to take him around as long as you're back by noon."

"Thanks, that'll be great," I said as I caught his keys that he casually tossed to me.

I can summarize the rest of the morning as a failed attempt to housebreak an inattentive puppy. I patiently covered all the bases while trying to instill confidence in the young officer, but although there was someone home, the light was out. To be completely honest, I felt that all the bulbs were broken.

Upon returning to VNN Headquarters, we went to see the Captain. I put on a face of assurance as I announced that Mr. Beasley seems to have a good grasp on the job. I held my breath as Bjorkman looked at Beasley and said, "If you agree, then it's all yours."

Beasley, being completely overwhelmed mumbled, "Yes sir."

"Good, good," said the Captain rising and shaking both our hands. "I imagine that you'll be heading home on leave now that you're off the hook," he said to me with a smile.

"Yes sir. I'm looking forward to it."

With that, the Captain hit his intercom and told Yeoman Norman to book me on the next MAC flight out to the States and to have Admin rush a set of orders for my thirty days home leave. I had finally hit the lottery but still had trouble grasping it as I headed back to my office to return Ed's keys and spread the news. Like they say, "Some days you're General Custer and others you're the Indians."

Two days later I was seated comfortably in seat 10F next to the window on a World Airways DC-9 chartered MAC flight bound for the "Big PX in the Sky," as most of the troops referred to the States. With interim stops in the Philippines, Guam and Hawaii, we eventually touched down at Travis Air Force Base in northern California. From there we were bused to San Francisco where we each boarded our respective commercial flights to our final destinations. During the two weeks with my family in New Jersey, one week in Minneapolis, and the final week in San Diego, I was constantly making excuses for wanting to do another tour in Vietnam. With all the anti-war controversy going on in the States and fomented primarily by the huge masses of unwashed Hippies, Liberals in government and the biased news media, it was difficult to explain why I was going back. During my brief stay in New Jersey, I took my Aunt Nell to a local coffee shop and sat in the first booth next to the cash register. In the course of our conversation the subject of my return to Vietnam came up and since I was wearing my dress khakis I naturally stood out among the other patrons. After a lack-luster brunch as we got up to leave, I was paying the check when the middle-aged cashier said, "I overheard you say that you were going back to Vietnam. Is it because of the money?"

HE CALLED ME A DIRTY 'BABY KILLER'!!

My aunt immediately pinched the back of my arm because she knew a nerve had been touched. I took a deep breath, looked the woman straight in the eyes and calmly said, "If you think that $65 dollars a month combat pay is big money and worth getting shot at, then yes, I'm going back for the money. By the way, your coffee sucks!"

We left without another word until we got into the car and my Aunt said, "I'm proud of you nephew," and gave my hand a squeeze. She at least got to see firsthand what spurred my decision and I was sure that she'd be able to explain it to my mother in terms that she'd be able to understand. This was the sort of treatment our military was being subjected to here in the States. At least in Vietnam when they shot at me occasionally, I got to shoot back, but no one ever spit on me or called me names. So it was with a great sigh of relief that I finally boarded a flight back to San Francisco and then on to Travis Air Force Base.

I can understand why many of my friends thought I was nuts, but the very thought of returning to the fleet and going through the endless drills and paperwork made it a no-brainer. I knew that sooner or later I would have a major career decision to make, but for the moment, I was going to enjoy my coming year as a River Assault Group Advisor.

PART TEN

BACK IN SAIGON

The trip back to Saigon seemed much shorter than the one going out, because I slept most of the way, waking only for meals and head calls. At exactly 0700 on Monday morning I presented myself to the Third Riverine Senior Advisor, LCDR Link Richards my new boss. His office was located on Avalanche Creek which is located behind the confines of the Vietnamese Naval Shipyard. I could see through the open door that he was already at his desk and upon my arrival, waved me in to have a seat.

"Well, how was your leave and did you have any second thoughts about extending your tour?" he asked.

"No way, in fact I was getting antsy to return after about a week or so. Believe it or not I was bored."

While you've been gone, a few things have happened, none of them earth-shattering. First, RAG 24 was transferred from Tan An City up to Binh Loi and attached to the Saigon Capital Military District Command. Your group will patrol the Saigon River from the Binh Loi Bridge north to Lai Thieu-Phu Cuong. Second, Senior Chief Shipp from RAG 27 has requested that he be assigned to your unit since he has also extended and you guys know each other. Is that OK with you?"

"Sure; most certainly. It'll be a lot easier for me to have an experienced backup like Gunner and besides, I like the guy. What happened to the original replacement for 24?"

"His name is Chief Truesdale and Shipp already conned him into swapping since they had known each other in the fleet. I asked Lieutenant Sanderson to meet us here this morning so he can bring you out and introduce you to the crew in Binh Loi."

No sooner was his name mentioned when in walked LT Sanderson. Noticing me, he said "I'm sure glad you're here so I can get the hell out of here," plopping onto the remaining chair.

"Sounds like your tour hasn't been up to your expectations," I said wryly. He either missed my sarcasm or didn't really care.

"Well let's just say that I have had more productive tours."

Now I've been in the service long enough to spot a malcontent when I meet one and this guy certainly filled the bill. After my time as an enlisted man, whenever I met someone in the civilian world who bitched about having been in the service, it was the guy who never got promoted. Everyone above him was a lifer or an asshole, when in reality he was the a-hole and non-producer who lived in a state of denial by griping.

LCDR Richards having sized up the situation, stood up and said, "You guys should head out now and get the turnover done."

With that polite dismissal, the two of us stood up and left the office with our mandatory "Aye aye Commander." Fortunately, Sanderson didn't see the quick wink that the boss had given me.

On the way out to Binh Loi in his Jeep, Sanderson gave me an abbreviated rundown on the unit's Commander, Exec and the rest of the officers, but oddly enough, nothing about the enlisted men. I filed this away for further reference because it seemed strange that he wouldn't comment on any outstanding sailors, of which there were many in the Vietnamese Navy. After about a half hour's drive through Gia Dinh's busy streets, we arrived at Binh Loi. We passed a medium-sized US Army compound, home of the 519th Signal Battalion and turned off onto a dirt road that paralleled the river. Off to the right and down a worn footpath, I saw a dark gray Commandament tied up to some antiquated pilings. To board the craft, we had to negotiate a ten foot board about a half inch thick and six inches wide. Now I weighed about 198 pounds, but Sanderson topped out at around 230 and I sincerely doubted that the board would hold him. Surprisingly enough, we both made it, primarily because he waited for me to cross first. The secret, I found out, was to take long, slow sliding steps to avoid setting up a harmonic up and down motion that would result in the board snapping in the middle.

As we made our way topside, I saw Chief Shipp and two Vietnamese Officers sitting in the shade of the canvas awning.

The Chief was the first to react and immediately jumped and grabbed my hand in his usual bone-crushing grip saying with a grin, "Good to see you again *Dai Uy*, welcome aboard."

I noted that he acknowledged Sanderson but didn't shake his hand and I could almost guarantee that the Lieutenant's handshake would have been like a wet oyster.

Shipp then introduced me to the older officer who had stood up and extended his hand. "This is Lieutenant Commander Gia, the CO of 24 and Lieutenant Dinh, the Exec." I shook both their hands as I mentally compared them to my last counterpart LTJG Minh of the Junks and I liked what I saw. Gia was somewhere in his late forties, about an inch shorter than me, stocky frame and a round face that was covered with character lines. Lieutenant Dinh, on the other hand was the same height, but slim as a rail with an elongated face that crinkled when he smiled. I immediately felt at ease as Gia invited us to sit down.

Instead, Sanderson stood fast and said that if I would go back to Saigon with him, he would turn the Jeep over to me. It was obvious that he wanted to get back to the city with no intentions of going with me on the turnover patrol upriver. I was to find out later from Gia that Sanderson had gone on two patrols down in Tan An, wound up in a small firefight and never rode the river again. Instead, he made frequent visits to the unit during daylight hours and occasionally met Gia at the RAG 24 office in the shipyard, while relegating the nightly patrols to his assistant, Chief Boatswain's Mate Tyler, who by now was back home . . . thanks to Chief Shipp's early relief. As we debarked, I could feel the coolness between Sanderson and the Vietnamese. It was evident that they considered him a "big dead chicken."

The return trip to Saigon was quiet, with Sanderson doing the driving. Upon reaching the McCarthy, he double parked in front, jumped out and said "I stand relieved," with a half-hearted salute. The proper procedure for this custom was for the person relieving to salute and say, "I relieve you sir," while the one departing says, "I stand relieved," and return the salute. Without even wishing me good luck, he spun on his heel and disappeared into the BOQ like he was about to have an attack of dysentery. So much for protocol and camaraderie!

I got behind the wheel, turned the Jeep around and headed back miraculously retracing my route through the dusty streets of Gia Dinh without once making a wrong turn. Arriving at Binh Loi, I pulled into the US Army compound, parked my Jeep in the shade and made my way on foot back out through the gates. Turning right, I followed the dirt road that branched off until I came across the footpath that led me down to the river. There, I once again negotiated the "plank" doing my darndest to imitate the light-footedness of a water bug, and boarded the Commandament. Both Gia and Chief Shipp were still sitting topside drinking tea as I made my appearance. Gia seemed surprised that I had returned so quickly and he expressed it simply by asking, "Back so soon?"

RIVER ASSAULT GROUP 24

Sitting down alongside the Chief and across from Gia, I said, "I've been waiting a long time to get here and I didn't want to lose any more before getting to work." This seemed to please the CO and I could see by the look of satisfaction on Shipp's face that things were indeed looking up for RAG 24 as far as the advisory effort was concerned. No further mention was made of Sanderson.

Since it was close to suppertime, the aroma of cooking rice wafted up from the bow where crewmembers were preparing the meal. Gia invited us to stay and eat with them, but Shipp quickly interjected diplomatically that he would take me over to the base and introduce me around. Besides, he knew that they hadn't prepared for any additional people since Sanderson never ate with them. It was fairly obvious that Sanderson had missed the class on "Getting Along With Your Counterpart" back in Coronado.

Once inside the compound, Shipp led me up a flight of stairs to the rooftop of the main building. It was originally a terrace that had been made over into a club, complete with a bar, kitchen and restrooms. It was open on four sides and a thick thatch roof of palm fronds provided protection from the sun and the elements.

We sat down at one of the many tables and a pert Vietnamese girl came over to take our order. Shipp ordered two beers and added, "You've got to try the hamburgers and fries up here *Dai Uy*." I took his advice, which was smart to do with Navy Chief, and thoroughly enjoyed the meal. We spent a good portion of the late afternoon discussing our new unit, the nearby Marine Advisors, the Army base and things in general. It proved to be very productive and I was pleased that Shipp had amassed all this information from Chief Tyler before he relieved him. It certainly made my relief of Sanderson pale by comparison and definitely increased my admiration for my new partner. By the time we returned to the Commandament, the crew was making preparations to get underway. Gia and Dinh his XO were already topside and upon our arrival, Gia said "*Chung Ta Di*," which meant "Let's go." The fore and after lines were snaked aboard and the deep growl of the two diesel engines broke the stillness of the evening as the propellers dug deep into the muddy water moving us away from the pilings. The helmsman held the wheel hard over to port as he maneuvered us into the center of the river and then headed north. I stood on the starboard side of the upper deck as a strong feeling of contentment filled my chest. This was what I had been dreaming about ever since I was transferred out of Poulo Obi. I was completely at peace with my surroundings and my new shipmates as the boat plowed effortlessly through the murky waters.

Although the distance from the Binh Loi Bridge to Lai Thieu is only ten and a half miles as the crow flies, it is actually about twenty two miles when you transit the meandering river. I stood almost the entire journey as I scanned the passing riverbank for anything unusual. From my Junk Force days whenever we entered a tributary, we were always on the lookout for sampams hidden under palm fronds or unnatural looking foliage. The VC were known to pull in close to shore whenever they heard our engines and cover themselves with any available greenery hoping that in the waning light they remain unseen. Gunner Shipp stood on the port side also scanning the shoreline, but it was difficult because of the deepening shadows and a moon that had not yet risen.

On these nightly patrols, both gun turrets were manned and the engineer remained below tending the engines. Two crewmembers occupied the helmsman station so that one man concentrated on the steering while the other relayed any commands from the CO. Yes indeed, these sailors were professionals and it was comforting.

Gunner explained to me that on these nightly patrols, we would sometimes have two FOMs accompanying us. One would be ahead of us close to one bank while the other trailed behind on the opposite side. Their positions would vary on each patrol so as not to be predictable, because patterns were what the VC were looking for. We would also alter our patrol start times for the same reason.

Off on the port side about two kilometers from the Lai Thieu Bridge, the landscape was blackened and desolate as far as the eye could see. The dead vegetation stood in mute evidence of the massive doses of Agent Orange defoliant that was dropped on the area. This was done specifically to deprive the enemy of cover for any attacks on the vital bridge

Once we arrived at the Lai Thieu Bridge, Gunner told me we would either tie up for awhile beneath the center span or we'd continue on up to the Phu Cuong Bridge before starting our return trip. I made a mental note to see if I could get a star-light scope issued to me so that we could see better in the dark. In Vietnam on moonless nights, you could barely see your hand before your face and only then did we light off our radar for safe navigation. The Vietnamese were never keen on using the radar equipment because they didn't want it to fail and have to be sent back to Saigon for repairs. The reason was that they never got a replacement nor did they have much faith in the Supply system to return the repaired unit any time soon. Ah, Asian logic; better to have the equipment aboard, working or not and never use it rather than to use it and possibly lose it.

This time, we turned around at Lai Thieu and began our return journey almost immediately, but I noticed that only one of the FOMs accompanied us. I was told that the other one would continue to Phu Cuong and then transit back later in the evening. What it amounted to was a chess match of sorts because the VC were always studying our patrol habits. I asked Gia where he learned his patrol techniques and he replied that he had spent a month at the Little Creek Amphibious Base in Virginia prior to taking command.

On the way back, we were more relaxed as Gunner and I sat alongside each other on the portside padded benches while Gia was down below talking to the engineer. I told the Chief that I didn't know what arrangements he and Lieutenant Kelleher had in RAG 27, but at least one of us had to be aboard on every patrol. I said we could alternate nights or we could ride together, whatever was agreeable and that was flexible as long as the Viets were happy. He replied, "I have no problem with that and we'll most likely be spending a lot of time together because I thrive on this shit."

"Sounds good to me" I said, "And if you need a few days off for any reason, let me know in advance so that I can cover it."

By the time we arrived back to Binh Loi it was almost midnight, and instead of returning to the pilings near the bank, we snugged up to the center supports of the bridge. The span was closed from 10 PM to 6 AM with a small contingent of ARVN troops posted on each end for security, so mooring there for the night made good sense.

Since it had been a long day, we both decided to hit the sack. The upper berthing had four bunks for the officers and advisors, while the lower section two steps down in the well deck was for the enlisted men. The top bunks in the upper section had the luxury of being next to the metal grating which allowed whatever breeze there was to cool the occupants and a canvas roll-down in case of rain. The lower ones had only the metal bulkheads and could become a bit stifling. As senior, I was afforded the top bunk on the port side, while Gunner had the one below me. Being an easygoing guy I said that he could use my bunk whenever I wasn't aboard. Hey, that's what shipmates are all about.

I must have fallen asleep the minute my head hit the pillow when I was rudely awakened some time later by a muffled explosion. I immediately jumped down from my bunk trying to get my bearings and my pants on simultaneously, when a soft voice coming from below said, "It's OK *Dai Uy.* That's only the night watch tossing a concussion grenade over the side to discourage sappers, just like down in Ben Luc. Remember?"

Being new to the world of river warfare, I had never thought about some enemy swimmer attaching a limpet mine to our hull and blowing us up while we slept. So the throwing of grenades into the surrounding water at unspecified intervals became all too clear and I learned to sleep through them from then on.

Early the next morning, I took the Jeep and headed back to Saigon where I had several things to do. Gunner decided to stay aboard and I said that I would more than likely return by early evening.

My first stop was NAVFORV where I drew an AN/PVS-2 hand-held starlight scope and also pursuant to new directives, traded my M-14 rifle for the M-16 from the Armory. Up until now, we Naval Advisors were only authorized to carry the M-14 whereas everyone else had been issued the newer M-16. Don't get me wrong, I'm not complaining, but I could never understand the politics involved in issuing weapons to the military. The M-14 is a heavier rifle and replaced the old M-1 Garand of World War II and Korea fame. It has a solid punch, but because of it's through and through capability, many preferred the tumbling bullet from the M-16 that tears big holes in the target. Many of the enemy managed to keep coming after being hit with the M-14's 7.62mm bullet, but not so those nailed by the smaller 5.56mm NATO round of the M-16. One of the earlier complaints of the M-16 bullet was that because of its lightness, foliage could easily deflect its flight. The M-16 is two pounds lighter and five inches shorter than the M-14. So we had been forced to lug the heavier rifle and ammo into battle. It was good enough for government work, I guess.

I then swung by the Personnel Office and received permission to move out of the congested McCarthy BOQ and advance up the social ladder to a two-man room at the Le Qui Don BOQ.

My next stop naturally, was to get my gear together and move out of the McCarthy. It only took me about a half hour to pack, say my goodbyes to the bartenders, waitresses and to Catherine at the front desk where I turned in my key. I asked her to please say goodbye for me to my maid Ba Tu. She said she would gladly do that and was happy for me although sad that I was leaving. I promised that I would come by from time to time to visit.

Once back in the Jeep, it was a short trip to Le Qui Don Street, from whence the BOQ derived its. It was a small three story building on the corner of a tree-lined residential area just a few blocks from NAVFORV. I drove into the courtyard through an open iron gate and parked in the shade. The first door from the right hand corner of the building had a sign posted on the wall indicating that this was the office, so I went in. Behind the desk sat an attractive girl in her mid-twenties, dressed in a modest mini-skirt similar to those worn by Co Mai at Headquarters. The exception was that she was about three inches taller and had a slight build which accentuated her pretty size B-cup breasts. Things were again looking up, I thought.

"Good afternoon," she said in almost accentless English. "May I help you?"

"Yes you can," I said. "I am Lieutenant Kay and have been reassigned here from the McCarthy."

"Have you been in Vietnam long?" she asked matter-of-factly.

I explained that I had been in-country a year and let it go at that.

"You can have the corner room just above this office on the next floor and your roommate is Army Captain Vlastoff. Here is your key. I hope you have an enjoyable stay with us and my name is Therese."

"Pleased to meet you Therese," I replied. Unlike the Splendid BOQ, my new home had no cafeteria or bar, so it was strictly bed and no breakfast. A redeeming factor however, was that it was directly across the street from the French run "Marie Curie School for Girls" that purported to provide a proper education for the future ladies of Saigon society. Another plus that I soon discovered was that I had an unimpeded view behind the walls of the girls during recess from my second floor balcony vantage point. Yes, things were looking up for this dirty old man.

My roommate wasn't in as I opened the door and sized up my new quarters. It was about a 12 x 20 foot room with two beds aligned adjacent to the three side by side windows. The bathroom and shower was at the rear on the left side and two wardrobes against the wall on the right seemed more than adequate. Two 4-drawer dressers lined the front left side of the room separated by one small desk. The air conditioning was quiet and efficient, unlike the thumping generator at the McCarthy. Dark blue faded curtains covered all the windows keeping the room cool and the sun at bay.

After stowing my gear, I took a quick shower and changed into a fresh set of greens. I left my soiled laundry piled atop the wastepaper basket next to my bed and hoped the maid wouldn't toss them out in the morning.

With my newly acquired Starlight scope, M-16 and a bandolier of extra magazines, I went down the stairs, jumped into the Jeep and headed back to Binh Loi feeling on top of the world.

True to my word, I arrived a little before supper and found Gunner topside reading a history book about ancient Rome. This took me by surprise until he told me that he enjoyed learning about world history.

When he saw me with my brand new M-16, he asked me how I managed to get my hands on one. I said that COMNAVFORV had authorized the changeover from the M-14 and that he could get his anytime. With that, he stood up, stretched and asked if it would be OK for him to go home to see Ann. "Reading about those decadent Romans made me a little horny," he said chuckling in his inimitable way.

"It's no problem," I said. "Take the Jeep and enjoy yourself."

"Thanks *Dai Uy*, I'll be back tomorrow after I pick up my new shooter and exercise my libido with Ann," he said laughingly over his shoulder as he scampered nimbly down the plank.

A few minutes later, Gia came aboard and greeted me. I told him about my move to the Le Qui Don and showed him my M-16. He held it admiringly and said it is a good weapon but he prefers the Communist-made AK-47 for its reliability. I had no reason to doubt him since I had heard the horror stories concerning the M-16's proclivity to jam during firefights.

"Have you had supper yet?" he asked.

"No, as a matter of fact I thought that the Chief and I would get some, but he opted to go home instead."

"I'm sure that he will get his supper and then some when he sees his Chinese mama-san," he said smiling. "In that case, why don't you join me for a bowl of '*Pho Ga*'?"

"I would like that very much," I replied as we disembarked and proceeded to a shop just up the road. It was a small place with two wooden tables in front and run by a gentle 40+ year old Vietnamese man. We would eventually name him affectionately as "Baby-San" and our conversations were always animated and spoken in a combination of French, English and Vietnamese with many corresponding hand and facial gestures.

The soup was just right; spiked with freshly squeezed lime, *Hoi-Sin* sauce and a fiery red chili concoction that added flavor to the bean sprouts, pieces of chicken and noodles. When the meal was finished, I quickly grabbed the check because I knew that Gia's monthly pay was nowhere close to mine. Since the Vietnamese military was grossly underpaid, commanding officers like Gia were given free rein to supplement their income through any means as long as it wasn't blatant extortion compromising their position.

From what I learned about this man, he was a straight shooter who took pride in being an officer, husband and father. He had earned his Ships Master's papers sailing on Vietnamese crewed, French owned merchant vessels and when the war erupted, he was quickly mobilized into the fledgling South Vietnamese Navy.

About an hour after we returned back aboard, he gave the order to get underway. "Now you can put your little starlight scope to a test and see what up to now was unseeable," he said hopefully.

The moon was a faint crescent and the stars were about as bright as they would ever be as we made our way upriver. I stood up forward holding the scope to my right eye as I scanned both sides of the riverbanks. The green image was fairly clear, but my arms started to tire holding the scope and the area of visibility left a lot to be desired. It was much too small for river work although it was more than adequate at sea in the Junks. I offered the scope to Gia for a look and after a short while, he agreed with me. I would have to see about getting a bigger scope when I returned to Saigon, if there even was such a thing

This trip took us all the way up to the Phu Cuong Bridge where we stayed until a trailing FOM arrived some twenty minutes later and tied up. We made our turnaround and as we approached the Lai Thieu Bridge, the second FOM joined up with us. This time, the small patrol boat stationed itself off our starboard bow at a distance of some 50 yards and ran a parallel course close to the shoreline. On the return trip, XO Dinh asked if he could use the scope, so I turned it over to him and sat down to enjoy the ride.

TAKING FIRE

We were about a half hour from Binh Loi when we heard three shots followed by three loud bangs slamming against the portside steel plating surrounding our command deck. I and Dinh quickly hit the deck as ensuing cracks of gunfire shattered the night air. Both gun turrets immediately swung to port, but Gia, who was peering over the armor plating, ordered them to hold their fire. It sounded like one AK-47 shooting at us in controlled 3-tap shots and a rifle firing single rounds. The attack continued for only a few minutes until we were out of range and I used that time to call Leatherneck One on the PRC-25 radio. The Marine Advisor answered immediately and I informed them that we were southbound on the blue and had taken hostile fire from the east side of the riverbank. He asked me if we needed any assistance and I replied that we had everything under control. He then asked me at what location did we get fired on and I replied that we were close to one of the bends but wasn't sure which one. I ended by saying that I would get back to him.

When I signed off, Gia said "The reason I did not return fire was because that was some VC trying a very old trick. They shoot at us from between the huts of sleeping villagers in hopes that we will return fire and perhaps kill some innocent peasants. That would give them some propaganda to use against us. I'm relieved to see that you did not react foolishly."

"To tell you the truth as soon as I heard the first round, all I could think of was Lieutenant Meyerkord, who was killed in 1965 down in Vinh Long with RAG 23. His unit came under attack and during the firefight he stood up to return fire with a .45 pistol and took a .51 caliber round in the head."

"Yes, I recall that incident clearly because the Commander of that unit was a classmate of mine at the Academy. He was never the same after losing his close friend and Advisor."

As we continued down the river towards Binh Loi, things returned to normal. The escorting FOM remained in position and stayed close to the opposite side of the river in case of any possible crossfire. Gia and I both resumed our seats as the XO handed me the Starlight scope shaking his head negatively and making a dour face. I guess he wasn't impressed with it either.

Once we tied up to the bridge, Gia and I went below to turn in while Dinh made a cursory tour to set the night watch. Although I was a tired, I couldn't stop thinking about how to solve the problem of nailing down a location in the event of another such occurrence. Sleep eventually did come, despite the sporadic whumps of the anti-sapper grenades.

The next morning I awoke to the sound of heavy rain pelting the topside canvas cover and the engines being lit off to move us back to the pilings. As I was in the process of jumping down from my bunk, the answer came to me as if in a revelation. I couldn't wait for Gunner to come back so I could run my idea by him, because I was sure that this was the solution. It wasn't the first time that I had gone to sleep with a perplexing problem, only to wake up suddenly with the answer. I was excited that the fix was so simple.

Once moored, familiar footsteps on the overhead could only mean that Shipp had returned. I made my way topside and sure enough, there was Gunner getting an earful about last night's events from the XO. Upon seeing me he said, "Looks like you had a little excitement while I was gone."

"Just a little," I replied. Then I related the radio conversation with Leatherneck One and the fact that I wasn't able give him an exact location of the attack.

"That's no big thing, just be glad they didn't have a B-40 rocket launcher or a recoilless rifle. Things could have been a lot worse."

"That's for damn sure, but I came up with an idea that will solve that problem." I spread out the US Navy's Hydrographic Office map of our area and started penciling in circles at prominent locations along our patrol route. I used the names of Snow White at the Binh Loi Bridge, the Wicked Witch at the Phu Cuong Bridge and the names of the Seven Dwarfs for the places in between. "I think that I can get some acetate sheets from the 519th and fill in the names and locations on an overlay for Leatherneck One and anyone else we need to inform. Then, if we get hit, we can report that it's between Dopey and Grumpy or whatever and they'll know pretty much where we are. How's that?"

"That's not only simple, it's ingenious and we can change the names around if we have to. I can see that your Old Man didn't waste his money when he sent you to college."

"It wasn't his money Chief, it was my Korean G.I. Bill that sprung for my education," I replied. "Let's get some coffee from the army and we'll check about acetate. They should have some on hand being a Signal Battalion and a Military Intelligence Group.

While we sat around having coffee in the base's mess hall, one of the Staff Sergeants with the name Tanner sat down to chat with us. "I hear you are the new Advisors on those VN boats. I'd met the assistant Petty Officer Tyler a few times, but never his boss; heard he was a mite anti-social."

"Just as well," remarked Gunner. "He should have been riding a desk in Saigon instead of these boats anyway."

After we became comfortable talking with the Sergeant, Gunner asked him if there was any chance of scrounging some acetate sheets from them to make overlays. He said that it wasn't a problem and we could have a whole roll of the stuff if we wanted it. I said that it would be great, but we only needed about six sheets or so. The Sergeant stood and said, "Hang tight here and I'll be back in fifteen minutes."

He was true to his word as he handed Gunner ten sheets of acetate, saying if we needed more to come see him anytime. We thanked him, finished our coffee and set off for the boat to work on our overlays.

After I finished marking the reference points on the chart, I put a sheet over the chart and transferred the points and repeated the process with a second sheet. Then I printed the names next to the points on both sheets; One for us and one for the Marine Advisors. Gia had come up quietly behind us and had overheard our conversation. After seeing what we were doing, said that he was impressed with the concept. I have just learned that Saigon District Command is establishing a Tactical Operations Center manned by a Vietnamese and an American sailor so that we can be in constant communications with them. This way, they will know immediately of any situation that arises and be able to react appropriately. That sounded good to me and it also meant that we had to provide another overlay for our new rep in the TOC and one for LCDR Richards at 3rd Riverine. Great! Now it was beginning to feel like we were getting some semblance of an organization in place that would make our job a lot easier.

Gia patted us both on the shoulders and said, "You two have accomplished more in the short time since you've joined us then your predecessors did all year long. It is refreshing as well as comforting to have you working alongside us."

"Speaking for the both of us, we appreciate the confidence."

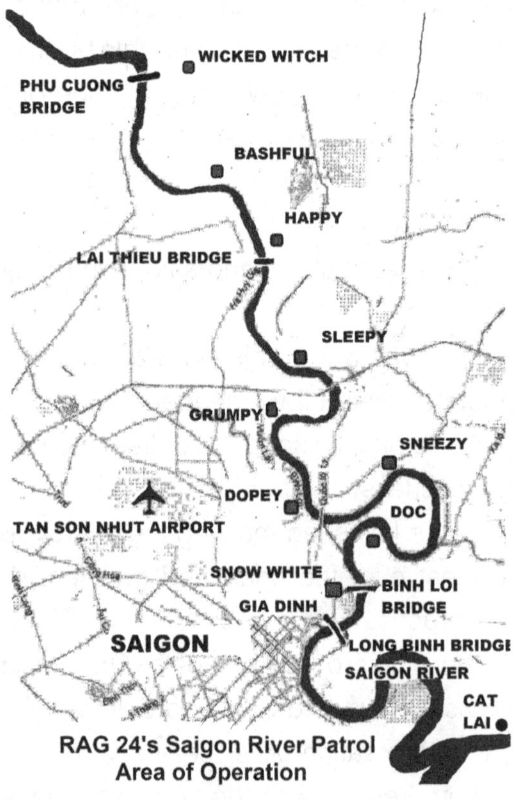

RAG 24's Saigon River Patrol Area of Operation

After Gia left to go below, I told Gunner that I was heading back to Saigon to try and trade the Starlight Scope for something bigger and while I was gone, see if he could drop the overlay off at the Marine encampment just up the road. I added that I would try and get back by late afternoon if possible.

I took off for Saigon desperately needing a hot shower and a change of clothes. Turning the scope back in at NAVFORV was no problem, but they had nothing bigger that they could give me. Instead, the Petty Officer gave me a request chit to fill out saying that he would pass this on to the US Army Electronics Command office up at MACV Headquarters. He said that those folks had all kinds of electronic gear and told me to write down what I wanted and for what purpose. I got the feeling that this was going to be just another drill in futility, so I filled it out as best as I could, thanked him and headed for the Le Qui Don.

After a good long soak in the rain locker, I shaved, brushed the fungus from my teeth and donned a set of freshly pressed greens that were hanging in my closet. It looked as if my new maid was on the ball having washed the gear that I had left. It had been a real effort not to have laid down for a short nap, but I knew from past experiences that if I did, I'd be down for the count. So instead, I drove down to my favorite "Le Corse" Bar and had a small steak, fries and a fresh green salad, washed down with a perfectly cold "33" beer. I noticed that the Napoleon card was still affixed prominently on the mirror behind the bar.

There was plenty of daylight left, so I decided to swing by the Dragon and see if Tuyet was working. The Gods must have been smiling down on me because she was the first one I encountered as I entered the place. As we sat down at a small table towards the rear, she bombarded me with a million questions about my leave, my family, how did I like my new job, etc . . . I said that I would answer everything providing she ordered me a cold beer and a "Tea" for herself. I was really impressed with how she looked and the manner in which she handled herself to the point that I was starting to form an attachment to her. I told her that I couldn't stay long because I had to get back to Binh Loi. She said that she understood. I found that she was very easy to talk to and felt more at ease in her company than anyone I had met in a long time. With a solemn promise to drop by when time permitted, I took my leave as she gently squeezed my hand at the door. The drive back to the boats was quick and uneventful as thoughts of Tuyet filled my mind.

Once back aboard the Commandament, I found the Chief sitting topside again reading another history book. After explaining the situation about the night scope, I told him that I wasn't too optimistic about getting a bigger one. He shrugged and said not to sweat it. Also, he had delivered the overlay to Marine 1st Lieutenant White and explained the reference points to him after placing the overlay on top of his chart. "I'll tell you one thing," he continued, "you made an impression on those guys when you called in about the shooting last night. He said you sounded relaxed and like one cool squid."

"He wouldn't have thought so if he had seen me scrunched down on the deck kissing the rivets."

"Well, there's nothing wrong with having a little respect from the Marines, is there? Besides, I informed him that we weren't cherries, with me on my third tour and you on your second."

"Good. You never know when you'll need their help or they'll need ours. I always like to know who has my back."

"Me too!" said Gunner in all seriousness.

"By the way, I also visited the Dragon and saw Tuyet. I think she's getting to me Senior Chief."

"There's nothing wrong with that," he said. "It sure sounds like you're on the verge of cohabitating with her, eh *amigo*?"

"The thought has crossed my mind. I'll know better when I meet my roommate at the Le Qui Don."

The next few days passed by uneventfully sometimes alternating on patrol and sometimes we went together. It all depended on how we felt and happenstance. This unit was a joy to be with because they took pride in everything they did. The camaraderie that developed between us was unbelievable right from the get-go.

RETURN OF THE SILENT VIPERS

On a beautifully clear Saturday morning, I was topside all decked out in my Saigon River Yacht Club attire which consisted of black t-shirt, khaki shorts, sneakers and no socks. Dinh had gone ashore to get a glass of iced coffee for breakfast and left me in charge while Gia had taken last night off to be with his family. A few days ago, Gia had put out the word to the crew that in the event he or the XO were absent, I was to be in command and for them to follow my orders. The fact that he had such faith in me in so short a time truly humbled me.

Since everything was quiet, I had given Gunner the weekend off and took the opportunity to clean my .38 caliber pistol just to have something to do. A Huey helicopter suddenly appeared from out of nowhere and began circling overhead. I looked up from under the canvas awning and saw the pilot rapidly pointing to his headphones. I quickly reached for the PRC-25 radio and turned it on. A voice came through saying, "Crazy Racer Eight, this is Somber Hero Prime, over."

"Somber Hero Prime, this Crazy Racer Eight, go."

"Crazy Racer Eight, we received Intel that a small group of Indians were in your vicinity and I dispatched a squad of my men to sweep the area to try and make contact. They are about 3 clicks north of your present position in the lariat bend of the blue. They encountered a feeder stream coming from the east and when the squad leader attempted to cross, he went under and didn't resurface. Request your immediate assistance. I am going back to base to refuel and then come back, over."

"Will do Somber Hero Prime, am on my way: Out." I grabbed my M-16, the radio and climbed down to the FOM nestled outboard. The 3 man crew jumped up when they saw me as I yelled for them to get underway, *mau len*, which meant "in a hurry."

It only took about twenty minutes for us to enter the big bend in the river referred to as the lariat and easily located the rest of the squad hunkered down along the riverbank. The Cox'n put the nose smartly onto the muddy bank as I stood up and asked who was in charge. A young Corporal stood up and said, "I'm the assistant squad leader, sir." He couldn't have been more than nineteen years old with a hint of peach-fuzz on his worried face.

"Show me where your Sarge went down," I said calmly.

He pointed to the near side of the feeder stream that looked to be ten to fifteen yards wide with a moderate current emptying into the river. I ordered the Cox'n to enter the stream and position his bow against the northern bank and hold it there. I motioned him to move over in the turret in order for me to get at the .30 caliber machine gun. I cranked back the lever to load the first round and then proceeded to fire short bursts spraying the brush in front of us. I kept up a sustained, methodical rate of fire covering a ninety degree arc until I was satisfied that we wouldn't be surprised by any bad guys on the other side.

As I climbed back out of the turret, a crewman handed me a 12 foot boathook from below. I lay down prone on the stern deck and proceeded to prod the stream bottom. My arm went into the water up to my elbow plus the length of the boathook, so I estimated the stream to be about fourteen feet deep. I could readily see how the Sergeant underestimated its depth. After several tries, my boathook hit something firm but soft. I looked up and said to the squad on the bank, "Which one of you is a good swimmer?"

"I am," said a lanky, lantern-jawed youngster. "I'm part sea-otter," he boasted as he started taking off his gear.

"Good, when you're ready, I want you to jump in upstream and let the current bring you down to the pole that I'm holding in position. Then I want you to go down the pole, grab a hold of the Sergeant's belt and pull him to the surface. We'll help get him out of the water, OK?"

He nodded his head as he took off his boots and socks and stood in his skivvies. The kid had a swimmer's physique and he confidently dove into the water with no hesitation. Following my instructions, he surfaced and let the current carry him down to the boathook. Wiping the water from his eyes, he looked up at me, smiled, took a deep breath and dove straight down into the muddy brown water. In less than a minute, he pushed the body of his sergeant to the surface where my eager crewmen quickly dragged the waterlogged body onto the deck. I reached down with a tight wrist grip and pulled the soldier out of the water by myself.

The sergeant had been a stocky young man with closely cropped blonde hair. He had an expressionless youthful face with blue eyes wide-open and sightless somewhere in his early twenties. An M-16 was strapped across his chest with a bandolier of magazines, plus a canteen and a K-Bar knife on his belt. That explained why he couldn't surface after he took that first step into the water.

A few minutes later when the chopper reappeared overhead, I said into the mike, "Somber Hero Prime, this is Crazy Racer Eight. Be advised that the body has been recovered and we are waiting for further instructions, over."

"Roger Crazy Racer Eight; request you transport the body along with the rest of the squad about a fifty yards north of your present position. There's a suitable clearing that we can land in and get the body aboard. Pass the word to the acting squad leader to have his men set up a security perimeter around the LZ and inform me when it's in place."

"Roger that," I replied into the mike as I ordered the Cox'n to back out and turn around to pick up the seven remaining men.

It was a sad looking group of young men that boarded the FOM and I felt compassion for them having lost their sergeant in such a useless accident. One soldier handed the swimmer his clothes as he patted his shoulder and said softly, "Good job, Tom."

I passed on the orders to the corporal and asked him, "Who's the brass calling the shots in the chopper?"

He replied, "That's Colonel Savage, our Battalion Commander."

Once again, the Cox'n deftly maneuvered the boat against the bank between two large mangrove trees. Four soldiers quickly disembarked and proceeded at a run to establish the perimeter, while the remaining three reverently picked up the body of their dead sergeant and carried him to the edge of the clearing.

As the security team spread out around the clearing, the man on the extreme right turned around and yelled back to us, "Hey, there's a bunch of Gook bodies here in the brush."

I quickly jumped down and ran over to him through the waist high grass and to my surprise, in a slight depression that had been carefully camouflaged with nipa palm leaves, found four Vietnamese bodies. Of the four people, one was an older man wearing mud-streaked black pants and a white shirt that was now covered in blood from an ugly head wound and a younger man wearing dark maroon pajamas with a gaping wound in his back. He was lying across the body of a young girl with his arms spread as if to protect her. The girl was wearing sun-faded black pajamas and had been shot once in the throat and once in the chest. Her once beautiful dark brown eyes remained wide open with the dull flat stare that only death can bring. The remaining young man was miraculously still alive, although he had received a nasty thigh wound just below his soiled tattered shorts. They all had well worn rubber flip-flops on their feet.

"Looks as if you caught them by surprise when you fired sir," said the trooper who discovered the bodies.

"Sure looks that way, but I don't feel too good about it just the same," I said sadly. "Somehow, I don't think that we navy men were meant to be involved in this close up and personal kind of fighting, but war is war I guess."

"I hear you Lieutenant," said the private. Just then, the unmistakable sound of the Commandament's engines broke the stillness of the morning as it approached the riverbank. After Gia came ashore, he got a rapid explanation of the events from the FOM's Cox'n and then made his way to where I was standing.

"I had just returned from Saigon when Petty Officer Mai told me that you had gone upriver with a FOM, but he didn't know why. That is when we heard the firing. I ordered the crew to get underway to investigate and be of assistance, if need be. I can see however, that none is needed and once again, I am impressed," he said smiling.

"All in a day's work," I quipped back.

"Maybe, but it looks as if you had a very busy morning regardless, eh *Dai Uy*?"

"Yes. But unfortunately we lost a young sergeant, although our luck wasn't all that bad because we have a wounded man here who you may want to question," I answered. I could see his eyes light up when he heard that we had a prisoner.

As we talked, the chopper landed in the nearby clearing and a tall gaunt looking Army officer climbed out and approached us.

"I'm Colonel Savage and am sincerely grateful that you were able to recover my man and assist my troops," he said as he extended his hand instead of returning our salutes.

Gia shook his hand first as I introduced him as the CO of the RAG unit, then continued saying "I'm Lieutenant Kay, Commander Gia's Advisor and happy to have been able to help sir."

Turning to look at the bodies, the Colonel said, "I'd be glad to take the prisoner off your hands and fly him back to my base."

Before Gia could respond, I quickly interjected by saying, "Thank you very much for the offer sir, but under the circumstances, we shot 'em, we got 'em."

He gave me a slow knowing grin as he replied, "I understand." Tossing us a crisp salute, he returned to the waiting helicopter. With the sergeant's body already aboard, the chopper lifted up gracefully nose down as its rotors thrashed the grass and blew sandy soil all over the place. The assistant squad leader then approached and thanked us for our help and said that they were going to continue the sweep for another few clicks just to be sure that there were no more VC around. Simultaneously, as the patrol was leaving, a crewman from the Commandament with our medic in tow arrived. Gia ordered the crewman to go gather any weapons from the bodies and the medic to examine and treat the wounded VC.

The search resulted in two vintage Russian made Tokarev and two modern Makarov 9mm pistols. During the process of searching for weapons, as the crewman pulled the man's body off of the girl, I immediately recognized the angry purple burn mark on the left side of the young man's face.

"Holy shit," I cried. "That's Khoi, the grandson of the Hoa Hao Hamlet Chief."

"Are you sure?" asked Gia furrowing his brow.

"Positive *Thieu Ta*, I could never mistake that distinctive scar in a million years and I can't imagine how the hell he wound up in this neck of the woods?"

"Perhaps his wounded friend may be able to shed some light on that," said Gia emphatically.

Two additional crewmen came ashore to assist in bringing the wounded prisoner aboard the Commandament, Gia said, "We'll leave the rest of the bodies here if only to intimidate anyone who may come to take their place." As he made his way back to the boat, he suddenly bent down and stared intently at a spot near the bank just to the right of where the FOM was beached.

"*Dai Uy*, come look at this," he said as he reached down and raised a woven grass and palm frond cover. Underneath, there was a hole containing a ceramic pot big enough to hold a crouching person. At the bottom of the pot there was a pencil and a small spiral notebook containing scrawled times and dates in numerical order.

"Do you know what this is?" Gia asked as he showed me the book as he shook the dirt from its pages.

Having seen similar spider-holes down in Camau during my tour with the Junks, I replied, "Yes sir, looks like someone has been keeping track of our comings and goings."

"Correct! Now we will have something of interest to discuss with our prisoner," he said with a big smile on his face.

He then pointed out the small horizontal opening just above the lip of the jar and about six inches below the cover that allowed the occupant to peer out over the river and be completely undetected. Man, were these people slick?

INTERROGATION, ORIENTAL STYLE

Once back aboard the Commandament, the helmsman reversed the engines and maneuvered the craft into the middle of the river. I was a little surprised that we headed northward instead of back to Binh Loi, but the reason was soon to become apparent.

The prisoner was brought down below to our sleeping quarters where he was bound to a chair with his arms tied behind him and both feet secured to its legs. A large piece of tarpaulin covered the deck with the chair positioned in its center. Gia sat on the edge of the lower bunk by the side of the prisoner and I climbed up into my bunk which gave me a clear view of an event that I had never before witnessed.

Petty Officer Mai with a soiled bath towel draped around his neck, sat almost knee to knee with the trussed up youth. He had a stockier build and was taller than the average Vietnamese sailor. With a malevolent scowl, he appeared quite threatening. There was definitely some Caucasian admixture somewhere in his family tree, I'd bet on it.

XO Dinh was seated quietly with his legs crossed at a small table located forward of the bunks and behind Mai. He held a pencil poised expectantly above a pad with carbon paper under the first sheet and was ready to record any information extracted. A copy of the report would be sent to the VNN Intelligence people upon conclusion of the interrogation.

Gia began questioning the youth in a soft and casual avuncular voice, asking him to identify the others in the group, where they came from and the reason they were in this particular area.

Mai sat motionless, staring at the youth who began to slowly move his head from side to side, muttering softly that he had no idea what they were talking about.

The questions were repeated over and over, resulting in the same head shaking denials. After a few more minutes of this, Gia leaned over and gripped the youth by the jaw as he put his face up close and said quietly, "I will give you one more chance to answer my questions honestly and if you continue to refuse, I will turn you over to Petty Officer Mai for his amusement."

He released the prisoner's face and leaned back on the bunk. Pausing for a moment, Gia took a deep breath and repeated the questions. Again, the reply was absolute denial, only this time he showed a bit of arrogance.

Gia frowned and nodded to Mai who then inched his chair even closer. The young man's eyes widened enormously as Mai brandished a wicked looking knife and in a quick upward motion, sliced the front of the boy's shorts open. Then with a calloused hand, Mai grasped the youth's penis while the other fished a one inch firecracker from his shirt pocket. Before the prisoner could react, Mai had pushed the thin firecracker almost all the way into the penis opening with only the fuse hanging out. Grabbing a handful of matted hair, Mai pulled the youth's head down so he could see the Zippo lighter that he had lit in his other hand. Now having the boy's undivided attention, Mai said menacingly through clenched teeth that this time he wanted straight answers and if for some reason he didn't believe him, he would light the fuse. It took only a microsecond before the kid started singing like a tenor auditioning for a part on Broadway. Who said harsh interrogation methods didn't work? What would you have done in his situation? Yeah, me too!

Sometime during the questioning, the helmsman had reversed course for home. Having successfully coerced the prisoner to spill his guts and the firecracker removed, Mai now held a cup of tea up to the boy's mouth as if nothing had happened. This signaled the end of the ordeal and that image will remain with me for the rest of my life.

There were two men wearing white open necked shirts and black trousers waiting for us as we tied up to the pilings. They were standing by a nondescript black Citroen sedan and by their body language; I tagged them as VNN Intelligence. Another giveaway was their untucked shirts which obviously covered their weapons.

Gia leaned out from topside and yelled to the two men that the prisoner was being made ready for transfer along with a report. He then asked them to be sure and leave a receipt for both. Ah, the paperwork never ends in this world because it's needed to cover one's ass!

Later, as Gia, Dinh and I were sitting topside enjoying some cold bottles of "33" beer that the XO had miraculously produced from somewhere, Gia said to me, "I'm sure you must be curious about what we have learned today from our young friend."

"Curious is putting it mildly. I still can't get over the fact that I killed a young boy that I had met down in Hoa Hao."

Gia replied, "I understand your feelings because killing an enemy in time of war is one thing, but killing someone you know is most distressing. Dinh will translate the information given to us and hopefully it will put to rest any of your questions."

THE VIPER'S TALE

"The prisoner is nineteen year old Ho Van Ninh who was previously a University student in My Tho. Last year, his younger sister married an American GI, infuriating him so much that he retaliated by leaving his family and joining the local VC. With no real experience, he was sent to Saigon to join a group from Chau Doc and that's where he met the people who were killed this morning.

The older man Chu Bay was the son of the late former Hoa Hao leader with whom he had been estranged for some time due to their serious political differences. Khoi, the grandson of the Hoa Hao leader had been living with him up to the time of his death. With no place else to go, he voluntarily chose to go with his uncle Chu Bay and join his band of rebels."

Dinh frequently had to refer to his notes about the girl whose name was Ngoc and her troubled path from her home up to the time she met Khoi and his uncle.

"The wounded Ninh stated that he had first met Chu Bay and his group when they shared a room above the *Pho Binh* shop in Saigon. The next day, he had been instructed to accompany Chu Bay's party to join Group 3 in Gia Dinh. They arrived at the designated location that from the outside appeared to be an old abandoned single story garage. A middle-aged man answered their knock at the back door and quickly admitted them. Within the dimly lit interior, the man led them past a military Jeep and two vintage Toyota sedans to a dirty partially glassed-in enclosure. Inside, there were five men gathered around a wooden table intently studying a large map of the National Broadcasting Station and the surrounding area.

The leader, who was introduced as Brother Nam, looked up at the newcomers and welcomed them saying that they had been expected. He then had them gather around the table.

Chu Bay introduced himself and his three traveling companions as additional chairs were brought and room was made for them at the table. Nam pointed at the map and said that the radio station was their assigned objective and that the attack would begin exactly at 3 on the morning of Tet using the three vehicles. He said that there was a platoon of paratroopers camped on the roof of the station, but that some of our men with machine guns would be prepositioned on the roof of an adjacent apartment building. It was felt that at that early hour they could be taken under fire while they slept.

Singling out Chu Bay, he told him that his group was to join him in breaching the station and taking control. He pointed to a lanky man with greasy looking hair and a faint pencil-thin mustache named Mister Danh, who was a radio specialist from Hanoi. He was to broadcast a prerecorded message announcing the fall of the Saigon puppet government that would signal the start of a glorious general uprising by the people.

Nam then looked around at each of them in the room and asked if there were any questions. When no one replied, he suggested that we all get some sleep before embarking on the mission to unite our country."

"From what I heard," said Gia as he interrupted Dinh, "the sleeping paratroopers were all cut down to the last man, but the so-called 'General Uprising' failed because the night crew at the transmitting station 22 kilometers away, shut down the link on a prearranged signal and the message never got out."

"That is true," continued Dinh reading from his notes. "When the group realized that the broadcast could not be sent, they rushed to their vehicles and returned to the garage to lay low. They kept a low profile in the ensuing weeks and although Group 3 remained intact, they were completely inactive. Then, in early April, Nam told Chu Bay to take his group in one of the cars and go to a hamlet called Vinh Phu. The small village is located just north of the Saigon River almost in a straight line from Xom Moi, a bigger and much larger village across and south of the river bend. In Vinh Phu, the headman would be expecting them and would provide shelter and other necessities. They were to remain there as long as necessary and blend in with the other villagers who would not pose a threat to them.

Their task was to maintain a log of the times and patrol habits of the River Assault Group assigned to the Saigon River between Binh Loi and Phu Cuong. In the very near future, there was to be a strong incursion by some troops from the north that would cross the river and make their way once again into Saigon. It was imperative that accurate times be recorded in order for them to cross the river safely.

One morning, Chu Bay and Ninh had been working a little garden plot near the river that they had cultivated while they waited for Khoi. He had been on watch all night and it was Ngoc's turn in the observation post and as usual, she was running late. She arrived almost simultaneously as Khoi and was out of breath as she blurted out that a squad of American soldiers was making its way towards them. She thought that someone in the village had informed on them, but she didn't know for sure. Chu Bay then ordered them to quickly take refuge in their nearby little foliage covered hideaway so that they wouldn't be out in the open. Once they were underneath, Chu Bay told them he didn't think it was safe to stay in the village any longer and they should return to Gia Dinh to turn over the information.

They had made a habit of leaving the book in their hidden lookout position in case they were ever stopped and searched on their way back and forth from the village. The other three remained silent as Chu Bay made his decision to retrieve the book and head for the garage in Gia Dinh. There they would turn over the book to Nam to pass on to his superiors. Suddenly and without warning, they were completely surprised by *Dai Uy* Kay."

Dinh then conclude the report by saying, "And that is when Petty Officer Mai put away his lighter."

"What do you think will happen to the prisoner?" I asked remembering the guy that flew out of the window at Headquarters after the TET attack.

Gia replied stoically, "Oh, the Intelligence people together with the National Police will pick up all those sleepers in the Saigon soup shop, the garage in Gia Dinh and the villagers in Vinh Phu. Then, they will interrogate them thoroughly and send the prospective long term residents to the internment camp on the island of Phu Quoc."

"I have to admit that I'm impressed," I said putting down my empty beer bottle. "But, let me ask you something now that I've seen how you guys operate. I'm curious to know if you've ever gone all the way and lit the fuse."

"Yes, as a matter of fact," replied Gia. "Last year in Tan An, some villagers came and complained to me about a local VC tax collector who had been harassing them. Not only that, he was also suspected of being a child molester. So either reason was cause enough for us to get our hands on him. Luckily, we took him by surprise one night after he had been drinking. We questioned him the same as we did today and tried to show him the error of his ways, but he was obstinate. I had never met anyone so hate-filled and spiteful like that deviate. When Petty Officer Mai cut his pants open and pulled out his penis, the man started thrashing wildly until the firecracker was inserted. He immediately settled down, stared Mai in the eyes and spit at him. I cannot recall if I nodded to Mai or not, but he lit the fuse. The tax collector then sat upright in a show of bravado and stared blankly into space as the rest of us watched the burning fuse. Moments later, there was a muffled pop and bits of penis and blood splattered all over. The agonizing screams that came from that bastard were probably heard all the way to Saigon."

"Whew! What did you do then?" I asked

"I shot him in the head with my revolver." said Gia.

Dinh then added, "It took the crew almost three hours to clean up the mess because there was shit all over the place. It was a long time before any of us slept in that compartment because there was always a faint stench down there."

"Now I understand why you had that tarp on the deck, but what was the towel around Mai's neck for?"

Dinh replied laughing, "To cover his crotch just before his dick exploded."

"My good friends," I said as I stood up and headed aft to urinate into the river, "This has indeed been educational for me, even with my degree in Anthropology, how will I ever be able to describe that in a text book if I ever go for my doctorate?" The sound of their laughter followed me long after I pulled my zipper down under the setting sun.

After the patrol Saturday night, I barely remember my head hitting the pillow again. It had been an extremely long day and the ensuing events had mentally drained me. I awoke the next morning to the familiar footsteps of Gunner on the deck above. Since I had fallen asleep in my clothes, I only had to slip on my flip-flops and went topside. "What are you doing back so early?" I asked him. "Didn't I give you the weekend off?"

"Yeah, I know. Ann had bought me a case of "33" beer and according to her, I tried to finish it all by myself heh-heh," he said laughing that short dry laugh of his.

"In other words, you got shit-faced."

"Yeah, and you know when I get like that, I get horny as hell. Good ol' Ann, she wasn't having any of that, so she took little Lorie and slept over fat Betty's place. When I woke up alone this morning, I was hung-over and pissed. I mean really, because I had wet the bed. If she was mad yesterday, she's really gonna be mad when she gets home, so I figured that I'd better get my ass back to the boat where it's safe."

After hearing his confession of sorts, I nodded priest-like and proceeded to tell him of yesterday's events. When I finally finished, he said, "Geez, how come all the good shit happens when I'm gone? From now on, we're sticking together."

"Well, that's up to you. I'm merely catching up for all the time I spent doing that damn Newsletter."

"By the way," Gunner replied. "This morning I had breakfast at the 519th with 1st Sergeant Greer. He lives by himself in one of those green trailers at the rear of the compound and said you and I were welcome to use his shower anytime we wanted. I thought it was a good idea because we wouldn't have to run back and forth just to clean up and we could bring extra gear back with us."

"That's great, but what will you do for your love-life?"

"No sweat, *Dai Uy*, there's a little whorehouse just up the road and it's called 'The Two-Story.' "Maybe you'd like to try it sometime when the pressure builds up, if you know what I mean."

After that little piece of information, I said that I was going went back down below to hit the sack again."

THE ARMY COMES THROUGH

The next week was uneventful except for the deal that we made one day with the Mess Sergeant who was a big strapping light skinned Negro named Moses. Whenever we ate in the Mess hall, we noticed at the end of each meal that the cooks were tossing the leftover food into the garbage cans. When we first met, he was impressed by us after hearing of our exploits on the river. When Gunner told him that not only were we there to interdict the bad guys, but that we would cover their backs in the event that the base comes under attack. At first I thought the Chief was laying it on a little thick, but in reality he was playing on the man's fear of danger. We told him about our Vietnamese sailors facing extreme hardships because they had to send most of their meager pay home to their families, which left them pitifully little for food. I added that they would supplement what rice they had with fish, grapefruit, coconuts and palm nuts gathered from the river banks. I neglected to tell him however, about the chickens that they occasionally 'liberated' from local villages.

"We even tried to share our C-rats with them," I added for effect. That was the clincher. Sergeant Moses asked hopefully, "Would your guys eat the left-overs from our lunch and suppers? If so, I can have my cooks put them aside everyday so you can pick them up. How's that sound?" he asked beaming

And that's how we started fattening up our crew. Needless to say their morale soared as they started bragging to other units that they had the best two Advisors in-country.

One Sunday morning, Gia informed us that there would be no patrol by the Commandament that night because the engineman Phi was going to change the oil and replace some clogged injectors. In its place, three FOMS and one LCVP would make the run at random intervals. He said that he would remain with the Commandament and that it would be able to get underway if need be. So with our day free, we headed for Saigon. On the way, Gunner asked, "Can we make a quick run out to Nha Be because I've an old shipmate out there who runs the Armory? I haven't seen him in awhile and besides, maybe we'll find something there that we can use."

"Sure, why not?" I said. The day was pleasant and with little traffic on the road, we made it to Nha Be easily. This was a fairly large base and home to a Repair Barge that was the mother-ship to the PBRs of River Division 51. I always marveled about the engineering that went into those fast little patrol boats. They were equipped with Jacuzzi pumps that propelled them through the water up to 29 knots, substantial firepower and a compartmentalized interior that made them virtually unsinkable.

We located the Armory where Gunner introduced me to his buddy, Chief Gunners Mate Sal Martino, also a Jersey boy. After some reminiscing, Gunner asked if he could poke around the shop. "What are you looking for specifically, Earl?" asked Martino.

"Oh, nothing in particular, I've always liked to scrounge around the scrap bin to see what I could salvage."

"Have at it, mate," he said and with that Gunner scurried off like a kid in a candy store with fifty cents in his hand.

"Hey, look what I found," exclaimed Gunner a little while later, holding up the carcass of a Honeywell Grenade Launcher. "What's wrong with it?" he asked Martino.

"Beats me; some guy off the barge tossed it yesterday."

Gunner pulled it out and set it on a workbench where he proceeded to open it up and examine its innards. "Everything looks OK, it's a little worn and some of the teeth on the sprocket are busted off. Have you got any spares around?"

"As a matter of fact, I do," he said as he produced a new sprocket still wrapped in Cosmoline paper. The two of them went to work on the launcher with the practiced expertise of two heart transplant surgeons and when they were finished, they stood back and beamed in satisfaction.

"Here you go *Dai Uy*, we got us a genuine launcher. Was this trip worth it or not?" asked Gunner.

"Yes indeed partner, and if you two get me into the Chief's Club, I'll buy the beer and burgers."

Both Chiefs agreed. Martino suggested that we leave the launcher and pick it up along with some ammo after we come back. With that, we three Jersey boys headed for the "Goat Locker."

Later, we dropped Martino off at the Armory and stowed the launcher and 3 cases of grenades in the back seat of the Jeep. We took off for Saigon with Gunner driving. Approaching the city limits I said, "You can keep the Jeep and drop me off at my BOQ. We can leave the launcher and the ammo safely inside my BOQ compound. Pick me up around 10 tomorrow and if you intend to get buzzed again on '33', make sure you don't drive, OK?"

"OK *Dai Uy*, he said almost saintly, like the altar boy that he had once been in his youth.

The next day at exactly 10 o'clock, I came down from my room and found him patiently waiting. "Have you been here long?"

"I got here about five minutes ago and I want you to know that I stayed sober last night just so you wouldn't worry."

"Ah, that's sweet but don't you mean that Ann hid your beer?"

"These friggin' Asian women have no idea how much stress we GIs are under."

I laughed as we loaded the launcher and grenades into the Jeep and departed. When we arrived at Binh Loi, there was an American civilian sitting in an Army Scout truck parked on the road near the pilings. When he saw us approach, he got out and said, "Are you Lieutenant Kay?"

"I am," I replied a little confused. He was the same height as me, grayish sidewall haircut denoting previous military service, white short sleeved shirt opened at the neck, chino pants and suede chukka boots.

"My name is Hal Schultz from USAECOM, the Army Electronics Command, and I'm here to deliver the Night Scope you asked for.

He opened the passenger side door and lifted a large cardboard box down from the seat.

"Great, we've been waiting for this. Those small hand-held units aren't worth a damn as far as I'm concerned."

"Well, in that case, you'll like this piece of equipment. The lens is 18 inches in diameter giving you an increased area of visibility and it's powered by a lithium battery, so there's no need for an outside power source. The scope is worth $35K and the battery runs $15 a pop. I've had it configured so that it can be easily mounted over a .50cal machine gun, which I assume that you have."

Since the beginning of the conversation, Gunner had squatted Oriental-style against a tree trunk. I thought he was probably trying to show Schultz that he was an old Asia-hand. As I signed the receipt, Gunner asked him rather sarcastically, "Aren't you going upriver with us tonight to give us a demo run?"

"No!" he replied curtly, "That's not in my job description."

"What, afraid of a little boat ride in the dark?" said Gunner snidely.

Schultz's face reddened as he turned on him and growled, "Listen up you scrawny little prick, I'm an ex-Marine Master Sergeant with two Purple Hearts and a Silver Star from Iwo Jima and a field commission on Okinawa while you were still shitting your diapers. Don't give me any of that chicken crap. I've paid my dues and you can address me as Major Schultz from now on, hear?"

That was the first time that I had ever seen old Gunner so completely speechless. He was as pale as a sheet as he stood up and mumbled his sincere apologies saying, "I thought you were just another one of those sandcrabs over here making a ton of money."

"Well, I am a civilian but I'm definitely not a money chasing sandcrab either. I'd be real careful not to make snap judgments in the future because you might piss someone off that's not as laid-back as me, boy."

As Schultz drove off obviously still rankled, I figured there was nothing to say because Gunner was embarrassed enough. I whistled to get Petty Officer Mai's attention on the boat and yelled for him to bring some help to get the gear aboard. Gunner grabbed one of the grenade cases and carried it aboard on his shoulder to physically escape and separate himself from his screw-up with Schultz. The subject never came up again as I was sure that he had learned a good lesson.

Gia came topside when he heard me whistle and was ecstatic when he saw the goodies that were brought aboard. "Where did you find these things?" he asked visibly excited.

"One of *Thuong Si's* buddies in Nha Be gave us the Honeywell and the army brought the new Night Scope that I had requested."

The three of us assisted by Mai, spent the next two hours mounting the scope atop the machine gun on the starboard side and the grenade launcher opposite it on the port side of the top deck. After being satisfied that everything was in order, we invited Gia to go with us for a couple of beers, but he politely declined. So the Chief and I spent the next several hours in the army club supping on BLT sandwiches and washing them down with copious amounts of stateside beer, eventually returned and crashed for the night.

JACKPOT!

The following evening we headed upriver with me on the new scope and Gunner seated near the loaded grenade launcher. Gia and the XO sat quietly conversing as the boat, with its burbling newly revitalized engines, pushed us northward. The current was ebbing at about 3-4 knots, so we had no trouble making headway.

As we entered the lariat bend where we had discovered the spider hole, I noticed a slight anomaly along the riverbank. I adjusted the focus of the scope and saw a sight that made the hair stand straight up on my neck. I whispered to Gia that there was a large group of people hunkered down behind the tree line and brush. Since there was no apparent movement, they probably assumed that we couldn't see them.

Gia, immediately grasping the situation quietly alerted the crew and said, "Steady on."

I picked up the radio and said softly, "Leatherneck One, this is Crazy racer Eight, over."

"Crazy, this is One, go."

"One, meet me at alternate push over." This meant that we should switch to the predetermined frequency that we had agreed on earlier to avoid a possible intercept by the enemy.

I switched to the new setting and heard him calling me. "One, I am between Sneezy and Doc heading up the blue." I answered. "Have many Indians massed on the north bank, probably waiting for us to pass so they can come across. Do you want a piece of this, over?"

"Roger that. Me and my little green men can make it to the south bank at that location in about 45 minutes. Will keep you advised and thanks, over."

"One, it's a go. My opposite intends to go just north of Sneezy, cut engines and drift down with the current to engage. That should give them enough time to be vulnerable mid-blue and for you to be in position, over."

"That's a Roger. Keep in touch and good hunting, out."

I relayed the information to Gia and Gunner, who was visibly animated at the thought of finally getting some action. Gia's eyes were bright, even in the dark of this moonless night.

"They picked a good night to cross," he said pensively as he stared into the darkness. "I ordered the FOMs at Binh Loi to proceed to the bend and remain there until I call them in. They will be the blocking force to close the net." As he spoke, the all too-familiar smell of burning charcoal permeated the air around us from the silent sleeping villages in the area.

Time seemed to stand still as we slowly made our way around the bend of the lariat and continued northward. Frequently checking his watch, Gia finally gave the order for the helmsman to come around and cut the engines once we were pointed downriver. We had given the Vietnamese Marines ample time to get into position as we slowly and silently drifted down river with the current.

What I saw through the scope was a multitude of dark heads bobbing in the river bathed in a pale green light that made the scene appear spectral. The engines were restarted in order to regain steerageway as Gia gave the command to open fire. Gunner cranked out the grenades from the launcher, which by the way puts thirty rounds in the air before the first one lands and detonates. I opened up with the machine gun whose tracers enabled me to aim with the scope and the forward 40 millimeter gun barked sharply and rhythmically spewing out instant chaos.

The Marines on the far bank were pouring a withering hail of bullets into the hapless men in the water who were floating on inner tubes, doors, sampams and any floating object that would support them. The FOMs with their .30 calibers picked off any remaining survivors that were trying to escape downstream.

The entire battle lasted only about fifteen minutes and the previous charcoal smell that had been in the air was supplanted by the smell of cordite and death. Strangely enough, the only cries that were heard during the melee came from us on the boats and the Marines. The enemy died silently in the churning water and it would take about three days before the river gave up the bodies of those who had sunk to the bottom.

Gia learned later that night from the Vietnamese Lieutenant Colonel in charge of the Marines, that we had intercepted a segment of the 9th North Vietnamese Army Regiment. The final estimate was that we had killed about a hundred and fifty men with no prisoners.

When we were finally moored under the bridge, Gunner, Gia and I sat topside quietly letting the adrenalin dissipate. Although it was a one-sided fight with no casualties on our side, the blood had roared in my ears. It's always been a mystery to me how in the heat of battle, everything seems to move in slow motion but with a clarity that's unattainable during normal times. When the high is over, your body is drained to the point where you just have to give up the ghost and lay down . . . which we eventually did.

The next morning, I got a call on the radio from LCDR Richards. He said we were the talk of the Third Riverine and that Captain Bjorkman had called personally to extend his personal "Well Done" to you and Chief Shipp. Then he asked me if we were OK. I replied that we were all well and the group itself was in exceptionally high spirits.

"Well, I'm glad that you finally got what you wished for," he said sincerely.

"Thanks Boss, I appreciate it because I couldn't have done it without you."

"Drop by the office when you get to town and maybe we can hoist a couple and shoot the breeze a little."

"Will do, Commander," I replied and signed off. Gunner, who had been listening, said sarcastically, "Now they'll all want to rub elbows with us and ride our coattails."

"Aw, he's OK Chief. Don't think that he doesn't wish he could be out here with us instead of riding a desk."

"Maybe so, but there are a lot of guys in-country that are just putting in their year, hoping to get some medals, their ticket punched for promotion and their asses out in one piece," he said knowingly.

"Too true," I agreed.

About a month later for that night's work, RAG 24 was awarded President Thieu's Prize of 35,000 Piasters (about $700US), given to each service for a significant accomplishment. With that money, Gia threw a party for the officers, Advisors and Chiefs and a separate one for the enlisted men. What remained was evenly distributed among the crew. Talk about a happy group!

VUNG TAU, VIETNAM'S RIVIERA

Another couple of monotonous and uneventful weeks passed by with Gunner and I sometimes alternating patrol with each other, when Gia told us to take another weekend off. He said that since the turkey-shoot upriver, things had been quiet and he thought the both of us needed a break, even going so far as to suggest our going to Vung Tau. Since neither of us had ever been there before, we happily agreed.

Fortunately, we both had a clean change of clothes from our last trip to Saigon, so we jumped into the Jeep and headed out. It was a beautiful day in June as we took Highway One and headed for the cut-off at Long Binh. I was driving as the road took us past the old Michelin rubber plantations on the left. We passed rows upon rows of stately rubber trees that were symmetrically aligned and that stretched back as far as the eye could see.

Suddenly, puffs of dirt began to appear on my side of the road as Gunner yelled out, "Hey, some bastard's shooting at us." I stomped on the accelerator and veered right as far as I could go hoping to get out of the kill zone. Someone was shooting at us from within the plantation, but the shots were falling short.

"How about that?" said Gunner as we once again were in the clear. "How'd you like to be nailed by some shithead taking potshots at us from behind a rubber tree?"

We eventually arrived safely in the resort seaside city of Vung Tau and we drove around until we found a secluded little hotel on the beach front. We checked in and were given a second floor room with two beds and an ocean view.

"Man, it'll be great to get some sleep without smelling the diesel oil or hearing grenades go off all night," said Gunner.

"C'mon, let's get something to eat and check out the night life," I said.

We found a little pseudo-Italian style restaurant just up the street and enjoyed a pretty passable plate of *pasta fra diavolo*, or spaghetti with a spicy hot sauce. Since Gunner and his sister had been raised by an Italian family as orphans and I had grown up with many Italian friends in Jersey City, the local atmosphere brought back many memories to both of us.

With our primary need taken care of, it was time to search for the second,—pussy. The sun had already set as we headed back down towards the beach. There was a slight breeze blowing in from the sea and mixed sounds of music could be heard coming from the many bars that lined the avenue. As we walked leisurely along, two young ladies came around the corner unexpectedly, so engrossed in conversation that they nearly bumped in to us.

"Excuse us," said the shorter of the two in accented English.

"Good evening ladies," said Gunner politely. "Is that an Australian accent I detect?"

"Yes it is Yank, do you have a problem with that?" she asked trying to appear belligerent.

"Not at all," replied Gunner in a soothing tone. "I was curious because I was once on a ship that put into Sydney for a few days and had the time of my life there."

"HEY MATEY, D'YA SPEAK ENGLISH?"

"In that case, how do you do?" piped in the other girl. "I'm Barbara and this here's Sophie. We're Army nurses and we're stationed at the Aussie base clinic here."

I added my two cents by introducing ourselves and saying that we were Advisors to a Vietnamese River Assault Group.

"Oh, that sounds exciting," said Barbara. She was about 5'9" tall, maybe 120 pounds with short cropped auburn hair, blue eyes, a cupid's-bow mouth and big tits. Sophie was a little shorter, blonde hair held back with a barrette, brown eyes, full petulant lips and much smaller tits. Both girls were sun-bronzed wearing identical khaki shorts, short-sleeved white blouses and open-toed sandals showing neatly painted toenails.

"We're just taking time off from the war for the weekend and it's the first time either of us has been to Vung Tau," I said. "Since we don't know anyone here, perhaps you'd care to join us for a drink?"

Barbara said boldly, "We'd love to," as she came and took my arm. Without a word, Sophie fell in behind us and took Gunner by the arm too. We walked for awhile, each carrying on with small talk until we reached a fork in the road. Directly nestled between the streets was a nice outdoor café with tables under a wide striped awning.

"This looks like a good a place as any," said Barbara as she gently pulled me to a table. Not catching the name of the place, I picked up the menu on the table and saw it was called "*Hy Lap*" which means Greece in Vietnamese. How's that for a coincidence?

A slightly stooped Caucasian old man with wispy white thinning hair came out and asked politely in heavily accented English, "What can I get for you?"

I took the lead by asking, "By the name of the place, I assume that you are Greek."

"I am," he replied. "My name is Stavros and I came here aboard that rusted old hulk that is high and dry on the beach. In 1953, I was Captain of the 'Ioannis K.' carrying olive oil, olives, cheeses and other foodstuffs from Greece. When I asked permission to off-load my cargo in Saigon from the Port Director, I was refused with no explanation. When I radioed back to my company in Piraeus, they ordered me to deliver, unload the cargo and return immediately. I couldn't convince them that this was impossible and we were at a stalemate with the Vietnamese government. I was then ordered to lay offshore in International waters until they could resolve the problem diplomatically.

The problem was never settled and after a few weeks of steaming slowly off-shore, we started running low on fuel. By this time, my crew was ready to mutiny, so I made my decision. I explained my plan to them and they agreed to a man. I turned the ship towards the beach, put all engines ahead flank and drove the ship about forty yards onto the sand, where she has been to this day. We abandoned the vessel and the crew scattered to the four winds. My company eventually dissolved, so I ended up staying here, got married and raised a family. The locals stripped the ship of everything they could carry away, leaving only the carcass of a once proud ship."

"Unbelievable," I said shaking my head. I explained that I was an American of Greek descent and that my people were from Sparta. He told me that he originally came from the large island of Andros in the Aegean Sea and that he had never returned home even though he missed Greece but not the miserly ship-owners who refused to pay the Port Director under the table.

When Stavros finished his narrative, Sophie asked him since he was Greek, did he serve any Ouzo. "But of course I have. What kind of Greek would I be without the nectar of the Gods?" he asked smiling. "Where did you hear about Ouzo?" he asked.

Sophie replied, "In 1954, Australia allowed boatloads of Greeks to immigrate because we were in dire need of shoemakers, restauranteurs, bakers, pastry makers, candy makers, farmers and fishermen. I grew up next to a Greek family so I know all about Ouzo."

"Wonderful," said Stavros. "Then the first round is on me."

A young half Vietnamese waitress brought a large bowl of hot roasted peanuts in the shell to the table and I guessed that she had to be the owner's daughter. By the time we finished our fourth round of drinks, we all were pretty well feeling no pain.

Gunner had been leaning over for the past five minutes urgently whispering into Sophie's ear. Finally, she turned around to face him and said, "That's the trouble with you Yanks. All you want is to get into my knickers with no subtle endearing talk or verbal foreplay. You guys just go for it."

'TOGETHER NOW SARGE...'WALTZING MATILDA'....

Gunner pulled back and looked her in the eyes and asked, "Sophie, have you ever been to Brooklyn?"

"No, I haven't," she replied looking a little befuddled.

"Me either," said Gunner. "Let's fuck."

Barbara and I doubled over with laughter as Sophie stood up and said, "OK you silver tongued devil, take me to your room."

I was at a loss for words as Barbara looked at me and said, "Let's go and join 'em because I don't want to sit here and drink all night."

So we did—and did it again early in the morning.

We woke up at around 0800. With the sun shining brightly in our window, the four of us grinned stupidly at one another. Then we treated Barbara and Sophie to a well deserved breakfast of coffee and fresh croissants over which we agreed to stay together for the weekend.

The rest of the day was spent doing a little sightseeing, since our "guides" had been here for almost a year. After a quick lunch at Stavros' place again, we headed for the beach. Gunner had his faded shark covered bathing trunks and I had found a reasonably priced bathing suit at a seaside shop. Barbara insisted on this particular one because its design was obviously French inspired. To attach the word "skimpy" to it would be an understatement because I had to shorten my stride in order to keep my genitals from falling out on the sides. If nothing else, it provided an air of expectancy among the four of us. Aside from that, we did get to see the remains of the "Ioannis K." It was actually sad for anyone who has sailed the seas, to see the pathetic remains of a once vibrant ship after being raped, ravaged and ultimately abandoned far from home.

That evening, the mattress gymnastics were renewed with more exuberance than the previous evening's attempts at solidifying Australian-American relations. In fact, by the look of the girl's happy glowing faces early the next morning, I'd say we were unequivocally successful.

We dropped the girls off at their base, foregoing breakfast in order to get a jump on the traffic for our return to Binh Loi. Before climbing out of the Jeep, promises were made to keep in touch as we agreed to do this again. This was followed by quick brotherly pecks on our cheeks for the benefit of the two bored Aussie guards posted at the entrance to their base.

On our return trip, there were no potshots taken at us as we sped past the rubber plantations and made it back in time to catch breakfast at the 519th messhall.

Once back aboard the Commandament, Gia remarked after seeing our smiling faces, "It looks as if your trip was enjoyable."

"As a matter of fact, it was. We met two Australian Nurses and educated them in the ways of a true sailor's weekend."

"I'm sure," he mused sagely and probably relieved that we diddled the round-eyes rather than the vulnerable Viet girls.

A few nights later, as I was sitting alone topside after finishing the nightly run upriver, as I gazed to the north, my blood immediately ran cold. There in the night sky, dozens of red flares illuminated the horizon, which signified an enemy attack was in progress. From the amount of flares, it had to be an all out offensive and as I was mentally trying to get a grasp on the situation especially after the enemy contact last month. Twelve white flares went up in the same area followed quickly by twelve green ones. Just as I was saying "What the hell?" out loud, it came to me that it was the fourth of July and since there was no such thing as a blue flare, those guys at Lai Thieu were substituting green ones. Red, white and blue, get it? So much for calendar awareness, I went below to hit the sack.

The next day after I explained my near heart attack because of the flares to Gunner, we heard that a FOM from RAG 30 had been blown up by sappers on the Long Tau Canal. The crew had set up an ambush site under a deep cut in the bank and unfortunately all three fell asleep. During the night, a VC swimmer attached a mine to the hull and when it detonated, rolled the hull up like a sardine can with the crew inside. They didn't have a chance.

The Commanding Officer of RAG 30 was LCDR Minh and he was a fire-brand when it came to fighting VC. The loss of his men and the boat infuriated him and in order to bring his point home, he ordered his men to shave their heads in mourning. His Adviser, LT Chuck Bart, was prematurely bald to begin with so no further scalping was necessary for him. His Assistant Chief Knox, on the other hand and much to his dismay, had to shear his curly locks. Rumor has it that he plans to go into hibernation until his hair grows back into its original and full condition.

An operation came up a week later where we had to pick up and ferry two companies of ARVN troops in a sweep around the southern waterways of Saigon/Cholon. Because of the high tide, we couldn't get the Commandament under the bridge even if we took down the awning and removed the topside shielding. The smaller LCVPs that we used to carry the troops were already on the other side, so Gia decided to bring one of the Monitors up to the east side of the Binh Loi Bridge where we could cross over and use it as our command platform. Boarding time was 0600 at Cat Lai, which was located on the Dong Nai River and about 22 kilometers northeast of Saigon. It meant that I had one of two choices; either stay aboard the Monitor at Binh Loi and make the trip to Cat Lai with the group, or go with Gunner into Saigon for a little R & R. Since Gunner was going home to his little Chinese bed-warmer, I could sleep in my air conditioned room and get up at o-dark-thirty to make the thirty-five minute drive to Cat Lai in the morning. It was safer this way with one of us riding shotgun.

After dropping him off, I went to my room in the Q to take a much needed shower and leave more dirty laundry for the maid. Putting on freshly laundered greens was one of the luxuries enjoyed by those troops fortunate enough to have maid service.

The supporting cadre assigned duties in the big city were known as "Saigon Warriors." They shed their sweaty uniforms at night and their maids washed them in the morning. The clothes would be dried, pressed and hung neatly in the closet by the time they returned that evening from another peril-filled day at the office. Who said "War is Hell"?

I had a slight buzz on from the local "33" beer that I consumed while making the rounds of my usual haunts that night. It's funny how any thought of putting food into an empty stomach has a lower priority than satisfying a thirst. I managed to beat the 2200 curfew (for a change) and crawled happily into bed in a room that I had all to myself tonight.

I got up at 0400, showered and donned my greens. Filling my canteen with drinking water from the recycled whiskey bottles that my faithful maid replenished daily, I remembered the Vodka debacle and laughed to myself. I grabbed my M-16 and my carry-all bag, went down and unlocked the padlock securing the chain around my Jeep's steering wheel and headed for Gunner's pad.

His Chinese girlfriend Ann owned a second floor apartment that was down the street from the Catholic Church that President Thieu attended on Tran Hung Dao. There was a small Buddhist Temple in the rear of her building and we couldn't help but notice the hard stares and surly looks we always got from the saffron-robed monks whenever they saw us. Not only that, but on several occasions we distinctly heard them speaking to each other in the dialect of the north. Odd huh, but then again, what did we know?

Anyway, Gunner was to meet me on the corner by the Catholic Church at 0515. As I motored through the empty, darkened streets, I could see stray cats and rats scuttling around the gutters and the garbage heaps and as I had witnessed before, the cats avoided the rats.

I approached the appointed corner and Gunner was nowhere to be seen. I gunned the Jeep straight ahead down Tran Hung Dao for a half a block, made a quick U-turn and headed back towards the pickup point. Still with no Chief in sight, I turned right at his corner and warily headed down the narrow street towards his alley. I kept my eyes moving from side to side searching the darkened doorways for anything out of the ordinary. Before I go any farther, I have to explain the following to you, the reader. There are myriads of small alcoves, stairwells, passageways and entrances leading to multiple dwellings packed to overflowing with humanity in Saigon. In most cases, a barricade or steel fence is erected at the entrances to provide some semblance of security for the occupants. The gates were sometimes topped with barbed wire and secured after the ten o'clock curfew. They would normally remain locked until five or six in the morning when a duty gatekeeper would do the honors.

The entrance to Gunner's alley had such a gate. I figured that he had probably forgotten to ask Papa-san to unlock it so he could get out early. As I approached the entrance, the dim bulb that exuded no more than five candlepower of light in the alley, barely silhouetted a body hanging from the top of the gate. For a moment my heart went up to my throat until I heard Gunner hiss out a string of profanities as only a Chief can do.

Gunner obviously had trouble trying to arouse old Papa-san from his rice-wine induced sleep and being resourceful, he had resorted to plan "B." He scaled the gate and was doing great until he cleared the barbed wire with a minimal of difficulty. He somehow got turned around and was coming down backwards when the topmost spike on the gate got snagged under his green jacket. There he hung, unable to go up or down with his eyes moving furtively from side to side like a caged gorilla. He had a death grip on his beloved chrome plated carbine in one hand and his rucksack in the other. Pulling up in front of the gate, I tried to suppress a grin at seeing him dangling helplessly on the fence like a butterfly on a pin.

"Hey *Dai-Uy*, get me the fuck down from here" he croaked.

I said "Gunner, why don't you just unbutton your jacket and slip out of it?"

It was comical to see the disconcerted look that came over his face as the obvious solution sank in. Anyway, I jumped out of the Jeep and took the carbine and rucksack from him. He was then able to brace his heels on the fence and undid his jacket. I managed to break his fall avoiding any injury except to his ego and freed his jacket from the spike. How we didn't rouse the entire neighborhood remained a mystery.

With a deep sigh of relief, he settled in the passenger seat assuming his usual position with his carbine resting on his right knee. When he had left RAG 27, he was presented with a sawed-off

M-30 chrome plated carbine with a modified pistol grip by LCDR Rac. The one sure thing was the carbine's gross inaccuracy. One could never predict where the bullet would go once it was fired at a target, but it looked impressive nonetheless.

On several occasions that Gunner rode with the gun proudly resting on his knee, a Vietnamese "cowboy" on a passing motorcycle would invariably take his eyes of the road as he stared at the shiny carbine. This usually resulted in a collision with whatever had stopped in front of him. Gunner took extreme pleasure in causing accidents with these "dumb shits" that he called "Crows" because they were attracted to shiny objects.

At other times, I would have to intercede with the U.S. MPs whenever they stopped us because of the carbine. They would attempt to confiscate it because it was considered an illegal weapon due to its alteration. I would then inform them as authoritatively as I could that it was a gift from a Vietnamese Navy Captain and would constitute a severe breach of military protocol to take it away from him.

We then headed out for Gia Dinh and Highway #1 that would take us to Cat Lai and our rendezvous with the boats. We arrived a few minutes before 6 after a quiet and uneventful drive from Saigon. The troops were just about loaded, which surprised me somewhat because on past operations, they would invariably be from one to two hours late. This one turned out to be a walk in the park with no contact being made with the elusive adversary. Truth be known is that "Charlie" had probably already been notified about the impending operation and they made themselves scarce.

We returned from the futile sweep through the rivers that bordered the Chinese inhabited area of Saigon known as Cholon. It is only three miles from the center of Saigon, but one is hardly aware of the subtle changes as you travel down Tran Hung Dao into Cholon. It is only when you reach the center of Cholon that you realize that you are now in Chinatown. The residents of this area are primarily from southern China and speak Cantonese, even though Mandarin is the official Chinese dialect. Other dialects encountered in this immensely populated area are Fukien, Hokien and Hakka.

The Bird's Nest

On the return trip, Gia came to where I was sitting half asleep on the forward part of the Monitor. He said, "I've decided to give my people a short break before returning to Binh Loi."

"Sounds good to me" I replied. "What did you have in mind?"

"There's a place just up ahead where an old friend of mine runs a little business. She's been a widow for about 10 years and her husband died during a practice jump with the Airborne. Fortunately they had no children, so it made the loss much less painful. Once the fighting escalated and more men entered the service, she decided to provide them with some little creature comforts at a reasonable price."

"Here's the place," Gia said with a little grin as the Cox'n turned the Monitor to starboard and gently eased the bow up against the bank. Two seamen quickly leaped ashore and secured the bow lines around a couple of sturdy coconut trees.

"I will let half the men go in now and the other half will get their turn when the first group finishes. Would you and the Chief care to have some beer? She keeps it very cold and the glasses are clean."

"I thought you'd never ask," I said, anticipating the icy liquid washing down my throat. It sure would be a welcome relief from the stale water that I had been drinking from my canteen.

Just as Gia, Gunner and I jumped down onto the embankment from the boat, a strikingly attractive Vietnamese woman, somewhere in her late 30s, appeared in the doorway of the main building. She wore her lustrous black hair tied up into a flowing ponytail that framed her slightly triangular facial features and hung down to the small of her back. Her jet black eyes were bright and alive under delicately defined eyebrows and long eyelashes. The nose was small and aquiline and had definitely been refashioned to conform to Western standards. Since the arrival of the Americans, many young ladies visited the cosmetic clinics to trim the epicanthic folds from above their eyes, straighten and lengthen their noses, and in some cases took a v-cut of skin from their cheeks or chin to give them a permanent dimple. Her lips wore a hint of pink as they parted into a girlish grin over sparkling white, perfectly formed teeth. The plain solid black Ao Dai and pants performed its magic by disguising the wearer's defects and accenting the assets. One could easily see the VPL (Visible Panty Line) through the thin material of the pants. A surprisingly slim waist and tantalizing small, perfectly formed breasts completed the picture.

"Long time no see, *Thieu-Ta"* she said in a soft delicate voice while her eyes gave Gunner and me only a cursory glance. "Where have you been keeping yourself?"

"Only the powers in Saigon and the VC have prevented me from having visited you sooner" Gia replied rather gallantly.

In that instant I sensed rather than saw a silent message pass between them. Gia introduced us to the owner as *Ba Ni* and I was surprised by the delicate diminutive softness of her hand as she offered it to both of us.

The "Bird's Nest," as the bar cum whorehouse was called, was typical of the small entrepreneurial efforts that had sprung up throughout the country. The building was constructed from green painted cinder blocks, various types of a wood and an aluminum roof. A palm frond covered overhang at the front of the building provided shade from the sun and cover from the rains. A few rickety rattan chairs surrounded a cigarette scarred table and a well-worn hammock strung between two uprights completed the outer decor.

The front room contained a small bar with a few stools, while the rest of the room was occupied by antiquated wooden tables and mismatched chairs. In Saigon, as in other large cities, the bars had juke boxes, however the further one got into the boonies the music was supplied by a radio cassette player or a tape deck.

Cassettes were almost always pirated from original tracks as this was a common practice in the black market that flourished so successfully. The "Bird's Nest" featured a large Sony boom box softly playing Vietnamese music while the six girls lounged about in their mini-skirts. Some were playing a game called "*Doi*" with little Chinese cards while others painted their nails or combed their long black hair.

A room in the back, which one entered through a curtain of beads, was actually twice as big as the front one. Here's where the girls provided the entertainment on four beds separated from one another by bamboo and plastic curtains. At the rear of the house there was a little kitchen area complete with a worn wooden chopping block, a chipped, stained enamel sink and a small propane stove. From there, a narrow passageway led to the toilet that consisted of a single standard porcelain basin within a cement enclosure resembling a shower stall. The basin had two ridged areas for placing one's feet securely which enabled you to be strategically positioned over a hole when in a squatting position. There was also a water spigot provided for minimal flushing and rinsing accommodations. Last but not least, the ubiquitous tin can nearby for depositing used toilet paper so as not to foul up the septic tank. The can would be dumped daily and the contents burned. The overhead of the toilet area was covered by palm fronds woven and lashed onto a wooden framework supported by thin latticework covered sides. Actually it was rather pleasant to answer nature's call out in the fresh air. On the other hand during rainy season, one could count on getting wet as the raindrops would find their way through the fronds. Add to this the flies, mosquitoes and a variety of scuttling rodent life and you have a picture of real country style living.

As we entered the bar area, several of the girls looked up and evaluated us as potential customers since they had never seen me or Gunner before.

"Don't tell me that you haven't any places like this in the United States," asked Gia smiling.

"If there are, I sure haven't seen them" I replied.

Three cold beers were placed on the bar in front of us and they couldn't have come at a better time. I was really amazed at how many attractive young girls were here considering that we were in what could be considered the "outback." In most bars, there may be one or two exceptional looking "hostesses" and the rest tail off from fair to "no way, thank you."

At that moment, my hormonal radar picked out a particularly unique young lady sitting in the far corner reading a Vietnamese love novel. What drew my attention to her was that she did not look up as we entered, almost to the point of indifference. Only after she heard my voice did she cast a glance our way. Her eyebrows were natural and finely tapered over soft dark brown eyes made up to perfection and cat-like. She was taller than the average Vietnamese female by at least four inches and her short black hair literally shone as it just reached her shoulders. Wide pronounced cheek bones and sparkling white teeth further enhanced her appearance.

Ba Ni, noticing my interest in the girl, leaned towards me and said in a conspiratorial voice, "Beware of that one, *Dai Uy*, we call her *Xoay Nuoc* which means 'Whirlpool.'" Because you are a friend of Gia's, I feel it is only right that I warn you. I gave her that name because once she pulls you down you will lose everything before you come back up. Would you believe that she is presently juggling three Americans at one time? One is a Colonel in the Air Force who was stationed at Bien Hoa Airbase and the father of her 3 year old son. He's back in the United States with his wife, but still sends her money every month. The second one is on staff at the Embassy in Saigon and the third is an Army Major stationed at MACV.

The nights that the Major has the duty, she stays with the Embassy staffer at his house. Nights when the Major comes to their apartment, she tells the Embassy man that she is going to visit her mother and son in My Tho. They all give her money and are more than happy to do so. The rest of the time she spends here waiting for a new prospect.

"Wow, that's an appropriate name for her although 'Barracuda' comes to mind as well," I said honestly impressed.

Ni nodded in agreement. "Feel free to choose any other girl and I guarantee that they are all clean."

"Thanks for the heads-up, but I think I'll pass," I said as I turned back around on the barstool. Gunner on the other hand had already disappeared with a consenting partner behind the beaded curtain. I'll say one thing for him; he was never one to let an opportunity pass by when it came to putting the lumber to some female—any female.

True to his word, Gia had given half the Monitor's crew about a half hour to do or not do at Ba Ni's establishment, then the other half. By the time we left, it was late afternoon and the buzzing insects seemed to come alive along the riverbanks. Gunner and the crewmembers who had taken advantage of the sexual release were all contented and silent. Gia told me that the XO would make the patrol run with the Commandament this evening so Gunner and I could have another night to ourselves. That was more than OK with us, so we disembarked at Cat Lai, retrieved the Jeep and drove back to Saigon.

BA-MI-BA BOOM

I dropped Gunner off and decided to get my usual quick snack at the USO. I would have lingered awhile longer after the meal, but the unrecognizable music coming from a dubious group of young musicians with long oily hair encouraged me to seek the relative quiet of downtown Saigon traffic instead.

Since it was relatively early, I decided to drive one block over and try out the New York Bar on Hai Ba Trung that a soldier at the 519th had recommended to me. I had to go a ways down the street to find a parking spot which was fortunate as I was to find out later. The soldier told me that there were several Eurasian hostesses working in that bar and since I was always interested in meeting new species of female, (strictly in an Anthropological sense), I decided to pay the place a visit.

It was as typical a bar as any other in Saigon, with the exception that there were three Eurasian girls doing the honors. I took the first stool with my back to the front window so I could see down the length of the bar. There were two American civilians and three Vietnamese ARVN soldiers quietly talking to two hostesses who sat behind the bar. This was where the girls used to stay during President Diem's morality advocate sister Madame Nu's push to clean up the bars. No touchy-feely or other public displays of affection were allowed. No wonder Diem and her husband had been assassinated.

The third girl behind the bar came up and took my order for a cold bottle of "33" beer and told me her name was Monique. She was very definitely half Gallic because of her green eyes and short light brownish hair. The rest of her was all Vietnamese in that she was slim and probably wore a padded bra. With her fairly good English, we made the usual small talk and eventually I bought her the obligatory "Saigon Tea." During that time, one of the ARVNs got up and left just as a young boy of about 9 or 10 entered carrying a shoeshine box.

As he canvassed the customers, I excused myself to go relieve my bladder. The toilet was all the way in the rear, through the beaded curtains and to the left of the back room. There were two enclosed toilet squatting stalls with flimsy doors for privacy, separated by a cement seven foot high wall.

While I was standing there casually letting my rented beer stream accurately into the round hole, the little boy exited the bar leaving his shoe box just inside the front door. The next thing I heard as I was zipping up my fly was a horrendous explosion. I was thrown against the cement wall and onto the toilet floor where I lay momentarily stunned. When I regained my senses, there was nothing but ringing in my ears. I managed to regain my feet after slipping on the wet porcelain basin and made my way back into the bar. The sight before me was like a scene from Dante's Inferno. The room was full of smoke, the front door and plate glass window had been blown out onto the street and bodies were strewn all around the littered floor.

I checked the two ARVN soldiers first and they were dead. One of the two Americans was lying grotesquely between two mangled barstools and he too was dead. The second American was trying to sit up holding his head which had a huge gash on the back. I found an old bar rag and tied it around the wound hoping to stem the flow of blood. Fortunately he was out of it and the fact that he was a lightweight, I was able to half drag him out of the bar onto the glass littered sidewalk. By now, an ambulance, a white National Police Jeep and an MP Jeep screeched to a halt next to the damaged parked cars in front.

Although all three hostesses survived the blast having been behind the bar, they suffered facial and upper body scarring that would prevent them from seeking future similar employment. Me,

I was OK and the medic said the ringing in my ears should go away since I was protected from the direct blast. I answered some questions for the MPs and when they were convinced that I was unhurt, offered to help me to my Jeep.

As I got behind the wheel, the older of the two MPs said, "It's getting so a guy can't have a quiet beer around here anymore, right Lieutenant?"

"You've got that right, Sergeant. I'll tell you one thing though, from here on in whenever I have to take a leak, I won't try and hold it . . . not after what happened tonight!"

After driving for about five minutes, I pulled off to the side of a dark, quiet street and turned off the ignition. I closed my eyes, slumped down in my seat and took several deep breaths. A cold sweat was covering my body that I figured had to be the adrenalin wearing off. On top of that, a strange thought had popped into my mind. What a great injustice to the heroes in Arlington National Cemetery if I had died in that blast tonight and was buried alongside them. What an epitaph, "Killed in action while taking a piss in a Saigon bar."

I finally pulled myself together after a few more minutes and made it to my BOQ without any further mishaps. When I entered the darkened room, I could just make out that there was someone in my bed. I snapped on the overhead light and had the first glimpse of my elusive roommate, Army Captain Vlastoff. Taken by surprise, he awoke with a start and quickly sat up in bed. Meanwhile, there was a diminutive young lady curled up in my bed under my poncho liner sound asleep.

"Sorry to wake you up like this," I said, "But it looks as if we have a slight problem here."

Still trying to wake up from an obvious deep sleep, which is common after intercourse, he stammered "I'm awfully sorry about this; I thought you'd be out for the night."

By now, the young lady awoke at the sound of our voices and sat up tightly clutching the poncho liner to her bosom.

Looking down at the Captain, I said, "It looks like you've got three choices. Bring her home, throw her out or take her back into your bed."

"I can't take her home because it's almost curfew and my bed is too small for both of us to sleep in," he whined.

"The bed was big enough for you to screw her in, so you should be able to manage all right, or you can let her sleep in it and sit up in the chair by yourself."

"Hey, I've got an idea; you appear to be a little smaller than me, so why don't you take a crack at her? She's pretty good in the sack," he volunteered.

"Thanks, but no thanks. I have an aversion about being second in the pool, if you know what I mean. Besides, I have already had one helluva day and I need to get some sleep."

As I was saying this, I went around to the other side of my bed and sat down on its edge to remove my boots. The girl, clad only in bikini panties and a bra, quickly uncoiled from under the covers and jumped into bed with Vlastoff. With that, I told him to turn off the light and I rolled over and went to sleep.

The next morning when I awoke, I saw that I was all alone. I had no idea what time they got up, what time they left nor did I really care. When I picked up Gunner and related my adventures from the night before, all he could say was that he'd never met anyone who could get into so many predicaments like me. He also added that I'd be better off in the future hanging out in the Golden Dragon because he was sure that Marie paid her protection taxes to the VC.

All things considered, that wasn't such a bad idea. An option that had been rolling around in my mind lately was whether Tuyet would consider moving in with me somewhere. It sure would solve a lot of problems, such as not having to play sexual roulette and having a warm bed to come home to.

On the way back to Binh Loi, I asked him how his evening had been. He replied grinning, "Not as exciting as yours. When I woke up this morning there was an aspirin stuck in my belly button."

"A what in your where?" I asked.

"Last night, I was running a low grade fever and because I sleep bare-ass with the ceiling fan right over my bed, Lan put an aspirin in my belly button to prevent air from getting into my body and making my fever worse."

"First time I ever heard that, but it was a good thing you weren't laying on your stomach," I said laughing.

"Yeah, only a Greek would think of that," he answered.

"Don't knock it," I said. "One of my female cousins in Greece would place an aspirin in her navel to prevent getting carsick every time she went on a trip."

"Did it work?" he asked.

"Usually it did, but only after she threw up."

I decided to swing by VNN Headquarters for a short visit with the guys before we headed back to Binh Loi and as we pulled into the compound, we confronted Co Mai coming down the stairs.

She came over to the Jeep as soon as she saw us and asked how we were doing.

I acknowledged by saying we were both fine and of course Gunner had to comment on how radiant she looked. My buddy: Ever the lecher.

When I asked her how the boys on the top deck were doing, she replied that there were all new officers now. The other people had rotated home except for Mr. Morrow who extended for six months as an advisor aboard an LSSL.

"Good for George," I said. "He finally got what he wanted.

But Gunner didn't think much of the new assignment because he said it was almost as bad as being aboard ship back in the US. Oh well, there was no pleasing some folks, I thought as we bid Co Mai goodbye and resumed our trip back to the bridge.

We arrived at the mooring just as a medium sized rain squall dumped a ton of water on us as we hastily climbed aboard the Commandament. Fortunately, neither one of us slipped off of the wet plank as we scuttled nimbly across like a couple of Chinese acrobats. XO Dinh was topside watching one of the FOMs that seemed to be in trouble. Upon seeing us, he said that the boat had lost power as it was returning from upriver. The current was carrying it rapidly towards the bridge as the three man crew was scrambling to get it under control. They were about fifty feet from the bridge abutments when we heard the engine cough and a dense cloud of black smoke erupted from the exhaust. The Cox'n tried to turn the bow upriver as the boat's screw was thrashing the water in a losing battle. One of the crew had been standing aft with the boat hook preparing to fend the hull off from the cement bridge piling just as the stern slammed into it viciously. The crewman lost his footing upon impact and went over the side into the churning mud-ladened water.

When the boat was finally under control and secured to the piling, the engineer and the Cox'n hurriedly scanned the water for the hapless sailor but he was nowhere to be found.

The three of us on the Commandament stared helplessly as we witnessed the accident unfold and all the while realizing that the man was gone.

"The screw must have got him," said Gunner softly.

"It would make no difference," said Dinh quietly. "He most likely did not know how to swim."

"Whoever heard of a sailor not knowing how to swim?" I asked.

"Most of the enlisted men who come from inland areas where there are no rivers, have no opportunity to learn," Dinh said.

"What about your Boot Camp at Camranh Bay? That's right on the ocean and a perfect place to teach them to swim," I replied.

Dinh replied, "That's true, but there is no such training."

"Then that's just pure bullshit," I said heatedly. "I can't believe that no one considered the ability to swim a necessary part of their naval training."

"Unfortunately, that is the way it is, *Dai Uy*."

"What are you getting so heated up about it?" piped Gunner.

"Suppose our boat hits a river mine and you're in the water hurt and unable to swim, wouldn't you like to know that one of your VN sailors could swim and help pull you out?"

"Well, when you put it that way, I can see your reasoning. But what can we do about it?"

"I'm sending a report up the chain of command about what happened here today with the recommendation that they include swimming classes at their Boot Camp. I'm sure they can provide a swimming instructor from somewhere, don't you think?"

"I say again, that's why they pay you officers the big bucks," he said chuckling.

The report was submitted and three days later I was relieved to hear that it was approved all the way up to the top and that swimming would be included in the recruit training. Hopefully, it would prevent any further unnecessary accidents.

True to form, the Saigon River gave up the drowned sailor's body three days later on the north side of the river on the other side of the bridge. As the body was being lifted out of the water, it was a gruesome sight. The body had bloated to the point that the clothes had stretched and appeared translucent. The tongue was huge, ugly and grey and protruded grotesquely between his swollen lips, while the eyes were wide open, colorless and opaque staring into infinity.

Gunner's original assumption was borne out in that there was a nasty gash on the side of the sailor's head where it had come in contact with the boat's propeller. In that respect, he died instantly thereby avoiding an agonizing death by drowning

"What are they going to do with the body?" I asked Gia who had stood alongside me watching the retrieval.

"They will return it to the family so they can prepare for the funeral," he answered quietly.

"I would think that it would be much better if the family did not see the body in such a horrible condition. That's no way to remember a loved one."

"I agree, but they are Buddhists and have strict customs to follow. Now at least the family can grieve happily knowing that he is in a better place."

A few days later Gia permitted half of the unit to attend the first day of the sailor's funeral, followed by the rest of the crew the next day. I accompanied Gia with the first group and Gunner would go with XO Dinh and the second group. Now I hate funerals with a passion and vowed that if it was within my power, I would be a "no-show" for mine. However, under the circumstances and because it was the right thing to do, I stood alongside Gia and the crew. I had never attended a Buddhist funeral but I had heard the all-night drums, cymbal crashing and the wailing of the reed instruments that kept me awake several months ago in Saigon.

The deceased's family and relatives were all dressed in white with white scarves tied around their heads. The cloying smell of joss sticks permeated the air as the instruments kept up a steady tattoo of sound in my ears. About halfway through the initial ceremony, Gia touched my arm and motioned with his head that we could leave. Once outside, he said, "The crew will remain here for several more hours, but we have performed our required duty and now we may leave."

The cool night air was refreshing as I sat in the back of Gia's Jeep as we were driven back to Binh Loi. Gunner was still up and had just returned from having several beers with 1st Sgt Greer up in the 519th club.

"How'd it go?" he asked quietly.

"When you've seen one, you've seen them all," I replied dryly.

"I'm not looking forward to it, but it's my job. The sad thing is that I didn't even know the guy," Gunner said wistfully.

"I understand, but after all, he was one of ours and it doesn't make it any easier."

THANKSGIVING

The Holiday was only a day away and the only thing that had happened was the blowing up of a section of the Phu Cuong Bridge on the 2nd of November. The US Army Engineers rapidly constructed a pontoon bridge across the river and completed it by the 6th of November thereby averting a major traffic and military logistic disaster of enormous proportions.

Our patrols continued as usual and the food from the Army mess was still being distributed to our boat crews. One boring day led into the next and the only significant event occurred when I ran into my roommate Captain Vlastoff on the 519th compound one afternoon. It was totally unexpected as I learned that he was one of the Operations Officers attached to the unit. Apparently, he had known who I was even though our paths hadn't crossed since I found his freshly-screwed girlfriend in my bed.

We engaged in a very brief innocuous conversation before I broke it off and headed back to the Commandament where I told Gunner of my meeting with Captain Vlastoff. He said that the guys on the base had already talked about him and what a big dipshit he was. I wholly concurred with their assessment. I very rarely take an immediate dislike to a person, but I had to make an exception in his case. Militarily, he didn't fit the mold and whoever promoted him to Captain must have been related to him. He was that kind of an individual, the proverbial square peg in a round hole. Oh well, I could live with it as long as I didn't have to socialize with the jerk and knowing that there was always the option of moving in Tuyet.

Changing the subject, Gunner asked me if I had any plans for Thanksgiving and if I didn't, he'd invite me for dinner at the Plaza BEQ. "They always put on a good feed and I don't feel like eating American food alone, so what do you say?"

I replied that no, I didn't have any plans and that I'd be honored to accompany him for a good turkey dinner.

The next afternoon, we arrived at the Plaza Bachelor Enlisted Quarters and made our way into the spacious cafeteria. The pleasant aroma of the freshly prepared food kick-started our salivary glands and we were ready to dig in. Standing in line with trays in hand, we made good time up to the serving counters.

On top of the chrome and glass covers over the steam tables sat two succulent roasted turkeys. The birds were prominently displayed at each end of the counter and reminded me of the famous Norman Rockwell painting of a family Thanksgiving Dinner.

As we finally made it to the turkey server, much to my chagrin I noticed that she was doling out processed turkey roll instead of the usual breasts, drumsticks and thighs. From that point on, I moved like an automaton as the servers heaped my tray full of stuffing, yams, cranberry sauce, baked ham slices, apple pie and ice cream.

Gunner led me to an open table in the rear and said angrily, "This is a severe case of quantity as opposed to quality. Just wait till I confront the mess sergeant about this crap and I'll bet dollars to piasters that the fuckin' kitchen help get to eat the real turkeys."

You're probably right, but what the hell, it beats C-Rats and Vietnamese Catfish, so let's try to enjoy it anyway."

On the road back, I noticed that Gunner was awfully quiet which for him was out of character. "Is something bothering you Chief?" I asked casting a sidelong glance at him.

"Well as a matter of fact, there is something and I've been trying to figure out a way to broach it," he said.

"I never met a Chief yet who couldn't spit out what's on his mind," I said good-naturedly.

"Yeah, I know, but this is different. Well, here goes anyway; I've been offered a billet with the Personal Response folks. They said that I'd be the perfect guy to meet the incoming ships and give them the cultural briefing. This way, they'd have someone with considerable in-country experience and who is able to answer any questions thrown at him. To be honest, since things have quieted down on the river, it's gotten pretty dull. I'll definitely miss our times together, but we can still get to see each other whenever you're in town."

"Wow that came out of left field Gunner. But, I respect your wishes and I can understand the lack of excitement after all your time in Vietnam. Does LCDR Richards go along with this and when did you figure on leaving?"

Lieutenant Dorsey from Personal Response spoke to him about it a week ago and he said it was OK as long as we had a relief for me. When I got to speak to Richards, the first thing he wanted to know was if everything was OK between us. I told him that things couldn't be better and then I leveled with him about Ann and my wanting to spend more time with the family. "The good news is that I found just the guy to take my place, Boatswains Mate First Class Montoya. He recently came to the PsyOps people and is chompin' at the bit to get into the RAGs. Naturally you will have the last word and if you agree, then it could happen ASAP."

PART ELEVEN

CHANGING OF THE GUARD

The next morning, Gunner and I drove directly to VNN Headquarters where I would get a chance to meet my prospective new assistant. I pulled up in front of the PsyOps office and Gunner jumped out and went inside. A few moments later he came out followed by a smiling, broad shouldered individual sporting a beautiful waxed mustache that reminded me of Salvador Dali, the late surrealist painter. BM1 Juan Montoya was about 5 foot eight, with a 38 inch waist, an 18 inch neck and a barrel chest that must have measured close to 56 inches. His green sleeves were folded up and strained around his massive biceps. Under his fatigue cap, his hair was black and closely cropped giving him a professional wrestler's appearance. The most noticeable feature however was his eyes; they were alive and seemed to light up as he stepped forward to meet me. As Gunner made the introductions, my hand disappeared in his calloused grip and I took an immediate liking to the man.

"Well Boats," I said, "What makes you want to be a River-Rat?"

Looking me straight in the eyes he said, "I had no idea where they were going to put me in until I got here. If I wanted to hand out goodies and PsyWar pamphlets, I would rather have worked in the

Charleston Commissary and stayed at home. I'm just not cut out for paperwork and I need activity to keep me busy."

"I can relate to that as I'm sure Senior Chief has already told you of my struggle to get here."

"He did, and that's why I'm sure that you can understand why I'd like to serve with you."

"It seems that you and I are cut from the same cloth Boats and because I put a great deal of faith in Gunner's instincts, it's OK with me. Let's do it."

"I promise that you won't be sorry and you can call me Poncho. My old Minesweeping crew hung the title of 'Poncho the Honcho' on me because we had no Division Officer and I was senior man in charge of the Deck Force."

"Poncho it is then. Let's go over to 3rd Riverine and tell the boss that it's a done deal so we can get on with this war."

As the three of us entered LCDR Richards' office he looked up from behind his desk and said, "I can see by your faces that you guys are OK with the switch."

"Yes sir," I replied. "Actually, I prefer keeping the both of them, but since it's not feasible, Montoya will do just fine."

As we departed the 3rd Riverine compound with Poncho in the back seat, I asked Gunner if he wanted a lift to his pad now that the relief was official.

"No," he replied. "If it's not going to be a problem, I'd like to go back to Binh Loi and make tonight's patrol with the both of you. This way, I can introduce Boats and say my goodbyes to Gia and the rest of the crew."

"That sounds like a good thing to do, especially since the crew had really taken to you," I said. Although Poncho was sitting quietly in the back, I could see in the rear view mirror that he was bursting at the seams with anticipation. Yes, I thought to myself, this is going to work out.

As the Commandament made its way effortlessly upriver, the usual soft chatter was absent after I explained to Gia and Dinh that Gunner was being relieved because his expertise and in-country experience was needed elsewhere within the Advisory Group. Poncho sat back quietly trying to fathom what the lack of conversation signified for his future. The Vietnamese probably had never before met an American whose mere presence exuded such physical strength. The silence was reminiscent of a loved one's funeral where everyone sat around the casket quietly thinking private thoughts and their own personal loss.

The return trip was a carbon copy of the one upriver with the exception that Gia spent more time conversing with Poncho in order to put him more at ease. I had no doubts that the crew would also eventually rally around the new assistant once they got over the departure of their beloved *Thuong Si* Shipp. After we finally moored for the night by the bridge abutment, Gia and Dinh excused themselves and went below to hit the sack. The three of us remained topside well into the wee morning hours quietly conversing about nothing in particular and listened to the occasional thump of the concussion grenades.

As the first rays of light crept skyward out of the east, the surrounding riverbanks slowly awakened to the chirps and calls of the myriads of birds nested in the foliage. As is common among shipmates the world over, time passed rapidly as we enjoyed each other's company and the quiet desultory conversation. Poncho said that he would remain aboard while I drove Gunner back to Saigon.

I dropped him off at Ann's and then went to my BOQ to shower and change clothes. Again, I was fortunate that my very obnoxious roommate was nowhere around, which made my shower more enjoyable.

During the following weeks, Poncho's integration into the unit went as I had predicted. He stayed aboard every night and took advantage of the First Sergeant Greer's generous offer to let us use his shower facilities. No matter what chores the crew would be involved in, he was there lending a hand and in many cases instructed them how to do the job better and easier. The mutual admiration between the crew and Poncho continued and strengthened as the days passed by.

I had stopped visiting the Golden Dragon when I came to the realization that monopolizing Tuyet's time at work severely cut into her earnings. Instead, I started taking her up to the Rex every Saturday where we watched the late afternoon movie. On Sundays we would sometimes go to the Zoo or out to "The Deer in the Woods" restaurant in Thu Duc.

Before we realized it, Christmas and New Years were upon us. The Holidays provided no break in routine for us on the river, whereas office workers and American troops on their bases got to celebrate. They had Christmas trees and decorations, with special Holiday meals and church services for those so inclined. Manning was scaled down to skeleton crews as they tried to forget for a few days where they were and why they were here. It was during this time that Tuyet and I finally agreed to move in together. She assured me that she would find us a suitable place.

It was early Monday morning when I arrived at Binh Loi only to find the Monitor on the other side of the bridge and Poncho on the top deck. He was working alongside a couple of crewmembers resetting the large hyperlon canvas awning. The sweat had already drenched his back and chest and his body literally glistened in the morning sunlight. One of Poncho's particular features that attracted the crew was the two beautiful Bluebirds tattooed on each side of his massive chest. They were a work of art I had to admit and that comes from someone who has never had one on his body. I came very close on two occasions in my naval career, but never succeeded in going through with it.

Wiping the perspiration from his brow, Poncho looked up at me and said, "We're heading over to Cat Lai for a sweep op with the ARVNs tomorrow morning on an island in the Soi Rap. We got the word last night from Radioman 2nd Class Bo Tanner, our new Navy Liaison Rep at District whose call sign is 'Blue Boy 1.' The XO will take the Commandament up to Phu Cuong along with two of the FOMs for tonight's patrol. It looks like we'll only need four of our LCVPs to carry the troops since the latest Intel reported only some small units in that area. Two of our other FOMs will join us in Cat Lai."

When I finally confided to Poncho about my decision to move in with Tuyet, whom he had already met and approved of, he said, "It's about damned time partner because you sure look like you could use some good female company on a steady basis."

"What, are you some kind of psychoanalyst now?" I asked with a grin.

"Darned straight, it ain't natural to go around hoarding all that semen in your testicles either. It'll put a crimp in your walk," he said seriously.

Later, as Gia came from down below, he looked well rested and eager to get on with the operation. Although our nightly patrols served a distinct purpose of denying the enemy an incursion into the city, Gia lived for any opportunity to have physical contact with them.

As Poncho put the finishing touches on the awning, Gia nodded his head towards him and gave me a smiling wink. I returned the smile and that's when I knew that nothing had changed in our relationship with regards to Gunner's departure.

While we were talking, an American Army Captain dressed in Tiger Stripe cammies called down to us from the bridge and asked if he could come aboard. Gia didn't hesitate as he nodded and waved him down.

"Hi, I'm Captain Greg Malko, the XO of the Advisory Team attached to the 2nd Vietnamese Ranger Battalion. We just relieved the Airborne guys just up the road from the bridge so I thought I'd better come over and get acquainted with y'all."

Malko was about my size, with short light brown hair showing from under his maroon beret and I put his age at about 25. He appeared to be in superb physical condition, as one would expect from a Ranger. On his left shoulder, he wore the distinctive patch of the Vietnamese 2nd Ranger Battalion, which depicted an enraged black water buffalo. That came about some years back when the VC tangled with a bunch of these Rangers who proceeded to kick their butts even though they were outnumbered 2 to 1. The VC later said that those soldiers fought like crazed water buffalo, thereby branding them forever to be known as "*Con Trau Dien.*"

I introduced Gia and Poncho to the Captain and said that I was surprised that the Airborne detachment had been relieved so soon.

"Ah, it's all politics. We never know from one day to the next where they're going to send us, but it doesn't matter as long as we get to tangle with the bad guys. Before the Airborne guys left, they passed on your map overlay that you had given to the Marine Advisors. I think it's a pretty clever idea."

"I'm happy to hear that it's still around and viable until we say otherwise. You'll have to give us your call sign on the net. Ours is 'Crazy Racer 8' until the end of the month then it will change to 'Thirsty Boats 4.'"

"Thanks, I'll put that in my notebook so I don't forget. Ours as of now is 'Black Bovine 2.' Well, I'd better be getting back."

"We appreciate your coming over and we'll probably get to see you at the 519th compound for a couple of beers after we return. We're heading for an op with the ARVN out of Cat Lai and we'll be back in a couple of days."

"Oh man, good luck with those guys. Whatever you do, don't let them get behind you."

"Don't worry, we won't. They have a nasty habit of pulling a disappearing act at the darndest times," I replied.

"Ah, I see you're familiar with them, especially those without Advisors assigned to their units. You can always tell by the way they lag behind," he said as he climbed over to the abutment.

The minute the Captain had made it safely onto the bridge, Gia ordered the Monitor's crew to get underway. On the way downriver towards our rendezvous at Cat Lai, Poncho spent some time familiarizing himself with the Monitor. When he finished, he came up to me and said, "Man this is one serious kind of boat but I don't particularly care for the sleeping compartment. It reminds me of a vertical sewer culvert."

"Absolutely, and you'll never see either me or Gia sleep in there even though there's plenty of room inside that 15 foot diameter cylinder."

"How come, you guys claustrophobic?"

"It's not that so much as it is if 'Charlie' hits us with a B-40 rocket armor piercing round, it doesn't explode until it penetrates the plating. Then anything inside is turned into instant tapioca, so we consider it healthier to sleep topside in the open. God forbid if we do get hit, the blast would throw us up and out into the water rather than slamming us against a half inch thick steel bulkhead."

"Whew! I'm sure glad you explained that to me because I would have never thought of it."

The trip to Cat Lai was pleasant and peaceful with the exception of a short rain squall that inundated everything in its path. The minute it passed, a blazing sun broke through the overcast and caused steam to rise from the river's surface.

Our other two FOMs were already tied up and the crews began smiling and waving at us as we made our approach to the pier. Once we were snugged up securely and the engines shut down, I made the suggestion to Gia that the three of us go over to the little shop and get some iced coffee. He smiled as he nodded and uttered his familiar '*Chung Ta Di,*' or "Let's go!"

Even before we sat down, little one-legged Vu came flying out to greet us with a grin as wide as a pumpkin's. I explained to Poncho how Vu lost his leg and his siblings and I could swear that I saw his eyes misting up.

"Damn, what a cross to hang on a good looking little kid like that," he said sadly.

"Yeah that's true, but you've got to hand it to him; he's a little trooper and it's not going to hold him back any."

Gia sat back and said softly, "It's unfortunate and there will be many more like him before this war is over."

After a good night's sleep under our respective mosquito nets topside aboard the Monitor, the three of us awoke refreshed as dawn's first rays began leeching into the fading black night sky. I had fallen asleep easily listening to the flocks of night birds softly chittering in the safety of their tree branches.

There was one thing that I had failed to mention about Boats' unique sleeping habits. When he would finally get into the deepest part of his sleep, he would erupt with a loud cacophony of grunts, snores, whistles and an occasional fart that I had ever heard. Never before had I encountered such consistency and quasi-melodic snoring for such long periods of time as I had painfully experienced with Poncho. Fortunately, we had come to a gentleman's agreement after the first night that he would stay awake until I had fallen asleep. Now that's a buddy for you in anyone's book.

After stowing our sleeping gear, Gia suggested that we should get some breakfast before the ARVN arrived, to which Poncho and I heartily agreed. We made it over to the coffee shop, but this time there was no Vu to greet us. His mother, who came out to serve us, said that the little guy was still in bed sound asleep.

Our breakfast fare consisted of a hot golden scrambled egg sandwich on toasted French bread along with a large cup of dark freshly roasted coffee liberally laced with condensed milk. The meal couldn't have lasted more than a half hour because we were anticipating an early arrival of the troops, which we should have known better. We were already back aboard the Monitor and the four LCVPs were standing by as the first glimpse of the two columns of lethargically shuffling troops made their way onto the pier . . . forty minutes late. It took another hour before all the boats were loaded and underway for our objective of Soi Rap Island which lay about 10 kilometers to the north of Cat Lai.

The two FOMs went ahead to position themselves as a blocking force on the far side of the island, while we in the Monitor led the flotilla of LCVPs to the landing site on the western side of the island.

The landing and off-loading of troops had all the appearance of Jews being herded into the concentration camps by the Nazis. Not only were they a bedraggled group, but some of them started making preparations to heat their rice once they set foot on dry land. It took a considerable amount of cursing and pushing by their noncoms to get them on their feet and moving inland. While this fiasco was going on, Poncho, who had been standing by the port side, spotted a large water snake swimming towards the landing area. As he grabbed his M-16 and was taking aim at the serpent, an ARVN Captain who had been with us overseeing the operation from atop the Monitor, pushed the gun barrel down while harshly hissing in English to Poncho that a shot would warn the VC of our presence. Poncho gave the officer his most menacing look as he said derisively, "Are you shitting me? The fuckin' VC knew you were coming before you ever set foot on the island and if you don't give a rat's ass whether one of your guys gets bit by a snake, then I don't either."

Visibly shaken by Poncho's outburst and disrespect towards an officer, the Captain beat a hasty retreat and joined his troops ashore. Gia ordered the landing craft to back off of the beach immediately. "If we leave the boats there, some of the ARVN will inevitably try to re-board. These people are a big embarrassment and fortunately not the norm of our other fighting services."

"We already know that, *Thieu-Ta*. There's not much that you can do about it, so don't let it get you down."

"I know and thank you. It's just that it gets me so angry at the ones who don't care enough to fight for their own country."

"Hey, we've got the very same thing back in the States with all those pot-smoking, lazy unwashed, longhaired, unshaved hippies who wear dirty underwear," said Poncho.

"Ah yes, I've seen pictures of them on the television and it is most disturbing. I cannot understand how anyone living in the United States does not jump at the opportunity to defend one's way of life. Your founding fathers were very good examples of that," opined Gia.

"My solution is simple," said Poncho. "If you don't like the country and you're not willing to put your life on the line for it, then get your ass the hell out. Go someplace else in the world and keep a low profile while you're smoking your dope."

"I'll second that," I replied. "Man, it does one good to vent once in awhile, don't it Boats?"

During the next three hours, not a gunshot was heard from the ARVN that we hoped were making their way to the other end of the island. A radio call from one of the FOMs let us know that the first of the troops were making their way to the beach and were obviously calling it a day. They were flopping to the ground and started to eat the rice from the plastic bags that they kept under their arms to keep it warm.

Gia ordered the landing craft to change places with the FOMs on the far side of the island so the troops could once again embark for the return trip to Cat Lai. All in all, another good exercise in futility by the master planners in Saigon.

We returned to Cat Lai and unloaded the "battle fatigued" troops without any further ado as Gia decided to moor the Monitor alongside the pier for the night. The three of us went ashore and ate steaming hot bowls of chicken pho soup and from there we returned aboard and turned in for the night. Although we hadn't done any strenuous physical work, the sheer frustration of the day's wasted operation allowed sleep to quickly envelope us.

A SAILOR'S TALE

Bright and early the next morning we undocked and headed back to Binh Loi. During the trip, Poncho and I were sitting topside while Gia was below-decks filling out his operational report to the Third Riverine Commander. "Hey Boats," I asked, "Where are you from in the States?"

"New Mexico, but I'm not sure if that is where I originated."

"What do you mean?"

"I was abandoned by my biological mother when I was about a month or so old. The family that raised me found me by the side of a dirt road in the southern part of the state wrapped in a dirty old blanket inside a cardboard box. The guy who found me was a

Montoya and he must have had some serious pull with someone because he managed to get me a birth certificate and a social security card. The rest is history."

"Wow, you must have had a Fairy Godmother watching over you."

"I don't know about a Fairy Godmother, but I had an uncle I wasn't too sure about."

"Huh?" I asked laughingly.

"Well, I had eight uncles from my adoptive parents and one of them was rumored to be gay although they never told me which one. However, when I was between the ages of three and four, my Dad instructed me to always look at him when a visiting uncle would ask lil' Juanito here to come sit on his lap. If my Dad smiled, it was OK but if he closed his eyes and looked down, I was to come to him instead. It took awhile, but I finally found out it was my mother's younger brother. He eventually got beaten to death some years later in a bar outside of Las Cruces."

"Boy, you carry some history. What made you join the Navy?"

"I got tired of working under the hot sun in the fields and wanted to see the world."

"And here you are."

"And it's exactly where I want to be," he said matter-of-factly. "Man, I'm sure glad you gave me the chance to get out of that PsyOps office. There was one squirrely LTJG by the name of Dawson who came up with the bright idea to put loudspeakers on all the RAG boats so that they could play a recording while on patrol inviting the VC to *Chieu Hoi*. When he presented his idea to Third Riverine HQ, the boss said that it was entirely up to the unit commanders."

"I've met the gent. He came aboard about a month ago and made his pitch. When he finished, I remember word for word what Gunner said to him."

"With all due respect, *Trung Uy*, asking us to go upriver with those loudspeakers blaring would be the same as driving a 'Good Humor' Ice Cream truck with bells a-ringing through East Los Angeles on a hot evening in July. It would be just a matter of time before the natives would come down and pick you clean."

"And besides," I added, "my counterpart wouldn't go for it . . . Trust me. Our job is to exterminate not negotiate. How many other groups have you approached?"

"Four," he answered softly

"And how many takers did you get?"

"None," he mumbled.

"There you go my friend. You get an 'A' for trying. Why don't we just let the flyboys keep on dropping those pretty pamphlets on the VC from the sky? They'll read them first then later use them for toilet paper in the bush and everyone will be happy."

With that, he sullenly disembarked and we were polite enough to let him get out of earshot before we cracked up laughing.

"Speaking of squirrels in PsyOps, whatever became of Chief Dozier? I heard he already had a wife back in Georgia but wanted to replace her with this young little thing from Saigon."

"Yeah, he'd go around soliciting the single guys who were getting ready to rotate home. He offered them 500 bucks if they would take out marriage papers with his girlfriend, take her to the States where he would pay for the divorce and give the guy another 500. But he never got any takers because no one could figure out where she would stay until he got home."

"YOU CAN'T REGISTER HER AS A WAR TROPHY!"

"I met her once at a beer-bash and I wasn't impressed. She had that high pitched voice that just gets under my skin. I found that these types of Vietnamese women are troublesome and whenever I run into one, I reverse course and move out smartly."

"Rumor has it," said Poncho, "that he is ditching his wife and plans on taking an extended leave so he can come back and take her out himself."

"I sure hope he knows what he's doing, but then again, he wasn't the brightest bulb in the marquee."

We finally arrived at the Binh Loi Bridge a little after noon. Boats and I disembarked and made our way on foot around to the 519th compound entrance. Since Dinh already had the Commandament moored to the stubby pilings on the riverbank, Gia said that he would be gone for awhile and headed out in his Jeep. Poncho and I decided to go up to the club and grab a few beers and a sandwich before returning aboard. Actually, we had planned on maybe taking a little nap onboard prior to tonight's patrol.

That evening when Gia returned, he announced to us that he had been promoted to Commander, along with his classmates Rac and Minh. I for one was pleased because if any one deserved a promotion it was these three men. XO Dinh then piped up merrily, "Now we'll have to have what you Americans call a 'Wetting Down' party."

It was still in that elated spirit of camaraderie that we got underway later that night for our patrol upriver. The few hours rest had done wonders for me and Poncho,

On the return trip downriver, Gia got me aside and said he had something to ask me and that he wasn't sure how to go about it. I told him to just let it out, whatever it was, hoping that I hadn't screwed up somewhere to his displeasure. Instead, he asked if I could lend him 80 dollars in military scrip so he could purchase the fare for his promotion party. Relieved, I told him that it was a done deal and that he could count on me for whatever he needed. Visibly moved and a little embarrassed, he shook my hand profusely. That was when I knew that I would definitely go to the wall for this man anywhere, anytime. The rest of the trip passed in silence and it was obvious that a great weight had been lifted from Gia's shoulders.

I never told Poncho about Gia's borrowing money because I felt it was prudent to maintain the CO's dignity and keep it between the two of us.

AN UNFORGETABLE EXPERIENCE

The next morning I took the Jeep and headed back to Saigon because Poncho said he would rather stay aboard. On the way back, I stopped at a little roadside shop in Gia Dinh and had a hot cup of coffee and a buttered croissant that really hit the spot. From there, it was straight through until I pulled into the BOQ.

I can only recall one thing about the shower that I had taken; it was long and extremely invigorating. The hot water loosened up my tightened back muscles and made shaving my two day stubble considerably easier.

I had just finished brushing my teeth when I heard a light rap on my door. I hurriedly wrapped a bath towel around my waist wondering who it could be because the maid had already made up the room. As I opened the door, I was surprised to see Therese the desk girl standing there. She was wearing a white cotton short sleeved shirt with a flared collar, pressed khaki pants and comfortable looking brown pumps.

"I wasn't at the desk when you arrived so I didn't know you were back until I saw your Jeep parked in the yard. I hope I am not bothering you," she said softly.

"No, as a matter of fact I just finished showering after a long night on the river. Is there something I can do for you?" I asked feeling a little self-conscious standing there in my towel.

"Yesterday a young lady left this envelope for you and I thought it better to deliver it in person rather than leave it down at the desk where it could get lost."

"Why thank you," I said as I took the white envelope.

After a slight pause, she asked quietly if it was all right for her to come in. Somewhat taken by surprise, considering that I was standing in the doorway practically naked except for the towel, I opened the door wider and let her in. She entered the room practically gliding over the floor and sat demurely on my roommate's bed. I placed the envelope on my dresser and sat down opposite her on my bed trying to keep the towel from opening.

Again, there was that awkward silence between us until she came over and stood between my legs, taking my head gently in her hands and pulled it to her bosom. I instinctively wrapped my arms around her hips and cradled her small buttocks in my hands while squeezing gently.

I couldn't believe this was happening as I breathed in the clean fragrance of her body. By this time my faithful and long time companion "peter" poked his head out between the folds of the towel and had hardened to the point where a flock of starving woodpeckers would have avoided contact at all costs. Feeling the pressure against her knees, she gently pushed me down onto the bed as she slipped off her shoes. With my head on the pillow and my mind racing at a million miles an hour, she knelt on the foot of the bed and gently took "him" in her left hand. With the other she gathered her lovely black hair and tossed it back over her shoulder.

She began by placing soft kisses on the sides and at its base, alternating with feathery flicks of her tongue that were as soft as a butterfly's wings. All the while, I was frantically trying to concentrate my mind elsewhere . . . . anywhere but here. I came to the conclusion that these young ladies, who attended the Marie Curie School for

Girls and had an affectation for taking on new French first names, might also have been schooled in the erotic arts as part of the curriculum. A pleasant thought to ponder considering what was presently going on here.

Back to reality, Therese was doing things to my buddy that had never been done to him before and she was definitely raising the art of fellatio to a new level. Each time that she sensed I was about to explode as she slowly slid her warm soft lips up and down its length, she applied pressure to the underside of his base and postponed the inevitable. I always had the opinion that most women would rather masturbate the man frantically while just barely encircling the head of the penis with their mouth in order to speed up the process. They most likely thought that although the act itself was repugnant, it would eventually lead to the roles being reversed and turn the man into the oral performer.

Finally, after what seemed an eternity while never breaking rhythm, she let nature take its course and I erupted like Mount Etna. I never dreamt that there were so many colored lights and shooting stars in my room as I watched her sit back up. Her cheeks were puffed out as she obviously had a mouthful of my semen and was looking for a place to deposit it. I told her softly that it was safe to swallow because it was pure protein and good for her eyes, hair and complexion. Not knowing whether to believe me or not, she bravely swallowed it and then kissed me with a ferocity built entirely out of passion.

Before I could take hold of her, she quickly disengaged and went into the bathroom where she rinsed her mouth out with water from the sink. I was grateful that she didn't go and retch into the toilet bowl which would have put a sad ending to something that seemed so perfectly natural and mind-boggling.

I wish I could have done something for you," I said in all honesty as she wiped her face and hands with a towel.

"Perhaps you will get your chance *Dai Uy*, but not this week because I am fertile. The last thing I need is a baby which my husband Anh, who is a Marine Captain, would not much appreciate since he has been on the Cambodian border near Tay Ninh for almost a year now. I knew when we first met that you were sensitive and would not be the type to forcefully take that which was not freely offered. That is why I came to you as I did and hope as a gentleman you can accept it and understand."

She was out the door and gone before I could fully realize what had just taken place. Nothing like this had ever happened to me back home and it merely reinforced my desire to remain here in Vietnam as long as possible.

Finally after a few nostalgic moments of reliving what had just transpired, I remembered the envelope on the dresser. It was from Tuyet and in it she said that she had quit her job at the Golden Dragon and was now working in her uncle's soup shop on Phan Thanh Gian near the circle at Petrus Ky. She said that he had agreed to let us use the small apartment over the shop as long as she worked as a cashier and could fill in for him and his wife occasionally watching the place.

I sat back on the bed and started thinking that moving in with Tuyet wasn't such a bad idea. We had been close friends from the moment we met and although we had never been intimate, I didn't think that it would present any problems. The physical attraction was definitely there and thinking back to Poncho's sage advice, I could use a steady and trusted bed partner that would put an end to the endless game of "VD Roulette" that was played with each sexual encounter.

Having finally made up my mind at this point anyway, I checked the address of the soup shop in the letter and put it in my pocket. Once back in the Jeep, I headed over to the small PX at the Meyerkord BOQ to pick up some toothpaste and mouth wash. While there, I noticed some posters announcing that there would be a "Happy Hour" tomorrow in the courtyard and Martha Raye would be there with some of her USO troupe. Since I had briefly met the actress/comedienne several years ago, I thought I would bring Poncho along to give him a break in his routine.

Arriving back at Binh Loi, I found him sitting topside at the 519th club with his meaty hand holding a large Rum 'n Coke and the remnants of a hamburger and fries in front of him. He was surprised to see me as I pulled up a chair and joined him. It was after one in the afternoon and all the Army guys were back at work or whatever they did on this base.

I related my experience with Therese as he sat there speechless and his eyes wide open with awe. When I finished, not having omitted anything, he finally said, "And she swallowed it too after you told her it was good for her skin, eyes and hair?"

"Absolutely Mate, I couldn't think of anything else to say."

"Man, that's beautiful and here I've been sitting all by my lonesome ogling two skinny waitresses."

"Oh your day will come, I firmly believe that," I said and then told him about Happy Hour at the Meyerkord tomorrow with Martha Raye.

"Sounds good to me, but that's an officer's billet and I'm just a lowly enlisted. How do I get in?"

"You will come as my guest. Remember, you and I are not 'Saigon Warriors' and that has to count for something, right?"

The patrol that evening to Phu Cuong and back went by uneventfully with XO Dinh in command. He said that Gia had stayed in Saigon to make the preparations for his party this coming Saturday and all the officers were excited.

The next day as we pulled into the Le Qui Don's courtyard, Therese was standing in the office doorway. She was wearing a pale lime green Ao Dai with black pants and one hand resting on her hip as she leaned casually against the doorframe. Her head was cocked to one side and there was a slight smile on her face as she looked directly at me and said, "Good morning gentlemen."

Before I could reply, Poncho said, "Good morning to you lovely lady. I've never seen you lookin' prettier, your hair's so shiny, your eyes are bright and your skin is gorgeous. What have you been doing to yourself?"

Obviously flustered, a slight tinge of crimson colored her face as Therese stood there speechless. I immediately nodded my head to her and said softly getting out of the Jeep, "I told you so," as she quickly turned and disappeared into the office.

Having changed clothes, I returned to the Jeep where Poncho was still sitting behind the wheel as he said, "She never did come back out Boss. I'll say it again man, you're one lucky sum'bitch," as he started the engine and we departed for the Meyerkord.

COLONEL "MAGGIE"

We lucked out by finding a parking spot underneath a massive Beech tree that was close to the entrance and keep the sun off our vehicle. The Meyerkord provided billeting for transiting military officers, government personnel and USO touring troupes arriving in-country. Today there was the usual number of people wandering in and out of the PX as well as the other shops that composed the little mall. We walked straight through to the rear of the building that opened up to a large area that housed twenty to twenty five patio tables. Each had an opened umbrella in its center to provide shade and there appeared to be about 40 mixed military and civilians happily enjoying their cool drinks.

Poncho and I found an empty table slightly off to the side but still close to the building as a young Vietnamese waitress promptly appeared to take our order. Boats opted for a beer but I was in the mood for a spicy Bloody Mary. Our drinks appeared in short order and I was surprised to find that my Bloody Mary was garnished with a large stalk of celery in it.

"Now I know why you ordered that pussy-drink," said Poncho. "You just wanted something to eat with your booze."

"You're too observant my friend. It's a habit I picked up at the Green Anchors in the Coronado BOQ where we had Rum Cokes with Queen Anne olives in them. Hell, a guy's got to eat sometime, right?"

"It must be an officer thing," he said shaking his head.

Just about then, a group of young ladies, who all appeared to be in their very early twenties, came out of the building led by Martha Raye. The girls were decked out in various colored shorts and USO emblazoned "T" shirts, while Martha was wearing a white cotton blouse open at the neck, tailored khaki slacks and a gleaming pair of paratroop boots on her feet. Everyone stood up immediately and gave them a rousing round of applause. She still looked good even after all these years of entertaining the troops during the Second World War, Korea and now Vietnam.

As the girls proceeded to mingle among the tables, Martha stood her ground and was taking everything in. Just as her gaze came towards us, I made eye contact and waved to her. This obviously piqued her curiosity and as she made her way over to our table, Poncho and I stood, saluted and said, "Good afternoon Colonel, would you care to join us?"

"Have we met somewhere before?" she asked looking me straight in the eye and returning our salute prior to sitting down.

"As a matter of fact we have, but I was a young teenager then and I doubt if you'd remember. My cousin's husband was related to your husband Nick Condos and we were allowed to come backstage after the show one night at the Copacabana in New York to meet you. Since you were the first famous personality that I had ever met, I was awestruck by the way you so graciously received us."

"Yes, I vaguely remember that evening. Good old Nick, when he and I first met I thought he was a damned Greek God and then after our marriage, I found out that he was just another Goddamn Greek. I'm joking of course because he was one passionate man, so much so in fact that I physically didn't know which way to turn."

Since I had heard that phrase numerous times before in my life, I feigned ignorance and let it slide by, although I could see she knew that I had caught its meaning. What an astute women.

After asking where we were from and what we did in Vietnam, she allowed us to order her a can of ginger ale. When it arrived, she admitted that she'd much prefer hard liquor but because she had consumed so much alcohol prior to her flight in from Guam to ease her fear of flying, it was time to give her body a rest.

"In fact just last night as I was getting into bed, there was a soft knock on my door. Who's there?" I asked.

A voice said softly, "I'm Major _______ with a chilled bottle of Mateus wine and I was hoping . . ."

"You were hoping that the wine would help you get into my pants. Well, you're too late Major because there's one asshole in them already, so go to bed—and that's an order."

With that, Poncho almost had a heart attack holding back his laughter and trying to keep the beer from gushing out his nose. Only Martha Raye could have pulled that one off so neatly.

She then stood up and said seriously that she'd better make the rounds of the other tables and check up on her girls.

As Poncho and I rose to our feet, she gave us each a warm hug and a kiss on the cheek saying, "Stay safe guys and thanks for the job you're doing."

I waited until Martha was a few tables away before I began to explain to Poncho that her husband at that time was Nick Condos. He and his brother Steve made up the Condos Brothers Dancing Team and had made several films at Fox where they were a personal favorite of its vice-president Darryl F. Zanuck. They were considered highly exceptional at a time most of the dance groups in Hollywood were colored. After their divorce, Nick stayed on as Martha's business manager

(Author's note: Martha Raye died in 1994 at the age of 78 and was buried with full military honors in the Special Forces Cemetery at Fort Bragg, North Carolina. Sleep well Colonel Maggie, you're in damned good company.)

COHABITATION

We sat alone at the table until we had both finished our drinks, which by the way, the celery stalk had hit the spot. I told Poncho that I wanted to swing by Tuyet's uncle's place and take a look before returning to Binh Loi and he said that he was fine with that.

Locating the shop was easy as it was the only eatery in the area and about half of its eight marble-topped tables were occupied by patrons happily shoveling noodles and soup into their mouths with flashing chopsticks and ceramic spoons. Upon seeing us, Tuyet quickly came to greet us from behind the counter, her entire face lit up in a big smile. She led us into the shop and introduced us to her uncle Dung Nam and his wife Co Bay, (pronounced Yoong Nam and Co Buy). We shook hands as Tuyet explained that the aunt was her mother's younger sister.

Nam was of typical Vietnamese height, in his early fifties, deeply tanned with a longish face, tobacco stained teeth and a shock of unruly white hair that stood up on his head. His most noticeable attribute was his perpetual grin and sparkling eyes. His wife, on the other hand appeared to be in her mid-thirties, plain but not unattractive with black hair streaked with gray and tucked in a bun.

Poncho and the uncle hit it off immediately, especially after Dung Nam made him sit down and brought him a big steaming bowl of beef noodle soup. No doubt, this man was destined to become a successful entrepreneur because he recognized immediately that Poncho was an "eater' and read him perfectly.

Tuyet was eager to show me the room over the shop that was to be ours. Inside the small kitchen area at the rear, there was a wooden staircase off to the right that led up to a 15 x 20 foot room that housed a small bathroom with shower, a double bed and a small dresser and lamp. It was compact, neat and very clean which I would have expected no less from Tuyet. She looked up at me expectantly to see what my reaction would be and was visibly relieved when I smiled and nodded my head in approval. That's when she jumped into my arms and gave me the hardest hug I had ever had.

"I am so ver' happy that you like."

Being the American pragmatist that I am, I asked "What is your uncle asking for the use of this place?"

"He asks nothing other than I work for him and even wants to pay me a part of his profits because he knows a pretty cashier will bring in more customers. This way, I can also send money home to my mother and children. Having someone upstairs at night will provide security for his shop, which means a lot to him."

"In that case, I could also get him an occasional item from the PX or the commissary as long as it doesn't get out of hand."

"Oh Bob, you make me so ver' happy," she said as she gave me another one of those bone-breaking hugs. "Oh, I almost forgot to show you this," she said conspiratorially as she pulled back a sliding panel behind the bed that led to the open latticework ceiling over the shop below. "This is where you must hide in case the National Police ever come to inspect the shop. If they found you, they would think you were here for a 'short-time' and would arrest my uncle or start taking money from him every week."

"Ah, the old extortion game," I said quietly shaking my head.

"And," she continued, "leave your Jeep where it will be safe for the night and come here by Cyclo or Taxi. If it is parked outside the shop, it might get stolen or it could attract the attention of the Police or the QCs." (The QCs were the *Quan Canh*, the Vietnamese version of our Military Police.)

"This is all do-able," I replied as we returned downstairs just in time to see Poncho wipe his face with a paper napkin, put down his chopsticks and pat his stomach in satisfaction. This brought an even larger grin to Dung Nam's face and although he shook his head vigorously when we attempted to settle the tab, Poncho managed to leave 300 piasters folded under the empty bowl.

I told Tuyet as she walked us out to the Jeep that I would spend tomorrow evening with her because we had to return to the boat tonight. In typical Oriental fashion she showed no visible signs of disappointment, instead a smile crinkled her eyes as she lightly blew me a kiss.

"Take good care of the *Dai Uy*," she said to Poncho as we pulled away from the curb.

"Never fear little lady,' he replied as he maneuvered the vehicle into the oncoming traffic and headed for Gia Dinh. "I'll say it again Boss, you're one lucky sum'bitch, you know that?"

That evening's patrol was uneventful until we came abreast of "ambush alley" on our return trip. Although we were pretty well immune to the random pot-shots taken at us from this village, we still kept our heads below the outer shield whenever we came into range to avoid any lucky shots. This night was no different. I had to admire the patience that Gia exhibited with this harassing fire because anyone else would have leveled the place by now.

Just before we turned in for the night and the boat was safely snugged up to the bridge pilings, Gia softly announced from his bunk that the "Wetting Down" party was to be held this Saturday evening at his friend's soup shop in Cholon. He also said that he had made arrangements with two officers from the Third Riverine Staff to handle the patrol that night so all his officers could attend.

The next day being Thursday, it was agreed that Poncho would take the patrol alone tonight while I went and "cohabitated" with Tuyet. I knew that it was a little selfish on my part, but Boats had mentioned that this union was long overdue and he genuinely liked Tuyet. For that matter, I don't think that there were too many people that Poncho didn't like because he was that type of an individual; easy going until you pissed him off, which wasn't often. He reminded me of an old bull elephant gently flapping his ears as he calmly grazed and protected his herd until something set him off. Then his eyes would turn a fiery red and focus directly onto you just before he pummeled your ass into the dirt. Yeah, he was all that and more.

I decided to return to my BOQ to take a little nap, shower and change clothes prior to going to my rendezvous. Before doing that however, I wrote a couple of overdue letters to my mother and friends while sipping a water glass a third full of dark Bacardi "Anejo" Rum that I kept under my nightstand just for medicinal purposes. Boy, was that a kick-start for the ticker.

Normally, you could hear a chestnut fall to the ground in this neighborhood because it was so quiet but the racket from the female students of the Marie Curie School across the street letting out let me know that it was seven o'clock in the evening. Schools in Vietnam were a year round function interrupted only by national and religious holidays. The normal school day commenced at eight in the morning until twelve noon when they left for a three hour lunch and siesta break. Then classes resumed from four until seven pm, six days a week. It was obvious that education was taken seriously in Vietnam.

Rumors had it however, that there was some sexual misconduct occurring regularly at the school between the French teachers of both genders and the matriculating daughters of Saigon's more affluent society. Naturally, the predictable French response to that accusation was a shrugged "*C'est la vie!*" or "That's life!"

There had been no visitors, maids or obnoxious roommates to interfere with my nap, so I had that to be thankful for. I got into my Jeep and drove to the Plaza parking it amidst the other military vehicles out front. I then flagged down a passing Taxi and after checking to see that there were door handles on the inside, hopped in and gave directions to the driver. There had been incidents in the past when a lone GI would get into a cab at night and find himself being driven up a dark alley where he would be beaten, robbed and thrown out into the street. The lack of interior passenger door handles ensured that the victim could not open the door and jump out once he was inside. Happily, this was not the case tonight.

I had the driver let me out on the corner and walked the few dozen yards to the shop. The place was almost full and as I entered and made eye contact with Tuyet behind the counter, I gave her an imperceptible shake of my head to keep her from greeting me. If the name of the game was to bring in more male customers because of the pretty young cashier, then it wouldn't do to let on that she was fraternizing with a "rich American."

Finding an empty table in the back, I sat and ordered a small bowl of rice soup from Nam who had evidently seen my quiet entrance and understood its logic. The place was doing a brisk business and Tuyet looked exceptionally well wearing a saffron yellow cotton blouse, a pair of loose black satin pants and a big smile that made her glow all over. Yes, Nam knew what he was doing when he brought Tuyet into the business. Smart, I told you!

I took my time eating my soup so that the place would empty out a bit and when I motioned Nam over for the bill, he took the money and subtly nodded his head towards the kitchen. When I was certain that no one was interested in me, I got up and made as if I was paying a visit to the toilet in the back and quietly took the stairs two at a time. I had to leave the door ajar in order to find the lamp in the darkened room. The thirty watt bulb cast a soft glow around the walls as I silently closed the door and sat on the bed.

Many people in Vietnam still slept on wooden platforms with no padding which was probably why they had such good posture, but thankfully this bed had a good firm mattress. I once had the misfortune of sleeping on a hard wooden platform bed upon coming to Vietnam and my ensuing backache guaranteed that I would never, ever do that again.

I got out of my clothes and placed them on the nearby chair with my socks in my boots under the bed as I slipped between the crisp smelling sheets. After a few moments, I sat up and took off my tee shirt, opting to keep my standard Navy issue white boxer shorts on so that I wouldn't appear overly horny to Tuyet.

Somewhere along the line, I must have dropped off because the sound of running water in the bathroom sink woke me up. Tuyet was standing there as the light from the bathroom silhouetted her body beneath her satiny pajamas. I watched in fascination as her left breast jiggled back and forth as she vigorously brushed her teeth. Her tiny buttocks were doing their darndest to keep up and it was pure poetry in motion.

Some sixth sense caused her to glance around and she noticed me looking at her.

"I did not mean to wake you up because you were sleeping so peacefully," she said softly.

"It's OK. I must have dozed off, besides I enjoy looking at you."

"Oh, you have never seen a Vietnamese girl brushing her teeth before?" she asked self-consciously.

"Actually I haven't, but you are special," I said.

Slightly embarrassed, she turned off the bathroom light and padded softly over to the bed, picking up a small red and gold satin bag from atop the dresser as she passed. Opening it, she withdrew a carved ivory Buddha encased in 18 carat gold on a fine gold chain. "I had this sent down from the Temple in Da Lat where it was blessed by the most senior Buddhist monk in Vietnam. I would like you to wear it to help keep you safe," she said as she placed it over my head.

Completely at a loss for words, all I could do was hold up the sheet as she quickly slipped in and nestled herself against me under my outstretched arm. Almost immediately, the one-eyed seed-spreader was awakening and attempting to extricate itself from within my standard Navy issue boxer shorts. At the same moment I felt Tuyet's entire body begin to tremble uncontrollably.

Before I could ask her what was wrong, she said almost in tears, "I am sorry. I am so nervous because I have not slept with anyone other than my husband and I so want to please you."

"That's OK," I said softly kissing the top of her head and holding her close. "We have lots of time and I want you to be relaxed so let's both get some sleep," I added just as my loyal erstwhile impaler went limp and allowed the blood to recirculate back into my body.

Sometime during the pre-dawn hours of the morning, I awoke to a familiar sensation. My love muscle had become so engorged, that I was sure there were no wrinkles left on my face as Tuyet was in the process of frantically mounting me. It was obvious that she must have awakened and put her initial misgivings aside as she was butt-naked and hurriedly guiding me into her moist vagina. Even in the subdued light I could see that she had large dark purple aureoles and erect nipples capping her pert pear-shaped breasts. As she bent over me, her long hair hung over my chest hiding her face as she increased her pelvic thrusts at a rate that reminded me of a jockey spurring his mount to the finish line.

And finish she did, with a momentous shudder that wracked her body as she threw her head back and grimaced almost in pain. She stayed in that position for almost thirty seconds as if to enjoy every last sensation and then dropped her head to my chest as her thighs began to shake. I felt the perspiration between her breasts against my chest and could do nothing but let her bask in the moment. I unfortunately did not climax because of the speed and ferocity of her attaining an orgasm and I was all right with that because I understood what it took for her to let go like that. I made up my mind not to tell her that she finished that journey by herself in order to avoid any future bug-a-boos in our sexual relations and with that thought in mind, gently rolled her off me. In seconds, she was nestled against me soundly sleeping.

Knowing that I probably couldn't go back to sleep, I figured that I might just as well head back to the boats. I silently got out of bed, got dressed and before leaving, leaned over and kissed Tuyet lightly on the cheek. She stirred ever so slightly and mumbled, groggily "Please do not think bad of me," and once again immediately fell back to sleep.

"No little one, I don't think badly of you," I whispered as I quietly closed the door and went down the stairs. The shop was empty and dark, so I let myself out locking the door behind me.

Hailing a passing cyclo was no problem and I quickly found myself in front of the Plaza heading for my Jeep. I undid the chained padlock around my steering wheel and checked to see that the lock on my gas tank was intact. A favorite trick of the VC was to tape down the spoon on a hand grenade, pull the pin and drop it into a vehicle's gas tank under the driver's seat. The unsuspecting driver would head on out until the gas disintegrated the tape freeing the spoon. Then "BOOM!"—Another statistic for the bean counters at MACV to include in their daily incident reports to General Abrams who had relieved General Westmoreland.

On the road back to Binh Loi, I couldn't help but wonder just what the hell we were doing here anyway because our enemy was being supplied with arms, ammunition and in-country Advisors by China, Russia and Cuba. With no Navy or Air Force to back them up, the Viet Cong, comprised of many rag-tag guerrilla groups along with their better equipped North Vietnamese Army comrades, proved to be a thorn in the side of the allies.

Whenever there was an attack by an enemy that hit quickly and melted back into the jungle, you could be sure that it was the Viet Cong. The NVA however, would hit you, dig in and slug it out toe to toe because they had trekked laboriously down to the South with orders not to return unless they were victorious. It was the old Spartan Code of "Return with your shield or on it."

Killing another human being up close isn't an easy thing for most people to do and Americans, as a rule shy away from it. I wondered how many split-second decisions to pull the trigger ended in disaster during wartime. Old vets agreed wholeheartedly, "When in doubt, shoot!" At least you'd have a chance to be the last one standing. I thought of this a lot lately when I thought about Khoi and the dead trooper lying on a stretcher in Son Ong Doc. I could only hope that those pictures do not hang over my conscience for the rest of my life.

My blood pressure had probably risen several points due mainly to the thoughts I was having and the frustration I was feeling. Could it be a delayed "Blue-Ball" reaction from not having shared in the climax this morning or was it because of the politicians in Washington who thought that they were better equipped to wage war from afar than our military leaders on the battlefield? Yeah, We had all the support in the world with the exception of course from the one place that mattered most, the people back home. Whatever it was, it was flushed from my mind when I reached Binh Loi.

Although it was only eight o'clock in the morning, I found Poncho topside and shirtless busily field stripping and cleaning both our M-16s. I had stopped carrying mine awhile back, although my snub-nosed .38 accompanied me wherever I went.

He was obviously surprised to see me back so early and had that quizzical look on his face. Before he could say a word, I said that everything had turned out just fine.

The look remained fixed.

"Honest," I said. "It was all I expected and more. You were right again Boats."

That's when he noticed the gold chain and a slow knowing grin began appearing under his waxed mustache. "Ah, I see something new has been added to your dog tags," he said.

"Oh that," I replied meekly. "It's an ivory Buddha from Da Lat that is supposed to protect me from harm."

"The only thing that it will protect you from *compadre* is other Vietnamese girls. Good ol' Tuyet has staked out her claim and by hanging that chain around your neck, it lets all the other females know that you have been spoken for. I guess that answers my question," he said resuming work on the weapons.

"Thanks for titivating my gun too," I said trying to change the subject by using some Boot Camp vernacular all too familiar to a Boatswains Mate.

"No sweat *Dai Uy*. That's the least I could do for a buddy who was busy getting his ashes hauled while I was aboard this floating Dempsy Dumpster."

"Now you're making me feel bad," I replied.

"Nah, I'm only kidding. I'm glad you two finally got around to the sexual part of your relationship," he said as he wiped the oil from his hands with a rag. "Now you can shoot this thing without fear of it blowing your head off."

We started our patrol just after 5 that evening rather than after dark because we were carrying a colored American dressed in greens with no insignias and a Vietnamese Army Colonel who came aboard with Gia.

Gia introduced Poncho and me to them as his Advisors without mentioning their names. He said that they would be riding along on this evening's patrol for some sort of a fact finding mission. It was OK by me because we occasionally had passengers whom we referred to as "straphangers" make the run with us. The important thing as far as I was concerned was for their safety. I had no desire to be responsible for the death or wounding of any VIP on my watch.

We passed "ambush alley" without incident although we took the precaution of telling them to keep their heads down until we safely cleared the area. It was probably not necessary this time because of our early transit, but we would have to be on double alert on the way back.

During the trip up, the American asked intelligent and subtle questions about the patrol area, enemy detection, collaboration with the locals and any significant problems encountered but not reported. I answered as best I could and to my relief, he, Gia and the Vietnamese Colonel appeared satisfied with my responses.

The one positive thing that I pointed out to them was the reopening of an old Pottery factory and the resumption of a sugar cane candy manufacturing site along the upper reaches of the river. Both industries had shut down after TET '69, and I considered it a good sign in the return to normalcy. Hopefully, our unit's presence in the area had contributed to that.

As we approached Lai Thieu, a sudden silence fell over our passengers as we came abreast of the vast area that had been defoliated by Agent Orange. It always seemed surrealistic to me in the daylight because it was black and barren as far as the eye could see. I wondered if Mother Nature would ever be able to recover from such massive destruction of her once lush and vibrant countryside. But war was war and everything supposedly had a reason.

Our passengers surprised us by disembarking at Phu Cuong but not before shaking hands and thanking us for a very informative trip. A US Jeep was waiting at the bridge to meet them and they were whisked away immediately. Gia appeared physically relieved to have gotten rid of them and as we got back underway, said "I think the American was some high ranking government official or a general traveling incognito, as they say in order to see what is going on in the field first hand. By the way, did you notice the West Point ring on his finger?" he asked with a small smile.

I hadn't and Gia's powers of perception continued to amaze me.

We killed about two hours tied up to a span of the Lai Thieu Bridge before returning back down river. During this lull, Gia told us what to expect in the way of food at his party tomorrow night and it only made Poncho and me eager to attend even more.

The pot-shooters at Ambush Alley apparently had taken the night off as we transited their area. Who knows, perhaps they were still sitting around their charcoal fires drinking their rice wine and smoking cigarettes. Whatever the reason, it was OK with us.

Although it was still a bit early when we finally secured for the night under the Binh Loi Bridge, we all decided to turn in because tomorrow night was the "party."

The next morning, Poncho and I strolled over to Baby-san's after we were safely snugged up against the shore side pilings. I had come up with the idea because it had been some time since we had seen him and he made an excellent glass of iced coffee.

His face split wide open with the biggest smile imaginable when he saw us approaching. As we sat down at one of the three outside tin tables, he pulled up a wicker chair to join us as we ordered the coffees. He turned in his seat and yelled back into the shop for his wife to bring out two "special" iced-coffees for his friends and one for him. How could you not love this guy?

When the coffees arrived, it was evident that his wife was extremely pregnant and moving slowly. Through the use of our Pidgin English/Vietnamese, garbled French and many gestures, we learned that the new baby was due any day now. We managed to convey to him that we were happy for them both and looked forward to seeing their new addition. As Baby-san translated that for his wife, she broke out in an enormous smile and her eyes teared up.

"She happy that you happy," he struggled to tell us as he shooed her back inside. "And, I happy too," he added proudly.

We paid our tab and doubled the tip that we left on the table as we took our leave, promising to return soon.

"It's people like these that makes our job easier," remarked Poncho as we retrieved the Jeep and headed back towards Saigon.

"You're dead on with that," I agreed. Our plan of action was for me to drop Poncho off at the Plaza where he could do the three standard Navy "S's," (Shit, Shower and Shave), while I went to the

Le qui Don to do the same. I would then pick him up around 6 and head into Cholon to Gia's party. This had been decided by using the formula for distance and direction of travel, otherwise I would have let him do the dropping off and picking up instead.

PARTY TIME

Smelling of "Old Spice" aftershave lotion and decked out in freshly pressed greens, I pulled up to the curb outside of the Plaza at exactly 6. Poncho was already there waiting for me as I knew he would be. The infuriating habit of us in the military always striving to be on time is almost an anal-compulsive reaction that is instilled into us in Boot Camp. That's why many of us were having "time" problems with our counterparts because to the average Vietnamese, time was irrelevant. Fortunately Gia did not fall into that category because he was obsessively punctual and insisted that the rest of his crew follow suit. In any event, we were not going to be late for his party.

We found the location only after a slight delay due to an accident where Tran Hung Dao opened up to Dong Khanh Street. Apparently, a cyclo-driver with a heavy-set Chinese woman sitting in the front-end loader part of his conveyance must have suffered a heart attack because he plowed headlong into a group of fifteen or so motorcycles and bikes that had jumped the yellow traffic light across his path. The collision resulted in a big pile of bodies and machines in the roadway. The 50cc motorcycle was the most common personal conveyance in Vietnam behind the bicycle which made up about eighty percent of the traffic in Vietnam.

This evening's pileup was only partially due to the impatience of the cyclists, although they probably didn't give the oncoming cyclo a second thought. The cyclo-driver was either dead or dying as his woman passenger was launched into the center of the pile with her shopping bags. There were about twenty people knocked over including some young children, but I didn't think other than the driver that there were any life-threatening injuries.

Before we could do anything, two National Policemen had arrived at the scene in their white Jeep, singled us out, hastily waved us around and sent us on our way. For once, we were both relieved that we didn't have to get involved and besides there was a large crowd gathering and I didn't care for crowds of any kind in Vietnam.

As we left the accident scene behind us, Poncho remarked, "It looks like your new Buddha is working already, otherwise we would have had a fat lady in our Jeep with us."

"Don't tell me that you believe all that stuff Boats."

"Well, too many things happen that I can't explain with religion and superstition being two of them."

"Well, let's hope for the sake of argument that it works."

The size of the soup shop surprised us in that it was set back within a wire fence enclosure complete with a Chinese guard who tended the front gate. It was easily five or six times larger than Tuyet's Uncle's shop. I parked the Jeep off to the side of the entrance alongside two other vehicles already there.

As we entered the front door, we saw three big tables placed in the form of a "U" at the rear of a large room. There were bowls, glasses, ceramic spoons, wrapped chopsticks standing in round cans and red paper napkins meticulously placed atop white cotton tablecloths. A blue banner with gold Vietnamese letters spelled out "Congratulations Commander Huynh Kim Gia on Your Promotion" and was hanging on the wall behind the center table. The biggest surprise of all was seeing Gunner Shipp sitting at the left hand table by himself. The moment he spotted us, he jumped up and came to greet us.

"Gia's driver dropped off a note at Ann's place inviting me to the party a few days ago," he said, "So here I am."

"Senior Chief, I almost didn't recognize you in your wash khakis," said Poncho who was all smiles.

"Me either," I added. "It doesn't look like being a 'Saigon Warrior' has helped you gain any weight."

"You can stow that 'Saigon Warrior' crap and as far as my gaining weight, it's hard to do being home every night with Ann.

"And you love every minute of it," I said smiling. How is Ann coping now that you're underfoot all the time?"

"It's what she always wanted and she's pregnant again."

"The 'Spider' strikes," said Poncho admiringly

"What's this 'Spider' business?" queried Gunner.

"Oh, it's just the nickname some of us hung on you because of the way you work on women, slow and deliberate like a hairy spider inching down its web to get to its prey," said Poncho.

"Heh, heh," came the soft dry laugh from Gunner that we were so familiar with. "I like that," he said smiling.

Just as I was about to say that Commanders Rac and Minh were also going to be here, in they came. It was getting to be like old home week as we all stood around warmly greeting each other. I introduced Poncho to both officers saying that this was Shipp's relief and they took to him immediately. A few moments later, Gia made his entrance along with his XO Dinh and three new additions to our unit, *Trung Uy* Dan, *Thieu Uy* Son and *Thieu Uy* Mang.

Gia was still wearing his old Lieutenant Commander's shoulder boards as is the custom until the new ones are presented. Once he introduced his new officers to the rest of us, he announced that it was time to get the party started.

The ten of us took seats at the tables with Gia, Rac and Minh at the center one, Gunner, Poncho and I on the left and the other four officers on the right. Three young waitresses appeared, each taking a table and placing ice-cold bottles of "33" Beer in front of everyone. This party was definitely starting out on the right note, I thought to myself.

While we were taking our first sips of the frosty beer, bowls of chicken soup were placed in front of us, along with small monkey-dishes holding quartered limes, small slices of red chili peppers, larger dishes of bean sprouts, cilantro, shaved red onion, sliced scallions, Thai basil and bottles of *Nuoc Mam*, Hoisin sauce and a chili pepper and vinegar mixture that would definitely take the varnish off of a doorknob.

Naturally, Poncho was in his element now that food and drink were being served. I had never met a man yet that enjoyed the epicurean way of life so much as this guy. He flat out enjoyed eating and drinking, which made him the perfect sailor.

Everyone in attendance except me didn't miss the amount of chili peppers and hot sauce that Poncho put into his soup. They were amazed and pleased at the same time to see him devour the peppers so effortlessly. They were starting to take their toll on him as he was perspiring profusely, but he never missed a beat.

When that course was finished, the empty bowls were taken away and replaced by individual plates of thin grilled beefsteak that had been pummeled and marinated in Magi and soy sauce to ensure tenderness along with a hefty serving of string beans sautéed in onions, garlic and butter.

It was a good thing that the chopsticks were replaced with knives and forks otherwise us Westerners would have been eating the steak with our bare hands.

The beer bottles were being replaced as fast as they were being emptied and as I glanced across to the table with the young officers, each had a bright crimson face, courtesy of the beer.

The final course was dessert; chilled bowls of Lychee Nuts that come from the Litchi tree native to southern China. They are not actually nuts but a type of fruit that grows in clusters of 20 to 30 and have a pinkish-red exterior and a leathery skin. The skin covers a clear, whitish flesh that resembles the inside of a grape and covers a large seed which is removed. The fruit is then served chilled in sweet heavy syrup.

At long last, the meal was winding down. Everyone was sitting back in their seats totally satiated by the tasty food that had been served. Again, the three waitresses appeared each carrying a bottle of Cognac that they ceremoniously set at each table.

"Ah, the *piece de resistance*," uttered Gunner, surprising me with his French as Commander Rac stood up clinking his glass with his spoon for attention.

"Gentlemen," he announced in his near-faultless English, "We are gathered here this evening to celebrate the promotion of not only a classmate of mine, but a very dear and respected friend. Along with my other classmate and close friend, Commander Minh, we often have been referred to as the 'Three Stooges' by some of our superiors and colleagues who sometimes frown upon the zeal with which we pursue the enemy. We do so because we want to rid our country of any and all forms of Communism as soon as possible and doing so with honor and integrity. This should be a lesson to you younger officers to take with you wherever you go. It will guarantee that no matter what happens, good or bad, you can look any man directly in the eye because you have remained principled.

I wish to thank our three guests, not only as Advisors, but as our good friends in attending this evening. To you new arrivals in RAG 24, I bid you welcome and good luck."

Without further ado, Commander Minh, will you please assist me in presenting Commander Gia with his new shoulder boards?

Minh stood up immediately with a big smile on his face as both officers removed Gia's old boards and replaced them with two new ones adorned by three gold stripes.

I could see Gia's deep emotion as he fought back the tears and bravely held them in check.

"Here, here," said Shipp standing up and applauding loudly as everyone else stood up and joined in. The waitresses and Gia's cousin, who obviously had done the food preparation, came out of the kitchen to partake of the moment.

After a few more seconds, Gia raised both his hands to silence the applause and said quietly, "I thank you all very much for your friendship and your professionalism for which I am extremely grateful. Now let's get to the cognac."

As we each finished our first quarter filled glass of cognac in a toast to Commander Gia, a waitress came out of the kitchen carrying two identical soup bowls. One of them contained the head and neck of a chicken, complete with dimpled skin, gray opaque eyes and set them in front of Gia. Since Gunner and I have both seen this before, I figured old Poncho was going to get the brunt of this joke.

Gia stood up and came around to the front of our table carrying both bowls with a serious look on his face. He placed the bowl with the chicken head directly in front of me, as I sat with Gunner on my left and Poncho on my right.

He stood there a moment and said, "This is a very old Navy tradition at these parties. I will cover one bowl with the other and then turn them around several times. When I uncover the chicken head, whoever has the beak pointing at him must perform a deed that I will address, understand?"

We all nodded in agreement. Poncho was really enjoying this but he failed to notice the slight chip on the edge of the bowl that was aligned with the beak of the chicken. That's right, the game is rigged.

Gia turned the bowls around several times and stopped. He paused for effect as he slowly lifted the top bowl revealing the beak pointing directly at Poncho. Loud whoops and laughter erupted as

Gia filled Poncho's glass half full and said, "Now you must drink this 'down the hatch' as you say in your Navy."

Without a moment's hesitation, Poncho downed the cognac while everyone in unison was yelling, "Yo, Yo."

Gia then turned to the table with his young officers and repeated the process. Naturally, the youngest officer, Ensign Mang got the beak. He struggled somewhat trying to down his drink trying to emulate Poncho, all to the accompaniment of more "Yo Yos" and laughter.

From there, the toasting resumed until all the cognac was gone. We older guys managed to fair pretty well, but such was not the case with the young officers and Poncho. Their faces were bright crimson and aglow with smiles that would shortly droop in sleep. We all somehow struggled through saying our "goodbyes" and then Gunner and I steered Poncho to my Jeep. The plan was for me to drop them off at the Plaza when I parked my vehicle and Gunner would ensure that Poncho made it to his room on the third deck. From there, Gunner would walk around the corner to his pad and I would catch a taxi to Tuyet's.

All that transpired as if it had been scripted. The soup shop was empty of customers as Tuyet and her aunt and uncle were in the process of closing as I walked in a little unsteady. They all turned to look at me and smiled, realizing that I had come from the party as I unceremoniously bumped into the doorframe.

"Help him upstairs," said her Uncle to Tuyet. "Co Bay and I will finish up down here."

The last thing I remember was Tuyet helping me take off my clothes as she pushed me onto the bed and removed my shoes and socks. "No pussy tonight," I thought as I got under the covers. But I was to be mistaken because our first early morning's go-round was repeated once again, only this time at a much slower pace.

That is until the last twenty seconds when she again became a runaway trip-hammer.

At the end, she threw her head back, clenched her teeth and leaned back digging her nails into my thighs as I felt her vagina muscles firmly squeezing and releasing me in spasms. It was as if she was trying to milk every last drop out of my body. Finally, we both collapsed completely spent and went back to sleep.

Early the next morning as I finished my shower Tuyet thrust a large glass of piping hot tea with lemon into my hands. Her face was aglow as she asked me how I felt and I answered by giving her a big hug and a kiss. "I feel super, how about you?"

"Me too, but I was ver' wet. What did you drink last night?" she asked as she began changing the sodden sheets on the bed.

"Ba-me-ba and cognac," I answered as I went on to describe the events of the evening and the accident on our way to the party.

An old sea-chantey came to mind at that moment that went, "A sailor's semen will go a streamin', whilst in the throes of a royal reamin'." How true, how true!

The taxi dropped me off in front of the Plaza and I walked halfway down the block to where I had parked the Jeep. To my surprise, Poncho was already sitting in the passenger seat happy as a clam at high tide.

"Morning Boats," I said climbing into the driver's seat. "How'd you sleep?"

"Like a new-born baby. Man that chow last night was out of this world, but that chicken-head had me going for a bit because I thought that I was going to have to eat the damned thing."

I explained the ritual saying that it's always a setup for the new guys. We've all been through it.

"And what's with the 'Yo Yos?"

"The Viets know that they can't drink like an American, so they try to see how drunk they can get us. It's all in fun."

"Something else that bothered me last night, one of the times that I went to take a leak, I almost fell and broke my ass in that stupid *binjo* ditch they call a toilet."

"It's the same type of hole in the floor toilet that third world countries still use and you were probably tipsy by that time anyway, right?"

"Yeah, I guess so but damn, why don't they use US style toilets?"

"Because they're used to them and that's what the French left them. That's what Tuyet and I have up in our place," I added.

"Bubba, that's unsat," he said with brow furrowed in thought.

"I remember the first time I ran into one of those things. I was a young sailor serving aboard a tanker that was deployed for six months in the Mediterranean with the Sixth Fleet. We made a port visit to Istanbul, Turkey where a couple of us went ashore on liberty. A young teenager attached himself to us as a guide and steered us to a sleazy nightclub that reeked of cigarette smoke and the drinks were watered down.

After our first drink, my stomach started to rumble, so I made a quick run to the toilets. Off to the side of the men's and women's doors, there was an old woman seated at a small table filled with several bottles. Once inside the dim room, I saw a ceramic basin set into the floor with a hole towards the rear and two grooved raised sections for your feet. A water spigot was attached to the wall behind it, but there was no toilet paper.

I quickly retraced my steps to my friends and mentioned the lack of paper to our young guide who explained in halting English that there is no paper. You wipe yourself clean with only your left hand, wash it under the spigot and the old woman will pour some aromatic rose water on your hands for five Kurus when you come out. The five Kurus was equivalent to one penny US.

Now I understood why the Muslims only use their right hands for eating out of the communal food bowl. To do otherwise would be an affront and could result in decapitation of that hand.

Saddled with that information, I returned to the toilet. The first thing I did was pull my white bell bottom trousers up over my knees so they wouldn't touch the unbelievably filthy basin. I then loosened my pants and simultaneously slid them and my skivvies down as I began to position myself over the hole. In the process of bending over, an enormous spurt of air and brownish liquid erupted from my butt and splattered the wall behind me.

That was it and I was lucky that it hadn't happened a few seconds sooner. I managed to perform the athletic ablutions with the water spigot and finished off by wiping myself dry on my handkerchief that I was taught to carry as a child. Whew!

As I pulled my pants up and got squared away, I turned to see how much redecorating I had done to the wall and was pleased to see that I surpassed an old high water mark by a good 3 inches.

Exiting the toilet, I motioned to the old lady to give me a double on the rose water, paid her ten Kurus and then returned to my buddies saying that I had had it for the night and left.

The moral to this story is that if you are ever with a woman anywhere in the Muslim world and you detect the scent of scented water on her hands, she has recently been to the toilet."

"You've got to be shitting me," said Poncho shaking his head.

"No, it's the honest truth. Luckily, Tuyet's toilet has paper available. There is also a water faucet with an eight inch length of hose attached to spray around in case you miss."

Poncho sat there silently for the rest of the trip probably digesting this latest bit of information. As we pulled into the 519th compound, the last guy I wanted to see was Captain Vlastoff making his way towards us.

"You missed all the excitement last night," he blurted out. "A rocket landed right across the street around midnight and hit the house of a US Embassy staffer killing his live-in maid's 86 year old mother. It scared the be-Jesus out of me."

"Yeah," I replied rather sarcastically, "A guy can get killed practically anytime, anywhere around here."

Obviously miffed because of my lack of concern for his safety, he stormed off in a huff.

"What a sorry ass," said Poncho.

"We had a similar attack before I moved in. A rocket landed behind the Indian Consulate and one in the front yard of Admiral Veth's house knocking the Marine sentry off the porch. Luckily there were no fatalities.

The VC lay out a map of Saigon, plot their geographical position and their targets for the night. Then using the tall radio station tower near the Catholic Cathedral as a reference point, they use a kid's plastic protractor to determine the azimuth angle between the tower and their position, the angle between the tower and the target and combine the two. Then, they set the launcher into the crotch of a tree, aligning it for the correct horizontal angle. The vertical angle for distance is basically a guess, but they're getting better."

"Man, these guys amaze me with their ingenuity," said Poncho.

"That's what makes it so tough to fight them."

The Beginning of the End

The next few days were fairly much the usual routine. I was taking every other night off so that I could be with Tuyet while Poncho remained aboard enjoying every minute of it.

One Friday morning as we were finishing breakfast in the Army messhall, Poncho asked me if there was a back entrance to Nam's soup shop.

"Sure, there's a small fenced-in back yard with a gate that leads out into an alley. Why?"

"Perfect. Because me and a couple of my PsyOps buddies are going to stop by tomorrow and deliver some stuff."

"What stuff?" I asked

"Trust me *hermano*, you'll see," he said without any further explanation. "Come on, take me to Saigon so I can do what I have to do and get back in time for patrol."

I had him drop me off in the middle of town as he drove off towards VNN Headquarters. I grabbed a passing taxi and went to Tuyet's wondering about Poncho's strange behavior and decided to wait to see what transpired.

Tuyet was surprised to see me so early, but relaxed when I told her I wanted to shower and take a nap. By now she was used to my strange sleeping habits during the day, especially after being out on patrol the night before.

Poncho arrived at the rear entrance with the PsyOps ¾ ton truck along with two of his buddies at 0900 the next morning. Since I was already up and having a cup of coffee in the shop, I went back and opened the gate to admit them at the beep of their horn. I could see that the truck was loaded with "stuff."

The three men climbed out of the cab as Poncho pointed over his shoulder and said, "This here's Gunners Mate First Class Roger Gainey and Utilities Man Second Class Chico Ruiz."

I acknowledged each man with a nod as Poncho climbed up into the back of the truck and started handing down the following: a brand new US style toilet complete with seat, various lengths of pipe, two bags of Quikcrete, tools, a caulking gun, Four double fluorescent light fixtures with lamps, a new large outdoor grill complete with a propane tank, three ceiling fans and five crates of 4x4 white ceramic tiles.

"Wow! Where did you guys get all this stuff?" I asked.

"Oh, I was still with PsyOps when I met this retired Marine Master Sergeant who runs the Property Disposal Office for PA & E contractors in Long Binh. He said that if I ever needed anything to come see him. When I heard that you and Tuyet still had one of those antique crappers, I remembered his offer. As for the rest, I figured the old guy could use it to spruce up the place."

"Poncho, I could kiss you, but I'll let ol' Nam handle that."

"Not so fast round-eye, if anyone is going to kiss me it'll have to be Tuyet or her aunt. None of that boy stuff."

When Tuyet and her Uncle and Aunt saw all the goodies, they darn near burst into tears.

Chico had installed the new toilet and connected the water to the tank in no time at all. As for the rest, Tuyet said her uncle could get some people to install everything else. He will close the shop for a few days so it can be ready for TET, but right now, he wants to thank his four American friends by feeding them.

After consuming the bowls of Beef Pho, Poncho and his two erstwhile confederates took their leave amidst another round of "thanks" from the grateful couple.

Later that night in our cozy loft, Tuyet outdid herself in the love-making department. I do not feel gifted enough to describe the emotions and physical accomplishments of that evening, except to say, "Man-oh-man, what a night!" It started me thinking again about my future because I could easily resign my commission and get a job over here with USAID or one of the many contractors. I wasn't ready to leave here any time soon, especially now that we had a decent toilet.

As February 12th approached, which was the beginning of TET '69, all units in-country would be "on-alert" to guard against any repetition of last year's attacks. The local population appeared to have forgotten that TET '68 and were more in tune with the coming holiday as fresh flowers and decorations began appearing everywhere. The mood was definitely up-beat while our nightly patrols on the Saigon River continued as usual.

Nam's Soup Shop was tiled half way up the walls with the top portion painted in a light tan color, liana vines were interwoven into the overhead latticework giving the impression of an open-air space and all the fixtures were installed in time for TET. With the new décor, the place was bringing in fresh new patrons.

Poncho was elated that he was able to bring joy to people whom he liked and for that, he would always dine there for free.

We were both aboard for the sweep of the river on the first night of TET and happily, it proved dull and uneventful. When we returned to Binh Loi for our nightly mooring, Gunner's Mate Mai came topside and invited us both to come to his home in Saigon.

"Now, but it's after midnight?" I replied.

"No problem *Dai Uy*," my family would be honored to have the both of you as our first guests of the New Year."

"Well, in that case, can do," I said as Gia who had overheard the conversation sat there smiling.

"You should go and enjoy it because there may not be another chance in the future," said Gia philosophically.

So the three of us piled into the Jeep and drove through the deserted streets towards Mai's house. As we neared the Lang Ong Buddhist Temple in Gia Dinh, I had a thought. Now would be a good time for me to kneel at its gate and offer a prayer for guidance regarding my future. The locals strongly believed that prayers made at the gates of this Temple would be answered if one was absolutely sincere. To my surprise, Poncho and Petty Officer Mai joined me with their own private prayers.

When we finally arrived at Mai's, it was after 1 am and the house was completely dark. I parked the Jeep in front and secured it as Mai tapped gently on the front door. It took a few moments before someone opened it wide after recognizing him.

We entered a large living room as people began coming out of their bedrooms still clad in their sleeping attire. Instead of indicating their displeasure at being awoken at this ungodly hour, they were all bowing and smiling once Mai told them who we were.

Poncho and I were given seats at the head of the table as Mai introduced his parents, his grandmother, three sisters aged from 10 to 16 and a brother who was 7. The father, grandmother, Mai and his brother joined us at the table while the rest of the women bustled in and out of the kitchen. Heaping bowls of fruits, candied coconut strips, plates of assorted nuts and cold bottles of Tiger Beer were set in front of us. Tiger was the alternative beer to "33" and came in larger bottles, much to our delight.

Once everyone was seated at the table, Mai translated the many questions posed to us by the family and in no time at all, they had our complete personal history—almost.

When we finally got up to leave, I reached into my pocket and pulled out two 500 piaster bills telling Mai it was for his sisters and brother. I apologized for not having any of the *Li Xi* red and gold envelopes used for giving money to children during TET. Again we were deluged with bows and handshakes.

On the way to the Plaza, I explained the tradition of giving money to children for TET and for just a measly 10 bucks; it was worth the night's experience. Poncho wholeheartedly agreed.

Once Poncho was safely in the Plaza, I figured there was no way that I would find a random taxi at this early hour, so I drove to Tuyet's and parked in the rear yard out of sight. Why didn't we think of this before and saved the cab fare?

I managed to slip into bed without awakening Tuyet who was fast asleep after a long day visiting her mother and children. When she woke up and found me sleeping next to her, she gave me a shove and said feigning anger, "Why you no wake me?"

Coming out of a deep sleep and rubbing my grit-filled eyes, I mumbled that I had been to a TET party at a sailor's house after the patrol and didn't want to wake her.

That seemed to satisfy her as she lay back down and nestled up against me. Being the boorish male that I am, I promptly went back to sleep.

The routine of going up and down the river continued even though scuttlebutt said that the enemy was gearing up for another large scale post TET attack. Having heard similar rumors on a daily basis, we would have welcomed an attack to break up the boredom. For me at least, I had every other night bedded down with Tuyet which in itself was never boring.

The morning of February 23rd, after my shower, I removed the Buddha and chain from around my neck and asked Tuyet if she could have it shortened. "The Buddha gets caught under my armpit when I sleep and I'm afraid the chain will break and possibly lose it."

"Can do easy," she replied as she tucked it into her pocket.

Back in Binh Loi that night after having a couple of BLT sandwiches topside in the 519th club, Poncho and I were walking back to the boat when we heard a muffled splash off to our left. Several tracts of small marshes paralleled that side of the dirt road adjacent to the base and rumors were always circulating about the VC stockpiling and caching bundles of weapons in such areas. It gave us pause and immediately stopped us in our tracks.

"What do you think, should we check it out?" asked Poncho.

"No, it's dark and we don't have any flashlights. Besides, tomorrow we can poke around in the daylight. I'll tell Gia and I'm sure he'll dispatch the crew to help us search the area."

Poncho agreed with my logic and we continued on without any further distractions. Once aboard, I recounted our experience to Gia who said that the crew would gladly help us search tomorrow.

He then told us that our departure to go upriver would be delayed until midnight. When we get to Phu Cuong, we will remain tied up until around ten in the morning and then return to Binh Loi. Then we can begin a search for the source of your mysterious sound.

"Is something going on?" I asked hopefully.

"It could be nothing, but there have been several reports of groups of people moving around the upper reaches of the river. Third Riverine has ordered us to alter our schedule this week as a precaution."

I looked over at Poncho and his eyes were almost ablaze with anticipation. He couldn't wait to mix it up with the elusive VC.

A few minutes after midnight, we cast off and headed upriver. There wasn't a cloud in the darkened sky and all the stars were shining bright and visible as we settled in topside for the trip. We posted one of the seamen called "Looky-Looky" on the night scope as we had done on numerous occasions. Poncho had given him that name because whenever either one of us were on the scope, he would suddenly appear and timidly ask "Looky-looky?" After his first look, he was hooked and he became very proficient letting absolutely nothing get by him.

Hey, that's what we were here for, to train and pass on some responsibility to the Viets. Sitting behind the scope for more than an hour was tedious for us, but he loved it.

We reached the Phu Cuong Bridge and tied up under the center span around 0215. The lights on the bridge were ablaze so we dropped the canvas covers on the outboard side of our bunkroom and turned in for the night, with Poncho diligently following our sleeping protocol of "Seniors first."

We all awoke coincidently around 7 in the morning and once we got topside, were greeted by a warming sun that was rising. One of the crew provided us with steaming cups of fresh coffee as Poncho said, "I sure could go for a loaf of French bread with some 'Laughing Cow Cheese' to stick on it."

"Me too," I replied. "Even a box of Dunkin Doughnuts would go good about now."

"Ah, I envy you Americans the way you can fantasize about food the way you do. Me, I think about rice, rice and more rice," Gia remarked stoically.

"That's understandable," I said.

"Yeah, please pass the rice," said Poncho patting his stomach.

At approximately 10 am, we slipped our lines and headed down river as planned. So far we had seen nothing out of the ordinary and I chalked it up to the usual paranoia generated by the paper pushers in Saigon. A little more than halfway as we were passing point "Grumpy" and turning southward towards "Dopey", a sudden whoosh filled the air. A B-40 rocket leaving a trail of grayish smoke, passed between our forward gun mount and our topside position from the right hand shoreline.

"Holy shit, somebody just fired a rocket at us," yelled Poncho excitedly.

"Come right and steer for the starboard bank," commanded Gia to the helmsman. He ordered the forward gun mount to commence firing in an effort to keep the enemy hunkered down and prevent them from firing another rocket. This was the standard operating procedure for an ambush on the river, turning into the teeth of the attack and laying down covering fire.

As we neared the bank, I could see several figures running further into the brush carrying a rocket launcher. I yelled to Poncho to get on the radio to Bo Tanner at District and ask for a helicopter gunship to assist. I grabbed two hand grenades and my M-16 and jumped onto the shore as soon as the boat squished into the embankment. My plan was to get close enough to toss a grenade or at least get a shot at the fleeing men. Unfortunately, our gunner was using 40mm armor piercing instead of point detonating rounds and they were ineffectual. I would make it a point to ream his ass out later when I got back because we had been having this problem with the gunners ever since Shipp had brought it to my attention. Armor piercing rounds unless, they hit something substantial, will keep on going and going, whereas, the point detonating rounds will explode upon contact, showering shrapnel all over the place.

Running hard, I could see flashes of the men running through the heavy vegetation and veering to the right ahead of me. Just to the right of that, I spotted a faint path through the brush and immediately headed for it hoping to gain some ground on them. Three steps in, the warning bells went off in my head just before the world turned topsy-turvy.

I never heard the explosion because I was in the center of its vortex, but I recall doing a somersault into the air as my visual horizon went into a spin. I landed hard on my back as dirt and debris showered down around me as I started using every curse word that I knew because I realized that I had been suckered.

I was in one hell of a predicament because I knew that I had stepped into a minefield and that there were probably more of them strewn along the path. I was fortunate in that I was thrown upwards rather than forward where I would have landed on another then another until I was a broken rag doll. I felt no pain, but looking down I saw that my heel was missing from my right foot. Another thought came to mind; it was the first time in months that I had my nylon innersoles inside my boots. They protect from stepping into a

Punji Stake pit and prevent the feces covered sharpened bamboo stakes from penetrating your foot that causes serious infection. They told me later that had I not had them in my boots, I stood a good chance of having lost my leg entirely because the heavy nylon redirected the blast.

At that point, I started yelling "Bosun's Mate" as loud as I could until I heard Poncho pounding his way to me. He pulled up short and I will never forget the look of pure anguish that came over his face when he saw me lying there. Immediately he had made up his mind to come in and pull me out until I stopped him saying, "Don't come in here Boats, there are more mines!"

He took a few seconds to evaluate the situation and said softly, "Can you turn your back to me?"

I said, "Yes," twisting gingerly on the ground just as I felt the first severe pain jolt my foot. It was a mother-stomper, believe me. I had never had a pain like that before.

Poncho reached over and grabbed me by my belt with one hand and my jacket collar with the other as he said, "On the count of three, ready?"

Not entirely sure about what his intentions were I nodded and as he reached three, I heard a huge grunt as he simultaneously dead lifted my 198 pound ass into the air and out of danger. He then hefted me onto his massive shoulders in a fireman's carry and quickly carried me back to the boat. Gia stood there with a pained look on his face when he saw the extent of my wounds.

Poncho then said as he gently lowered me to the deck that the dickheads didn't have a MedEvac chopper available because they were busy with the 25th Division up at Cu Chi. The Navy's HAL-3 out of Nha Be is sending two gunships to see if they can catch up to the runners. So, we're going to have to bring you back to Binh Loi. Gia already asked the Vietnamese Ranger detachment to call the 519th to have an ambulance standing by.

The Commandament backed away from the bank and headed home pushing the engines for all they were worth. Poncho sat on the deck cradling me in his arms as sine waves of pain continued to ravage my leg.

I had no concept of time because I was busy bracing myself against the recurring pain. Gia had he helmsman drive the bow into the embankment close to where the waiting ambulance was parked so that I could be off-loaded easily. The two Army Medics, with the help of Poncho, immediately put me on a stretcher.

One Medic gently removed my boot to examine the wound and said, "In a way you're lucky LT, the blast cauterized the wound so there was minimal loss of blood and it looks like it was a booby-trapped grenade and not a mine that did this. Had it been a mine, your leg and your family jewels would have been gone."

The other Medic proceeded to bandage my foot after which the three men mule-hauled me into the back of the ambulance where Poncho sat on the deck and cradled me once again. This time, my arm was draped behind his neck and each time a pain spasm hit, I squeezed his massive shoulder.

QUICK EXIT

Before we arrived at the Third Field Hospital in Saigon, I had given Poncho my wallet, the .38, watch and college ring for safe keeping. I remember the ride into the city only in that is was bone-jarring and painful but not our arrival at the hospital. Poncho later told me that I had finally passed out.

When I came to, I was lying on a gurney in an open passageway as one of the mama-sans who worked at the hospital stopped and silently looked at me. She was sad-eyed as she slowly shook her head and gently squeezed my arm with her tiny brown gnarled hand. That's when the thought came to me. I looked heavenward and said softly, "Lord, I asked for guidance in deciding my future, but couldn't you have given me a less painful sign?"

Eventually I was wheeled into a cold operating area where two surgeons began debriding my wounds. They skillfully removed bits of shrapnel, damaged tissue and applied antibiotics and bandages to both legs. I hadn't realized that my left leg had been hit too because of the lack of pain from there. When they were finished with me, I was moved to a ward with other wounded personnel where I promptly fell asleep.

The next morning as I was trying hard to ingest some breakfast eggs and grits, Poncho, Lieutenant Commander Shope and Tuyet came into the ward. Tuyet was the first to reach me with tears in her eyes as she chokingly said, "You were not wearing this," as she held out the Buddha and chain in her hand accusingly.

I looked up at Poncho who could only gaze skyward and shrug his shoulders at Tuyet's distress. LCDR Shope broke the tension by asking me how I felt.

"All things considered, I feel much better after a good night's rest and the pain is tolerable, thank God for whatever drugs they pumped into me."

"I was told that you'll be flown to the Naval Hospital in Yokosuka, Japan this afternoon for further treatment and from there, to another Hospital in the States. I'll keep your personal belongings in the Advisor's safe at Third Riverine until you let me know what you want me to do with them," said Shope.

"Just keep them there, because I'll be back, and that's a promise," I said looking squarely at Tuyet.

"For your information, your relief has been assigned and he's already in-country. His name is Lieutenant William Blakely and he'll be aboard in two days," said Shope.

"That's great Commander and Poncho here will take good care of him, won't you Boats?"

"Poncho grabbed my hand and said, "You know I will. If you ever need me, just give a holler and I'll be there and, by the way, take a look at what you did on the ride in." He unbuttoned his shirt and revealed a large purple bruise where I had been squeezing his shoulder.

"Damn, did I do that," now realizing how much pain I had been in after the shock wore off.

As Poncho was re-buttoning his shirt he said, "And another thing, when the Medics brought me back to Binh Loi in the ambulance, one of the young guys came up and told me to check out SFC Girard because he was keeping your boot for a souvenir.

This Girard character was a fat, lazy black supply puke who everyone called 'Honeybear.' I stormed into his office and when I saw your boot sitting on his desk, I completely lost it. He jumped up the minute he saw me and I swear he shit his pants as I grabbed his shirt and was about to punch him out. Lucky for him a bunch of guys followed me in hoping to see the show. When the smell hit me, I decided he wasn't worth it, so I took your boot and threw it out into the river as far as I could."

"Thanks Boats. Some guys just don't get it,' I said.

With that, they left but not before Tuyet gave me a big kiss as her tears fell on my face.

Within hours, a group of us were bussed to Tan Son Nhut and loaded aboard an Air Force MedEvac flight bound for Japan. As the plane's wheels lifted off the tarmac, I craned my neck to watch the passing landscape through the window. It was then that I sadly thought to myself, "Goodbye Vietnam, it was a helluva ride while it lasted . . . but I'll be back."

EPILOG

After several months of rehabilitation, I was outfitted with a below knee prosthetic leg and retired from the Navy on 1 November 1969 on the Permanently Disabled Retired List. By the end of the month, I had returned to Saigon and was working for Vice Admiral Zumwalt as a civilian. By his direction, I established and headed up the Vietnamese Navy Disabled Veterans Section at Naval Forces Vietnam Headquarters. As a footnote, Gia had given Poncho my $80 in US currency and it was in my wallet when I returned

In 1973, with the withdrawal of US military combat forces, I joined the Defense Attache Office, Saigon where I remained until a few days before the country's fall in April '75—

But that's another story!

Quotation by an unknown source which best sums up the Vietnam War:

"We won the war on the battlefield but lost it back home on the college campuses and on the streets."